Arnulfo L. Oliveira Memorial Library

THE CRASH OF RUIN

The Crash of Ruin

American Combat Soldiers in Europe
during World War II

Peter Schrijvers

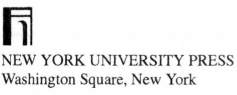

NEW YORK UNIVERSITY PRESS
Washington Square, New York

First published in the U.S.A. in 1998 by
NEW YORK UNIVERSITY PRESS
Washington Square
New York, N.Y. 10003

This book is printed on paper suitable for recycling and
made from fully managed and sustained forest sources.

Library of Congress Cataloging-in-Publication Data
Schrijvers, Peter, 1963–
The crash of ruin : American combat soldiers in Europe during
World War II / Peter Schrijvers.
p.   cm.
Includes bibliographical references and index.
ISBN 0–8147–8089–X
1. World War, 1939–1945—Psychological aspects.   2. World War,
1939–1945—Campaigns—Western Front.x.   3. Soldiers—United States–
–Psychology.   4. United States. Army—Military life.   I. Title.
D769.2.S34 1998
940.53'114—dc21   97–14751
                                                                CIP

To the American soldiers
who stayed at the bakery in Peer, Belgium:
John J. Beddingfield, Jr,
Lionel Bernstein
and
James K. Dumas

Contents

List of Abbreviations

AWOL	Absent Without Leave
DP	Displaced Person
ETO	European Theater of Operations
FFI	French Forces of the Interior
LST	Landing Ship Tank
MP	Military Police
MTO	Mediterranean Theater of Operations
POW	Prisoner of War
PX	Post Exchange
SHAEF	Supreme Headquarters of the Allied Expeditionary Forces
VD	Venereal Disease
VE	Victory in Europe
WAC	Women's Auxiliary Corps

List of Endnote Abbreviations

AD	Armored Division
ADP	Armored Division Papers, US Army Military History Institute, Carlisle Barracks, Pennsylvania
CU	The Carl Ulsaker Papers, US Army Military History Institute
ID	Infantry Division
IDP	Infantry Division Papers, US Army Military History Institute
MCC	The Mina Curtiss Collection, Yale University Library, New Haven, Connecticut
MD	Mountain Division
MP	The George E. McIntyre Papers, US Army Military History Institute
Q	Questionnaire
RC	The Raab Family Collection, US Army Military History Institute
RP	The John J. Roche Papers, US Army Military History Institute
SC	The World War II Survey Collection, US Army Military History Institute

Preface

The first seeds of this book were sown during a stay in the American Deep South in 1985. It was my first trip to the US and the purpose of my visit was the long-awaited reunion with the members of a B-26 crew who had stayed with my grandparents at Peer, Belgium, after an emergency landing early in 1945. For five weeks my hosts treated me with that wonderful southern hospitality and, needless to say, I had the time of my life.

Yet, I could not quite understand why, at saying goodbye, my American friends insisted that I accept sweaters and socks as gifts for my family. I had brought a huge suitcase full of clothes and liked to believe that I had been well dressed during my vacation. I therefore could not help musing that perhaps these gifts were inspired by the age-old images of ragtag European immigrants pouring into Ellis Island. Still, I was aware that these men had seen modern Europe with their own eyes only 40 years ago. Surely they knew that twentieth-century Western Europe was far more developed than Sicily and Poland had been in the nineteenth century?

It was only when my American friends visited Belgium a few years later that it dawned on me how much World War II had done to distort their image of Europe. My family and I noticed with shock that to the American veterans of that war our modern highways and up-to-date supermarkets appeared to be at least as impressive as the ancient castles and cathedrals we had intended to show off. Yet, even then, I kept wondering to what extent these men were surprised by our progress because they were veterans who had seen Europe in ruins and to what degree because they were Americans who had come to think of the Old World as stagnant.

So intrigued did I remain by this puzzling question that I decided in the course of my historical training to turn the GIs' perception of Europe during World War II into the subject of my doctoral research. I wanted to find out how their mental image had been distorted by the exceptional conditions of the war, in what way it had been influenced by the more traditional American prejudices toward the Old World, and how it had become molded by the interaction between both factors.

It therefore seemed most logical to focus my research on those Americans who had been closest to the war in Europe: the combat ground forces. Determining which GIs could be classified as combat soldiers, however, proved to be a rather tricky question. I finally opted to let the GIs themselves decide the issue. US Army wartime surveys showed that more than 70 per cent of both the frontline and the rear area soldiers agreed upon full combat status for the men in the infantry rifle and heavy weapons companies, the soldiers in the tank and tank destroyer companies, the combat engineers, the medical aid men, and other frontline troops.[1] I decided to add only the combat chaplains and a few carefully selected combat correspondents to this group. If I occasionally also considered the testimony of a few people who do not belong to these categories in the strictest sense, I did this only where it proved relevant to the combat experience.

I have gratefully made use of the statistical data that the Research Branch of the War Department's Information and Education Division diligently collected among the American troops at home and abroad during World War II, wherever it applied to my research. It is impossible, however, to reconstruct the soldiers' perceptions and experiences solely on the basis of numbers, percentages, and brief categories of answers, as a consequence, I have only been able to discover the important emotions and thoughts that hide behind them through a painstaking culling of the GIs' most personal expressions: diaries, letters home, poems, songs, jokes, cartoons, and memoirs.[2]

It is true that nations often reveal themselves most fully in encounters with foreign cultures.[3] Only very few of the American combat soldiers were college graduates used to writing lengthy papers; most were boys and men who had barely ever written a letter. Yet, taken together, the observations of these accidental and awkward commentators have managed to teach me as much about America as they have about my own European world.

Acknowledgements

If I have succeeded at all in answering the question about the GIs in Europe that first occurred to me during that hot summer in the Deep South in 1985, I owe this in the first place to my Ohio State University mentor, Professor Allan R. Millett. Not only was he instrumental in offering me the opportunity to research my subject in the US; his firm guidance has also enabled me to complete a project on which I might otherwise have labored an eternity. I also owe many thanks to the other members of my advisory committee, Professors William R. Childs and Susan M. Hartmann, as well as to Professor Mark Grimsley.

The Ohio State University library staff has simply been wonderful. My archival research at the Yale University Library was made pleasant by the courtesy of its staff. Most agreeable, however, were the five weeks that I spent at the US Army Military History Institute in Carlisle, Pennsylvania. The professionalism with which its staff – and in particular Dr Richard Sommers, Mr David Keough, Mrs Pamela Cheney, and Mr John Slonaker – advised me as a researcher was most instructive; the hospitality with which they surrounded me as a foreigner heartwarming. I would like to thank the Institute in particular for awarding me its Advanced Research Grant.

Special thanks should go to my publishers and editors. To Mr Niko Pfund, editor in chief of the New York University Press, who already showed an interest in my work when it was nothing more than a title and an intention. To the reader for the New York University Press. To Mr Tim Farmiloe, publishing director of Macmillan Press, for sharing Mr Pfund's enthusiasm. And to Aruna Vasudevan, assistant editor at Macmillan Press, for being as empathetic as conscientious.

I can only single out a few of the many other people to whom I have become indebted in the course of my doctoral odyssey. Professors Vic Doyen, Emiel Lamberts, and Lode Wils from the Catholic University of Louvain, Professors Burt Noggle and Charles Royster from the Louisiana State University at Baton Rouge, Professor Luc De Vos from the Royal Military Academy at Brussels, and Dr Richard White from Australia for their inspiration, advice, and encouragement. Vic Nuyts for being a kind Maecenas. Jaana from Finland, Frédérique and Bernadette from France, Steve from Louisiana, Christina from Norway, and Greg from Ohio for their friendship. And last but not least, my sister Karin for her professional linguistic advice, my parents and family for believing in me, and my girlfriend Elle for her love.

From Age to Age ...
The Crash of Ruin Fitfully Resounds

William Wordsworth
Descriptive Sketches, 1791–92

Part I
Nature

1   Nature

Even a cursory glance at the letters, diaries, and memoirs of the American combat soldiers reveals that their view of the Old World focused first and foremost on the natural surroundings. The GIs often found themselves fighting rain and cold before they had time to worry about the enemy soldiers, and many learned to know Europe's soil and woods much more intimately than they ever would its civilians. This can hardly be surprising, for the GIs had a love-hate relationship with nature. On the one hand, nature was their most persistent opponent. Brusquely torn from the shielding environment of their homes, the Americans were made to battle the elements for months on end with no other protection than the clothes on their backs. On the other hand, however, the natural surroundings also constituted the soldiers' most reliable ally. Frontline men knew that a smart use of the ground and a good eye for the terrain formed a crucial key to their survival.

The American soldiers fought in a war that was total. World War II rarely, if ever, gave them the chance to see Europe as tourists. A soldier in France, who had not been at the front long, promised his family that he would lend them his eyes through his letters in an effort "to see the beauty and to help me ignore the horror and ugliness of war." But neither he nor the other combat soldiers in Europe would succeed in that attempt. The war tainted every aspect of the Old World. Nature was no exception; it too degenerated into a soldier's reality. Frontline men had no eye for breathtaking vistas and romantic panoramas. For a private in Lorraine these were inexorably narrowed down to:

> a goddamn-muddy-field where a man's feet were always wet, a sonofabitch-of-a-sky that threatened rain, a pain-in-the-ass-of-a-woods from which a Heinie sniper could fire at us and stay hidden for hours.[1]

Scenery and the elements could prove helpful as well as hostile in battle, but whatever the circumstances, the GIs invariably interpreted nature in the context of the war.

Spring, the season of new life and hope, always tends to be most painfully incongruous with war. The killing looks more perverted than ever when it takes place under a cozy sun, in a balmy temperature, and amidst budding flowers. Spring, however, would remain largely absent from the GIs' perception of Europe's nature. The American soldiers experienced the war years as nothing but an endless succession of menacing clouds, suffocating rain, and biting cold. To them, the elements seemed to confirm that the Old World had somehow become predestined to be history's battlefield. Europe, concluded a GI in the cold of Colmar, was a "tragic earth."[2]

3

EARTH

When the GIs arrived at the front, pup tents and shelter halves disappeared from sight. They were too conspicuous and offered no protection against bullets or shrapnel. Under fire, earth remained the soldiers' only shield. Infantrymen usually envied the armored forces until they saw the first remains of a burned-out tank and its charred crew; after that, they were content to put their trust in the sheltering earth. "As a farm youngster, the land meant either hunger or bread to me," a soldier from Texas observed. "Now its shape is the difference between life and death."[3]

The GIs never had to live in the elaborate and static trench systems of the Great War's Western Front. Nevertheless, up front they too spent much of their time in Europe dug in: whether they were pinned down on the beaches of Salerno, Anzio, and Omaha or under siege at Bastogne; whether they were crawling up Italy's boot or slogging through Lorraine and the Hürtgen Forest. Even during breakouts and pursuits, the GIs inevitably rushed from foxhole to foxhole.[4]

Foot soldiers always stayed close to the soil. They ran heads down, they stooped, they crouched. When enemy salvos resounded, they instinctively dropped to the ground and flattened themselves, pressing cheeks, knees, and ankles against the earth, burrowing into the sand with belly and thighs. Under fire, the slightest hole, depression, or crevice beckoned, and infantrymen considered tank ruts and ditches the next best thing to pillboxes. When bedding down, or during other long halts, soldiers simply disappeared beneath the earth. Day after day, GIs hurriedly dug holes, using shovels and picks, entrenching tools, helmets, and bare hands. They excavated slit trenches to lie down in, foxholes to sit or stand in. When the advance bogged down completely and enemy fire intensified, the men constructed dugouts for the long haul. Such underground shelters could look like veritable homes, with roofs of corrugated steel camouflaged with sod, floors covered with mattresses and rugs, and walls with stoves and chimneys. When the GIs were not digging holes, they were enlarging them, strengthening them, improving them. They spent so much time turning up dirt and living in holes that they complained in letters home they felt like prairie dogs.[5]

"Me future is settled, Willie," cartoonist Bill Mauldin had GI Joe say while he was digging yet another slit trench. "I'm gonna be a expert on types of European soil." The American soldiers had come to Europe to fight, not to sightsee. Up front, they obtained most of their impressions of the Old World from ground level or below. Their worm's eye view showed them the particulars of Europe's sand, clay, and sod before it taught them more about the people and their society. Moreover, the combat soldiers analyzed Europe's earth almost exclusively in the context of the war. They were, after all, not overseas to marvel at the land, they had come to liberate and to conquer it. The GIs therefore did not discuss it in terms of panoramas and vistas. For frontline men, the significance of the Old World's earth simply lay in the security it could offer against the destruction of battle. A medic who was digging in during the fury of Normandy, for instance, could hardly be expected to pay attention to the richness and charm of the lush, green pastures that surrounded him:

I tried to think of some better means of protection. Even if the hole were deeper, it would not have helped. I looked up at the mound of earth that I had shoveled out when I made the hole and felt like pulling it in upon me.[6]

When sand changed into rock, digging in became impossible and Europe's earth lost much of its protective quality. In the mountains, soldiers felt more naked than ever. The Americans were surprised at finding so many of them in the Old World. They were awed by the volcanic mountains of Iceland. Instead of desert and jungle, they saw coastal ranges drop sharply into the Mediterranean from French North Africa.[7] Sicily's surface turned out to be almost all mountainous, with rugged peaks in the north and massive Monte Etna in the northeast. "The further we went the higher the mountains were," said a chaplain of the 1st Infantry Division. "There was no end of them in Sicily."[8] Things only became worse for the GIs who invaded mainland Italy. They were dumbstruck to find that Europe's so-called soft underbelly proved to be "pregnant with hard mountains."[9] Across the Alps, the GIs slogged their way from the mountains of the Massif Central, the Jura, the Vosges, and the Ardennes to Hitler's "Eagle's Nest". Those Americans who pushed all the way into Austria spent even the very last days of the war amidst some of the most imposing mountains of Europe.

War tainted the mountains as it did most of Europe's scenic splendor. During the Gustav Line breakthrough, for example, a surgeon of the 88th Infantry Division observed in his diary that massive artillery fire made the beautiful Italian mountain ahead of him look like "a volcano with craters bursting forth from all its sides." Mountains that had once enthralled walkers, alpinists, and skiers could only make the GIs cringe. "We also saw the snow-capped mountains today," a private wrote from the Vosges, "and instead of looking beautiful (which they are) they only fill us with the dread of a tough fight ahead."[10] Marching in column over steep, narrow trails on the edge of cliffs and gorges was a nightmare. It took men of the 88th Infantry Division six days during the Gustav Line breakthrough to reach Itri, which was only ten air miles across the Monti Aurunci Ridge. Soldiers gasped for air at high altitudes. They developed "climber's disease," and swelling and throbbing calf muscles and heel tendons disabled them for days.[11] The Americans almost constantly used pack mules to carry supplies in the mountains of Sicily and Italy. In the campaign on the mainland alone, they received help from 11,000 such animals. Nevertheless, so many mules perished on the treacherous trails that the GIs themselves were often forced to drag food and ammunition uphill on hands and knees. On top of all that, the impact of enemy fire increased in the mountains. Shells splintered rock into jagged shards that formed a vicious sort of shrapnel. At the same time, the impenetrable surface prevented the soldiers from disappearing below ground. They could only build beehive-like parapets of rocks and boulders to create at least some protection. To make matters worse, evacuation of the many wounded was a grueling task in mountainous areas. Hand-litter carries could take many hours and exhausted the bearers. Frequently, stretcher squads had to be strengthened with cooks, company clerks, and partisan volunteers. Medics used mules extensively to help carry stretchers; they even had to employ tackles in some cases. As a result, casualties often suffered more from the journey than from their wounds.[12]

The GIs were soon assigning new names to Europe's mountains that better reflected what they meant to soldiers in wartime. There arose a "Crazy Hill" and a "Million Dollar Mountain" in Italy, a "Red Hill" in France, a "Bogeyman" and a "Purple Heart Hill" in Germany. But it was the endless series of nameless hills and mountains that caused even more suffering. Correspondent Richard Tregaskis noted that on the tags attached to the wounded in Italy, medics often simply scribbled "hill" after the caption "Place where injured."[13] The soldiers knew most of the hills they occupied only by number. The army replaced the poetic names of Europe's mountains by impersonal digits. In Sicily, Monte Basilio became Hill 1035 and Monte Timponivoli Hill 1209; in Italy, Monte Camino was known as Hill 963 and Monte Sammucro as Hill 1205. The numbered hills were as menacing as they sounded. American soldiers met fierce resistance on Hill 1034 in Sicily, suffered tremendously on Hill 1205 in Italy, lost many comrades on Hill 87.9 during the Siegfried Line campaign, fought hard for Hill 310 in Lorraine, and were severely tested on Hill 313 in the Ardennes.

War cast a dark shadow over most of Europe's natural beauty. It transformed the picture-postcard mountains of tourists into the towering deathtraps of soldiers. As if to emphasize that metamorphosis, Monte Vesuvius, dormant since 1906, erupted again in full force in 1944. Many American soldiers entered Europe through the harbor of Naples under the volcano's dark, giant clouds of ash. In the Old World, nature seemed to conspire with man to present the continent to the GIs as a cauldron that would never stop boiling over.[14]

VEGETATION

In the winter of 1943–44, trains rushed men of the 88th Infantry Division from Magenta to Oran on their way to the Italian front. The GIs passed an endless series of colorful vineyards and orange groves planted by the French. "I long for peacetime," a combat doctor sighed in his diary, "so that I could stop here and really enjoy this glorious panorama." Up front, the GIs would get to know the Old World's vegetation as intimately as its earth. But the meaning of its flora, like that of its soil, would be determined only by the vicissitudes of battle. One American described how he experienced the scenery of the Alsace as an infantryman who lived in constant fear of German mines:

> Danger is sunk in the pastures, the woods are sly,
> Ingenuity's covered with flowers!
> We thought woods were wise but never
> Implicated, never involved.[15]

All of Europe's landscape, however, turned out to be involved in the war. The soldiers used some of it to their advantage. Enemy fire, for instance, taught them in no time how to become invisible in vineyards and olive groves, how to tuck themselves into hedgerows, and how to melt into woods. Yet, plant cover hid as much danger as it offered security. In the front lines, the soldiers' eyes searched restlessly for movements in still landscapes and for inconsistencies in the pattern and color of weeds and trees. Even the sweetish smell of dripping resin contained the ugly memory of recent enemy shelling and the stark warning of more to come.[16]

Perhaps nothing proved to be a more stubborn natural enemy to the GIs in Europe than the hedgerows of the Norman countryside. The hedgerow is the most persistent feature in the Cotentin. For centuries the Norman farmers have been enclosing each plot of land with living fences. These are half earth, half hedge. At the base they consist of earth that varies from one to four or more feet in thickness and three to twelve feet in height. Out of the earth grow hedges of hawthorn, brambles, vines, and trees that can be one to three feet wide and three to fifteen feet high. As the fields are irregular and tiny, the hedgerows follow no logical pattern and are innumerable.[17]

American soldiers complained that their invasion training had prepared them for storming beaches but not at all for hedgerow warfare, which was, according to an officer of the 29th Infantry Division, "as distinctive in its way as mountain warfare."[18] The GIs soon came to detest the hedges as much as the mountains. The lush vegetation hampered the adjustment of artillery fire and limited the use of armor. The impenetrable fences divided the battlefield into a sea of compartments. These formed natural defensive positions that the enemy exploited to the utmost. The small, fenced-in fields formed myriad traps. The dense foliage provided perfect camouflage, especially for snipers. In addition, the narrow, sunken lanes that ran between the fields and under the hedgerows created perfect trenches for enemy soldiers lying in ambush.[19] According to a Texan from the 9th Infantry Division, the hedgerows in Normandy were so thick that "[i]f you had dammed up the gates you would have had a land of catfish farms."[20] The GIs had to construct periscopes for peering over the hedgerows. To advance, they literally had to cut their way through the living fences. Men became entangled in the thick foliage and lost contact with their comrades. In the heat of the Norman campaign, Ordnance units eventually improvised expedients to help the combat soldiers break through. They supplied bazooka projectiles with more sensitive fuzes, for example, that were able to blow gaps in the hedgerows. But the hedgerow cutters they placed on tanks proved most decisive. These allowed the vital armor to slice through the matted roots of the embankments and to offer support to the infantry at last.[21] On 1 July 1944, a corporal of the 743rd Tank Battalion wrote home: "The 'Battle of the Hedgerows' continues as near to jungle fighting as anything I can think of." War changed the bocage, so charming a scenery in peacetime, into what the GIs soon called "this goddam country."[22]

And then there were Europe's woods "You hear everyone say, 'Soon we'll see trees!' How we have missed them!" That was the feeling in December 1943 among the men of the 5th Engineer Combat Regiment who had been stationed for more than a year on the barren volcanic rock of Iceland and were now on their way to England.[23] They would soon learn in battle, however, that Europe's woods were as dangerous and treacherous as the hedges of Normandy.

The American soldiers could not help feeling small and fragile in the oppressive atmosphere of the ancient forests they knew from Old World myths and legends. When the 14th Armored Division arrived in the bridgehead across the Lauter River in December 1944, a disquieted captain decided to send patrols through the gloomy woods around Soultz-sous-Forêts:

> This woods made me think of Little Red Riding Hood and the big bad wolf ... It was almost dark in these woods through the day because the trees were tall and close enough together to shut out the light.

The GIs who entered the vast Hürtgen Forest felt like walking into "a green cave, low-roofed and forbidding." Its silence, remembered a medic, was "awe-inspiring."[24]

Once the solid masses of green had swallowed the GIs, the silence was quickly shattered as the forests aided and abetted the enemy in unleashing their destruction. Thick foliage hid snipers. Tree tops exploded with the shells and showered fragments that reached inside the foxholes. Tight webs of roots often prevented the vulnerable men from digging in at all. Firebreaks beckoned the soldiers, but enemy fire was usually zeroed in on them and many intersections became known among the GIs as "Purple Heart Junctions." Europe's fairy-tale forests changed into some of the worst killing grounds of the war. The Hürtgen Forest absorbed unit after unit from mid-September to mid-December 1944. It devoured five divisions: 23,000 men were killed, wounded, or missing; another 8,000 fell prey to combat exhaustion and the elements. The dense evergreen forests of the Ardennes in turn brought the American troops so much havoc and suffering that John S. D. Eisenhower entitled his book on the Battle of the Bulge *The Bitter Woods*. But the war also transformed many of Europe's smaller wooded areas into vicious death traps overnight. Few GIs escaped picturesque woods like the Forêt de Gouffern, the Bois d'Amélécourt, the Forêt de Château-Salins, or the Bois des Valets without scars. Many of their comrades never emerged from them at all.[25]

The war reached into every nook and cranny of Europe. It climbed to the tops of its mountains and spread to the darkest corners of its forests. And everywhere it ensured that the GIs would come away with a distorted and dismal picture of the Old World. The fog of war obscured the beauty of its landscape as much as it would the merits of its society. In April 1945, a corporal of the 76th Infantry Division briefly halted on a hill to overlook the Rhine panorama and its many vineyards. The fleeting moment only caused him to realize with pain how much Germany "had perverted even this glory to politics."[26]

What made Europe's nature look even more tragic, however, was that the perversion of its beauty did not remain limited to that of the present war. The GIs were keenly aware that it had also taken place on numerous occasions in the past.

Of that endless series of Old World wars, none had etched itself more firmly on the American mind than the Great War of 1914–18. Ironically, its memory was unlocked time and again during World War II by one innocent-looking flower: the poppy. Poppies seemed to be everywhere in the European war theater: they grew knee-high at Kairouan, Béja, and Mateur; they waved by the thousands at Anzio; they radiated color in the Norman fields.[27] The flower fascinated the GIs. A tank driver in the Mediterranean enclosed a poppy in a letter to his mother and, the day after, another one in a message to his father. Near Saint-Lô, a medic plucked one beside his foxhole: "The bright red petals and black seeds. The green leaves. I dissected them carefully and examined their fibers closely."[28] Some GIs had never seen the flowers before, others thought they looked quite different from the ones in America. But the poppies rarely failed to remind them of the famous Great War poem "In Flanders Fields", and the GIs were quick to identify them as "the death flower."

In the Flemish pastures, the poppies had blown "amidst the crosses row on row" and had become the symbol of war's insanity. Only 25 years after the Great War, the American soldiers rediscovered the bright red flowers overseas, and again they were swaying gently around Europe's dugouts and graves. This time, however, they appeared to be telling the GIs not only that war was insane, but also that it was an inevitable part of the Old World's nature.[29]

LIGHT AND DARKNESS

In the front lines, soldiers did not measure time by the clock. They only thought in terms of daylight and darkness. But war changed even the meaning of sunrise and sunset in the Old World. On 10 August 1943, soldiers of the 3rd Infantry Division landed under cover of night in the rear of the Germans on the northern coast of Sicily. When they reached Monte Brolo, they started digging furiously in a race to get below ground before the sun betrayed their presence. Similarly, men of the 501st Parachute Regiment who dropped near Hiesville in the morning of 6 June 1944, rushed out of the fields to find cover before daylight could reveal their position. All along the European front lines, the GIs learned to fear daylight. Tension gripped the soldiers as soon as the faint, spooky light of dawn spread over the terrain. Daybreak was known as "the critical hour:" it was the time when troops attacked most often and ran the highest risk of being attacked. The arrival of light announced another full day of furious battle as it made the enemy clearly visible again and one's own position most vulnerable. During the day, soldiers who were not attacking or pursuing simply stayed below ground. The only other cover could come from natural fog or man-made screens. Chemical units were especially active in Italy, where the mountains offered the enemy perfect observation and where American troops employed smoke pots and fog oil extensively during amphibious operations and river crossings. During several weeks, for example, special units at Anzio shrouded the area in a thin haze that appeared half an hour before dawn and did not lift until half an hour after sunset.[30]

Although night brought its own tensions and fears, most soldiers accepted the shielding blanket of darkness with a sigh of relief. The patrols and raids that both sides organized under cover of night were still nerve-racking, but darkness mainly offered the GIs the opportunity to undertake activities within their own lines that proved too dangerous during the day. A platoon leader of the 7th Infantry Regiment at Anzio remembered that his men never moved around in the daytime and that he received replacements only at night. When his unit was at last relieved, he knew most of his men only by their voices. In many combat areas, enemy fire made it impossible for groups to gather during the day and even forced chaplains to postpone church services until night.[31]

Combat soldiers became conditioned to extinguish all lights after dark. The tiniest point of light flaring up amidst pitch blackness could work as a magnet attracting death and destruction. GIs on board ships to Great Britain were told that a lit match could be seen by submarines 15 miles away and consequently were only allowed to smoke below deck. Allied ships appeared before the North African coast for Operation Torch with their portholes painted black, and when the American troops left the landing crafts, they had to pass two rows of blackout curtains before facing the surf. Paratroopers flew from England to Normandy in unlit cabins; the windows had blackout curtains and the soldiers had to stop smoking once they arrived over the Channel. The headlights of trucks that carried troops to battle on the Continent were painted black except for tiny crosses of light. Candle-lit cans, with letters punched in the sides, served as road signs. Upon nearing the actual front, the soldiers had to descend from the vehicles and then continue toward their positions in single file and pitch darkness.[32]

Up front, light was even more anathema to the soldiers once night arrived. Near dusk, GIs in foxholes quickly smoked a last cigarette and hurried to complete letters home. Smoking was often not allowed at night and men who did steal an occasional smoke had to make sure they hid the flare of the match under a blanket and the glow of the ashes in cupped hands. Only soldiers who stayed in cellars were fortunate enough to be able to use candles to write letters after sunset, provided they blacked out the windows. In the field, soldiers crawled under raincoats to study maps with flashlights and medics worked on the wounded under shelter halves to hide the light. Orders often also forbade the use of fire to heat dinner rations, which were not very palatable cold. Despite freezing temperatures, men were forced to extinguish makeshift stoves in dugouts when sparks from the chimney threatened to give away their position. Veterans also knew better than to use rifle fire at night; they preferred to throw grenades at patrols to prevent the muzzle flash from revealing their whereabouts. Seasoned troops even liked beards because they helped to camouflage pale faces in the darkness.[33]

As a result of these measures, frontline men spent much of their time in the Old World in a darkness that was absolute. When soldiers of the 168th Infantry Regiment moved into line for the final assault against Hill 609 in French North Africa during the night of 21 May 1943, they had to hold on to the butts of the rifles ahead of them.[34] Darkness became even more persistent during Europe's winters, when velvet blackness closed in by mid-afternoon and lingered long through the morning. The Army guides had warned the GIs that much of Europe lay farther north than the US and that a country like Ireland, for example, lay "about exactly opposite Labrador." At the front, the Americans found out why the GI guides had called attention to the short winter days of the Old World. Paratroopers who defended Bastogne around Christmas were amazed that each day brought about "sixteen hours of night." Even when dawn eventually broke, winter did not allow much light. "Dawn came with its usual maddening slowness," a private in the Saar Valley observed in December 1944. "You'd wonder if it actually was coming on or if your eyes were merely growing more accustomed to the dark."[35] But nowhere was the blackness more stygian than in Europe's dense forests. During the battle of Biffontaine in October 1944, Japanese-American soldiers could only move through the Vosges forests at night by putting one hand on the shoulder of the man in front. GIs in the Hürtgen Forest formed chow lines for evening meals by holding on to one another's belts and shuffling toward the voices of the cooks. They never saw what they had for dinner.[36]

In the front lines, light that did pierce the night could only mean trouble. Enemy lights and flares were a constant matter of concern to American guards and patrols. During one of the nights of the battle for Long Stop Hill near Tunis in 1943, several observation posts of the 1st Infantry Division nervously reported that they had seen a strange light appear over the German positions. Before the command post could check the news, however, the tense observers hastily apologized for having mistaken the rising moon for an ominous signal. Lights often meant that an attack was imminent. As soon as the Germans across the river at Beaufort in Luxembourg jumped off for the Ardennes counteroffensive on 16 December 1944, for example, GIs of the 60th Armored Battalion found themselves blinded by huge searchlights shining from the enemy side.[37] Two days later, a combat engineer in a replacement depot at Liège jotted in his journal:

> About midnight a bunch of Kraut planes came over & I thought, this is it! Here's where we get it! They circled around & around & dropped flares & brother that makes you feel as naked as a jaybird. Everything lit up bright as day.[38]

Whenever the Allies themselves took the initiative at night, they created what was known as "artificial moonlight." Huge searchlight batteries focused on cloud banks hanging low over the front so that the reflected light made it possible for assault troops to identify their objectives.[39] The only other flashes that could light up the dark skies at the front were caused by artillery fire. A lieutenant of the 8th Infantry Division described the eerie effects brought about by friendly and enemy fire in an otherwise pitch-black Hürtgen Forest:

For an instant as each gun fired, the sky would light up with a blinding flash. After the sudden, brilliant burst of light, it was hard to adjust your vision again to the darkness. Circles and stars danced before our eyes, and you had to struggle to keep from losing your balance. Far off on the horizon answering reports from the enemy's big guns appeared like quick little flickers of heat lightning.[40]

Yet the war did more than plunge Europe's front lines into pitch darkness. Total war not only hurled army against army, but also society against society. As a result, entire countries had been forced to live under strict blackout regulations for years. When the GIs arrived in Europe, the civilians were still scrupulously smothering all light at night in the hope of keeping death and destruction away from their homes. It took GIs who arrived in Great Britain straight from the US quite some time to adjust to a country that was "universally Stygian by night."[41] On Christmas Day of 1943, an impressed Catholic soldier wrote to his mother that even midnight Masses were out of the question in England because of the strict blackout. By the time American troops left Britain for French North Africa, illuminated cities had become so strange to them that they clambered on deck to gaze nostalgically at the blazing lights of cities like Tangier and Ceuta in Spanish North Africa while sailing through the Strait of Gibraltar. But once the GIs had passed these neutral zones, Europe's total darkness restored its grip without mercy. Combat soldiers who withdrew for rest and reorganization often found the rear in the European war theater to be not much different from the front lines at night. Those who returned to England, for instance, simply relived the scenes they vividly remembered from battle on the Continent: blackout became total when dusk arrived, hooded lamps marked road intersections, civilians shuffled through streets with cupped flashlights, and searchlights slashed the skies. World War II turned all of Europe into a battlefield and so made the Old World look like a truly dark continent to the American soldier.[42]

THE SEASONS

Summer

Europe's summers never managed to enchant the American soldiers who waded toward the beaches of Sicily, Normandy, and the Riviera. Most of them had no idea of what autumn and winter would bring to the mountains of Italy and the forests of Western Europe. A mere inkling of what the Old World's darkest months had in store might have made it easier for them to bear the sun-drenched skies. As it was, the GIs mostly focused on the particular discomforts with which summer tended to harass soldiers.

The American soldiers who were destined to invade Europe learned what a scalding sun meant in combat for the first time during the campaign in French North Africa. According to one private, the last months of the war in Tunisia in the spring of 1943 turned out to be "hotter than a New York street at two o'clock on an August afternoon."[43] Many GIs were surprised to find that Sicily was no less sweltering and that an almost African sun burned over Italy in the summer. Armored troops perhaps suffered most under these conditions. In the summer months of Italy, the temperature inside a tank could climb to 130 °F. But even the milder summers of Western Europe caused complaints about the heat. Perspiring infantrymen in England during the summer of 1944, for instance, grumbled at the US Army for having sent them overseas in uniforms made of warm wool rather than light cotton.[44]

The sun in turn baked the earth into a dry crust. Dust was a companion that proved to be as inseparable from summer as it was from war. Shuffling infantry columns, swirling truck convoys, and roaring tank spearheads created veritable curtains of dust. In some European villages, the civilians found themselves forced to form bucket brigades that spread water on the roads to settle the dust from the many passing vehicles.[45] Blasting shells and bombs too kicked giant clouds of dust up in the air. A sergeant described in a letter home what had happened when waves of American bombers had paved the way for the Normandy breakout in August 1944:

> A wall of smoke and dust erected by them grew high in the sky. It filtered along the ground back through our own orchards. It sifted around us and into our noses. The bright day grew slowly dark with it.[46]

At times the dust clouds in North Africa were so thick that they made the GIs feel safe enough to move around freely despite the omnipresence of the mighty *Luftwaffe*. But dust also bothered the soldiers in countless ways. In Italy, signs along the roads warned chauffeurs to drive slowly because dust clouds would attract enemy artillery. The powdery dirt covered men from head to toe. It blackened faces, clung to eyebrows and beards, irritated eyes, and made mouths feel gritty and throats thirsty. The fine sand penetrated everything. It would get into tanks even when they were buttoned up and forced crews to clean guns endlessly.[47]

Summer brought yet another plague upon the soldiers: insects. Heat, combined with the chaos and filth that followed in the wake of war, multiplied their numbers. GIs noted that millions of flies literally speckled the air in French North Africa and soon the joke went that the aggressive mosquitos looked for the blood group on the dogtags before striking.[48] A lieutenant wrote from Sicily that "the flies were so thick you could eat them," while a sergeant claimed he had never seen more mosquitos than in Normandy and swore some of them were "as big as blackbirds."[49] Frontline men were only rarely able to shower and insect powder often did not reach them at all. As a result, they spent much time picking lice from their clothes. Moreover, soldiers were often forced to hide in deserted houses infested with fleas, and they rarely objected to sliding between old sheets even when these crawled with bedbugs. "Since hitting this country," a soldier of the 3rd Infantry Division in Italy complained, "I've been bit by everything but a mule and a mad dog."[50]

Under such conditions, parasitic diseases easily spread among the soldiers. Mites caused contagious itches and ugly crusts: some 8,000 GIs with scabies were admitted to hospitals in the MTO, another 25,000 to those of the ETO. Fleas in sandy areas were responsible for a brief virus disease that caused fever, headache, swollen eyes, and malaise. Hundreds of cases of sandfly or pappataci fever landed in hospitals of the ETO, thousands in those of the MTO. But the worst parasitic disease by far was malaria. It was known to be widely prevalent in French North Africa but did not become a problem for the American troops there because the campaign ended before the onset of the season. The disease did become a serious worry, however, during the 1943 summer campaign in Sicily. Netting and gloves were judged impractical in combat; Atabrine tablets had therefore been distributed with rations as early as April for the island campaign. Unfortunately, several problems occurred. Dosages were wrong at first and supplies sometimes did not reach the front lines at all. But, most importantly, soldiers avoided taking the bitter pills, while line commanders showed laxity in supervising them. The GIs only realized the seriousness of the threat when it was too late.[51] "Malaria has become rampant and place is being flooded with fevers," an alarmed surgeon jotted in his diary at Nicosia on 6 August 1943.[52] Fevers soon outnumbered battle casualties in Sicily. In a period of two months, the Seventh Army reported no less than 9,892 malaria patients on the island, compared with 8,375 wounded men. By the time the GIs moved to the Italian mainland in September 1943, the US Army had left nothing to chance. Special units treated the disease's breeding grounds systematically and troops were forced to take Atabrine more conscientiously. The measures curbed the incidence of malaria in Italy, but the disease was to remain a serious problem. The Fifth Army's 1943 peak reached 193 cases per 1,000 in October; its 1944 peak was still 94 per 1,000 in June. All in all, MTO hospitals recorded no less than 75,000 malaria admissions throughout the war. Curiously enough, thousands of GIs also fell victim to malaria in Western Europe. Soldiers with temperatures of over 100 °F stumbled into aid stations in Normandy and feverish men collapsed in the snow of the Bulge. All of them, however, had contracted the disease in the Mediterranean and suffered one or more relapses across the Alps. ETO hospitals reported 15,000 admissions for malaria in 1944 and another 12,000 in 1945. Europe's summers thus caused suffering among the American soldiers until long after the heat had simmered down.[53]

Autumn

To men who could rarely change their clothes and had little opportunity to find shelter indoors, wetness was a curse. Yet the GIs in the front lines seemed destined to get soaked incessantly in the Old World. Those who waded or swam to the invasion beaches spent their very first hours in Europe with chattering teeth. To slow down the Allied advance, the Germans regularly flooded large areas: they used water as a shield in several places in Italy, in much of Holland, and in the Ruhr Valley, for instance. In the course of their retreat, the enemy also systematically blew up all the bridges over rivers and canals. The GIs often preferred to wade across streams anyway, even when bridges had remained standing, for fear that enemy artillery was trained on them. Moreover, some of the Allied replacement bridges were constructed about a foot under water to make them invisible from the air. On top of all that, time and again mines drove soldiers from roads and fields into marshes and streams. The Germans had sown so many explosive devices in the Hürtgen Forest, for example, that GIs who were chilled to the bone preferred to wade through icy rivulets rather than to risk losing a foot or a leg. Whenever combat soldiers became drenched, clothes and shoes dried irritatingly slowly. Sloshing socks blistered feet and soaked pants chapped behinds and galled groins. At the front, wet soldiers were condemned to feel clammy during much of the day and to shiver throughout the night.[54]

But it was when autumn arrived in the Old World and rain started falling that the GIs abandoned even the hope of ever feeling dry again. In 1942 Great Britain immediately introduced the Americans to what rain could mean in Europe. The Army guide to Northern Ireland clarified that thundershowers should not be expected, but rather "gentle drizzles." It added, however, that this drizzle occurred some 200 days a year and that the climate was damp and chilly much of the time. Likewise, the guide to England warned the GIs that they should expect "almost continual rains." It concluded resignedly: "Most people get used to the English climate eventually." But many GIs did not get used to it easily. "So far as I'm concerned they can give this country back to the Indians," a private wrote from Britain to his sister in October 1942. "I've seen some miserable weather that beats even Kentucky. It rains every day."[55] Not surprisingly, the Americans who left Britain for French North Africa in the fall of 1942 looked forward to the sun of the Mediterranean. Serious disappointment awaited them, however, as the start of Operation Torch happened to coincide with the onset of the rainy season. Moreover, in North Africa rain did not come as drizzle, but in the form of violent cloudbursts and torrential downpours. "The fall rains started the day we landed," observed a discouraged chaplain of the 1st Infantry Division, "and slowly, but surely, became worse."[56] Not long after the end of the North African campaign in 1943, the GIs became acquainted with the Continent's autumn. They encountered the first heavy rains while still in Sicily late in August 1943. When they finally moved on to the Italian mainland in the fall of 1943, the Americans hardly recognized the sunny country they had heard so much about. "Ireland was wet," a medic put in his diary in November 1943, "but Italy is putting that country to shame."[57] On the other side of the Alps, precipitation was pestering the GIs long before autumn set in. In Normandy and Brittany, for instance, rain fell rather abundantly even during the summer months of 1944, and soldiers from the Deep South soon learned that an August shower in France could be a lot colder than October rain in Georgia. The autumn of 1944 itself turned out to be exceptionally wet. In Belgium, for example, the liberation months of September, October, and November had seen more rainfall only twice since the beginning of the century. The season only served to confirm earlier impressions among the GIs of the Old World as a vast vale of tears.[58] "We wear huge boots and float around

Europe," a private in the Vosges told his parents in November 1944. "Rain reigns here. Alla time."[59]

And it brought nothing but misery to the soldiers. In French North Africa, the GIs initially welcomed overcast skies because they shielded them against Axis air attacks. Once the Allies had gained air superiority, however, the men in the front line only wished to see clear skies. Rainy days prevented air support and slowed down columns and convoys. They seemed to benefit only the German defenders and GIs soon referred to them as Hitler or Kraut weather.[60] Rain also caused untold personal hardships for the combat soldiers. The GIs experimented with all kinds of clothing to stay at least somewhat dry. The long woolen issue overcoats soaked up so much moisture that men walked "stooped at the waist as if they carried the burden of the world on their backs."[61] The raincoats of rubberized cloth repelled the rain but caused such profuse sweating that the soldiers felt wet anyway. The poncho was the GIs' favorite piece of rainproof clothing, not only because it allowed body ventilation, but also because it covered most of their equipment. Keeping rifles dry proved especially frustrating. Soldiers tied handkerchiefs around the triggers and bolts, stuffed cleaning patches in the barrels, and pulled condoms or wax paper from the ration crackers over the muzzles. Fashioning a livable foxhole in heavy rain required even more ingenuity. GIs first covered the pits with fence posts and raincoats, then they threw sod and pine boughs into the holes to soak up the ground water. Sometimes, surface water made digging in simply impossible, and it ended up that soldiers spent entire nights squatting on trunks or rocks with nothing but ponchos pulled over their heads.[62]

The GIs' health suffered considerably in the wet and chilly weather. Ninety-six per 1,000 soldiers were admitted to hospitals in the MTO and a similar number in the ETO for common respiratory diseases, most of them from October through February. Ironically, in the ETO this disease rate was highest in 1942 and 1943 when the GIs were still training in Great Britain. During combat in the ETO, the peak occurred in October 1944 when no less than 372 soldiers per 1,000 had to be treated in hospitals for common respiratory diseases. In the MTO, such admissions reached their highest point in January 1944 with 215 per 1,000 soldiers.[63] Rain also severely affected the morale of the men in the front lines. In November 1944, a lieutenant scribbled in his journal while the battle for the Bois d'Amélécourt was raging in torrential rains:

> I have never had much fear of dying if I could be warm and dry. ... But under such conditions as today and tonight, I can think of it only with an attitude of the greatest dread.[64]

In some parts of the Old World, the GIs welcomed the first autumn rains because they took away the suffocating dust at last. Unfortunately, the rains proved so persistent that they gradually transformed the dust into mud, which eventually became one of the GIs' most detested natural enemies. The Americans were forced to live and fight in mud for so long that they became veritable connoisseurs of the numerous varieties that reigned in the European war theater. The GIs analyzed and described Europe's mud in painstaking detail. In Iceland it was "sizzling hot," in England "soupy," and in French North Africa "gumbo," whereas in France and Belgium it varied from "thin paste to huge chunks;" in Germany it proved "dense, heavy, sucking."[65] Europe took on the looks of a giant sea of mud. At times, it appeared to the Americans as if the slimy substance was burying the Old World like molten rock had once smothered sinful Pompeii. In the Gothic Line, for instance, GIs saw how mud slid downhill "like a slowly moving stream of lava;" in Lorraine, shell fire sent "geysers of mud into the air;" and in the Bulge too "[c]akes of mud were rising up like lava."[66]

The mud slowed down the Allied advance more than the rain itself. American engineers desperately tried to keep the traffic flowing. They used immense quantities of rock and gravel to drain the road surfaces. In Italy they even crushed valuable Carrara marble to cover the muddy roads to the front. Nevertheless, innumerable fields and roads changed into quagmires that greedily swallowed vehicles. Half-tracks had to wrench themselves out of slush with cables tied to nearby trees; tanks lost tracks in the deep mud; mired jeeps had to be left behind in the clinging soil. During the battle of Santa Maria Infante in 1944, the tanks of an entire company of the 760th Tank Battalion bogged down in a marshy area near a creek; it took engineers and armored bulldozers an entire day to pull the much-needed assault weapons out of the unrelenting mud.

Men, however, suffered more than machines in the slimy substance. They dragged themselves through deep ruts, with clothes and shoes grown heavy with mud, and never felt dry or clean. Line men spent battle intermezzos scraping clumps from their leggings with bayonets and removing gobs from their buddies' clothing. The mud also attacked their equipment. Rifle sights clogged, operating rods jammed, barrels split. Heavy mortar battalions were unable to support the troops at Anzio because accurate fire proved impossible when the base plates sank into the area's slop. The drenched soil also delayed the digging of foxholes. Soldiers tried in vain to shake the sticky earth from their shovels and often lost precious time scraping the mud from the entrenching tools with their hands. Mud's stubborn presence in Europe placed not only a physical burden on the combat soldiers, but also a mental one for which no one seemed able to offer relief. On more than one occasion, the Old World's mud was so deep it even prevented the GIs from kneeling when chaplains attempted to celebrate Mass in the field.[67]

Rain and mud proved so persistent and abundant in the Old World that the GIs came to suspect that the cataclysmic war had something to do with the exceptionally bad weather. An American from a well-to-do east coast family, who had toured France several times before the war, hardly recognized the country when he returned to Normandy as a lieutenant of the 2nd Armored Division. "It is pouring rain and has been raining intermittently for days," he wrote despondently to his mother early in July 1944. "I've never known France to be like this before."[68] From all over Europe, GIs reported that the weather appeared to be behaving abnormally. When a private of the 34th Infantry Division in Italy called a December day in 1943 "one of the wettest days in history" he did not intend it only as a manner of speech.[69] GIs near the Siegfried Line in October 1944 claimed that natives had told them it was the worst weather in 80 years. American soldiers in Alsace-Lorraine presumedly learned from French authorities that the rainfall had not been so heavy in 200 years. In December 1944, the Third Army, by express orders of general Patton himself, distributed a quarter of a million prayers among its soldiers. The prayer beseeched the Lord "to restrain these immoderate rains" so as to enable the Allied soldiers to crush the enemy's "oppression and wickedness."[70] Some GIs, however, could not help wondering whether the Old World's wickedness, or at least its vicious warring, was somehow to blame for the Noachian flood. After all, the doughboys in 1918 had believed that the seemingly constant rain in France was caused by the tremendous blasts of the artillery, and they had even nicknamed the biggest guns "rainmakers."[71] Moreover, Europe's sodden fields painfully reminded the GIs of Flanders' muddy meadows and of the traumatic war the doughboys had fought in the Old World only a generation ago. A private confessed to his parents in a letter sent from France in October 1944: "This is just like the first war – mud three inches deep. It's too terrific to describe."[72] The oppressive weather triggered flashbacks that accentuated Europe's recidivism unrelentingly throughout the war. While a column of GIs trudged through Germany on a February day in 1945, the gloomy atmosphere jolted a private into recalling the war that should have ended all wars:

> Sometimes against the rainy sky and flailing trees you caught a dim silhouette of the men. It looked like a scene from the First World War, showing the doughboys slogging through the mud.[73]

As with the poppies of sunnier seasons, the rain and mud seemed to reveal to the GIs that war was inseparably intertwined with the Old World's nature. As happened so often during World War II, Mauldin spoke for many of his comrades when he gauged the deeper significance of Europe's slimy earth:

> Mud, for one, is a curse which seems to save itself for war. I'm sure Europe never got this muddy during peacetime. I'm equally sure that no mud in the world is so deep or sticky or wet as European mud.[74]

Winter

Soldiers in the front lines who were exposed to the elements for weeks and months on end, feared cold even more than rain and mud. Traditional Old World snowscapes had always featured nostalgically on American Christmas cards, but the GIs could only worry about the arrival of winter in a Europe at war. The mere thought of it depressed the combat soldier. Early in October 1944, an infantry officer in the Alsace wrote in his journal:

The weather has been unspeakably bad also, and what with the dawning realization that the war may continue through the winter, it has been sufficient to lower my previous high spirits.[75]

The Old World certainly impressed itself on the minds of the American soldiers as a chronically cold place. The first GIs who came to the aid of Europe were sent, rather ominously, to Iceland, where many of them had to be hospitalized or removed from the island because of weather-related mental problems. In Britain, dampness and the lack of sun made the weather seem cold the year round. In 1942 the GIs in Britain were still wearing their winter uniforms in August. The winters were quite mild, but small coal stoves were the only source of heat in the sheet tin barracks, and shivering American soldiers were forced to keep their outdoor clothes on indoors and even in bed. "I think I'll always think of England as a place where I huddled by the fire to keep warm," a chaplain wrote to his wife in January 1944.[76] Those GIs who had expected the Mediterranean climate to be comparable to that of southern California throughout the year felt cheated more than once. During the campaign in French North Africa, heavy snow fell in the mountains and at the higher altitudes of the coastlands water froze in the canteens at night. Sicily's summer nights made the GIs shiver even when sleeping in woolen clothing under extra blankets, and Mauldin declared the winter of 1943–44 the coldest in Italy's history.[77] A private who arrived in southern France in the winter of 1944–45 was astonished to see women wearing fur coats. "If this is the warm part of Europe," he wrote to his parents, "I'm not looking forward to the rest of it this winter."[78] The winter in Western Europe indeed turned out to be harsh, although it was not at all exceptional. It is true, for example, that January of 1945, with an average minimum temperature of –6.3 °C, was one of Belgium's coldest in half a century (it had been colder only in January of 1940 and 1942) and that in the winter of 1944–45 the Belgian Ardennes received more snow than usual. Yet, apart from January 1945, Belgium's liberation winter was warmer than that of many previous years, and even the first weeks of 1945 can hardly be called Siberian by any objective standard.[79] But in the eyes of the American soldiers, who had to work and sleep in the snow without much protection, winter took on a different dimension. "I guess the winters here are like the ones back home," a private from Massachusetts reported to his mother in November 1944, "but when you are living out it isn't too good." Some of the GIs who were rushed to the Bulge as reinforcements in December 1944, for instance, sat on open trucks for 16 hours, wrapped only in blankets. By the time they arrived in Belgium, frozen men were crying from pain and had to be carried from the vehicles. In such circumstances, it was no wonder that a soldier of the 84th Infantry Division called Belgium "the coldest place on earth."[80] That several American units ended up in the mountains of Bavaria, Austria, and Bohemia during the last weeks of the war only served to strengthen the GIs' perception of an arctic Europe. There, hail, sleet, snow, and cold harassed them until May 1945. Many GIs left the Old World convinced that it was the coldest continent on earth.[81]

Winter in Europe held few redeeming qualities for the GIs. They were glad that the cold took away the stench of decaying flesh and that the snow hid the ugly scenes of death and destruction. But apart from that, winter only added to the soldiers' suffering. King Winter knew as many tricks as the rain to hamper the Allied advance. He hardened the mud, but at the same time made roads slippery and played havoc with motorized vehicles. During the Battle of the Bulge, soldiers had to warm up motors at least twice a night if they wanted their vehicles to start in the morning, and even then only urinating on the carburetor and battery could do the trick. Moreover, heavy snow made mine detection nearly impossible and slowed down nervous troops.[82]

The cold also affected the GIs' personal equipment. The men had to urinate in barrels and on triggers to get rifles and machine guns operating again. They slept with canteens on their bodies to prevent the drinking water from freezing, while medics carried plasma under their armpits. Ration cans froze solid and could not be eaten when fires were forbidden.

It was the GIs' clothing, however, that caused most problems. The combat soldiers were dissatisfied with several items of their winter uniform. To begin with, there was a serious shortage of camouflage suits for use in snowy terrain. That proved particularly inconvenient during the Ardennes counteroffensive, when soldiers were forced to ask civilians for white cloth and had to improvise suits from materials as diverse as sheets, flour sacks, and cheese cloth. What turned out to be much worse was that the winter uniform in several ways also failed to protect the soldiers adequately against the biting cold. The long woolen overcoat proved impractical at the front, while the field jacket, worn underneath it, was too thin by itself to shield against the cold. The GIs also disliked the woolen Army gloves because they were short-wristed and soaked up moisture. They were equally dissatisfied with the woolen caps that did not offer enough warmth under the steel helmets. Most serious, however, were the complaints about the footgear. American soldiers arrived in Europe with ankle-high, leather shoes, worn with canvas leggings. Because it was tedious to remove them, combat soldiers frequently kept them on for long periods, thus opening the way for foot ailments. During the war, the Army therefore switched to the production of combat boots that were intended to replace the service shoes and leggings. The boots were similar to the shoes, but they had a cuff and buckle top that increased their height and eliminated the clumsy leggings. Frontline soldiers found the boots very comfortable and practical, but they lamented that they received them too late in the war and that only rear echelon troops profited from them. To keep not only the cold but also the snow and the rain out of the permeable leather, the Army eventually also designed rubber overshoes. The problem with them was that they were too heavy for long marches so that combat men often discarded them. The Army then developed so-called shoepacs that came with woolen ski socks and were intended to replace shoes or boots in cold wet conditions. Unfortunately, most frontline men did not receive those shoes until late in January 1945 when the worst weather had already passed.[83]

The American combat soldiers responded to the many deficiencies of the winter uniform by improvising warm clothing as best as they could. They wrapped strips of blankets under their uniform, filled their clothes with newspapers, and scavenged the wool-lined windbreakers worn by tank crews. They pulled socks over their hands and wore towels or tank crews' cloth caps under their helmets. Men in service shoes took combat boots from dead GIs and fought over paratroopers' jump boots. GIs wrapped their feet with paper and stuffed the overshoes with straw to keep out the cold. Soldiers without shoepacs wrapped their shoes or boots in blankets or burlap. The GIs also turned to the home front in their frantic search for more warmth. Worried loved ones responded with vigor and sent a stream of winter packages to Europe. The parcels most often contained long-sleeved, turtlenecked, woolen sweaters, scarves and gloves, face hoods and ear muffs, heavy woolen socks and foot jackets. When winter approached in 1944, a company commander of the 2nd Armored Division decided to play safe: he ordered – and received – a pair of boots from L. L. Bean in the US.[84]

Warm clothing was of vital importance to soldiers who worked and lived outdoors almost constantly. Even when tank crews wrapped themselves up in several blankets, the metal cold of the vehicles still penetrated their bodies, and some preferred to sleep outside on the warm motor. Infantrymen huddled in foxholes to escape the icy winds. Straw became a valuable commodity at the front as it kept the holes warm and dry. Frozen men experimented with all kinds of heat sources. To thaw their hands they lit dubbin cans or C-ration cans with dirt on the bottom and fuel poured over it; to warm a canteen of instant coffee they burned the waxed K-ration boxes. During the winter of 1944–45, woolen sleeping bags with zippers were issued in large numbers, both in the ETO and the MTO, to replace the traditional two blankets. But although the frontline men found them much warmer than the blankets, they were often afraid to use them in forward foxholes for fear of being trapped during an alarm. Moreover, in the middle of winter many line men had to get by not only without sleeping bags, but even without foxholes. Digging in was a demanding task when several feet of snow had to be removed before the frozen earth itself could be tackled. In the Belgian Ardennes, some GIs resorted to digging small holes with pickaxes and planting quarter pound blocks of TNT in them to loosen the earth. More unfortunate comrades, however, had to scrape at the soil with entrenching tools for countless hours, spending most of the night exposed to enemy fire as well as the bitter cold.[85]

Clothing inadequacies combined with unfavorable operational conditions to make cold a serious competitor to enemy fire as a major cause of casualties among the Americans at the front. Dawn after dawn, GIs woke up feeling frozen, rheumatic, and feverish. "I awoke with ice in my veins," wrote a private who was dug in somewhere in Lorraine,

> my chin trembled; my hands shivered like tuning forks. But worst of all, the cold had settled in my spine. I seemed to be bodiless. I was a bundle of icy vibrations.[86]

Hospitals in the MTO treated almost 3,000 GIs for excessive cold, those in the ETO no less than 27,000. Winter undermined the soldiers' health in many ways. Pneumonia struck some 2,500 GIs in the MTO and more than twice that number in the ETO. Epidemics of heavy colds swept the combat troops. Many of the men in icy foxholes could barely whisper because of laryngitis. Racking coughs became a real danger in the front lines. Some soldiers managed to quell their coughs with massive doses of pills before they went on patrol, others had to be sent to the rear for fear that they would betray their unit's position. In addition, frostbite relentlessly attacked the men's skin. The wet woolen gloves froze around hands and caused such deep, painful splits at finger joints that soldiers became unable to lace their shoes or button their pants.[87]

Worst of all, however, was what Europe's winters did to the GIs' feet, with 10 per cent of the American battle casualties in Italy and 9.25 per cent of those in the ETO being the result of what was officially known as "cold injury, ground type." This was a painful foot disorder that resembled frostbite. The problem usually started with a tingling, burning sensation, followed in a few days by numbness and swelling. Untreated cases could lead to gangrene and amputation. The injury was the result of prolonged exposure to cold, aggravated by moisture as well as inactivity and constriction of the feet, possibly also by lowered metabolic rates due to fatigue and lack of hot food and drinks. It occurred most often in combat units, and the highest rates were invariably found in the infantry divisions.[88]

Like autumn, with its rain and mud, winter refused to let the memory of the Great War rest. The peculiar foot disorder was a case in point. It had been very common in the trenches of France and Flanders and it was there that it had received the name "trench foot." The GIs spontaneously adopted that name during World War II and used it much more commonly than either "frostbite" or "immersion foot." As a result, more than 46,000 Americans were treated for trench foot in hospitals all over Europe in a war their fathers had pledged they would never let happen again. It was, therefore, no wonder that it appeared to the American soldiers as if the Old World's diseases would never go away.[89]

Spring

American troops remained in Europe long enough to go through the cycle of seasons more than once. And, invariably, the dark skies, the rain and mud, and the cold and snow faded into the gentleness of spring. There was something comforting in the certainty that nature would keep its promise even in the middle of a cataclysm created by man. On 18 March 1945, a sergeant in Germany wrote in his journal:

> Spring. I suppose not even a war can change the seasons. In the middle of a shooting war the sap is going to rise in the trees, the grass is going to turn green, & flowers will bloom.[90]

No one was more sensitive to spring's promise of new life than soldiers who were constantly haunted by death. The GIs watched closely how the reborn sun cherished nature until the grass turned green again and the blossoms reappeared. The soldiers themselves felt regenerated as they basked in the warmth of the new light. "But this beautiful sun," a private in the Alsace wrote to his parents in March 1945, "it's a life saving sun for the whole damn world."[91]

No one listened more closely to spring's message of hope than soldiers who had lived with despair for so long. The balmy air lulled the nerves and the soporific season made the GIs feel lazy and merry. Several weeks after D-Day a medic's unit was still trapped in Normandy, but the spring climate could obviously do miracles for his and his comrades' spirits:

> The soft, warm sunshine and fresh, invigorating sea breeze offered a wonderful start for the new day. There was an air of gaiety within the outfit for everyone was whistling and humming.[92]

In the end, however, no one was more aware also of the irony of spring in the Old World than the soldiers who were fighting amidst its ruins. Europe had turned itself into a wasteland that seemed to scoff at the promise of new life. "The night was one of those mild June nights that poets write about," observed a paratrooper who landed behind Utah beach in the darkness of 5 June, "but this was neither the time nor the place for poetry."[93] On the Anzio beachhead, the GIs could hear the song of birds, but only when pauses in the artillery fire allowed them to. In Italy's valleys and Normandy's fields, combat soldiers noticed how the sweet fragrances contrasted perversely with the acrid odor of powder smoke and how the pastel blossoms only succeeded in bringing out more harshly battlefield's ashen reality. When the sun finally removed Europe's blanket of snow, it uncovered the grisly bodies that had been overlooked by the graves registration units. When warmth mellowed the air again, it released the sickly smell of decomposing corpses and carcasses. Never was the stench of death more pungent in Europe than in the season that had traditionally heralded rebirth.[94]

In the eyes of the American soldiers, spring did not seem to hold a message of hope for the Old World anymore. Nothing could have been a stronger exhortation for lasting peace in Europe than the First World War. Nevertheless, after barely 25 years, the continent had plunged itself into yet another great war. That conflict proved to be an even worse cataclysm than the one still painfully fresh in people's memory. Spring after spring came and went in Europe during World War II without the traditional promise of better times. The American soldiers experienced quite the contrary. Rather than bring an end to the bloodshed in the Old World, each new spring increased the violence as clear skies and warmer temperatures enabled fresh offensives. Allied troops first used the spring of 1943 to engage in a final, bloody struggle with the Axis forces in North Africa and then feverishly switched to preparing for the Sicilian invasion. Among the paratroopers training in Britain for

D-Day, tension rose as early as January of 1944: that was when the days started lengthening noticeably and the approach of optimal fighting weather became irreversible.[95] In the spring of 1945, the GIs braced themselves once again, this time for the offensive into the lion's den itself. That spring appeared to be a season of hope at last. The American soldiers had little doubt that the new campaign was the final one and that the war would be over in a matter of weeks. Early in April, however, the GIs were shocked to find that they had barely begun to uncover the heart of Europe's darkness as they happened upon the first concentration camps in Germany. In the middle of spring, the horrible discoveries cast new shadows over Europe, far more ominous than any the GIs had witnessed in the preceding seasons. When the war ended in May 1945, it looked to the American combat soldiers as if the Old World had become stuck in the autumn of life forever.

The wartime condition of Europe's nature influenced the American combat soldiers' perception of that continent in two important ways. First of all, total war prevented them from seeing much of Europe's natural beauty. For decades, Americans had visited the poetic Italian valleys, the ritzy French Riviera, the fairy-tale Rhineland, and majestic Austria; almost all had gazed at it enrapturedly. World War II, however, did not leave a stone unturned in perverting Europe's scenic splendor. It permeated its soil, it implicated hedges and trees, it disturbed the role of day and night, and it affected the meaning of seasons. What the GIs therefore inevitably retained of Europe's nature was not its pastoral charm, but the obscenity of the battlefield. Total war did not allow the American soldiers to obtain a tourist view of Europe and distorted their image of it into one that was exceptionally negative.

But the American soldiers' perception of Europe's nature did not just stop at the scenic surface; it also cut deep into the character of the Old World. The soldiers realized, of course, that they were seeing a world in trying circumstances and that the ugliness of an otherwise beautiful continent was solely attributable to the ravages of total war. That, however, not only failed to prevent the negative image of Europe, it also was not the essence of the matter to the GIs. They wondered why the Old World had allowed such a cataclysmic war to happen in the first place. Europe's very nature hinted at the clue to this mystery. The natural surroundings constantly reminded the GIs that World War II was anything but an isolated incident in the history of the Old World. They did this in particular by relentlessly bringing to mind the other great war that had devastated the Old World only years ago. The poppies, the rain, the mud, and the trench feet of World War I never seemed to have disappeared from Europe and thus helped to convince the American soldiers that war was simply endemic to that continent. This in turn helped to confirm a more deeply rooted American view that the GIs held of the Old World: that of a place doomed to suffer chronic warfare because it was afflicted by a string of seemingly incurable diseases, of which tyranny, poverty, intolerance, and vice were only a few.

The experience of World War II, the memory of the Great War, and the traditional American prejudices against the Old World thus meshed in the minds of the GIs. To be sure, World War II was responsible for the ultimate perversion of Europe's natural scenery, but that war itself only seemed to be the culmination of a long process of rot. In other words, World War II merely appeared to be bringing about the crash of a world that had already been ruined from within. And the American soldiers were convinced that this time they were witnessing the final collapse from which the Old World would not recover. Their perception of Europe's bludgeoned armies and of its wrecked society would serve to strengthen that conviction considerably.

Part II
The Soldiers

2 The Soldiers – Introduction

When the minds of the American frontline soldiers were not preoccupied with Europe's natural surroundings, their attention inevitably shifted to its soldiers – both allies and enemies. Once the GIs had properly dug in, they started wondering what kind of men their European allies were, as they relied on them to protect their flanks. Having melted into the hedges and woods, the Americans waited anxiously to learn what kind of people the Axis soldiers were who had been trained to kill them.

At first glance, individual as well as national distinctions between the men in the different armies appeared to have been erased. The military's proclivity to standardize equipment and to issue uniform clothing made everyone look alike on the surface. Soldiers – countrymen, allies, even foes – seemed to have become interchangeable. They were reduced from "people with recognizable characteristics" to "shapes created by accoutrements."[1]

The accoutrements of men at war did not differ much. GIs who had lived and fought with each other for months on end only managed to identify specific buddies in the fog of battle by their silhouettes, the manner they wore their helmets, or the way they carried their guns. More importantly, the US Army had to go to great lengths to ensure that its soldiers would be able to recognize the enemy. During the last briefings for paratroopers in the afternoon of 5 June 1944, dummies wearing German uniforms stood guard near the sand table facsimiles of the drop zones, and GIs were ordered to dress as German soldiers and visit the line company tents. Replacements who arrived at the front in northeastern France in September 1944 were first marched to a field with a large outdoor stage on which an officer gave an hour-long demonstration of German weapons, equipment, and clothing. But only the most seasoned veterans became adept at picking out the enemy in grey days and dark nights, often on the basis of details as minute as how they carried a gun.[2]

To many GIs the visual uniformity of the soldiers of different nations remained confusing throughout much of the war. At times, for example, the Americans took on the appearance of their British comrades-in-arms. This was particularly true during the early stages of the American participation in the war. The GIs who descended from the gangplanks in Northern Ireland early in 1942, wearing uniforms and equipment reminiscent of the Great War, had an uncanny resemblance to their British counterparts. They had not yet been issued pot helmets and instead wore the British-style tin hats, known as dishpan helmets. In North Africa, the American newcomers sometimes had to rely on a variety of British supplies. Men from the Big Red One's 18th Infantry Regiment, for instance, were given British underwear, battle dress, and shoes during a rest period in Tunisia early in 1943 and were sent back to the front in a mixture of British and American uniforms. Now and then such exchanges of clothing were used purposely to confuse the enemy. Americans relieving British troops near the Garigliano River in the winter of 1944 were told to pretend they were British in order to mislead German observers and Italian civilians; they were issued dishpan helmets to aid them in that challenging task. As late as October 1944, Dutch civilians mistook American airborne troops patrolling across the Lower Rhine near Renkum for Tommies because of their particular helmets.[3]

Helmets were the cause of still more confusion. If the dishpan helmets had made them look like the British, the Americans soon found out, to their embarrassment and detriment, that their new pot helmets looked suspiciously similar to the German coalscuttle. It took the British quite some time to get used to allies looking like Germans. An American lieutenant who acted as liaison between the 1st Infantry Division and the British 78th Infantry Division in North Africa barely escaped being shot at by soldiers from the Hampshire Regiment. He was only allowed to pass their roadblock after careful examination of his identification papers by guards who had become alarmed by his companion's helmet and his own overseas cap, both of which reminded them of German headgear. By the time of the Sicilian campaign, the British had still not grown used to the new American helmet. While covering the advance to Messina, war correspondent Richard Tregaskis was given the advice to wear a British helmet to avoid being mistaken for a German.[4]

The GIs themselves at times confused their countrymen with Germans. Paratroopers who had jumped into Sicily were fired on when they tried to hail an American reconnaissance jeep carrying soldiers who had never seen US airborne troops before. But exactly how convincing the Americans could be as Germans was probably best demonstrated by men of the 83rd Infantry Division who were advancing toward Honvelez, Belgium, during the Battle of the Bulge. When they passed a German patrol after dark, it silently joined their column. The Germans were captured before their mistake had time to register.[5]

When facing each other in the front lines, Europe's slimy earth often added the finishing touch to covering up the differences between friend and foe. "The enemy lives in the same kind of mud that we do too," a Japanese-American soldier of the 44th Infantry Division wrote to his parents from the sucking fields near Sarreguemines, "so sometimes it is hard to tell the difference between all the mud-covered soldiers."[6]

No matter how similar the conditions of war made soldiers of different nations look, however, the Americans in the course of time clearly noticed that hidden underneath the uniform layers of clothing and comparable coats of mud were people with distinct national characters and cultural attitudes that made them behave differently – even under fire. Yet, despite those remarkable differences, the American soldiers were affected most deeply by what Europe's armies – both Allied and Axis – proved to have in common. While the soldiers from the New World and their Soviet comrades from the East were growing stronger spectacularly as the war dragged on, all of the European armies were weakening dramatically. The GIs became convinced that the Old World's military strength had been suffering for a long time from deficiencies that were seemingly inherent to armies fielded by that continent. They watched with awe how World War II delivered the coup de grâce to Europe's legendary forces.

3 The Allies

The conflagration that erupted 25 years after the outbreak of the Great War had the unmistakable dimension of a global conflict. The events of a world at war made individual lives appear vulnerable, even insignificant, and none more so than those of the soldiers on the battleground. Instinctively, fighting men looked for strength in numbers. Hope for survival seemed to lie more than ever in becoming one with a larger body of human beings. One of the favorite pastimes, for instance, of men of the 90th Infantry Division in England in the last weeks before the invasion of France was to sum up over and over again the American divisions they knew had already joined them. "We didn't like the idea of being too much alone in this big show," one of the division's surgeons commented, "and we longed for plenty of company."[1]

The Americans received just that from allies from all over the world, a cosmopolitan experience that did not fail to impress even the soldiers from the New World's melting pot. A private from the 42nd Infantry Division wrote to his parents in California, after he had arrived in Marseilles from New York in December 1944:

> I never saw so many different uniforms in all my life. Everything from French Arabs with turbans and black smith red fezes on their heads, long scars on their foreheads and cheeks, still sticking to their tribal custom of so-called facial beauty by cutting gashes in them, to Russians and Poles from the Polish army who wear forest green uniforms that look much like a ski-suit.[2]

The experience was not just a cosmopolitan one; it was a comforting one too. The American soldiers wanted to be reassured that they had not become the world's lone crusaders in a Europe that had fallen prey to dark and powerful forces. During his training in Camp Gruber, Oklahoma, in November 1942, a lieutenant of the 825th Tank Destroyer Battalion listened with great satisfaction to the news of how the British had beaten Rommel at El Alamein, the Russians had launched a counter-offensive at Stalingrad, and the Americans had landed on Guadalcanal. "We sense the all-embracingness, the inter-connectedness of this war," he wrote to his wife. "It is truly a world war. Nearly every continent, every ocean, every people is involved."[3]

The feeling of international comradery had an inspiring effect on the Americans. A GI who witnessed an Allied parade on a square somewhere in North Africa in the summer of 1943, felt chills go up and down his spine as he listened to the national anthems of the French, the British, and the Americans. The sight of the three nations' flags filled him with "a unique feeling of solidarity." The fact that people from all over the world had joined the Americans in arms to fight for a common cause impressed the importance and validity of that cause on the GIs. A soldier concluded in a letter from Casablanca to his father that the Allied army was "shining democracy in khaki trousers and high brown shoes" and "a melting-pot symphony of human liberty and equality." Allied solidarity at the same time imbued the GIs with greater certainty about whose cause would ultimately prove victorious. "[T]he fine unity shown between the various nations – the French, the Canadians, the Americans and the British," a Jewish sergeant wrote home from Italy. "That's what spells success."[4]

Gradually, however, the American soldiers became disappointed with the role their European allies were still able to play up front. The main armies that fought on their side, the British and the French, appeared to be increasingly disintegrating under the strain of the conflict's unremitting demands. In comparison to the vigorously expanding New World and Soviet militaries, the Old World allies seemed to be shrinking in importance with each new year of war.

THE BRITISH

The GIs often called the British soldiers "Tommies," but their preferred name for them was "Limeys." Whatever nickname they attached to them, the Americans had a hard time fathoming the British soldiers. More reserved than their extroverted and sociable cousins, they often struck the American soldiers as aloof and unapproachable. A soldier of the 34th Infantry Division who helped unload British matériel from North Africa at Bari, Italy, in the fall of 1943 wrote in his diary that they were "nice fellows" but that "they don't mingle with us much." Cartoonist Bill Mauldin considered the average Englishman to be "a pretty good egg," although he felt frustrated by his "unholy fear of making a friend until he has known the candidate for at least five years."[5]

When the American soldiers started arriving in Great Britain in 1942, the surrender at Singapore and the reverses in North Africa had thoroughly shaken their confidence in the British soldiers. In November 1942, only 59 per cent of the GIs in camps in the US rated the British soldiers' fighting ability as good or very good. That was probably why the Army guides to Great Britain thought it wise to remind the American soldiers "that no criticism has ever been made of the gallant, stubborn fighting of the ordinary British soldier." The GIs were warned not to pretend they had "won the last one" and not to tell the British "their armies lost the first couple of rounds in the present war."[6] Nevertheless, in pubs across Britain Americans could soon be heard asking to be served beers "as quickly as you guys got out of Dunkirk" and proclaiming that "yellow" was the fourth color of the Union Jack.[7]

The news of the British turning the tide at El Alamein late in 1942, however, slowed down the erosion of American confidence. "Whatever their fighting qualities," a private of the 1st Armored Division in Northern Ireland wrote in his diary, "the British don't know when they are licked."[8] The reputation of the Eighth Army in particular soared. When American troops found themselves in dire straits in North Africa a few months after El Alamein, much of their hope was pinned on the hardened British veterans. A chaplain with 1st Infantry Division troops on the defense at Medjez el Bab, Tunisia, early in 1943 recalled that "of course, we never had our minds off of the excellent advance of the British Eighth Army." A GI who met some Desert Rats in North Africa at the end of the campaign wrote home that they were a "rugged bunch" and that he admired them.[9] But the British soldiers who advanced from the west with the American troops also managed to carry away the appreciation of the GIs. "I have met and talked with a number of British soldiers," a GI from New Jersey wrote home. "I have yet to see one that I could find fault with or criticize in any way. They're a nice bunch of guys. Good soldiers."[10] By the end of the North African campaign, confidence in the British soldiers had been much restored. Troops of the 45th Infantry Division received pamphlets on Sicily while on their way to invade the island some weeks later. When the fact that the information had been prepared by the British gave away that they were to join the GIs, this was received by the men aboard ship as "cheering news."[11]

At the time of the Americans' arrival at the front late in 1942, many British soldiers had already been in the field for years, and their experience showed. The British not only seemed to possess a wiry toughness, they also displayed an iron discipline that filled many Americans with awe. A lieutenant who acted as liaison between the 18th Infantry Regiment and the British 6th Armored Division in Tunisia remembered running into an MP sergeant-major of the 8th Hussars who came close to the kind of soldier Patton was dreaming of: "His shoes were shined, his web equipment was freshly blancoed, his brass shone and his uniform was spotless." A few months earlier, when the lieutenant had been attached to the British 78th Infantry Division, he had noticed how soldiers "of every rank shaved religiously every morning, good weather or bad, with hot water or cold," and he had considered himself fortunate that "those Spartan regulations" did not apply to the American army.[12] The GIs regarded several British items of clothing and equipment as more efficient than their own. The British uniforms were better adapted to the hot climate of North Africa, for instance. While the Eighth Army men only sported cotton shorts and shoes in the summer of 1943, Americans complained that they were wearing woolen olive drabs with hot, tight leggings. Even during the following summer in Italy, GIs were still stung by the fact that the British summer uniforms, which had short sleeves and left knees bare, were much more comfortable than their own. The Americans also admired the practicability of several pieces of British weaponry and equipment. Among them were the fine six-pounder 57 mm gun (which made the American standard 37 mm antitank gun in North Africa look like a "pea-shooter"); the powerful trucks with tractor-size wheels; the peculiar, small-tracked Bren gun carriers; the lighter and more compact gas masks; and the warm tents with bamboo poles and comforter-like sides.[13]

The experience of the British initially weighed so heavily that the American newcomers, who still had to prove themselves in the field, felt insecure and at times even inferior. The American setbacks in North Africa did much to strengthen these feelings. British government reports revealed, for instance, that its troops derived

quiet satisfaction from the Kasserine Pass debacle in February 1943.[14] And after
the battle of Fondouk Gap in Tunisia in April, British soldiers were singing:

> Our cousins regret they're unable to stay today.
> For the Germans are giving them *hell*[15]

Even worse than the songs the Americans knew their allies were singing behind
their backs was the British silence about it all in their presence. A wounded lieutenant
of the 1st Infantry Division suffered the humiliating experience of having to listen
to the news of the reverses at Kasserine Pass on a radio in the British 95th General
Hospital in North Africa. Afterwards, he was irritated by the fact that the British
patients, in their conversations about the war situation, remained "so conventionally
polite, as if trying to ease the blow," especially since he knew they were keenly
aware that the Americans had been cocky enough to believe the war would be over
in a hurry once they stepped into it.[16]

Long after the North African campaign, American feelings of insecurity could
occasionally raise their head in the presence of British troops. A GI who watched
the changing of the guard during a visit to London in September 1943 described
the close-order drill to his parents as "all faultlessly executed, of course, and
wonderful to an American soldier." A month later, a captain of the 29th Infantry
Division, who had just arrived in England and was watching British troops at
Tidworth Barracks, admitted he felt "overly concerned with what impression we
were making on the British." He feared that they possessed "a smarter and fitter
appearance" and that "the crash of their hobnail boots and stomping, arm-swinging
march style" compared unfavorably to "our simple, but no less precise, drill
movements." Even elite troops of the 82nd Airborne Division, sailing from Italy to
England in 1944, could not help feeling like "a mob of pirates" in the company of
the "neat and spotless" Scottish, Irish, and Coldstream Guards.[17]

Yet, gradually, the American soldiers started noticing cracks in the appearance
of British superiority. Ancient traditions seemed to stand in the way of maximum
efficiency in the British military. Myriad small things, of course, caught the eyes
of the GIs: the clumsy salute with palm out at the upper forehead; the trouble with
drivers neglecting to stay on the right-hand side on the Continent; the ludicrous low
shoes, knee-high socks, and kilts of the Scottish soldiers.[18] There were, however,
age-old conditions in the British army that reflected deeper chasms between both
countries and appeared to be particularly detrimental to the British army in the minds
of the Americans. Strange salutes and funny kilts could be laughed away, but the
GIs had a much harder time accepting the implications of Britain's strong social
hierarchy. They were stunned by the gulf that separated British officers from other
ranks and amazed by the distinctions that existed even between NCOs and enlisted
men.[19] At times, the Americans were convinced that the British had managed to
preserve the aristocracy's leading military role from as far back as the days of
Agincourt. Moments before the take-off from England for Operation Market-
Garden, the commander of the 506th Parachute Regiment reminded his men that

the units of the Guards that would join them were the best in the British army and that "[y]ou can't get in them unless you've got a 'Sir' in front of your name and a pedigree a yard long."[20]

Aristocrats or not, the GIs regarded the British officers as colder and more snobbish even than their subordinates, and American opinions on them ranged from "quite Colonel Blimp-ish" to "very stuffy."[21] The treatment the officers received in the British army was considered to be royal, even by American officers. No Americans could have been more baffled than the officers who were ordered to British units at the front for temporary liaison duties, there to be promptly assigned batmen by their hosts. A lieutenant of the 85th Infantry Division, sent to a Dominion unit at the Arno River in Italy to look for a place in its sector that could be crossed on foot, was stunned when he was appointed "a kind of servant" who cleaned his clothes, made his bed, took care of his weapons, and woke him up with a cup of tea in the morning. A junior officer of the 95th Infantry Division who was assigned to a British unit near Venray, Holland, to prepare its relief, received a similar treatment. He could not help but note "that the United Kingdom may have become a democracy but it was careful not to carry the ideal too far."[22]

The American soldiers were also mesmerized by the exotic appearance of colonial troops that came from all over the British empire. On many of the British ships that transported Americans to Europe – often colonial liners or freighters – colored staff served the officers. A battalion surgeon, traveling from Oran to Naples on the *Neuralia*, admitted in his diary that he felt "like a king" when waited on in the dining room by "Hindu personnel."[23] The British Eighth Army in Italy consisted of troops from places as diverse as India, Ceylon, Basutoland, Swaziland, Bechuanaland, Mauritius, the Seychelles, and the West Indies. The GIs were fascinated by Indian soldiers with long black beards manning British vehicles in the streets of Naples and by Sikhs wearing turbans under their helmets at Cassino. In the end, however, such unusual scenes only served to strengthen the American image of the British army as a military fossil.[24]

The outdated traditions, rigid structures, and imperialist anomalies of this Old World army made it look unsuitable for the total wars of modern times. The British troops had already teetered on the brink of collapse during World War I and the GIs became more and more convinced that the British army was not able to cope with the tremendous pressures of World War II either. As the war dragged on, the British men began to look less and less soldierly. GIs of the 88th Infantry Division, who watched British soldiers move up in battle column to relieve them during the Gothic Line breakthrough late in 1944, were tickled to see among them men smoking pipes, fellows carrying canes, and others carefully observing the surroundings through horn-rimmed glasses. Apart from their quaint mannerisms, GIs often also found the British physically unimpressive. Tregaskis reported from Centuripe, Sicily, that the British soldiers "were sturdy and sunbrowned, but short men by comparison with the Americans." The soldiers who marched into the Gothic

Line looked "chubby and pink cheeked," and a 3rd Infantry Division soldier, while on leave in Naples, found the British to be "husky men with blithe, red faces."[25]

Already much weakened economically by the convulsions of the Great War, the additional demand for resources to counter new worldwide strategic threats was pushing the British nation and empire to the breaking point. Thriftiness was born out of years of scarcity, and the frugal British formed a stark contrast with the Americans, who seemed to bathe in a wealth of matériel. "God help the Tommy who loses his Enfield rifle," Mauldin wrote jokingly. He noticed that the British were often appalled by the amount of discarded equipment the GIs carelessly left behind in their areas. "You blokes leave an awfully messy battlefield," he had a weary Tommy, carefully holding his rifle, say in a cartoon to an equally weary Willie and Joe, heavily laden with weapons and ammo. Mauldin was hardly the only one to notice the material discrepancies between the British and the Americans troops. When in the fall of 1942 American Rangers departed Corkerhill Camp near Glasgow, they left behind everything not deemed essential. They did not even bother to turn it in at the supply tents, but simply abandoned it in the mud: rations, tents, helmets, rifles, grenade fuses, ammo, and personal items such as books, sweaters, and toilet articles. A detail of British Pioneers was sent over to clean up the area. A lieutenant of the 1st Infantry Division who witnessed the scene found it "too embarrassing to even look them in the eye." The difference in material wealth led to painful episodes more than once. The same lieutenant who had been embarrassed by the waste at Corkerhill Camp later saw the American Red Cross hand out free books, cigarettes, razor blades, handkerchiefs, towels, and toothbrushes to Americans only in a British hospital for officers in North Africa. He noticed it left the British wounded "a little miffed" that their Red Cross did not provide a similar service. Gradually the GIs realized how heavily the British had come to rely on America once again to fill the shortages caused by war. A tank crewman wrote to his family after he had witnessed the British move victoriously into Bizerte in May 1943:

> This may come as a surprise to you, but the English 8th Army is the most over-rated army in the world. They should be good after fighting for four years and equipped with the best of American equipment.[26]

Even more indicative of British economic wretchedness was the striking difference in soldiers' pay. The Army guides to Britain reminded the GIs that both their wages and soldiers' pay were "about the highest in the world."[27] The disposable pay of a newly enlisted GI in Britain in June 1942, for instance, was £3.50 or $14, whereas his British counterpart only had £0.87 or $3.50 to spend. British service pay was low not only in comparison with that of American troops but also with the wages of British civilian workers.[28] The GIs were urged by the Army guides to treat this issue with the utmost sensitivity since they carried "the greatest sources of potential trouble right around with you in your billfold" while the British were "pretty touchy" about the matter.[29] But the inequality of pay remained an object of curiosity among the Americans wherever they met British soldiers. Men of the 1st Infantry

Division in Scotland in 1942 had a hard time believing that British liaison officers could play card games in earnest "for the ridiculous stakes of a penny or tuppence." Others had difficulty accepting the injustice and took up the cause of their comrades-in-arms. A soldier writing home from Algeria early in 1943 explained that the Tommies' pay was "a big joke," and he added rebelliously that he could not understand why they tolerated it: "When you consider that on the average most of them have been in 3 and 4 years you wonder how their families manage to live."[30]

No matter that some GIs expressed their sympathy, their money in the end talked the loudest. The Americans had been warned that, apart from insulting his army and boasting about their pay, "swiping his girl" would threaten the friendship with Tommy most.[31] Nevertheless, British soldiers overseas became particularly concerned about what was happening at home between their girlfriends and wives and the well-off GIs. "But during my absence long and grim," they sang with much melancholy to the tune of "Lili Marlene,"

> The Yanks had bought, with lime and gin
> My good-time English sweetheart,
> My faithless English Rose.[32]

They realized that what little pay they were able to send home was negligible and that American money might therefore prove an irresistible seducer. Rumors soon spread that "British girls flocked like bees to a honey pot around the free-spending Yanks."[33] In one British song about home, called "The Second Front Song," the words were those of resignation:

> And every time I think of her, with grief my body fills.
> But she'll do all right so long as there's a Yank to pay the bills.

The fact that they were losing the economic battle with their American cousins caused a humiliating feeling, as was shown in "The Second Front Song" where it described the experience of a Tommy who finally returned home. On the train to his house

> The seats had all been taken by the chewing gum brigade.
> They smoked their Camel cigarettes and petted with their janes,
> And looked at us like we were something crept out of the drains.[34]

A US Army survey of September 1942 revealed that almost nine-tenths of the GIs thought highly favorably of the British civilians, but that half of them gave evidence of a lack of friendliness with the British soldiers. This worried Allied leaders who were preparing for a combined invasion and feared an increase in mutual resentment with the build-up for D-Day. So much so, that in November 1943 they felt the need to start an "inter-attachment" scheme, aimed mainly at promoting exchanges between small groups of British and American enlisted men. About 10,000 soldiers were exchanged under this provision before D-Day, and the overall results were favorable as working and living together did breed a better understanding. But it only went so far. A mere handful of the 1.7 million GIs in Britain on the eve of

D-Day ever received this kind of preparatory exposure. And many of these men were stared in the face by inequalities so painful that even a better understanding could not make them go away. The British soldiers, for instance, turned out to have such a hard time reciprocating American hospitality that the British Treasury agreed in July 1944 to provide a small expense allowance for troops visiting or entertaining GIs.[35]

If British purchasing power could not impress the Americans, their gift for restraint never failed to do so. It was a knack that came to be especially admired when displayed under fire. No matter how destructive the situation they faced, the British somehow always managed to reduce it to only "a bit" of trouble. Upon nearing the furious fighting at the Volturno River, Tregaskis was cautioned by British troops to leave his jeep because there was a "[b]it of mortaring up there." British tank crews working on defensive positions near Nijmegen in a desperate attempt to stay put during Operation Market-Garden described the situation to a soldier of the 82nd Airborne Division as a "bit spotty." Throughout the war, the British never lost their equally admired sense of humor either. An officer of the 2nd Armored Division's reconnaissance battalion, who made contact with the British under a heavy barrage at the front lines not far from Caen, was directed to a wood by a sign reading: "Visitors, please park your vehicles here." 200 yards further down, a sign politely advised: "Visitors will please crawl from this point."[36]

At times, however, British restraint seemed to take on rather excessive forms and indeed looked very much like carelessness to the Americans. The GIs who were relieved by Tommies in the Gothic Line were surprised to see that they kept the roofs and windshields of their vehicles up, a habit that was contrary to American safety rules and regulations. A private of the Third Chemical Mortar Battalion could not understand why some of the Coldstream Guards' tank crews took the risk of sitting in the open with berets instead of helmets during the fighting near Münster in 1945. Neither did the British soldiers refrain from singing or striking matches and building fires at night. When an aggravated African-American soldier asked the British during the battle for the Ruhr why they disregarded the blackout precautions, they stoically replied: "Jerry knows we're here, old chap."[37]

Americans found this behavior hard to explain. Some were convinced it originated in the British temperament. A chaplain of the 29th Infantry Division concluded at the end of the Normandy campaign that the character of the British had been molded by their country's many wars and that making "'fun and games' of warfare, to underemphasize, to say little, to endure cheerfully, to pursue an end unflaggingly, to place honor ahead of all" had become "the *sine qua non* of the successful warrior." A surgeon of the 88th Infantry Division who observed the British in Italy likewise imagined that to them war was "just another big game" in which it did not matter "how long it takes, as long as you win."[38] And, believed many Americans, as long as they could fight it in a comfortable and civilized manner. A stunned officer of the 1st Infantry Division, for instance, watched the nearly surreal spectacle of British artillerymen lugging a collapsible canvas bath at the front near Medjez el

Bab early in 1943. Another Big Red One officer, attached to the British in Tunisia as a liaison late in 1942, was aghast when he found the officers leisurely discussing the purchase and preparation of a Christmas goose while an attack was coming up. They could not but make the American feel "like living in another world."[39]

To an extent, British behavior under fire did undoubtedly result from their temperament. Perhaps, too, it was the kind of bravado that could only have been developed by a long tradition of warfare and Michael Howard was right in saying that "too many of [the British army's] members looked on soldiering as an agreeable and honorable occupation rather than a serious profession."[40] Yet, some of the carelessness was a symptom of an army forced to overexert itself in what was one of the most challenging fights for the country's survival it had ever faced. British units thus had to be kept in the front lines for protracted periods. Veteran divisions from North Africa, for instance, proved cocky but unprepared and fatigued once they ran up against the Norman bocage and its determined German defenders. Losses became ever more difficult to replace. By October 1944, the 21st Army Group had found no other way than to break up the 50th and 59th Infantry Divisions to provide other units with new blood, and by the end of the year almost 27,000 airmen had been transferred to the Army.[41]

Moreover, training in the British army did not remain as consistent and effective as in the German army. Untested infantry quickly betrayed its inexperience during the treacherous hedgerow fighting in France. The performance of junior leaders in particular declined as some of the best non-commissioned officers had either not survived earlier campaigns or had hastily been given officer status. Green infantry officers arrived en masse and soon the casualties in their ranks, and especially those of the company commanders, rose dramatically. With experience and leadership dwindling rapidly, carelessness inevitably increased. Tank commanders, used to fighting with their turrets open in the desert, became easy prey for German snipers in the European foliage. So did inexperienced company commanders in the bocage, who proved unaware of such small but fatal facts as that their map boards flashed in the sun. Soldiers who lost NCOs and officers in turn tended to bunch together, causing mortar and artillery fire to claim unnecessarily large numbers of casualties.[42]

In the eyes of the Americans, the British army's exhaustion did not only manifest itself by costly carelessness, but also by an at times enervating caution. Ironically, the seeds of the GIs' frustration in this matter were sown by something so seemingly innocent as the British tea ritual. The Americans had grown used to seeing Tommies move up to the front with the ever-present white enameled tea cups dangling from their field packs. They had even come to accept the carefree British habit of having their "spot of tea" in full view of the enemy, a habit that dumbfounded GIs commented on from the Gothic Line to Nijmegen. But when tea time – preferably at ten in the morning and four in the afternoon – happened to coincide with war's more pressing demands and the British insisted on brewing their spot of tea anyway, the Americans lost their patience. Troops of the 83rd Infantry Division, involved in the Battle of the Bulge near Rochefort, failed to understand why their relief by the British 53rd Division suddenly ground to a halt on the morning of 1 January 1945. A hurried investigation revealed that, since it was ten o'clock, the British column had halted in the middle of the road and the soldiers were engrossed in boiling tea on their small, one-burner gasoline stoves.[43] Such incidents unfortunately did more than just make the Americans lose patience with British troops, they also made them lose confidence in them. When, during Operation Market-Garden, troops of the 82nd Airborne Division were attacked by German heavy tanks near Nijmegen and requested urgent British armored support, the Americans "cursed the British Lion" as it was about four o'clock and they doubted their allies would show up in time, knowing they "never passed up teatime."[44]

At Nijmegen that day, the British did arrive in time and were immediately forgiven. Nevertheless, the erosion of American confidence continued to spread. A soldier of the 1st Infantry Division concluded from their many stops for tea that the British "weren't as forward as us in doing things." The GIs knew, of course, that drinking tea would not make the British lose battles, but an officer of the 35th Infantry Division observed:

> because they did stop for tea, or for other causes on occasion, at what appeared to be inopportune times, the thought developed among us that they did not always go as far and as fast as they might have.[45]

The Germans, of course, were quick to play on the American suspicions. A pamphlet intended for US troops relieving British units during the Ruhr River campaign tried to dupe the GIs into believing that their allies were leaving the area because the air was too "heavy with lead." And it suggestively added: "As always, under these conditions, the British prefer to let you do the work."[46]

The erosion of confidence in the British troops gained much force in particular with the delay at Caen, when many GIs at the front lost their patience with "those bastard Limeys" for not getting hold of one of the key towns in Normandy.[47] Ever since the planning stage of Operation Overlord, British military leadership – haunted by the memory of the Great War and faced by manpower shortages – had been convinced of the need to use its soldiers as sparingly as possible and to depend on air, artillery, and tanks whenever feasible.[48] Although the Allies in general would later be criticized for abandoning risk-taking and for an overreliance on firepower and matériel,[49] the American soldiers increasingly considered avoiding risks to be a particularly British tendency, and they became more and more impatient with it after Caen. When men of the 101st Airborne Division asked British soldiers, whom they were relieving at Driel during Operation Market-Garden, why they did not fire at the Germans – who could clearly be seen moving around and digging in – they listened in disbelief to the British commander, who pointed out that the Germans would just fire back at them.[50] An officer of the 95th Infantry Division, who was sent ahead to Holland in February 1945 to prepare the relief of a British division near Venray, observed the opposite extreme. Day and night, the British directed an almost constant artillery barrage against the Germans across the Maas River. A British officer explained that they were short on manpower but had plenty of ammo and hoped to knock out as many Germans as possible without risking casualties. The American kept all comment to himself, although he was convinced "that about all this blind firing accomplished was to plough the ground, fell some trees, and maybe knock off a squirrel or two." A few months later, when witnessing the British take Bremen, the same officer found that the British were still employing similar tactics: "to minimize casualties by inflicting massive destruction on the enemy before closing with him."[51]

By then it had become painfully clear to most American soldiers that for the British, who were scraping the bottom of the barrel, war was not all "fun and games" and victory could not come soon enough.

THE FRENCH

Where the GIs had a hard time measuring the British soldiers, they found the French – sporadically referred to as "Frogs" – to be irritatingly ambiguous from the very first time they met them under fire. The uncertainty surrounding the French response to the Allied landings in their North African colonies during Operation Torch on 8 November 1942 left American soldiers confused even as to whether the French soldiers were allies or enemies. Most GIs thought of the French as friendly until they were actually shot at by them. Men of the 509th Parachute Regiment, whose planes were fired on by French antiaircraft guns on the way to La Sénia airport near Oran, were forced to perform "a tremendous feat of mental gymnastics" to adapt to the fact that the French proved hostile. Even then, the Americans had a difficult time accepting the unexpected turn of events. A company commander of the 4th Ranger Battalion felt "let down" in French North Africa because he "didn't relish the idea of slaughtering people who were not really our enemies."[52]

The Americans disliked having to fight the supposed French allies, but they did not seem to be at all intimidated by them. "We train like hell to fight the Germans and they send us to fight the French," a Ranger exclaimed upon learning on board ship at Glasgow that Algeria was the destination. His complaint betrayed disappointment as well as disparagement. Aboard a Polish ship transporting troops of the 1st Armored Division to North Africa, a sergeant was so worried about "the carefree attitude" of some of his men that he found it necessary to awake them to the danger ahead by painting a stark picture of "a tough fight" with the French that some of them would not survive.[53]

Only the French Foreign Legion succeeded in making many Americans jittery. The Legion, created in Algeria in 1831 and composed of mercenaries from all over the world, was preceded by a reputation forged in the field, enhanced by legend, and embellished by Hollywood. A combat doctor of the 88th Infantry Division imagined the legionnaires to be all "incorrigibles," while a Jewish corporal from New Jersey pictured them as professional soldiers without any "thought at all about tomorrow or the day after." Even a paratrooper could be made apprehensive by soldiers who were thought to believe "[t]heir lives were behind them." Little wonder that 1st Infantry Division troops, digging in near Oran during the first days of Operation Torch, felt "discouraged" when told to expect an attack by the Legion from its headquarters at Sidi bel Abbès; the GIs seriously doubted that they would be able to stand up against "one of the toughest fighting forces in the world."[54]

But if Hollywood had kept the legend of the Foreign Legion alive, recent history had clouded the Americans' memory of the grandeur of the bulk of the French armed forces. The Army guide to France tried to make the GIs understand that a "great French tradition has been justifiable pride in a long and illustrious military history." Yet, despite such efforts, America's soldiers did not set course to the shores of French North Africa with the old images of La Fayette's valor, Rochambeau and de Grasse's daring, and Napoleon's conquests in mind. Instead, they arrived in the colonies with the fresh memories of the exhausted and mutinous *poilus* of the Great War and "the spectacle of the apparent ruin of military power" in 1940.[55] The past decades had made it hard for the GIs to imagine that the French had ever been good soldiers. Even American terminology confirmed the impression of French military ineffectiveness when it referred to absurdly rigid disciplinarians as "martinets," accused soldiers who were absent without authorization of having taken "French leave," and suspected proponents of a purely defensive strategy of being "Maginot-minded."[56]

All this made the Americans wonder whether the French were made of the right fiber to be soldiers at all. The GIs were well aware that the French had proven their mastery in art, fashion, and cuisine. Traces of this could be found even among the French on the battlefield. A GI in Algeria, for instance, considered French officers "the most grandly dressed of all three Allies." They appeared "dapper" to many others, with their "epaulets and with a stiff, pointed, waxed mustache and imperial à la Napoleon III." Some Americans opined that the French made even the British look "sloppy."[57] And cooks at Fort du Nord, a Foreign Legion citadel in Algeria, convinced American Rangers that the French could indeed perform culinary miracles when they transformed the tasteless C-ration hash into delicious meals with the help of herbs, garlic, and onions.[58]

Whether such sensitive natures could withstand the pressures and cruelties of war, however, was a matter of American conjecture. To begin with, the French physique appeared to be rather delicate. The average stature of the French soldier proved so much smaller than that of the GI that a quarter of the first American deliveries of clothing items could not be worn. Thereafter, average US sizes were lowered considerably for French troops.[59] Moreover, some Americans feared that the French were also endowed with a rather fragile mental state. The commander of a paratroop battalion felt reassured when he discovered that the French colonel who commanded the troops at Tébessa, Algeria, late in 1942 was a confident man who inspired his subordinates. "Since many of the latter possessed the excitable temperament so often found in Frenchmen," the American recorded, relieved, "his presence was indeed fortunate."[60]

The conduct of the Gallic soldiers during the early stages of Operation Torch did much to strengthen the impression of French military ineptitude. Their fluctuating sympathies made them look like men on whom the Americans would never dare to rely with full confidence. The same French commander who was praised for his leadership at Tébessa, for instance, was also lauded because he "changed not a particle whichever way the winds of war blew our fortunes" whereas "others altered from time to time."[61] The Americans were not particularly impressed by French expertise and stamina in combat either. Logistical planning had not been adapted to modern mobile fighting and the French army still depended on a good deal of foraging during campaigns. Its supply branch was traditionally composed of men from the lower classes and the integration of large service units with combat divisions remained socially unacceptable. The French also tended to cling to static, defensive fighting and turned out to be no match for the Allied mechanized maneuver warfare that combined different arms.[62] Rangers who attacked Arzew on 8 November 1942 ran into French soldiers who had been taken by surprise so completely that they had entered combat only half-dressed. Later that day, they came across several Frenchmen who had cracked under Allied artillery fire. The astounded Rangers watched how they "huddled together in mortal fear" and could not stop "whimpering." Within three days after the Allied landings, the French in North Africa surrendered.[63]

In the eyes of the American soldiers, the French had made the North African operation look like "a real comic-opera."[64] Not even the more than 1,400 casualties the French had inflicted on the Allies before the armistice of 11 November 1942, nor the valor they would display at the side of the GIs during many later campaigns, could entirely take away that impression. French troops made it possible for the US to reduce its combat manpower in Europe by eight to ten divisions, which in turn allowed the Americans to avoid higher casualties. From the start of the Tunisian campaign to the end of the war in Europe, the French themselves lost 23,500 killed and 95,500 wounded in action in the ground forces alone.[65] Nevertheless, in a letter written in April 1945, a private of the 100th Infantry Division told his parents that although the French were "good guys" and "good soldiers," it was hard to take them seriously. He had spent some time with them during a rest in Stuttgart, where they had been driving everything "from Austins to buses" while wearing an exotic mixture of American and French items of clothing and equipment. They had all seemed "mad," he admitted, and every single one of them had been "an individual scream."[66]

If anything contributed to the comic-opera effect of the war waged by what was left of the French military, it was the deplorable condition, often the sheer absence, of its matériel. The outdatedness of French weaponry and equipment struck Americans the very moment they set foot on North Africa's shores. The German armistice agreement of 1940 that had emasculated the *Armée Metropolitaine* had also crippled the *Armée d'Afrique* to a force of 100,000 men with military stocks that would not last longer than three months and were of World War I vintage; some equipment even dated back to the 1890s.[67] The results were all too apparent. A lieutenant of the 1st Infantry Division was most puzzled by the old-fashioned French ambulances that picked up wounded GIs in Algeria, while a chaplain of the same division could not help being intrigued by the "armored vehicles of ancient types" with which the French dared fight against, and later with, the Allies in North Africa. Likewise, a forward artillery observer was stunned when he discovered in November 1942 that the French mostly had 75 mm howitzer "museum pieces" and "1917 ammunition" at their disposal.[68] Soon after the surrender of the French in North Africa, America started rearming their forces and later also those raised in continental France. It furnished every possible kind of weapon, from nearly 200,000 small arms to over 5,000 combat vehicles and some 1,400 aircraft. But even under the American rearmament program the French often had to settle for substitute weapons because of production shortages. French troops only received, for instance, small quantities of the more efficient M1 rifles and carbines and were forced to fight with the older M1903 Springfield and M1917 Enfield rifles throughout the campaigns in Europe.[69]

The state of French motorization was most appalling of all to the Americans. A combat engineer of the 3rd Infantry Division could hardly believe that the howitzers he and his comrades faced on D-Day in French Morocco were mule-drawn. At Les Trembles in southern Algeria, a lieutenant of the 1st Infantry Division also looked on in disbelief as the battery of a French artillery regiment left town for Oran. At the head of the convoy, French officers and NCOs rode beautifully groomed horses. They were then followed by Arabs who sat on horse-drawn caissons that pulled old howitzers or two-wheeled carts with hay or rations. To the stunned American "the whole unit looked like an apparition from the days of Napoleon III."[70]

The undeniable proof of the dilapidated state of French transportation, however, was what became known among the Americans as the "forty and eight." The memory of this standard French railway boxcar – marked "Hommes 40, Chevaux 8" on the sides, indicating its capacity to hold forty soldiers or eight horses – had been engraved on the mind of the American generation that had fought in the Great War. The GIs therefore reacted incredulously when their fathers' trains pulled in at French stations once again to carry American troops off to Old World battlefields. A doctor in the 88th Infantry Division, who was transported by such a train from Casablanca to Magenta on the way to Italy, refused to believe that those "Toonerville trolleys" had not been "long extinct."[71] To the GIs who had assumed that these trains had all been relegated to the distant colonies, the "quarante-et-huits" used to whisk off troops from Brittany and Normandy to the front lines in Western Europe looked even more like ominous chimeras. The long hours in the French boxcars were invariably miserable and the subject of many a detailed description by indignant GIs. The jolting rides on the dirty wooden floors were rough, and in bad weather an icy cold pervaded the drafty boxcars. Above all, the cars always seemed to be overcrowded with men who had no room to lie or even sit. Men from the 26th Infantry Division, on their way to the Lorraine front in November 1944, experienced how, with only 35 men, one boxcar already proved "insufferably crowded." Engineers en route to Italy could only solve the congested situation on a French train in North Africa by making hammocks out of their blankets. "From the amount of space we had and the smell that pervaded our boxcar," a sarcastic private noted on his way from a replacement camp to the war in France, "one would have judged that there were both men and horses ... in our gondola."[72]

It was still more painful to watch the humiliating impact that France's lack of means had on the appearance, well-being, and morale of its own soldiers. When the GIs in North Africa first marched off with their new allies, the French often fought in British battle dress. By the summer of 1943, however, the Americans had almost entirely taken over the economic support of the Free French Army from the British. From then on, it was the US that carried responsibility for clothing the French troops, from woolen trousers to overcoats. In each case, the French soldiers had no choice but to don the dress of the army that offered the best conditions. Unfortunately, the frequent changes of uniform made them look more like mercenaries to the GIs than liberators.[73]

French army pay too was most depressing. One GI wrote home from Algeria in January 1943 that the Gallic soldiers were "paid so little that it's one big joke." Exactly how ridiculous French pay must have been in the eyes of most American soldiers became glaringly clear when the GI added it was even a "much bigger joke than the English."[74]

Even tobacco, always the soldier's solace, was scarce among French troops. When paratroopers handed out cigarettes to French soldiers in Algeria late in 1942, they noticed that the men were overjoyed and that some refused to smoke them immediately, but instead "put them away with the care one takes with a precious stone."[75] French soldiers would remain dependent on the Americans for tobacco throughout most of the war. They had to settle, however, for only half the American allowance, made up of off-brands the GIs did not like.[76]

French food rations could not keep up with war's demands either. In May 1943, a GI in North Africa actually claimed that the French disliked the German POWs because the Americans fed them well while they had to live on the poor rations the French government issued. The French remained responsible for feeding their own forces from locally produced foodstuffs from November 1942 to the autumn of 1943. The Americans agreed to provide the French expeditionary forces that would join them in Italy with at least the food their government could not provide from local sources. Despite that American aid, the French faced a serious food crisis by the end of 1943. They failed to get the items they had promised to deliver – such as flour and macaroni, produced in Africa – to their troops at the front in sufficient quantities. Whereas an American received a daily ration of almost five pounds, a Frenchman could hope to eat only about three and a half pounds a day. The French suffered from poor quality rations too; they lacked sugars and fats and almost never received fresh or frozen meat. In March 1944, general Giraud reported that the troops felt less and less like eating because of the monotony of their food, and the French High Command expressed fears that the ration deficiencies were contributing to the worrisome number of cases of trench foot. By 1 June 1944, the Americans felt obliged to step in and assumed full responsibility for feeding the French in Italy. They continued to bear that burden when French forces moved into their homeland, and were still feeding 360,000 French soldiers by 1 March 1945.[77]

The US provided the French with numerous other items on credit. From recreational equipment such as rugby balls and basketballs to packages of dried plasma, penicillin ampoules, and hundreds of thousands of insect powder cans to help rid the French of the lice that plagued them in Italy. Taken together, the Americans furnished the French armed forces with supplies and services worth more than $2¼ billion. All this made it abundantly clear to the GIs that the French soldiers were being kept in the fight only by the mercy of their allies.[78]

But the French not only desperately needed their allies for supplies and services, they were also forced to rely heavily on the native volunteers and conscripts from their colonies to help fill their manpower shortages. When French troops landed in the Riviera in August 1944, it was estimated that they had replacements for about two months to maintain a strength of some 200,000 troops. The manpower pinch only lessened when newly liberated Frenchmen were absorbed as replacements or formed into new units during the advance. But by that time, the share of the colonial natives in the French armed forces, especially those from West Africa and even more so those from North Africa, had become impressive. Of the 560,000 men under arms on 1 September 1944, approximately 295,000 were colonial natives. In the French expeditionary forces only half of the 260,000 men were whites.[79]

The sight of the picturesque but poorly equipped colonial troops their exhausted ally threw into battle only served to bolster the GIs' opinion of the French military as an artifact of an era long gone, desperately trying to survive in a new world. The first troops a combat engineer of the 3rd Infantry Division ran into after he had waded ashore in French Morocco on D-Day were "very black and very tall" Senegalese troops in "fancy uniforms." Later that day, he also encountered Moroccan Spahi cavalry, nervously watching his unit from a rise of land, as if uncertain about the meaning of this latest invasion by whites: "Their robes looked clean and colorful. They carried long rifles and their horses' bridles and saddles were very ornate, with silver, and they flashed in the sun." The confrontation seemed to have come about as if by a rift in time. "To say that we were dumbfounded," the engineer from Illinois admitted, "was to put it mildly."[80]

Most intriguing to the Americans, however, were the 22,000 Moroccan Goumiers or Goums who joined them in the fighting in Italy and France. The Goums, whose name was sometimes mistaken for "Goons" by the GIs, were tough men who were recruited from the Berber tribes of the Atlas region and thus excelled at mountain fighting in particular. They always seemed to smile and neither cold, rain, nor snow appeared to bother them. But they also looked terribly out of place in a modern, mechanized war. *Tabors* of Goums, commanded by white French officers, would trudge past or ride by on well-groomed horses. The men wore flowing striped robes and their long hair was braided in pigtails. Some herded goats, others carried the animals with feet lashed together around their necks. "It was," wrote a regimental commander from the 88th Infantry Division, "as if troops of the last century had been reincarnated and suddenly appeared by our sides."[81]

The Moroccan soldiers soon acquired an odious reputation among the Americans. In North Africa, the GIs learned that the Goums liked to mistreat Italian POWs, not simply to humiliate beaten enemies, but also to punish defeated white colonizers. Perhaps that helps to explain some of the Goums' misconduct in Italy. In his memoirs, a counterintelligence officer of a US infantry division, for example, reported an endless series of horror stories from tearful Italian civilians of how their houses had been pillaged and their wives and daughters dragged to the woods and raped by Goumiers.[82] A GI who watched the soldiers near Castelforte in 1944 claimed "they looted everything that was lootable."[83] Americans who fought in the Itri Valley in the spring of 1944 were literally begged by Italian peasants to help stop the raping by the Moroccans and to send doctors to treat the victims.[84] Whatever the precise reason for their behavior, the GIs became intimidated by the Goums' "appearance of slyness and cunning" and rumors soon flew about unchecked.[85] One persistent story insisted that the Moroccans, who carried large machete-like knives, were paid 50 cents for each enemy ear they brought back from the front lines. The rumor soon escalated. During the Sicilian campaign, Goums were believed to have cut off the heads, arms, and legs of German soldiers. The Americans preferred not to take risks with their peculiar allies. In the spring of 1944, soldiers of the 88th Infantry Division in the Gustav Line put bands of adhesive tape on the rear of their helmets to identify themselves to the Goums operating on their flank.[86] A corporal from that division could only conclude that the Goums he had seen in Italy were "savages" and "mercenary degenerates" who "gave war and soldiers a bad name."[87] That the French had to enlist the aid of such troops in their fight for liberation seemed to say more than anything else about the deplorable state of their military.

Perhaps even more shocking to the GIs than the conduct of the Goumiers was the poor training, equipment, and armament with which the French allowed their colonial troops to enter battle. The Spahi cavalry that challenged men of the 3rd Infantry Division in French Morocco on D-Day, for instance, faced semi-automatic Garand rifles, machine guns, and 37 mm cannons. The unit's soldiers could hardly believe they were expected to train all that firepower on vulnerable riders and their horses. "We all hoped they would just go away," confessed one GI, "because if they charged there was sure to be a good deal of carnage."[88] The Goums, on the other hand, were equipped with old rifles of French manufacture for which sufficient amounts of ammunition were not available anymore. A private of the Third Chemical Mortar Battalion was shocked to see that the Moroccans went into battle at Castelforte with nothing more than old bolt-action rifles and long knives.[89] The seeming indifference with which the French permitted the high degree of unpreparedness among their colonial troops sometimes bordered on the immoral in the eyes of the Americans and left many indignant. A regimental commander of the 88th Infantry Division who observed the Goumiers in the Liri Valley in 1944 immediately noticed that they had "small appreciation of some of the modern implements of war."[90] A surgeon from the same division confirmed this when he saw them roast goats over large bonfires for their evening meal in the Gustav Line, making themselves vulnerable to German artillery from miles away. To make matters worse, the Moroccan soldiers had a penchant for walking into minefields, totally oblivious to any warning signs. American surgeons regularly had to amputate the feet of Goumiers who had neglected to observe the ground or had walked through clearly indicated minefields to pick oranges.[91]

The American soldiers became convinced that without their help the French would never have regained their country's freedom. The GIs found them confused, disheartened, and wretched in North Africa. They saw them fight valiantly but always begging for equipment in Europe. They witnessed how they dragged native colonial troops into a battle that was not theirs, just to fill France's own depleted ranks. Even the white officers of the units of French Africa, proud of their more unconventional and adventurous careers on the overseas frontiers, did not conceal their contempt for the units of Old World France that had succumbed so easily in 1940 when they finally linked up with them for the liberation of the *métropole* in 1944. They thought it only fitting that among the first French soldiers to enter Paris as liberators were those who wore the red *calots* of the Spahis and the fezzes of the *Chasseurs d'Afrique* and who had never before set foot in the old mother country.[92]

The soldiers from the even more distant American frontier, however, believed none of the French deserved the gestures made by the American leadership in allowing them the honor of taking several of the prized cities in their mother country. A private of the 5th Infantry Division, for instance, who had been involved in the heavy fighting for Fort Saint-Privat near Metz, was outright livid when the Americans in the end allowed "a platoon of Frogs" to accept the surrender of the German garrison. When a lieutenant of the 3rd Infantry Division entered the southern suburbs of Strasbourg on 26 November 1944 and discovered that the French 2nd Armored Division was already there, the disappointed Montanan maintained that only "good hearted Uncle Sam" could have arranged this. Yet nothing proved harder for the American soldiers to swallow than the news that the French had been accorded the privilege of capturing Paris. For months the GIs had been looking forward to their grand entrance into the fabled City of Lights, only to learn at the very gates that most of them, with the exception of the 4th Infantry Division, were to bypass it. "When we heard that a French Armored Division was going to take Paris," a soldier from the 1st Infantry Division wrote, "that made it worse." He believed, like many of his comrades, that the Americans had offered them "a big prize for nothing," because the French "hadn't done much of a job fighting for their country."[93]

When the GIs entered World War II, the size and unity of the Allied coalition strengthened their belief in the rightness of the cause and the prospect of victory. In the front lines, however, the Americans grew more and more convinced of the ineffectiveness of their European allies and increasingly noticed how dependent they had become on the US for everything from food to guns.

The GIs who saw their British and French allies in action came to believe that all that was left of the reputation of these mighty Old World armies was the fading memory of past grandeur. Tactics and equipment were often outdated, social class continued to fragment the ranks, and poorly trained and motivated colonial troops were still being used as cannon fodder. To the Americans, it seemed as if these European armies were desperately trying to hold on to the glorious past and stubbornly refused to adapt to the wars of modern times. The GIs knew that the Europeans had already reached a breaking point during the Great War, and it appeared to them that they had never fully recovered since. World War II confirmed in a most humiliating manner the impotence of armies that clung to the ways of the Old World. As a result, at the war's end the American soldiers largely viewed the Allied victory as an American–Soviet success in which British and French efforts had been barely more than token contributions.

4   The Enemies

The GIs experienced the typical physical symptoms of fear when they eventually faced battle with the Axis foe. Upon nearing the front, hearts pounded and pulses beat rapidly. Some soldiers shook, perspired excessively, experienced a sinking feeling in the stomach, or felt weak or faint. Others suffered from muscular tension, vomiting, or involuntary urination or defecation. Tense soldiers chewed gum or stuffed snow into their mouths to detach their tongues from the roofs of mouths that had turned dry from fear.[1] "Each measure of our journey toward the front," observed a private of the 99th Infantry Division who traveled from Le Havre to the Monschau sector in the fall of 1944, "had affected my nervous system like the gradual turning of a key on a mechanical toy."[2]

The front was the great unknown. The GIs hoped they would prove courageous in the face of danger. They wondered if they could withstand the strain of battle. They prayed they would never let their comrades down. They doubted if they could handle pain. They asked themselves if they were ready to die. But behind each question, inevitably, hid the unknown face of the enemy. Who was the man on the other side of the line who personified the difference between life and death?

The American soldiers never regarded the Italians as a serious menace and stopped worrying about them altogether when they abandoned the Axis camp in 1943. But the Germans seriously intimidated the GIs for a long time. The memory of the Great War slaughter had much to do with this. Moreover, by the time the Americans entered the European battlefield during World War II, the Germans had acquired the reputation of well-nigh invincible supermen. That tenacious reputation would only slowly erode. However, when the formidable German army at last collapsed, the event proved to the GIs more than anything else that the long era of the Old World's military dominance had come to a close.

THE ITALIANS

When the Americans set foot in Africa in November 1942 as a first step on the way to Europe's liberation, they entered a continent in which the Italians had been roaming aggressively ever since the invasion of Ethiopia in 1935. In those seven years, however, much had changed for fascist Italy. Its ambitious *Mare Nostrum* policy had turned the Mediterranean into a sea of Italian suffering and humiliation. By 1940 the Italians had so run out of breath in North Africa that they had been left with no choice but to accept the arrival of their German brothers-in-arms. These had quickly overshadowed the Italians in importance. For the Americans who waded through the Mediterranean surf on D-Day, North Africa had become synonymous with Rommel, and their focus was therefore on subjecting the German foe. The Rangers who sailed from Glasgow to Algeria for Operation Torch, for example, felt that they had been trained to beat the Germans and it irritated them that they would have to waste energy on eliminating French resistance first. Remarkably, in their train of thought the Italians were not even cause for irritation. They had disappeared from the GIs' sight altogether.[3]

Yet the Italians had anything but vanished from Africa when Operation Torch commenced. When Rommel had arrived in Tripoli early in 1941, there had still been more than 140,000 Italians in Africa. His German forces had been joined by four Italian divisions of some 37,000 men, while more than 100,000 Italians had guarded the rear and flanks as well as the logistical arteries. The Italians thus remained a substantial component of the Axis forces that faced the Allies in 1942.[4]

From the testimony of the American soldiers, however, one would never have surmised that much. The GIs found the Italian opponent to be indeed numerous but not at all formidable, and if the African campaign brought the Italians back to mind it was mainly as objects of ridicule. It was not long before the GIs in Africa automatically assumed resistance would collapse at the merest hint of Allied determination when encountering Italian troops. The Americans grew increasingly convinced that the Italians simply did not feel like fighting anymore – and even less like dying – for whatever cause they once might have agreed with. An unaccompanied chaplain, for instance, who went looking for dead GIs high up in the hills near El Guettar, to his great surprise returned with four Italian soldiers who had been waiting like sheep for someone to surrender to. Many more unarmed chaplains managed to bring in Italian POWs in North Africa, proving convincingly that the Italians did not need prodding to give up.[5] By the end of the African campaign, the Americans could not shake the impression that they had subdued an Italian army of POWs rather than one of combatants. A combat artist, attached to the 1st and 9th Infantry Divisions, left Tunisia with only one image etched on his mind: that of "Italian prisoners, packed together like sardines, urinating and vomiting from the rumbling trucks." The war in Africa destroyed the last remnants of what might have been left of Italian military dignity in 1942. A paratroop commander who had seen action in North Africa tried to assuage the fears of those Americans who joined his battalion at the end of the campaign by convincing them that "[i]f the enemies facing you are Germans, they are just as nervous as you are" and by reminding them that "[i]f they are Italians, they are twice as nervous."[6]

The Sicilian campaign in the summer of 1943 confirmed what most Americans had believed since, and even before, the victory in Africa: the Italian military had reached the point of total disintegration. In Sicily this was more glaring because the Italian tragedy now unfolded at home, for all their countrymen to see. Photographer Robert Capa described the campaign on the island as a 21-day race with the Italian army in the lead. Not even native soil could convince the Italian soldiers to dig in their heels. Men of the 82nd Reconnaissance Battalion of the 2nd Armored Division, for instance, when entering a Sicilian village late in July 1943, received a phone call from Italian soldiers in a town some miles ahead; the men asked the GIs to accept their surrender and to come and pick them up. Soon the American spearheading forces could no longer keep up with the many Italian soldiers scurrying to be brought to the safety of prison pens. The GIs just stashed their arms in peeps and jeeps, told them to walk to the rear, and pushed on. Not even the main body of the divisions that followed managed to control the flood of Italian POWs. Soldiers of the 1st Infantry Division who captured large numbers of Italians near Nicosia had to order the enemy's officers to march their men to the town themselves and to report to the nearest American command post. The Italian defeat had reached absurd proportions. Faced by an Allied thrust into the heart of the mother country, the fascist regime finally collapsed in September 1943. The aspirations of Mussolini's Italy to recapture the Roman glory from the days of old had failed abjectly.[7]

To be sure, not all elements of the Italian armed forces gave a disastrous performance during the African and Sicilian campaigns. The artillery in Africa gained respect from enemies and ally alike; parachute units, such as the Folgore Division, displayed great courage; and a regular force like the Savoia Grenadiers Division as well as the mobile Ariete and Trento Divisions fought stubbornly. The Italian forces that managed to impress the GIs most were the Bersaglieri units. With a tradition going back to the old Piedmontese army, composed of carefully selected troops, and equipped with greater numbers of artillery and vehicles, these units sometimes exceeded the performance of the German forces in Africa.[8] A soldier of the 4th Ranger Battalion who had battled against them at Sened Pass in Tunisia in 1943 remembered them as "big shots" while he was on his way to Sicily, and hoped that he would not encounter them again on the island. He did, however, and more bloody clashes with the Bersaglieri left him convinced that they were indeed "Italy's toughest troops."[9]

Still, a few elite units did not manage to change the course of the war for Italy. Instead, they put the weakness of the Italian army as a whole into an even harsher light. The American soldiers only had a little inkling of what caused the poor performance of the enemy's military. Above all, the inefficiency of the Italian equipment leaped to the eye. A lieutenant of the 1st Infantry Division who seized a motor tricycle in Sicily and converted it into a command post carrier, considered it to be a "typically funny-looking gadget of the poorly-equipped Italian Army."[10] Lack of sophisticated technology and an unimaginative leadership had indeed delayed the research and development of military production. As a consequence, soldiers were often sent off to war with hopelessly antiquated equipment. The standard rifle had been shouldered by Italian soldiers ever since 1891 and was inferior to that of every other major power. Of the almost 8,000 artillery pieces in possession of the Italian army at the outbreak of the war, less than 250 had been produced after 1930; only from 1941 on had small quantities of excellent guns become available. Motorization had been neglected to a large extent; armor was lacking almost entirely. In the few mobile units, commanders had to manage without compensated vehicle compasses and were forced to leave their armored cars to take bearings with hand instruments. Communication systems were downright primitive. For tanks on the move, for instance, the Italians had not yet engineered workable long-distance voice radios.[11]

With its weak industrial basis, Italy also failed to produce the quantities needed to realize its grandiose designs. Its total military output for 1939–43 did not weigh heavily on the international scale and there were shortages of almost everything, from munitions to trucks and aircraft. Italy produced fewer tanks during the entire war than Germany threw into battle against France in 1940. Overall military production barely sufficed to keep 20 divisions equipped for combat.[12]

The GIs also identified the rapidly deteriorating relationship with the Germans as an important factor of Italian disintegration. Although the arrival of the Germans in North Africa in 1941 had given the Italian army new hope and had in effect improved its performance, many Italian soldiers had become fed up with the Germans' domineering attitude on the battlefield by the time they faced the American troops. Soldiers of the Trento Division, for example, who surrendered to GIs in Tunisia after having been surrounded by their tanks, claimed they had been shot at by the Germans while marching to the American lines as POWs.[13] The Italian soldiers thus found themselves caught between two fires, and combat photographer Capa noticed that they often "ran in every direction" because they were afraid of both the Allies and the Germans.[14] To many Italians it was discouraging to realize they had been reduced to vassals forced to spill blood for what now appeared to be a German cause, and as a result they appeared to have few qualms about turning their backs on the war. A chaplain who talked with Italians captured during the battle of Maknassy in Tunisia in the spring of 1943 learned that they had wanted to surrender earlier but had been prevented from doing so by a stubborn German officer. When the chaplain asked them why the German had changed his mind after all, the POWs smilingly replied that they had killed him when he had dozed off.[15]

The Italian military debacle had many underlying reasons. The fascist regime not only depended on men rather than machines, but with half of the country's population peasants, the army also relied heavily on the uneducated and the illiterate. In addition, training was neglected and expected to be compensated for by intuition and individual courage. Experienced regular junior officers and NCOs were in short supply. Moreover, officers formed a separate caste – career officers were often nobles, especially in elite units such as the Folgore – and went to war with personal servants, more comfortable uniforms, and more and better food and drink than the common soldiers, whom they did not manage to inspire at all.[16]

But the American soldiers were not aware of exactly what was wrong with the Italian army in organizational terms, and did not particularly care either. They had made up their minds that what caused this army to be incompetent in the first place was the Italian character. In other words, the GIs blamed the Italian blundering mainly on flaws of disposition. What was disadvantageous in the Italian temperament, according to the GIs, was that it was southern. If the French troops already betrayed a certain degree of excitability, the Latin soldiers from Italy were hampered by outright overemotionality. This, the American soldiers believed, inescapably made the Italian army unstable and unreliable in more than one way. Its soldiers were epicures who disliked long-lasting rigorous discipline, their lightheartedness made them unresponsive to organizational demands, and their sensitive mental make-up could not sustain courage long in the face of war's horrors. In short, the Italians reminded the Americans somewhat of children. A platoon leader of the 2nd Armored Division, for instance, could only feel embarrassment when some of the Italians he captured in Sicily were "crying hysterically like snivelling babies."[17]

The Italian soldiers also appeared to be a shade effeminate. The physique of the rather scrawny Italians proved more unimpressive even than that of the British or the French.[18] Moreover, their mannerisms looked most unmanly. French soldiers at times already raised American eyebrows. When cartoonist Bruce Bairnsfather showed a smartly dressed French officer kissing a GI, he squashed all rumors by assuring in the accompanying text that it was "only Private Homer Smith being awarded the Croix de Guerre for gallantry." In comparison with the stylishly dressed French, however, Italian officers looked like genuine dandies who surrendered "not just en masse but pomaded and scented."[19] The GIs regularly captured officers in immaculately pressed uniforms that displayed colorful rows of service ribbons and decorations. They were surprised to discover that even the undaunted Bersaglieri wore feathers in their hats.[20] As a result of the elaborate Italian costumery, things often were not what they seemed. When the low-ranked commander of the insignificant Sicilian town of Menfi surrendered to men of the 82nd Airborne Division, for example, he looked like "a four-star general in a comic opera uniform." Mauldin was quick to translate the GIs' impressions into another marvelous cartoon. A proud private who turns in a most impressively uniformed Italian officer is told bluntly at the prison compound: "That's no general – you got the chief of police."[21]

All this did not mean to the Americans that the Italians were worthless people; just that they were not cut out for the soldier's life. Gifted artists they were. According to a sergeant in Sicily, even the Italian dugouts were "works of art" in comparison to the solid but unimaginative German constructions. Like the French, the Italians also had a "reputation as the surviving custodians of the cuisine." But above all, the Italians were considered to be born singers, predestined for the opera in which they were known to excel. In June 1944, an American combat engineer visited an Italian town on a pass. He immediately became enraptured by the magnificent voice of a young Italian soldier in a tiny music store. More GIs soon gathered around him. When an Italian-American soldier picked up a violin and joined in, Latin musicality made the engineer "spellbound" for "about 45 minutes of the merriest day I've had in my Army career."[22] As if their sensitive nature had not already made them quite unfit for war, many Italians had also retained enough of the classical features of their Roman ancestors to make them almost too good-looking to be maimed. A combat artist who saw Italian POWs march by near Salerno beach was above all touched by the eyes of the starved and malarial soldiers that looked "wildly beautiful." Amidst the ruins of the Sicilian town of Gela, a Ranger was mesmerized by the scene of a handsome young Italian sergeant lying spread-eagled in a puddle of his blood at the entrance of a majestic cathedral. Italians appeared to be characters from an opera; they never struck the Americans as real soldiers.[23]

The Army guide to Italy admonished the GIs not to "be critical of the Italian soldier as an individual or as a fighting man." Not only was it "unbecoming in a soldier to belittle his opponent," it would also backfire because it "minimizes his own victory before he has gained it."[24] But these were words in the wind. As the Americans could not bring themselves to accept the Italians as genuine soldiers, they never experienced them in battle as truly hated foes either. "[B]eing out in the front," a lieutenant of the 2nd Armored Division wrote from Sicily to his mother, "we could never tell when we'd run into the Germans or, *mirabile dictu*, an Italian force that would be willing to fight for even three minutes." This was actually a treacherous situation, the officer explained, because he and his men were gradually letting down their guard instead of constantly assuming that "a real enemy lay in wait ahead." A chaplain of the 1st Infantry Division was approached by civilians somewhere in Sicily; they warned him and his companions that there were soldiers in the valley they were about to enter. "Since they were Italian," the clergyman admitted, "there wasn't much interest in bringing them in." Only when the villagers insisted that some Germans were down there too, the unarmed Americans "stopped immediately to get the matter straight." In such circumstances, the Italian soldiers did not create a climate that fueled fierce enmity. "You can't work up a good hate against soldiers who are surrendering to you so fast you have to take them by appointment," Mauldin observed humorously but poignantly. And, as the Army guide had predicted, it made the taste of victory over this particular opponent rather bland.[25]

On 8 September 1943 the Italians surrendered to the Allies. Merely a month later the Italian government declared war on Germany and turned Italy into an "allied cobelligerent." This realignment only served to add yet more weight to the American conviction that Latin people were unsteady and unreliable. If French wavering in North Africa had irritated the GIs, the irresolute Italian vacillating between allegiances left the Americans entirely distrustful of their cobelligerent. Even as allies the Italian soldiers would keep many of the derogatory names they had been assigned earlier in the war by the GIs. They thus continued to be called Ginnies, Guineas, or Ginzos, sometimes also Wops, and less frequently spaghetti stranglers. Most often, however, they were referred to as Eyeties, a name that resulted from the mispronunciation of Italian as Eye-talian.[26]

Following the armistice, the Italian soldiers were transferred from the shadow of the Germans to that of the major Allies. With more than 600,000 men imprisoned by the Germans, some fascist forces continuing the fight on the side of their Axis comrades, and the troops under the command of the Allies exhausted and discouraged, the Italian contribution to the Allied effort in the field remained limited. Only a small combat force, never more than a division, joined the Allies. More important were the numerous service units, composed of labor troops, military police, mechanics and repairmen. Most operated in Italy, but some 1,000 of the 35,000 officers and enlisted men who had been recruited among the 53,000 Italian POWs in the US were sent to Western Europe in Quartermaster and Labor Supervision companies. These men served under American officers and NCOs. They did wear large *Italia* patches on their sleeves but had to remove them once they entered Germany for fear of retaliation by their former comrades.[27]

As the Italians were not a logistical priority, they remained poorly equipped for the remainder of the war. Moreover, many of the deficiencies that had earlier characterized their forces did not disappear simply because of switching sides. American troops, for instance, witnessed the failure of the 1st Italian Motorized Group during the first attack on San Pietro Infine in the morning of 7 December 1943. The blundering Italians neglected to make a ground reconnaissance, did not dispatch combat patrols, showed little attack discipline, and when the assault battalions eventually ran into machine gun and mortar fire, they simply froze in their tracks and remained paralyzed.[28]

Most American soldiers only saw their Italian allies in action as the drivers of mule trains in the murderous mountains of their home country. Even on those occasions, the Italians proved poorly equipped and inadequately dressed for the miserable weather. An appalled GI wrote from Italy to his parents in the wet fall of 1944 that he would never forget "a sad scene when they were even using burlap sacks for their feet and begging our soldiers for shoes." To the GIs, the Italians had not seemed much of an enemy and they would never seem much of an ally. The opera characters had changed into tragic personae.[29]

THE GERMANS

The American combat soldiers rarely referred to the German soldiers simply as "Germans" or "the enemy." They did not often call them Nazis either. The front lines did not allow the luxury of either neutrality or political subtlety.[30] The most popular GI epithets for the German soldier were Jerry and Kraut. Jerry was borrowed from the British; it was a slang word for chamberpot, which the German helmet was thought to resemble. The Americans came up with Kraut, which was derived from sauerkraut, the name of the popular German dish. Throughout the war, however, a whole array of other names emerged, expressing every possible shade of fear, anger, and contempt the GIs experienced while facing the enemy. The Germans became Huns, Heinies, Hermanns, Fritzies, Dutchmen, Boches, Katzenjammers, Lugerheads, and Squareheads. They turned into monkeys, dogs, rats, swine, pigs, and hogs. They were Supermen, Herrenvolk, clowns, jokers, Arshmen, bastards, and sons of bitches. To the GIs, the German soldier proved to be an enemy with more than one face.[31]

The Ghost from the Past

It never occurred to Americans on their way to the European front to think of the Germans as anything less than fearsome opponents. The Great War had not only become part of the modern memory of the Old World, in the minds of the GIs too, the German soldier proved to be a troubling ghost from a traumatic past.[32]

Soldiers of the 87th Infantry Division, who were billeted in the schoolhouse of the Belgian village of Tillet in the days following the Battle of the Bulge, studied the large canvas map of pre-1914 Europe with a keen interest. The map fascinated them, one of the GIs claimed, because it was "a simple, pleasant, nostalgic one" that represented "the Good Old Days."[33] The Great War had come to symbolize an equally great Divide. The War to End All Wars turned out to have had more success at ending what had remained of western innocence. Not many illusions had survived the war, certainly not those of battle and warfare as tests of manhood and national character.

To be sure, at the outbreak of World War II there had been no lack of patriotism in America, nor had the appetite for adventure been lost entirely among its young men. But, as a captain of the 29th Infantry Division observed, these feelings were "not hyperstimulated as in 1861, 1898, and 1917." A chaplain who sailed to Northern Ireland with an armored division early in 1942 noticed "no laughter or song, none of the wild excitement commonly pictured as the way men leave home to sail forth to war." Instead, the troopship swallowed its load in the dark of night and hurried off to Europe stealthily. So vast was the increase in cases of mild psychoneurosis among troops who were being processed for shipment overseas that the phenomenon became known as "gangplank fever." Soldiers of the 34th Infantry Division who arrived at the Virginia port of embarkation in September 1943 found themselves immediately surrounded by MPs armed with submachine guns to prevent them escaping before boarding. The scene formed a sharp contrast with the old newsreels of soldiers sailing away like heroes, and by the time these GIs climbed the gangplank to sail from Newport News to Italy, they felt "more like prisoners than soldiers." America's memory of "when Europe had last blown itself up to no lasting purpose," the captain of the 29th Infantry Division sensed, "was still heavy and sour."[34]

The GIs had not been allowed by their fathers' generation to forget the Great War. They had been forced to participate in the nationwide groping for its meaning and implications, and the experience had marked them too. A lieutenant of the 3rd Infantry Division, whose father had been a doughboy, could not erase the images he had seen as a child in the official pictorial history of America's participation in the Great War. The book had always lain about in the house and he had become so impressed by the pictures of "dead men sprawled over thickets of barbed wire" that not even his training with bangalore torpedoes at Camp Wheeler, Georgia, entirely succeeded in removing his "irrational fear" of barbed wire. During the Normandy breakout, an officer of the 29th Infantry Division was shocked to see a German patrol emerge from the morning fog dressed in the uniforms of 1914–18. The exhausted officer realized in time that he was hallucinating and recalling "the sepia-toned pictures of the Kaiser's army" from an illustrated volume on the Great War he had pored over as a boy.[35]

Some of the most celebrated literary creations of the interwar years too had pondered the issue of the Great War, and many of America's future soldiers had been brought up on them. Thinking of *All Quiet on the Western Front, A Farewell to Arms*, and *Journey's End*, a lieutenant who arrived at the Italian front in 1944 as a replacement for the 36th Infantry Division felt terribly out of place because he realized his generation "was not easily persuaded that modern war made sense at all." The literary images of the war had become imprinted on the minds of some GIs as sharply as the horrible photographs. An overwhelmed lieutenant of the 825th Tank Destroyer Battalion, for instance, wrote to his wife in the fall of 1944, after having passed Verdun on his way to the front, that he had now seen with his own eyes "the haunted wasteland of the battlefield."[36]

The work that had caught the essence of the era and the attention of most, however, was *All Quiet on the Western Front*. Erich Maria Remarque's bestselling novel *Im Westen nichts Neues* had been published in 1929. It had not only been translated into English almost immediately but had also been made into a successful American movie a year later. Many GIs were therefore familiar with the story and its message and had been deeply affected by it. A lieutenant of the 35th Infantry Division, who was shocked by the death of a comrade near Saint-Lô on one of the quietest days since the landing in Normandy, was inevitably reminded of Remarque's story and recorded in his journal: "He fell on a day in which there was so little activity that the newspapers reported the front with the line, 'All Quiet on the Western Front.'" Similarly, when the Battle of the Bulge had run its course, a medic of the 100th Infantry Division wrote to his wife: "Darling, all seems to be temporarily 'quiet on the western front' and now I've come to the full realization of what that can mean."[37] So powerful had been the message of the book that the GIs could not understand why the German soldiers had not been equally impressed by it and had allowed a similar tragedy to happen again. A corporal of the 76th Infantry Division reproachingly asked weary German POWs in a prison cage in Luxembourg in February 1945 whether they had perhaps never heard of Remarque's novel. He was surprised to find that some indeed had not. Because it portrayed the German army in a negative way, the movie had been kept from the screen in Germany and Austria under Nazi pressure in 1930 until a number of cuts had been made; the book had been banned since 1933.[38]

But the memories of the Great War were more numerous and more vivid even than the images and sentences on paper. The visible traces of the previous cataclysm had not been erased by a mere three decades, and they haunted the GIs wherever they went in Europe. In fact, they became apparent as soon as the Americans crossed the ocean. A soldier of the 4th Infantry Division, on his way to Liverpool aboard the *George Washington* in January 1944, was excited when he realized that the same ship had carried President Wilson to the Versailles peace conference. Other troopships also contained the memory of the Great War within their hulls. Like the *George Washington*, the *Edmund B. Alexander* – formerly the *Amerika* – was a German passenger liner that had been seized in April 1917. The *Siboney*, *Orizaba*, and *George S. Simonds* had transported thousands of doughboys to France in 1917–18. Newer ships, on the other hand, had been baptized *St. Mihiel* and *Chateau Thierry*.[39]

Moreover, many veterans of the war were still alive, and they had engraved their experiences in the memories of the young soldiers. Not a few GIs sailed to Europe with good advice from former doughboys. During a heavy barrage in the battle of Santa Maria Infante, for instance, a shaken corporal of the 88th Infantry Division suddenly remembered the express warning of his uncle to stay put in one hole no matter what. Some GIs kept up a correspondence with Great War veterans throughout the war. The old soldiers did not have to be members of the family. An officer from the Ozark Mountains in Arkansas, for example, exchanged thoughts and experiences from Europe with several doughboys he knew from his farm community.[40]

Overseas, GIs recognized the scenes of veterans' stories that had been repeated almost ritually within their families. When the 3rd Armored Division raced through the Argonne Forest, for example, a private from Missouri was instantly reminded that "Uncle Gus was gassed with mustard gas in that battle."[41] The GIs were especially keen on retracing the footsteps of their fathers. In England, two Americans brimmed with pride when they learned in the fall of 1942 that they had been assigned to the "Fighting First," the division in which both their fathers had served in 1917–18. In November 1944, a corporal from Seattle proudly announced in a letter to his family: "Like my Dad twenty-five years ago, I've landed 'somewhere in France.'" The element of competition was almost unavoidable between fathers and sons. "Tell Dad he hasn't anything on me," a private in Northern Ireland wrote to his parents, "I've made it over and I'm coming back some day just like he did."[42] Sons nevertheless gratefully clung to whatever security their fathers were still capable of offering in the trying times ahead. Many GIs sailed to Europe with their fathers' Great War bibles now in their own breast pockets. They would not have parted with them for anything in the world except peace.[43]

Veterans of the Great War were still around even as active participants in World War II. Almost all of the famous, high-ranking American commanders had obtained some military experience in the previous world conflict. But Great War soldiers could be found throughout the ranks. Soldiers en route to Algeria from the US in 1943 were dressed down by a colonel because it was dirty below deck and could not compare with when he had sailed over during the last war. A regular sergeant in a rifle company of the 1st Infantry Division was known to carry with him, in a piece of velvet and waterproof covering, his Purple Heart and Silver Star from the Great War as well as the German Occupation ribbon. When soldiers of the same division witnessed how another sergeant who had managed to survive the firestorms of 1918 was killed on a beach near Les Andalouses, Algeria, in the first hours of the second great war, no other foreboding could have discouraged them more.[44]

Not just veterans but entire units relived the past as if time had been distorted. The 3rd Infantry Division's patch showed three white stripes on a blue background; they represented its involvement in three World War I campaigns in France. The unit's nickname was "Rock of the Marne" and its unofficial motto "Nous resterons là – We are staying here." In August 1944, it seemed as if the division had indeed never left France when it started slogging its way from the Riviera to the Alsace. When the 8th Infantry Division was operating near Brest in that same month, it was assigned the barracks of Pontanezen as a target, the very camp in which men of the division had been quartered during the last war. Soldiers of the 90th Infantry Division who captured Gerolstein in the winter of 1945 were puzzled by the happy excitement of the German civilians when they noticed the GIs' shoulder patches. The Americans soon found out that the division's command post had been established in their town in 1919.[45]

The shadow of the Great War hovered eerily over much of Europe's battleground. The GIs could not escape its chilling effect even while the Old World was ablaze again. A sergeant of the 28th Infantry Division who was able to visit Verdun in the winter of 1945 was impressed by "the proliferation of World War I monuments." But even the tiniest villages showed wounds that had not yet healed. A *Yank* correspondent who was trapped in Theux during the Battle of the Bulge found the small Belgian village to be typically European with its ancient stone church, houses, and a few stores "clustered around a square in which there was the inevitable World War I monument."[46] At times, the GIs seemed to be taking over all too literally where their fathers had left off. In November 1944, the 825th Tank Destroyer Battalion camped on the Verdun battlefield and some of the GIs found shelter in its mildewed bunkers. A month later, green troops of the 87th Infantry Division who relieved units near Metz were dumbfounded when they were led into the long trenches of the nightmarish past. It was no wonder that the two European wars appeared to form a continuum to some American soldiers. "It made me feel good to think about those American Boys who are sleeping under the sod here from the last war," a GI wrote to his girlfriend from Lorraine on 11 November 1944. "Many people thought they died in vain but they didn't, they but led the way for we here now to follow."[47]

Battle itself, of course, was also surrounded by the opprobrium of the Great War. Almost unavoidably, the GIs marched to the front accompanied by the horrible memories of the immobility in the trenches, the frontal attacks, the hand-to-hand combat, and the mass slaughter. A replacement who was sent to a mortar platoon at the French–German border in September 1944 had expected to find clearly delineated, opposing front lines. Instead, he needed time to adjust to the sight of individual foxholes irregularly spread out over fields with only a few patches of woods separating them from the enemy. Another replacement, in Lorraine, was surprised that the troops had not put up barbed wire around their foxholes. Green troops who joined men of the 4th Infantry Division in the Vosges were particularly concerned to find out if bayonets were being used.[48]

But even while in training camps back home, the GIs had expressed more serious worries about warfare in Europe in a song called "Bombed Last Night." Its second stanza ran:

> Gassed last night, gassed the night before,
> Gonna get gassed again if we never get gassed no more.
> When we're gassed, we're sick as we can be,
> 'Cause phosgene and mustard gas is too much for me.[49]

Lyrics of this kind caused nervous laughter, for the thought of having to descend again into the yellowish gas clouds of the European cauldron was indeed too distressing for most. But the grim reality had to be faced. The War Department was convinced that the German military was thoroughly prepared for chemical warfare and that its stocks of war gases were plentiful. Its gruesome inventory of German tear, vomiting, blister, and choking gases listed cyanogen chloride, hydrocyanic acid, arsine, and nitrogen mustard. The field manual on the rules of land warfare informed the GIs matter-of-factly: "The practice of recent years has been to regard the prohibition against the use of poison as not applicable to the use of toxic gasses."[50]

The GIs could not avoid preparing for the worst. In 1941 a lieutenant who had been assigned to teach a course on chemical warfare at Camp Wheeler, Georgia, dutifully traveled all the way to North Carolina to interview a doctor who had treated gas casualties during the Great War. When the American troops were ready for war, they boarded the ships to Great Britain loaded with gas masks and protective skin ointment and dressed from head to toe in gasproof clothing. A sergeant stationed in England in 1942 told his family in Delaware that he was writing their letter with his gas mask on because they were required to wear them half an hour a day to get used to them.[51] Men from the 1st Infantry Division who were getting ready in Scotland for the invasion of North Africa received "anti-gas ointment, shoe impregnate for protection against mustard gas, and British-made, apple-green oilcloth gas caps."[52] On the eve of the invasion of France, the GIs in England put on new uniforms impregnated with chemicals to neutralize blister gas. From the War Department's pocket guides to Europe the soldiers learned that a gas warning sounded like "gahz!" in French and "gahss!" in German.[53]

When the war had been going on for some time, however, green troops were disquieted to find that the veterans had become rather callous about the gas threat. Replacements who entered the battle of Cassino left their gas masks behind only reluctantly when told to do so. New soldiers arriving at the Lorraine front had to be ordered by an officer of the regimental headquarters itself not to carry their gas masks into battle. As gas attacks did not materialize, the masks soon became superfluous baggage that was tossed away. Among the first things that began to appear along the road when soldiers of the 1st Infantry Division marched from Arzew to Oran in November 1942 were gas masks and capes. A combat doctor in the Italian Gustav Line kept catching up with his unit simply by following the trail of discarded equipment and gas masks. Some GIs cut up the masks' hoses and fitted the rubber sections around their dog tags to eliminate the clicking noise. Others held on to the mask containers, which made handy carriers for rations, mess kits, razors, tobacco, or pictures from home. By late 1944, so few Americans carried gas protection that when men from the 26th Infantry Division were rushed from Lorraine to the Bulge, they were issued masks to distinguish them from German infiltrators who wore GI uniforms but had been unable to obtain American gas masks.[54]

Yet the memory of the Great War, coupled with the uncertainty surrounding the Nazis' intentions concerning gas weapons, remained capable of turning callousness into panic almost instantly throughout the war. American soldiers liked to believe that the Germans would not dare use gas because the Allies controlled the air and would retaliate against their cities. But at times when the going was tough, the GIs nevertheless feared that the enemy would turn to more drastic measures anyway. During the fighting in Normandy, several gas scares were triggered by seemingly insignificant events. Men of the 101st Airborne Division near Carentan and combat engineers near Sainte-Mère-Eglise, for example, panicked because they mistook smoke screens or phosphorus clouds from their own artillery for poison gas. When GIs of the 90th Infantry Division in the Siegfried Line near Dillingen captured Germans who carried brand-new gas masks, rumors soon spread that the enemy had become desperate and willing to use gas.[55] Troops who were caught off guard by the violent German outburst in the Ardennes in December 1944 also took the risk of gas attacks seriously. A sergeant of the 1st Infantry Division, dug in near the Belgian town of Büllingen, nervously scribbled in his small notebook during a briefing that there was the "Possibility of Using Gas" because the "Nazis Party disregard Civilians." The fear of that kind of fanaticism prevented the GIs from excluding the German use of gas even while fighting on their home soil. As late as 28 April 1945, a tank driver of the 13th Armored Division recorded in his diary that they had broken off their push abruptly because they had mistaken American artillery smoke for German poison gas.[56]

The specter of the Great War never faded away entirely during World War II. It constantly reminded the GIs that a relapse from the present horrors into the madness of the past was no more than a few steps away. In September 1944, a medic who was digging a foxhole near a zigzagging trench of the last war, close to the French–Belgian border, stared at the green grass around him. "Twenty-six years ago it had been oozing mud and flying clods," he contemplated. "Two minutes from now it could again." The American combat soldiers in Europe were well aware that they were fated to wage a tough war against a valiant German foe.[57]

The Valiant Foe

"We whopped 'em all right, but it wasn't easy. They was hard fighters. Don't ever kid yourself about that." It was the advice a soldier from the 3rd Infantry Division had been given as a youngster by a neighbor farmer in Texas who had been gassed during World War I.[58] But by the time America entered World War II, neither the memory of the Kaiser's army in the Great War nor the endless newsreels of confident Nazi troops goose-stepping all over Europe had left much room for kidding about the German foe among the new generation of American soldiers. A survey conducted among ground and air force troops in nine US camps in November 1942 showed that 82 per cent of the men rated the fighting ability of the German soldier as very good or good. The GIs were well aware that the German army had been training and gaining battlefield experience for many years. The first lesson new members of the 509th Parachute Regiment learned from a battalion commander who had lived through the North African campaign was that the German soldiers were "businessmen who know their business" and "have the finesse of experience." Soldiers of the 35th Infantry Division who arrived in Normandy a month after D-Day admitted that they were nervous, not only because they were faced by real combat for the first time, but also because they would soon encounter "an already battle-wise enemy."[59]

In comparison with the German opponent, the GIs felt embarrassingly green. To be sure, the American republic's refusal to sustain a large standing army and its alternative tradition of rapidly fielding impressive fighting forces of citizen-soldiers in times of threat, instilled a measure of pride in the GIs. They derived satisfaction from the notion that they were "not professional military men," but "a bunch of soda jerks and grocery clerks" called on to defend their country against "the best Hitler can send – and beating them".[60] Yet, that same notion also gave rise to much uncertainty and insecurity among the GIs. After all, experience had made Hitler's best formidable. Would soda jerks and grocery clerks truly be capable of beating them? By the time they arrived at the front, some Americans wished they could have felt less like civilians and more like soldiers. Green troops of the 34th Infantry Division who disembarked in Italy in September 1943 had received about five months of training. When they were told that they would receive two more weeks of practice before meeting the seasoned enemy, the men were shocked because they were convinced they needed much more combat preparation and felt "as if a death sentence had been postponed two weeks." Likewise, it was probably not much of a pep talk for replacements who arrived in northeastern France in September 1944 – barely ten days after they had left the US – to hear from an officer of the Third Army that their brief 17 weeks of basic training would be compensated for by the fact that, unlike the more experienced enemy, they at least were fighting for ideals worth believing in.[61]

In battle, some German forces impressed the American soldiers more than others. Rommel's *Afrika Korps*, for instance, had acquired fame in America even before its soldiers had set foot in French North Africa. The Tunisian tug-of-war and the Kasserine Pass debacle only intensified the awe for the field marshal and his men among the GIs. Instead of being "a beaten dog," an artillery observer commented, "he was slapping us around like schoolboys. It was discouraging and humiliating but, more than that, it was fantastic."[62] Rommel was the only German commander in the field who became widely known by name among the GIs. Their letters and diaries did not refer to Kesselring, Blaskowitz, or von Manstein, but Erwin Rommel was mentioned often and a regular personality cult developed among friend as well as foe. So legendary had Rommel become by the end of the African campaign that an admiring lieutenant from the 813th Tank Destroyer Battalion wrote to his father in Indiana, with unadulterated pride, that he had been drinking at a French farmer's house from the same wine the famed German commander himself had enjoyed only a few weeks earlier. For the remainder of the war, German POWs would part with pictures of Rommel as reluctantly as GIs were eager to get them.[63]

After the African campaign, the paratroopers became the most admired German soldiers. They resembled the GIs' image of Hitler's model troops more than the *Waffen SS*. A battalion commander of the 29th Infantry Division, for instance, who saw a paratroop POW at Saint-Lô, judged the "big, fine-looking youngster in his early twenties, blond and sturdy" to be a typical sample of the German military elite. An officer of the same division who watched the paratroopers in action near Saint-Lô claimed that they were "among the most dangerous fighting men of the war," while a lieutenant who got to know them at Cassino was convinced that they were "as tough as any that Hitler had."[64] Most others agreed. They described the paratroopers as "a young, tough-looking lot" and as "fierce, stubborn, crafty, ingenious warriors" who were "almost sullen in their determination."[65] The line between their determination and outright fanaticism sometimes proved to be a thin one. Soldiers of the 90th Infantry Division who were hit by a counterattack in Normandy, for instance, talked about "a wild pitched battle" against "fanatical, screaming paratroopers." Most GIs, however, looked upon the paratroopers as dedicated professionals rather than fanatics and grudgingly admitted a kind of respect. A Jewish tank operator of the 4th Armored Division felt "ambivalent about beating the enemy" for the first and only time during the war when fighting the 5th Parachute Division south of Bastogne. That was, he admitted, because the German paratroopers "were simply too gallant for a man of any sensitivity to destroy without some twinge of bittersweetness."[66]

The *Waffen SS*, on the other hand, was despised more than it was feared. Although the SS undeniably displayed daring in battle, they commanded little respect from the GIs because their behavior seemed to spring from unhealthy fanaticism rather than commendable courage. To a company commander of the 2nd Infantry Division who lived through an attack by the 12th SS Panzer Division during the Battle of the Bulge, the enemy looked "possessed" and "suicidal." A Japanese-American soldier, involved in ferocious fighting with SS troops in the Alsace, was convinced that the enemy was "doped up."[67] The SS soldiers were reputed to be extremely cruel and ruthless and very reluctant to give up. Even after they surrendered, Americans found them to be "arrogant bastards."[68] A soldier who fought SS men in the Colmar pocket could only compare them to "a nest of rattlesnakes."[69]

Yet, whether they were elite units or not, most German forces seemed to share a number of qualities. Foremost among them was efficiency. Though German *Gründlichkeit* had long been proverbial in America too, it did not fail to amaze the GIs time and again during the war. To an extent, the efficiency of the German soldiers was seen as the result of experience gained from many campaigns. When a German medical team was captured during the Normandy breakout and was told to give emergency care to the men of the 29th Infantry Division, the unit astounded the Americans with its "assembly-line precision" and "the efficiency of long practice." Soldiers of the 94th Infantry Division, who were introduced to the ways of the enemy before they entered the battlefield at the end of the summer of 1944, were impressed to hear from veterans that the German soldier had even learned to duck to the ground according to a studied routine: he never ran but crouched, carried his rifle on the left side, dropped to the ground on his right hand to spare his knees, and refused to pop his head up again.[70]

But the GIs attributed the thoroughness of the enemy in battle to more than just experience. It also seemed to be a trait that was somehow inherent to Germans. All over Europe, for instance, Americans could not but admire the dugouts and shelters the Germans had built to withstand Allied firepower. Of course, being thrown on the defensive, the Germans had had plenty of time to come up with sturdy constructions, from trenches in Italy that were "very well constructed in 'Old War' fashion" to foxholes in Normandy covered with cement slabs rolling on metal tracks.[71] Nevertheless, the GIs suspected the Germans of a building zest that went beyond mere safety precautions and instead betrayed a compulsive methodicalness. Mauldin reported that one of the dugouts at Cassino was made of "a four-foot layer of dirt and rocks on top, then a section of railroad ties, a thinner layer of stones, a layer of crisscrossed steel rails, and beneath that a ceiling of more thick wooden ties." Smaller shelters often boasted walls that were smooth and vertical and even panelled with doors taken from houses.[72] Efficiency appeared to surround everything the Germans undertook. At Brest, for instance, the bombed French port facilities were a shambles, but not the German wartime constructions, including the submarine pens, which were, noted a GI, "massive – on a scale that is particularly German."[73] The German soldiers' graves too looked more elaborate than the others. They were often embellished with large wooden crosses that contained detailed information and with mounds that were covered and bordered by stones. A corporal of the 76th Infantry Division was particularly impressed by the "clean rows of young men" at a "neat and Prussian" temporary cemetery in a field near Reims. Even in death the Germans seemed to appreciate methodicalness.[74]

That very methodicalness appeared to be what had enabled the relatively small European nation to make a bid for world power. In their Army pocket guide, the GIs read: "The German will justify his defeat by charging that it took a world coalition of United Nations to do it, that Germany stood alone against the world. Don't bite!"[75] But, especially when confronted with the quantity and quality of the German army's equipment, it was not always easy for soldiers from the cradle of industrial mass production to deny that Germany had generated power of a dimension that far surpassed the country's modest size.[76]

The kinds of German equipment that carried away the GIs' admiration and caused them to scoff at similar American-made articles were legion. "One thing you have to give the Krauts," a combat engineer wrote in his journal. "Some of their equipment is damned good & a lot of it beats the hell out of ours."[77] German flares went up without noise, showed no traces, and managed to hover over the battlefield for nerve-rackingly long periods. The GIs agreed that they were about the closest thing to daylight. They also feared the enemy's famous field glasses, which were rumored to be able to count the buttons on their jackets. Those GIs who did carry gas masks had often exchanged theirs for the German ones which were deemed better in several ways. The Americans also searched eagerly for German stainless-steel eating sets, which consisted of a fork and a spoon, placed in the handle of a combination of knife and can opener. They looked even more eagerly for the German rifle cleaning kits, which had brushes, oiler, and patches handily attached to a chain-link, whereas their own kits consisted of loose elements, including a clumsy cleaning rod. Most popular, however, were the *Esbit Kochers*, pocket cooking stoves that resembled small aluminum tobacco cans and contained heating tablets the size of sugar cubes. Men of the 90th Infantry Division in northeastern France in the fall of 1944 used to joke that it was time to capture some more Germans whenever they ran out of such tablets. During the battle for the Hürtgen Forest, the American army itself decided to distribute the miniature stoves that had been captured in German supply dumps.[78]

German clothes were particularly well designed for their purpose and – as could be expected from an enemy with battle experience in Russia – especially effective against cold weather. Since the American soldiers lacked camouflage clothing, they envied the Germans their excellent snow suits, which not only concealed them, but kept them warm at the same time. During the Battle of the Bulge, a correspondent at Saint-Vith noticed that several GIs were wearing the enemy's flowing white capes with hoods. It was not uncommon either to see GIs at the front wearing the much sought after German rabbit-fur jackets. Moreover, they preferred the lined leather gloves of enemy officers to the US Army item and were also jealous of the wool-rayon caps with turn-up flaps and the toques the enemy wore under their helmets to cover their necks and ears. Officers from the rear did not always tolerate the field adoptions. They made the soldiers look like scavengers and, more importantly, they caused dangerous confusion. Already during the first weeks of the Normandy campaign, for instance, a company of the 101st Airborne Division had suffered the loss of a sergeant who had put on a German poncho while on night guard. He was bayoneted by a sleepy soldier who took over duty and mistook him for an enemy.[79] The commanders, however, were powerless to stop the practice. A colonel who visited the 14th Armored Division at the front in Germany in March 1945 arrived just in time to see a company roar by to Oberhausen. Dressed in American, German, and civilian pieces of clothing its soldiers could not help but remind the flabbergasted officer of "a damn Cocksey's army."[80]

Appreciative as they were of much of the German equipment and clothing, nothing impressed the GIs more than the enemy's weapons. German artillery for one wreaked terrible havoc – from Hell's Corner at Dover to Monte Cassino's Purple

Heart Valley.[81] The gargantuan caliber of some of the guns was enough to awe the Americans. A medic in the Anzio beachhead wrote in his diary that "Anzio Annie," the 280 mm railroad gun that was zeroed in on his sector, made the ground shake like an earthquake, leaving holes ten feet deep and fifteen wide. The sheer noise of the shells that 16 inch naval guns fired inland from the island of Cézembre near Saint-Malo – resembling that of "a freight train with a trailer on it" – caused the GIs to cringe.[82]

What struck most fear into the hearts of the Americans, however, was the tremendous accuracy of the German artillery. The 88 mm piece in particular was the most dreaded of all German weapons and Mauldin dubbed it "the terror of every dogface."[83] The gun became notorious. It had been designed to be effective against aircraft, armor, and personnel. Its high muzzle velocity eliminated the familiar long, moaning whistle of other shells. Instead, it merely triggered a short, sharp sound "like the scream of a madwoman" that barely left time to drop to the ground. So accurate were the 88s that the soldiers began to imagine that their projectiles could "all but go around corners."[84] The areas the guns covered invariably turned into bloody killing grounds. GIs made mention of an "88 Lane" near Mateur, an "88 Street" at Dillingen, an "88 Junction" near Wiltz, and an "88 Corner" at Olzheim, to name only a few. As early as the North African campaign, American soldiers were singing "Those 88s Are Breaking Up that Old Gang of Mine."[85]

The multi-barreled rocket launchers or *Nebelwerfers* were dreaded too. The Americans knew them as Minnie Werfers and as Screaming, Screeching, or Moaning Minnies, Meemies, or Mamies. The hellish noise they produced could be heard from miles away. Horrified GIs outdid themselves in trying to capture the true nature of the weapon's scream. In Normandy they described it as "ten thousand wildcats fighting," near Bastogne as "lions roaring," and at the Siegfried Line as "hysterical banshee wailing." A soldier who heard the weapons at Monte Trocchio in the winter of 1944 said they inevitably "chilled the blood." All agreed they were among the worst morale busters at the front.[86]

German mortars taxed the American soldiers in quite a different way. Their projectiles, some of them as large as 120 mm, were silent until right before they hit; even then they only made the slight sound of "a sighing yawn."[87] It was the sneakiness of these weapons that made them dangerous and mentally destructive. Moreover, they were known to be deadly accurate. As a result, some GIs found them worse than regular artillery, and not a few combat soldiers snapped under sustained mortar barrages.[88]

The crack of small-arms fire, on the other hand, sounded like "static on a forgotten radio during an electrical storm."[89] It could not compare with the artillery's pandemonium, but was no less threatening. What the Americans envied the Germans most on all fronts was their excellent gun powder. Their own "spewed out billows of smoke;" the puffs would hang over their heads for what seemed like an eternity, giving away their positions and forcing them to keep on the move constantly. Yet, to the frustration of the GIs, the German powder somehow proved to be perfectly smokeless.[90]

The American soldiers became particularly unnerved by the 9 mm Schmeisser machine pistols. Their cyclic rate of fire was so high that the sounds of the shots simply blurred into each other. When the guns went off, they reminded the GIs of canvas being torn. Most soldiers referred to them as "burp guns." Their furious speed impressed the Americans. During the battle of Altavilla in Italy, Tregaskis reported that they "squeaked loudly, offensively" and "stung my auditory nerves to anger." An officer recorded in his journal during the Battle of the Bulge that they had "the most hateful, deadly, menacing sound in all the world."[91] But the burp gun also occasioned frustration for a reason other than its aggressive rattle. The GIs became discouraged by the comparison of the enemy's gun with their own. At Altavilla, Tregaskis noticed that the Schmeisser went "Brrapp!," while the American guns answered with a slow "Bap-bap-bap-bap-bap." An officer of the 2nd Infantry Division was disheartened to hear that the German "Brrrrrrrrrp" was only being challenged by the "Put-put-put-put-put" of American machine guns that sounded like Model T Fords. Throughout the war, the stammering response of their own machine guns to the challenging chattering of the German ones never failed to trigger some kind of insecurity among the GIs about the quality of their own equipment. So sensitive did the issue of the burp gun's sound become that Tregaskis, for instance, was careful to cover up the audible inequality between both weapons when he reported from the Volturno front, where one could discern "the rapid, yet confident, German gun contending with the more deliberate, yet equally assertive, American tone."[92]

No matter how deadly artillery and small arms proved to be, however, nothing was dreaded more by the Americans than the German tank. From the beginning of the war, the GIs showed disappointment with some of their antitank weapons. The 37 mm antitank gun, for instance, much in use in North Africa, proved grossly inadequate for tackling German tanks. It could "not even dent the door of a Model T Ford," denounced a lieutenant of the 3rd Infantry Division, "let alone a Mark 6 tank."[93] The bazookas did not escape criticism either. They were not readily enough available and the GIs wanted to see more of them. When so many *Panzerfauste* were captured during the drive from the Ruhr to the Rhine that men of the 84th Infantry Division were trained to use them instead, some soon claimed that the German antitank weapon was more efficient and powerful than their own 2.36 inch bazooka.[94]

There was no argument over the superiority of the German tanks. The German experiments of the 1930s had paid off handsomely in the form of four types of *Panzer Kampfwagen* by 1939. Of these, the heavier *Pz. Kpfw.* III and IV – solid tanks, gradually modified by thicker armor and better guns – were encountered until the end of the conflict. During the war, two new and much improved types rolled from the assembly lines. The sturdy *Pz. Kpfw.* VI or Tiger was thrown into battle against the Russians in 1942 and against the western Allies early in 1943 in Tunisia. The tank was protected by a front vertical plate of 102 mm and a turret wall of 82 mm thickness and was usually equipped with the dreaded 88 mm gun. Late in 1943, the Germans also introduced the sleek *Pz. Kpfw.* V or Panther. Modeled after the Russian T34, with sloping armored plates, heavy armament, and high speed, it was probably their best armored vehicle.[95] In the eyes of the Americans, the tanks became the embodiment of German engineering. The GIs only had to look at their own tanks to suspect that they were inferior. After the Allied victory in North Africa, a tank driver complained to his family that operating an American tank was like "driving a 1934 model car in 1942." The Shermans could not convince the GIs that they were being supplied with state-of-the-art tank technology either. To an officer in Normandy, who compared them to the lower-slung enemy tanks, they appeared "awkwardly high and vulnerable." But that was not the only deficiency the GIs could detect in the Shermans. A soldier of the 9th Infantry Division, for instance, noticed that the suspension system and bogies of the Panther were less fragile, and quieter. Moreover, he observed that the engines of both the Panther and the Tiger "purred like a Ford V-8 whereas the Sherman HAD a Ford V-8 and sounded like a P47 at takeoff."[96] The combination of thick armor and heavy guns made coming out in the open against Tigers in particular sheer suicide for American tank crews. In Normandy in August 1944, the Germans introduced the colossal King Tiger, a tank that became instantly notorious. A front glacis plate of 150 mm and a turret front of no less than 180 mm thickness made its armor simply impenetrable. A medic remembered that whenever "one began to groan every one of our men automatically stopped breathing."[97]

All in all, the German army managed to impress the GIs with everything from its *Esbit Kochers* to its *Königstiger*. Looking back on the quality of the German equipment, clothing, and weaponry he had encountered across Europe, a lieutenant of a tank destroyer battalion wrote to his wife in February 1945: "if Jerry were here with his whole army instead of facing Russia with most of it, we might be fighting till our hair is grey."[98]

The German soldiers in more than one respect proved themselves opponents worthy to be remembered. That probably helps to explain why the GIs were so eager to frisk or "desouvenir" German POWs in search of mementos. Perhaps they shipped home items as varied as helmets and caps, boots and belts, swastika flags and SS sabers to show material evidence to family and friends of their encounter with the famed enemy. Maybe they collected the fetishes merely for themselves, as reminders for years to come of how lucky they had been to survive the endless series of ferocious battles against a soldier unsurpassed by any other. Whatever the exact reason, the compulsive search for German mementos was testimony of the GIs' fascination with this valiant foe.

The soldiers' taste for souvenirs from the battlefield could border the macabre. They would hold on to bullets and jagged pieces of shrapnel that had barely missed them. Surgeons would remove the ones that had found their targets, rinse them, and hand them to those GIs fortunate to have survived. In the frenzy to acquire souvenirs from the war against the Germans, combat soldiers were even willing to risk their lives needlessly. In the Po Valley, for instance, with the end of the war in sight at last, a soldier of the 88th Infantry Division was mortally wounded when a *Panzerfaust* shell exploded in his hand. He had been trying to pry it open in the hope of taking it home.[99]

The German soldiers themselves had most often been cleaned out completely by the time they reached the rear as POWs. "It was an unwritten law with us on the line," admitted a soldier of the 1st Infantry Division, "that any prisoners we took ourselves he was ours to take any thing of his you wanted."[100] That often included personal belongings the GIs were supposed to leave untouched: money, snap shots, *Soldbuchs*, and even letters from home.[101]

Experienced troops knew exactly what they wanted from German prisoners. Their watches were very popular, for instance. The rigors of battle were hard on the GIs' watches; they came undone, were smashed, or got crushed. But watches – especially those with illuminated dials – could not be missed long in the front lines: they marked shifts on guard duty, timed German artillery, and synchronized attacks. Occasionally, a few army watches reached the front lines in PX supplies. Some combat soldiers asked their families to send them the watches they had safely stored away at home; a few received new ones as Christmas or birthday gifts.[102] Soon, however, it became a more practical habit to declare a wristwatch "a legitimate item of military equipment" and to look for famed German brands among the POWs.[103]

German field glasses too were much sought after and both enemy prisoners and dead were searched for them. The GIs complained that only officers and NCOs received binoculars and that even squad leaders had to get by without these vital instruments. Moreover, the quality of the German binoculars was well-known. A reconnaissance lieutenant of the 2nd Armored Division never operated without them during the war, claiming that his Zeiss glasses were "about three times as good as the GI variety."[104]

The most prized trophies, however, were the German pistols. Not many GIs were issued sidearms, but they were practical and soldiers preferred them over their rifles for guard duty, for instance. German pistols were excellent souvenirs too. They were rather rare and the GIs claimed they were all superior to the American .45 automatic. Both standard German pistols, the Lüger (*Pistole* 08) and the Walther (*Pistole* 38), were the fashion, but the Lüger was unquestionably, as one infantryman called it, the "'HOLY GRAIL' of souvenirs."[105] American soldiers would sometimes literally risk their lives to get hold of one. On D-Day in Normandy, for instance, a lieutenant of the 101st Airborne Division was outraged when, during a vicious fight with German paratroopers at Brécourt Manor, one of his men crawled out onto a field under heavy MG fire only to obtain a case he thought contained a Lüger. Most soldiers shipped the pistols home, but some created a lucrative business, selling them for drinks or money to replacements, artillerymen, the rear echelons, and airmen. By the end of the war, Walthers were worth $75, Lügers $100. Combat soldiers gave away these cherished souvenirs as gifts only to those they held in the highest esteem. An officer would present his best NCO with one; soldiers would give them to the surgeons who had saved their lives. Men of the 8th Infantry Division, for example, rewarded soldiers of the 709th Tank Battalion for their vital assistance in the hellish Hürtgen Forest by tossing German pistols in their hatches. Frontline soldiers grew so attached to the pistols that they refused to leave them behind under any circumstances. Sometimes they were wheeled into operating rooms clutching them to their chests. Unfortunately, the men would also carry them in their pockets while visiting towns during rest periods. There they would injure themselves or threaten others in brawls. During rest and reorganization for the 101st Airborne Division in France following the Battle of the Bulge, the dangerous practice had to be discouraged by fining those caught with enemy pistols no less than $25.[106]

With or without mementos, the American soldiers were bound to remember the valiant German foe. "By God, they were soldiers!," a paratrooper exclaimed when he saw German POWs singing and marching "with pride and vigor" in France as late as 1945.[107] Many GIs were impressed by the Germans as the epitome of what fighting men should be. Most importantly, in the eyes of the Americans the Germans held an advantage throughout the war simply because they seemed to have soldiering in their blood.

The Army guides to the Axis countries told the GIs that fascist propagandists claimed that "democracies were decadent and their men could not fight," while Americans were alleged to be "simple-minded boys who made poor soldiers."[108] The GIs paid no attention to the enemy's accusations of decadence and simple-mindedness, but they could not help harboring doubts about their worth as soldiers throughout the war. A lieutenant of the 29th Infantry Division wrote to his wife during the Battle of the Bulge that combat veterans ascribed to the Germans "certain astute qualities – in fact so many you wonder who is winning the war, we or Jerry."[109] The difference in the attitude toward discipline was a case in point. The Germans seemed to derive a natural satisfaction from the kind of discipline that was totally alien to Americans. When Mauldin entered the captured town of Vittoria in Sicily, for instance, he was struck by the fact that the German POWs were "marching briskly, in perfect step," whereas their American guards were just "shambling along." The military appearance of the Germans – even while POWs – not infrequently forced the GIs to take a second look at themselves. A company commander of the 2nd Infantry Division who was negotiating with the commander of the Leipzig police force about its surrender, surprised himself when he tried to make his heels click. He also caught himself "unconsciously imitating the stiff military bearing of the Germans." But the American soldiers realized that they did not have it in them to become perfect imitations of the rigid German disciplinarians. The day after the German surrender in Europe, a soldier of the 13th Armored Division at Braunau complained that the captain was trying to mold them into garrison soldiers again and that he wanted "to show Germans we can outdrill their army." "We can't," wrote the exasperated GI, "and everybody knows it except him."[110]

The GIs also learned from their Army guides that fascist propaganda insisted that American decadence had bred softness. It was a stigma that the GIs especially disliked but that somehow seemed to be confirmed by the embarrassing fact that the German soldiers often preferred to surrender to them rather than to European resistance fighters or Soviet soldiers. It troubled the American soldiers to discover that what they had regarded as fairness was interpreted by the enemy as softness and something to take advantage of.[111] "I hope the Russians and the European underground exterminate every damned Nazi and German militarist," an angry GI wrote in his journal during the bitter fighting in the Norman bocage. "I am afraid that we Americans will be too lenient."[112]

In the end, nothing proved more effective to dispel American self-doubts about their soldierly qualities than praise from the valiant Germans themselves. A captain of the 1st Infantry Division, for instance, was proud to be able to write from Sicily to his family that German POWs time and again admitted they dreaded the sight of "The Big Red One" shoulder patch. The GIs did not just cherish the nicknames the Germans gave to their divisions; they fought over them with other units. Soldiers from the 2nd Armored Division, the 4th Armored Division, and the 30th Infantry Division alike claimed that it was their unit that had obtained notoriety among the Germans as "Roosevelt's Butchers." German acknowledgments of prowess could only have that kind of importance to the American soldiers because they came from the mouth of an enemy who had earned a high regard himself.[113]

Even by the end of the conflict, the respect for the valiant German foe had not entirely dissipated despite all of the war's viciousness. On 11 May 1945, GIs of the 26th Infantry Division cut off the legs of their winter long johns and went swimming in a river on the border between Austria and Czechoslovakia. They had barely hit the water when stentorian singing in the nearby town drew their attention. The Americans hurried to the road, just in time to watch about 200 German soldiers march by in perfect parade order, their shoulders back, their feet kicking high, and their eyes looking straight ahead. "For a few minutes, they had grabbed the brass ring," a wet GI observed, "and we, the victors, were left standing by the roadside in our underwear, fighting the urge to applaud."[114]

The Fiendish Foe

The GIs rarely felt the urge to applaud the Germans in the thick of battle, where they became acquainted with a very different face of the enemy. In the fierceness of fighting, the distinction between skilled determination and blind fanaticism was quickly blurred and soldierly expertise easily interpreted as deviousness. As a result, the war unmasked the Germans as foes who were as fiendish as they were valiant. "The very professionalism of the krauts which makes the American infantryman respect the German infantryman," noted Mauldin perceptively, "also makes him hate the German's guts even more."[115]

It was, after all, this professionalism that was responsible for the ruthless killing of too many a comrade. The German soldier usually remained merely an abstract enemy until he killed a buddy. From that moment on, he was no longer a soldier but a murderer and would stay so for the remainder of the war.[116] The absence among the Americans of inveterate historical animosity toward the Germans was amply compensated for by the sum total of personal scores that the GIs increasingly itched to settle as a result of the war itself. "Maybe we don't share the deep, traditional hatred of the French or the Poles or the Yugoslavs toward the krauts," Mauldin remarked, "but you can't have friends killed without hating the men who did it." Few frontline men escaped those feelings. Early in April 1945, 87 per cent of the combat infantrymen of four divisions in Italy claimed that they had seen a close friend get killed or wounded in action.[117]

Nothing could trigger a more fierce hatred in a GI, however, than the news that a family member had fallen in battle. Too many Americans had been sent overseas in uniform to make this a rare occurrence. A soldier of the 101st Airborne Division, for example, was relieved from combat duty near Carentan in June 1944 after the army had learned that no less than three of his brothers had been killed. Inconsolable siblings were determined to get even before the end of the war; a few actually joined up for that express purpose.[118] "I was like a maniac," admitted a paratroop sergeant who learned that his brother had been killed at Cassino. "When they sent me into France, they turned a killer loose, a wild man."[119]

That death in battle was "not a pleasant, natural death, but an unimaginable kind of mutilation" made the killing of brothers-in-arms even harder to accept.[120] Since the anger that this caused could not be vented on the nature of battle itself, it was directed instead at the German soldiers, who became suspected of inflicting the kind of suffering that was senseless even in war. Awe for the Germans' methodicalness easily turned into accusations of diabolicalness when it proved to result in wholesale slaughter on the battlefield.

Some of the methods the Germans used to eliminate their opponents were more detested than others. No German weapons became more hated by the GIs than mines and booby traps. Land mines were used extensively for the first time in World War II. The Germans turned into masters of mine warfare when they were forced on the defensive and attempted to delay their pursuers by all means possible. The Americans took heed of these weapons belatedly. Only in August 1943 did mines and booby traps become a major subject in engineer training centers, while 90 per cent of the infantry veterans complained as late as the beginning of 1944 that they had too little training in how to find and handle the devices. In the meantime, reports from North Africa had already indicated that the Germans were using mines on a scale large enough to suggest a new weapon in warfare. Between late February and 13 April 1943 alone, American engineers located over 39,000 mines in Tunisia. Later, similar minefields were found all across the European continent. Some of the most extensive ones lay in Normandy, while in Italy certain areas contained so many antipersonnel mines that they could only be cleaned up by bulldozer operators and engineers wearing flak suits. In the course of the war, the Germans developed a multitude of new mines at a furious pace: Topf mines, Riegel mines, Mustard Pots, bottle mines, Stock mines, vicious "Bouncing Betties" that discharged a hail of steel ball-bearings at waist or chest level, nasty Schu mines that mangled foot, ankle, and shin bone, and powerful Teller antitank mines. All mines known to exist in 1940 were encased in metal, but the Germans rapidly increased the number of nonmetallic mines during the war. Made of wood, glass, concrete, bakelite, even paper and cloth, they were virtually impossible to locate with standard metal detectors. This, combined with the fact that in retreat the Germans abandoned placing mines in systematic patterns and resorted to scattering them randomly, had a tremendously demoralizing effect on the American troops. In addition to the mines, the Germans booby-trapped anything that curious or unwary troops were likely to touch, from fruit trees to Lügers and from haystacks to pencils. After the German retreat from Normandy, for instance, American engineers removed no less than 300 booby traps at Lessay, a village of only 2,000 people. The Germans continued to excel in mine warfare until the end of the war.[121]

The Americans had a hard time accepting these weapons as legitimate instruments of war and explained the German preference for them as a manifestation of innate cruelty and cunning. They refused to see them as efficient defensive weapons and instead considered them to be "dishonest," "wicked," "infernal," and "diabolical."[122] A GI who explained to his family what kinds of mines the Germans had been using in the North African campaign mistakenly believed that those "devilish, fiendish devices of war" were "things that we don't dare use."[123] It was one thing to the GIs to use mines on roads and trails to hold up troop movements, but to mine tomato patches, vineyards, and swimming holes in order to harm people indiscriminately was "just sadism." These were not the methods of ordinary soldiers, but the "Nazi specialties" of a debased enemy.[124]

Sniping was regarded as another such method. German snipers pestered the Americans from the moment they landed in North Africa. Tales soon circulated of German sharpshooters receiving bonuses and three-day passes for each officer they killed. As a result, American officers scraped the white bars off the front of their helmets or covered them with mud, and they preferred not to wear the typical officers' trench coats. On the eve of the Normandy invasion, paratroop officers and NCOs respectively painted vertical stripes and horizontal ones on the back of their helmets to be on the safe side.[125] The American soldiers regarded sniping as an especially treacherous way of killing. And although the US Army employed snipers too, it did not strike the GIs as contradictory to regard them as skilled specialists, while condemning the enemy's expert marksmen as "unspeakable villains."[126]

The GIs found evidence of several other German methods of killing that suggested they were dealing with a perverted enemy. From Normandy to Aachen, for example, they reported that the Germans used wooden bullets for ammunition. Although normally less harmful than standard ammunition, the slugs could cause messy, painful wounds when they hit the bone and shattered into a multitude of splinters. That result enraged medics and gave life to the rumor that the wooden projectiles worked on the principle of the dumdum bullet, which had been forbidden by the law of war.[127] The German soldiers also did not hesitate to use the many antiaircraft weapons that were at their disposal, especially on home soil, against the Allied ground troops. So terrifying and destructive were the 88 mm pieces and the 20 mm four-barreled guns that the GIs refused to believe these weapons were permissible on the battlefield and again accused the Germans of violating the international rules of warfare.[128]

The American soldiers' claim that the rules of warfare had lost their meaning to the Germans did not only concern their choice of weapons. More and more, they also charged the enemy with violating other codes of behavior in battle.[129] This seemed to be the case even with regard to the use of the Red Cross. To be sure, from Cassino to Saint-Lô there were instances of Germans agreeing to call truces that lasted up to several hours and effectively allowed medics from both sides to care for the wounded without being bothered in any way. Other than that, however, the fog of war easily obscured the presence of the Red Cross on battlefields and often hampered the German respect for it. Yet the GIs refused to accept that their medics, who displayed red crosses on both helmets and arm bands, were killed only by accident. They insisted, for instance, that German snipers zeroed in on areas with potential casualties – such as minefields – and then purposely singled out the medics, using the crosses on their helmets as targets. The Americans had a whole list of other complaints about the German disregard for the Red Cross. Medics were killed when they tried to remove wounded or dead comrades who had quickly been booby-trapped or surrounded by mines. They were ambushed by vengeful German wounded. The *Luftwaffe* knowingly strafed ambulances. At Anzio beach, the GIs became convinced that the Germans were shameless enough to be using the red crosses on the hospital tents as targets for their artillery.[130]

An enemy who did not respect the Red Cross was capable of every dirty trick in the book. Americans charged the Germans on numerous occasions with abusing the white flag, for instance. They were said to fake surrender so as to be able to kill approaching GIs with hidden pistols or grenades released from their armpits when raising hands. At Monte Porchia in Italy on 6 January 1944, German tanks more than once attempted to get closer to armor of the 760th Tank Battalion by flying white flags. At Nieder-Olm and again at a village near Hof, men of the 90th Infantry Division were ambushed by enemy soldiers when white flags hanging from German houses turned out to be ruses. The growing German reputation of deceit had made soldiers of the 84th Infantry Division so distrustful by November 1944 that they refused to leave their shelters at the Wurm River to help a soldier who kept crying throughout the night that he was an American whose leg had been blown off. The GIs' agonizing dilemma lasted until the moaning stopped hours later.[131]

Even more disquieting than the diabolical weapons and fiendish tricks the Germans were using in battle was the disrespect with which they were increasingly rumored to treat POWs. As early as November 1943, 13 per cent of the American infantrymen in Europe claimed they had personally seen the Germans fight or treat

POWs in a dirty or inhuman way; another 24 per cent said they had heard such stories from others. As the war dragged on, more and more stories began to circulate among the GIs about German atrocities against POWs. In Sicily, paratroopers were said to have been tied to trees, doused in gasoline, and burned. The Normandy campaign gave rise to several new horror stories. It was whispered that in the Utah sector the mutilated bodies had been found of paratroopers who had been tortured before their execution. Some were said to have been lying along the roadside near Sainte-Marie-du-Mont, their pants pulled down and their genitalia shot or cut away.[132] "I'd rather be killed than captured," a combat engineer confided to his journal near Carentan in July 1944, "I've read & heard too much about the way the Krauts treat prisoners. I *know* I'm not made of the stuff to stand being tortured."[133] The Americans also heard that the enemy routinely killed soldiers for possessing German belongings. Rumors claimed that GIs had been found shot in the mouth with the Lügers they had carried and that the souvenir pistols, wrapped in swastika flags, had been displayed on their chests as a warning against stealing from German soldiers. The GIs did not find these tales at all unlikely. Troops who found themselves cut off in the bridgehead across the Saar River at Dillingen in December 1944, for example, hurriedly dumped all the German items they were carrying before the enemy had the chance to take them prisoner. An 18-year-old Arkansan of the 84th Infantry Division was so frightened of the enemy's wrath in case of capture that he decided to part even with the German blanket he had taken to keep warm during the bitter winter of 1945. The fear of capture reached an all-time high, however, during the battle of the Ardennes, when news of the Malmédy massacre spread like brushfire. After Malmédy, the GIs deemed the Germans capable of anything. Early in January 1945, for instance, soldiers from a company of the 42nd Infantry Division were told by their commander during a nasty counterattack near Strasbourg to make sure they kept at least one round in the chamber to shoot themselves with when threatened with being taken alive.[134]

If the American combat soldiers responded to the Germans' valor with a mixture of fear and respect, the enemy's fiendishness increasingly cultivated hatred in the front lines. US Army surveys established a clear relationship between vindictiveness and the witnessing of atrocities. But the anger of the GIs who had only heard about atrocities from others grew too. An officer of the 35th Infantry Division confided to his journal early in January 1945 that the news of the SS murders at Malmédy had enraged the men: "A hatred such as I have never seen has sprung up among us against Hitler's armies and all of Germany."[135]

Such hatred was largely absent among the American combat soldiers at the outset of the war. Indeed, US Army reports from the North African campaign found it necessary to warn about this shortcoming. The GIs entered the conflict with a vivid impression of the Great War, but without any personal battle experience. The temptation to imagine war as "playing a game on a vast scale" – involving a skilled and determined yet fair and courteous opponent – therefore remained difficult to resist at first.[136] Soldiers of the 101st Airborne Division, for instance, who were training in southern England for D-Day, were impressed when they witnessed the sinking of ships at Torquay by German torpedo boats darting in and out of the harbor undauntedly. "We couldn't help but cheer the display of sheer guts and bravery," said one, "despite the fact that it was committed by the enemy."[137]

Chivalry, however, was one of the first casualties among the GIs in the front line.[138] The paratroopers at Torquay had not seen action yet. Those of the 509th Parachute Regiment had, and one of their commanders had been urging newcomers ever since North Africa to "forget good sportsmanship on the battlefield" because battle was "not a refereed football game but the dirtiest game yet devised by human minds." Mauldin too was quick to learn at the Italian front that "you don't fight a kraut by Marquis of Queensberry rules." And he emphasized that up front this was true no matter what kind of German troops the GIs faced:

> Our army has seen few actual Nazis, except when they threw in special SS divisions. We have seen the Germans – the youth and the men and the husbands and the fathers of Germany, and we know them for a ruthless, cold, cruel, and powerful enemy.[139]

If the rules of good sportsmanship were tossed overboard rather quickly in the front lines, hatred proved to be an increasingly helpful emotion as the war against the ruthless enemy dragged on. A combat doctor of the 88th Infantry Division noted in his diary during the Po Valley offensive in April 1945 that the eyes of the soldiers had become "red from hate and fatigue." By that time, 28 per cent of the enlisted men surveyed in four infantry divisions in the MTO claimed hatred for the enemy helped them a lot when the going was tough, while another 34 per cent admitted it helped them to some extent. Also in April 1945, 41 per cent of a cross section of the GIs in the ETO said they strongly hated the German soldiers.[140]

Hatred in turn spurred the lust for revenge. American soldiers who joined the chase after the fall of Rome, for instance, confessed to "a bitter hatred of the Jerries" as well as "a burning desire to avenge what they have done to us." That kind of craving, an infantry division's counterintelligence officer observed, reached a climax "in the environment of disorder and deprivation common to life at the front" and usually indicated "the great difference between green troops and veterans:"

> Men who have lived in the zone of combat long enough to be veterans are sometimes possessed by a fury that makes them capable of anything ... It is as if they are seized by a demon and are no longer in control of themselves.[141]

A paratrooper in Normandy was overwhelmed by such a frenzied rage that he crawled up to the German soldier he had just killed and tried to take his long, blond hair as a scalp. Only enemy rifle fire managed to stop him and bring him to his senses. "Deep inside, something primitive stirred within me," was all he could say to justify his attempt. Combat soldiers could also explode into a fury en masse. This is what a GI of the 84th Infantry Division witnessed at Linnich in February 1945, during a heavy barrage on German positions across the Ruhr:

In the middle of it all, a lone German machine gunner decided he'd had enough. He fired a long burst of tracers at his tormentors. It was his last mistake. Every tank, every antiaircraft gun, every machine gunner within range returned the fire. Waves of tracers and flat-trajectory rounds swept toward the hole, engulfing it in a single continuous explosion. We cheered lustily.[142]

There were times when the enemy's fiendishness so blinded the GIs with anger and hatred that they could not be prevented from taking revenge even on unarmed POWs. During Operation Market-Garden, men of the 101st Airborne Division captured a few dozen German soldiers while on patrol across the Lower Rhine at Renkum. Many of the POWs were veterans from the Eastern Front, and when they nervously asked a private if they would be shot, the GI assured the Germans that "such things aren't done in the American Army."[143] Yet, despite the private's assurance, capture by American combat soldiers did not always guarantee German soldiers safe passage to the rear. A medic who was searching for POWs to help as litter bearers during the siege of Metz, for example, was told bluntly by the American infantrymen that they were "not fighting that kind of war right now." Likewise, a private from the 87th Infantry Division admitted: "Time and time again in combat we heard, 'The boys aren't taking any prisoners today,' and that always meant the prisoners were being shot down."[144]

When asked to evaluate the 1st Infantry Division's treatment of captured German soldiers in the front lines, a sergeant's laconic answer was: "They were very good enemy prisoners or they was dead." Unfortunately, there were numerous circumstances that could make American combat soldiers decide that POWs were undeserving of the humane treatment guaranteed by international law and explicitly stipulated in the GI field manual.[145]

To begin with, of course, the killing of POWs took place in the general climate of hatred that was born out of battle. That climate could already be pervasive on the eve of combat. In the hours before D-Day, for instance, major general Maxwell D. Taylor, as well as junior officers, incited the men of the 101st Airborne Division not to take prisoners.[146] In the front line itself, adrenaline rushes often prevented the GIs from calming down in time to respect the rights of prisoners. "I was so scared and upset," confessed a GI to whom a German had surrendered during the battle of the Ruhr pocket. "I swung at him with my rifle butt. I was lucky I missed his head. In combat you are like an animal fighting to survive."[147] Combat soldiers found it especially hard to accept the surrender of those enemies who continued to resist at close range until they ran out of ammunition and then had the nerve to beg for mercy. General Patton himself delivered an inflammatory speech to officers of the 45th Infantry Division prior to the invasion of Sicily in which he "urged the killing of enemy troops who continued to resist at close quarters, even if they offered to surrender." Some regimental commanders in turn repeated that message verbatim to the enlisted men.[148]

Those Germans caught using weapons the GIs particularly despised ran even higher risks. Snipers, for example, often could not count on any mercy whatsoever. The Americans disposed of them most thoroughly. They used bazookas to remove them from trees and tanks to eliminate them from houses. Men of the 87th Infantry Division claimed that they shot snipers who surrendered in the Thüringer Forest "without hesitation." A sniper apprehended by soldiers of the 761st Tank Battalion after having killed two medics was executed on the spot by one of the unit's officers himself.[149]

The GIs also immensely disliked finding American items on POWs. In such cases, they often suspected the Germans of having stolen from prisoners or, worse, of having robbed the dead. A German captured in GI combat boots during the Battle of the Bulge, for instance, was ordered to remove them immediately and to walk to the rear through the snow in his stocking feet. With one punch, a soldier of the 14th Armored Division broke the nose of a prisoner who carried in his pocket no more than a few American cigarettes.[150]

But the German POWs had most to fear from those GIs who had seen buddies get killed. Men of the 84th Infantry Division managed to subdue a tank operator only after he had already killed two of the POWs they were herding to the rear. He turned out to have just arrived from the Bulge's Verdenne pocket, where he had lost too many good friends. A tank operator of the 13th Armored Division, on the other hand, made contact with infantrymen near Duisburg who had recently lost several good men and were out for revenge. On 17 April 1945, the dismayed GI noted in his diary that the foot soldiers had gone "crazy" and were "getting bloodthirsty, bayoneting, shooting, beating."[151]

The chances of surrendering Germans making it to the rear reached all-time lows whenever news of enemy atrocities against American POWs seeped through. In response to the stories of brutalities in the Utah sector, a surgeon of the 506th Parachute Regiment wrote to his wife that they too were now fighting dirty and taking "very few prisoners compared to the number we could have."[152] The Americans reached a true boiling point, however, when they got wind of the massacre committed by the SS at Malmédy. "In the heat of battle, prisoners were sometimes killed," a soldier admitted. "We knew that. But this was mass murder."[153] In more than one place, American combat troops reached the silent understanding that they would get even by not taking prisoners either. A private of the 5th Infantry Division observed that the Malmédy massacre had made everyone "nervous." He claimed that, as a result, the men from his unit who were told to take POWs to the battalion headquarters in the rear shot German soldiers on the way "again and again for quite a while."[154] After Malmédy, SS soldiers in particular were singled out for acts of revenge. The GIs started looking under the POWs' right arms; those who were branded by the SS tatoo were "not treated kindly." A sergeant of the 10th Mountain Division in Italy, for example, admitted that he and his comrades "didn't take many SS to the stockade." Men of the 90th Infantry Division at the Saar River took revenge on the SS in such a systematic manner late in December 1944 that headquarters had to issue express orders to take SS soldiers alive so as to be able to obtain information from them.[155]

Combat officers could do little to prevent the killing of prisoners, what with tempers running high and confusion reigning in the front lines. At the little Italian village of San Biagio in 1944, a soldier of the 350th Infantry Regiment in a frenzy managed to shoot one of the surrendering Germans in the stomach in the presence of the regimental commander himself. A paratrooper of the 101st Airborne Division who was wounded in Holland in October 1944 was told by his captain to get treatment and to take a batch of prisoners with him to the rear. But the officer suddenly remembered that the wounded soldier had a reputation of roughness with POWs. He had to force the disappointed paratrooper at gun point to hand in his ammo. The man was allowed to keep only one round in his gun so that the other POWs could defend themselves if he fired at them once. The officer personally checked with the prison pen that evening to make sure the Germans had arrived.[156] But combat officers could rarely spend that much time on guaranteeing the security of POWs. Moreover, some found it much easier to sympathize with their own men than with enemy prisoners. A sergeant of the 95th Infantry Division killed three surrendering Germans – including a medic – in the Saarlautern bridgehead in December 1944 in revenge for the killing of a good friend by a sniper. Still, the NCO never received more than an admonishment from his commander. At Rothau in the Vosges, a lieutenant who demanded court-martial for a sergeant who had killed two German POWs was told abruptly by his captain that the man was one of his best NCOs and that he would not punish him. "Trouble is," the disquieted lieutenant put in his diary, "that some of our best men are also the most murderous."[157] When one of his sergeants emerged from a cellar during the battle for Bendorf in March 1945 without the three Germans he had just taken prisoner, a company commander of the 2nd Infantry Division realized that a war crime had just been committed in his own unit. "They are going to win the war, however," he consoled himself, "so I don't suppose it really matters."[158] As a result, many unarmed German soldiers perished without much ado amidst the anger and hatred of battle.

Worse even than the anger and the hatred the fiendish German foe provoked, however, was the gradual dehumanization he underwent at the front. This, more than anything else, made the killing less and less hard for combat soldiers. German POWs, for instance, were not always killed out of blind revenge. Sometimes the GIs eliminated them merely because they formed a practical nuisance. Armored spearheading forces rarely had the time or means to bother with POWs at all. The job was left to the infantrymen, who had to walk them to improvised pens several miles to the rear. But, during battle, caring for POWs often proved to be too much of a burden for them as well. A foot soldier in Italy tried to take 11 Germans to a prison pen during the advance from the Volturno River to the Winter Line in October 1943. He discovered that his own regiment had already moved out; another regiment bluntly refused to accept his POWs. When he was told to walk them to the divisional stockade much further to the rear, the GI feared he would then lose touch with his company up front. He finally decided to leave the POWs standing in the road and hurried to his unit.[159] In such circumstances, men of the 90th Infantry Division thought it "a relief" to find all the German soldiers of a resistance post at Hof dead, "because it meant we didn't have to worry about coping with prisoners." Soldiers of the 12th Armored Division, on the other hand, had the misfortune of capturing three German soldiers alive at Herrlisheim right before being ordered to move out immediately. Not knowing what to do with the POWs, they killed them. "Human life," a soldier of the division confessed, "can become a mere matter of logistics."[160]

The process of dehumanization in the front lines was responsible for a growing indifference toward taking lives in general. Combat soldiers only crossed the threshold of killing an enemy face to face with extreme hesitancy, sometimes even avoiding it at the risk of their own lives. At Béja in Tunisia, for example, a private came across a young German soldier in a foxhole who did not notice him. The GI could not bring himself to kill the soldier just like that. He was thinking about speaking to him first or throwing a rock to draw his attention, when a German patrol spotted him and took him under fire without a second thought.[161] Breaking the commandment against taking lives proved to be a horrifying experience. A Ranger in Tunisia who killed his first person in a hand-to-hand fight at Sened Pass could not help vomiting; afterwards, he felt haunted by a "stained, sodden, guilty" feeling. Shame too was part of the confusing jolt of emotions that followed taking an enemy's life for the first time. In December 1944, a young soldier confessed in a private letter to his father that he had killed his first man face to face. "He was a blonde kid," the tortured boy wrote, "maybe even younger than I – and he probably had a father and mother too." In a postscript he added: "Don't tell Mom about that German kid. I don't want her to ever know."[162]

To most GIs, the only way to avoid getting lost in the confusing maze of feelings that surrounded the killing was to stay out of it altogether. "[Y]ou must squelch your emotions almost to nil," a chaplain of the 29th Infantry Division wrote to his family after the fall of Saint-Lô, "or you'd go nuts." Whether they were aware of it or not, many other soldiers went through that same process. "More and more," an officer noticed toward the end of the battle in Normandy, "emotion seems to leave us and we function more as machines."[163] As the war dragged on, combat soldiers stopped resisting the inevitable step by step, suppressed their scruples one by one, and gradually accepted being part of the merciless business of killing.

In the front lines, the GIs soon learned to equate killing the opponent with averting death from oneself and one's comrades.[164] From that new perspective, the fury of artillery raining destruction on the enemy could suddenly become "as deep and quieting for the mind as the bas notes of a musical piece."[165] War's peculiar and crude logic accomplished remarkable transformations in soldiers who had entered battle as frightful sinners. During the massive bombing for Operation Cobra in Normandy, for instance, men of the 35th Infantry Division "cheered and prayed," and an observer at Les Foulons reported that the GIs "gloried in it." Waiting for a concentrated artillery barrage to take place on the Germans near Roccagorga, Italy, an officer settled himself against a rock "to enjoy the slaughter." The veteran had arrived at a point where he felt "nothing other than an intense desire to kill as many of the enemy as possible."[166]

By the time so many Germans had been eliminated so easily that they had stopped looking human, the killing did not feel like murder anymore; it rather took on the appearance of a hunting trip. "This beats the pheasant season at home all to pieces," a corporal in North Africa wrote to his parents, "as it is always open season here." "It is just about like going rabbit hunting in the hedgerows," another corporal wrote home during the Normandy breakout. Infantrymen who participated in reducing the Verdenne pocket during the Battle of the Bulge, as well as paratroopers who trapped German forces near Randwijk during Operation Market-Garden, described their bloody encounters as "duck shoots." On 22 April 1945, a private informed his parents: "I actually think that I have shot at my last Jerry Rat in Germany." Those Germans who survived the hunts were marched to POW stockades that were appropriately known among the GIs as "cages."[167]

The combat soldiers eventually reached a point where animals roused their pity more easily than Germans. After having shot a German soldier in the Hürtgen Forest, a lieutenant was amazed to find that he "could stand there and watch him die and feel absolutely no qualms of any kind." "This seemed particularly strange to me," he realized, "for I was a man who had never gone hunting simply because I had neither the urge nor the heart to kill an animal." A GI who passed Saint-Lô on 22 July 1944 recorded in his journal that the rubble had not yet been cleared and that "the cows, hogs, dogs and Germans lie dead and stinking." The enemy had come to rank low on the ladder of living species.[168]

As the killing gradually lost much of its meaning for the American soldiers, so did the enemy dead. Graves registration details and chaplains worked hard to remove the dead from sight as soon as possible. But death was so pervasive on the battlefield that it never allowed itself to be hidden entirely. Killed soldiers could not be picked up while battle was raging and, afterwards, bodies were frequently overlooked in high grass, brush, woods, and mountains. Moreover, because there was a shortage of graves registration units, the enemy dead were taken care of only in between the removal of GI bodies, if there was time at all. A new company commander for the 2nd Infantry Division, who arrived at the Siegfried Line in October 1944, was shocked to find the unburied bodies of German soldiers carelessly strewn across his sector, their identification papers still on them. The battalion commander simply informed him that there was no graves registration unit available.[169] Likewise, a battalion surgeon of the 88th Infantry Division recorded in his diary upon arriving at Anzio beach in May 1944: "[T]he decaying enemy dead have not yet been removed, and their stench is sickening."[170] In the valleys and mountains of Italy, the GIs occasionally stumbled over enemy soldiers dead so long they had become fully dressed skeletons.[171]

Dead German soldiers kept staring the Americans in the face throughout the war. But the message they conveyed changed as battle experience increasingly hardened the GIs. At first, the ignored enemy dead, lying where they had fallen – discolored, bloating, decaying – filled the men with horror and repugnance and made them turn their eyes away as quickly as they could. Those who caught their first glimpses of mangled bodies were filled with sickening revulsion. When they pushed inland at Brécourt Manor on 6 June 1944, men of the 4th Infantry Division "puked their guts out from the sight of the distorted and riddled bodies." An African-American tank gunner, who was confronted by his first enemy dead near Vic-sur-Seille in November 1944, was struck "numb with fear and remorse."[172]

Death, however, fascinates the living. The initial revulsion triggered by mangled bodies rather quickly turned into curiosity. "An urge to examine them seized me," admitted a medic who stared at the remains of enemy soldiers in Normandy. The same company commander of the 2nd Infantry Division who at first had been shocked by the German dead at the Siegfried Line, gradually felt his eyes "drawn irresistibly toward them." GIs at Brodenbach near the Moselle River silently watched three dead Germans lying nearby. "We wondered idly where they'd been shot, although with all the holes and blood on their uniform we knew almost without looking," said one of them. "Still, we were curious, so I turned the first one over." The men then proceeded to examine the other two bodies in detail.[173] Similar examinations were repeated elsewhere in the front lines, as if they were rituals designed to dispel the mysteries that shrouded suffering and death in battle, and aimed at helping soldiers come to grips with what seemed their likely fate. GIs near Rohrbach-lès-Bitche in the Alsace rolled over a dead German lying face down in a gutter and scrutinized his gruesome appearance and the nature of his wounds. "We felt," one of them explained, "that the sooner we got used to looking on death, the better off we'd be."[174]

Once the enemy dead stopped holding mysteries for the GIs, they became "incapable of stirring any emotion except perhaps satisfaction."[175] The GIs remained troubled by the sight of their own dead throughout the war. Their faces were too familiar, their backgrounds too similar. Moreover, dead countrymen were indications that the war was not going the way it should.[176] Whenever he approached a new body, an American soldier in Lorraine, for example, could not stop worrying whether it would be an American or a German. But each time he noticed the German helmet or boots, he experienced "a surge of relief and then a wave of satisfaction." The German dead were mere strangers and the frozen lifelessness of the fiendish foes caused a pleasant sensation of security. All that a GI could think when he came across Germans who had been killed by mortar fire near the Maginot Line was "that here were six Krauts who wouldn't be shooting at us."[177] Whenever the war stagnated and progress stopped being measurable in miles, the GIs coldly resorted to body counts to put their minds at ease. During a burial detail the morning after a furious German counterattack near La Vacquerie in June 1944, a chaplain of the 1st Infantry Division was consoled to find "three or four Germans for each of our men killed." An officer of the 35th Infantry Division recorded in his journal after a fierce fight at Grémecey in November 1944 that there were many American dead. But he was relieved to be able to add that they formed "only about one third the number of the Germans," who were lying around "like watermelons in Georgia."[178] Dead Germans eventually remained noteworthy only as confirmations of the fact that the Allies were winning the war.

Beyond that feeling of satisfaction, the German dead stopped generating any emotion whatsoever. So commonplace did they become that they appeared to form an inextricable part of the European landscape and GIs stopped removing them altogether. Men of the 8th Infantry Division who took a town in the vicinity of Bonn, for example, refused to pay attention to the body of a German soldier lying near their house until much later when the smell became a nuisance; then they callously ordered some civilians to take him away. In the Gothic Line, the commander and junior officers of the 350th Infantry Regiment repeatedly had to prod the soldiers to bury the German bodies. Even so, the veterans remained "reluctant to expend any unnecessary energy on such unimportant matters."[179] When the GIs did comply, often they did not dig graves but hastily covered the bodies with some dirt. Across Europe, German boots could be seen sticking from the mud because the enemy had simply been "dumped in abandoned foxholes and covered unceremoniously." The incessant rains of the Old World easily washed away the earth, causing the decomposing corpses of the enemy to protrude from the soil on many a battlefield.[180]

In the end, the German cadavers only retained meaning for the hungry, wandering pigs that feasted on them. At the Maas-Waal Canal near the Dutch-German border, so many enemy dead had been left rotting in the mud that the men of the 82nd Airborne Division were powerless to keep away the hogs that swarmed to the killing field. A company commander of the 2nd Infantry Division, who inspected his unit's positions at the Siegfried Line in October 1944, stared at a dead German whose intestines had been torn out by pigs in a bloody, knotty mess. Next to the remains, one of the veterans was digging his foxhole with sublime indifference. Like many other American soldiers, he had lost any urge to treat the German enemy as a valorous foe who deserved humane gestures like burial.[181]

The Burned-Out Foe

As the war progressed, the American combat soldiers, torn between assigning the German soldier Olympian prowess and diabolical deviousness, were surprised to discover that the enemy was, in fact, no less human and vulnerable than they themselves were. It was a still greater revelation to find, as the war drew to a close, that the formidable German army was even more exhausted than the decrepit armies of the other European belligerents. The ultimate face with which the GIs caught the German soldier was that of a foe who had become totally burned-out.

Although it proved all too easy -- or necessary -- in the front lines to forget that the German soldiers were indeed human, an infantry counterintelligence officer observed that most GIs were "incapable of supporting over a long period the devil image of the enemy." He noticed that whenever the physical distance was reduced, the American soldiers were startled to discover that "the enemy, too, seemed nearly human."[182] The GIs tended to be surprised – and somewhat disquieted – to discover that the German foe shared the universal characteristics of ordinary human beings. A combat doctor who read some of the letters left behind by German soldiers in the Italian Gustav Line noted in his diary, with an air of revelation, that the enemy was "apparently just as homesick as we are." Likewise, GIs who had been fighting bitterly at the Rhône-Rhine Canal were startled to find that the surrendering Germans were "more exhausted than we," while it took a combat engineer until north of Rome to discover that the German soldier "ends life much like we do."[183]

The worst shock of recognition, however, came with the realization that even God and religion played an important role in the ranks of the German soldiers. By 1943, 75 per cent of the American soldiers were convinced that the Nazis would abolish freedom of religion in America if victorious.[184] It was therefore no wonder that the GIs at the front were intrigued by the fact that they were being attacked by German fighters plainly displaying white-bordered crosses on their wings and by tanks showing large black crosses on their sides.[185] Moreover, not only did German medics wear white tunics with huge red crosses on the back and front, in which they looked "like crusading knights,"[186] but enemy soldiers also wore belt buckles on which a slogan unashamedly exclaimed that God was on their side. The *Gott mit Uns* buckles of the German army shocked more than one GI. The Americans could hardly believe that the German soldiers were willing to use His name on their uniforms at all, and thought it truly perverted that they dared to pretend He was actually on their side. A combat artist with the 1st Infantry Division in Sicily, who came across a wounded German soldier near Troina, immediately cut off the man's belt buckle. "I thought it was time," he explained, "that 'Gott mit Uns' changed sides."[187] Yet the GIs soon learned that the worship of God among the German troops had not simply been relegated, as some had imagined, to a mere "pseudo-religious touch" on belt buckles. GIs who searched prisoners, for instance, often found religious medals and badges as well as rosaries and prayer books. To the GIs, that God could not be denied the right to be also in the midst of the Germans hinted more than anything else at the enemy's humanity.[188]

An enemy who was merely human had to be vulnerable too. The further the American soldiers managed to push back the Germans, the more that fact was borne out. "And so you dig your hole carefully and deep, and wait," said a paratrooper who had already withstood the test against the German foe both in Normandy and Holland when he arrived in Bastogne on 19 December 1944, "not for that mythical super man, but for the enemy you had beaten twice before and will again."[189]

Gradually, the GIs could see for themselves that the Germans were not immune to making mistakes either, despite their much admired and feared efficiency. In fact, the Americans came to believe that the Germans' biggest weakness stemmed from that high degree of methodicalness itself. They grew convinced that such discipline could only have been attained in a regime that had created the kind of soldier who was "too stupefied to have any thought of his own."[190] How else could several hundred badly shaken Germans who surrendered at a fort near Dinard in Brittany still manage to file by "in parade formation," under the watchful eye of their officers? How else could German POWs who came under fire from their own artillery after the fall of Koblenz break "into an orderly run" rather than a panic, even though they were terribly frightened? And how was it otherwise to be explained that in the Anzio beachhead German soldiers were seen attacking American positions "geometrically massed" and "in perfect alignment," marching behind the bellowing officers and NCOs "to the certain death of sheep following the leader to the slaughter pen?"[191]

German methodicalness could give rise to an astonishing predictability in an otherwise cunning enemy. German soldiers were known, for instance, to count the number of artillery rounds available for the day and then to calculate how many could be fired at what intervals. Soldiers of the 1st Infantry Division in Tunisia, dug in south of Medjez el Bab, were shelled for days on end at regular hours in the morning and evening and could set their watch by the five o'clock barrage. The GIs obligingly employed the reputation of German precision to their advantage. During the street fighting in Aachen, men of the 2nd Armored Division timed the intervals between the first three barrages of a German mortar team; for the rest of the day they could rely on moving freely during those same time spans.[192]

Despite their admiration for much of the German equipment, the American soldiers never lost confidence in the superiority of their own matériel. Eighty-two per cent of the enlisted men and 76 per cent of the company grade officers of the divisions that had fought in North Africa and Sicily believed that all or most of their equipment was better than that of the Germans. The Americans became increasingly aware of all kinds of deficiencies in the German equipment and clothing. While the GIs considered helmets of vital importance and even slept in them, the Germans were often captured wearing only long-peaked, soft caps. Whatever the reason – some POWs claimed they had thrown their helmets away because they were too heavy – it made the enemy appear careless and negligent. When cotton and wool became scarce in Germany, field uniforms had to be made of low-quality wool, mixed with various fibers such as rayon, and the result was that more and more German soldiers looked shoddily dressed. Throughout the war, the German foe remained easily identified by his ankle-long overcoat, whereas the US Army switched to field jackets that allowed the soldiers to be more mobile. The GIs considered the heavy, double-breasted, six-button German overcoat, which was narrow at the waist and flared at the bottom, outdated and clumsy in combat. Belgians who were liberated by the 9th Infantry Division told the Americans how surprised they were by the silence of their footsteps as they had grown used to the intimidating cadence of the German hobnailed boots. The GIs themselves soon also learned to be alarmed by hobnails crashing on stone, and they failed to understand why the Germans had not yet switched to the soft, quiet rubber soles of some of the American footgear.[193]

As American combat experience grew, German weapons were revealed to suffer from inadequacies too. Despite the weird and agonizing sound of the *Nebelwerfers*, most GIs eventually agreed they lacked the accuracy of artillery and were not very deadly. German rifles were solid and accurate, but many still consisted of bolts that had to be operated manually. Moreover, the side effect of the high cyclic rate of the enemy machine guns was a tendency to climb. The Americans were most relieved, however, to find that the monstrous King Tigers – essentially designed for defensive warfare – behaved very clumsily in the field. Their great weight, low speed, slow-turning gun, and poor visibility when buttoned up made them much more vulnerable than they appeared at first sight.[194]

More and more, however, the GIs realized that the problems of the German army went much deeper than mere flaws in the soldier's mental makeup or the equipment's design. Germany had been caught unprepared militarily and economically in 1939 for a long industrial, total war. Eventually, it was plain for the Americans to see how burned-out the German army was becoming as a result of the war's tremendous attrition, both in terms of its matériel and its manpower.[195]

The demise of the *Luftwaffe* formed the first convincing proof for the GIs of how fast the war was gobbling up Germany's military equipment. The American soldiers witnessed the spectacular effects of attrition on the German air force firsthand. From Iceland and North Africa they still reported that the air was the Germans' favorite element, and no GI stationed there denied that the Allied air force was being outnumbered by German planes. A chaplain who lived with a unit of combat engineers at Budareyri in Iceland, for instance, made mention in his journal of 25 different air alerts in a period of barely a month and a half during the autumn of 1942. In North Africa, the enemy bombed and strafed so frequently that soldiers of the 1st Infantry Division at El Guettar had to shave hurriedly in between runs to the trenches.[196] As late as March 1943, a soldier of the 1st Armored Division at Maknassy complained that his unit drew "bombers like molasses does flies." Above all, the GIs in North Africa learned to hate the terrifying JU 87 *Stuka*, which sounded "worse than a person being tortured to death."[197] Apart from the 88 mm gun, the dive bomber was the most feared German weapon in Africa. The skies seemed infested with *Stukas*. Americans who were under attack from the dive bombers three times a day for two weeks at Fondouk Gap in March 1943 appropriately baptized the area "*Stuka* Alley."[198] In the valley of Tébourba, even a brief religious service could be interrupted more than once by *Stuka* air strikes. It inspired the GIs to sing new words to the tune of "The White Cliffs of Dover:"

> There'll be Stukas over
> The vale of Tebourba
> Tomorrow when I'm having tea,
> There'll be Spitfires after –
> Ten minutes after
> When they're no bloody use to me.[199]

But, gradually, the Germans were forced to sing a different tune themselves. The high attrition of their air fleet, which had started over France and Britain and increased as the Reich's perimeter expanded to the south and east, combined with an aircraft production that lagged more and more behind that of the Allies. As early as the last quarter of 1942, the Anglo-Americans outproduced the Germans by 250 per cent in single-engine fighters and by more than 20,000 per cent in four-engine bombers. In the meantime, the skills and experience of new pilots declined so fast as a result of the curtailment of training programs that by 1943 the Germans lost as many fighters due to noncombat causes as to the efforts of their opponents. Allied raids over Germany further depleted the enemy's air force as well as its fuel reserves.[200]

All this caused the German planes to become fewer and fewer until they were in effect a rare occurrence in the skies over Europe. Late in 1942, an American lieutenant wrote home from England that the German air raids were not "any pink tea" but that "Jerry doesn't come over as often as he used to."[201] The full impact of attrition on the German air force began to be felt during the summer of 1943. A lieutenant of the 2nd Armored Division in Sicily wrote to his mother that he rarely saw more than five or six German planes at a time, and that their attacks were merely "wasp-like" and "of the nuisance variety."[202] By the time the Allies landed in Normandy, they had firmly established air superiority over Europe and the *Luftwaffe* had stopped being a serious factor in the war. In almost every entry of a diary belonging to a sergeant of the 1st Infantry Division, German planes were mentioned until the summer of 1943 in Sicily. When the NCO arrived in France on 8 June 1944, however, it was not until 20 June that he mentioned in his journal having seen the first German planes – eight in total – come over in formation during the daytime. The few German planes that were still operational rarely ventured out in daylight. Only when night set in, could a few timid enemy reconnaissance planes be heard here and there, at times dropping a flare, perhaps even a few bombs. GIs all over Europe mockingly called them "Bed Check Charlie."[203]

Eventually, Germany was forced to switch to the production of qualitatively inferior aircraft in a desperate attempt to keep up with Allied production levels. To the American soldiers, it seemed as if the very noise of the German engines echoed the demise of the opponent's air force. They had fun comparing the sound of "Bed Check Charlie" to that of an old lumbering engine or a Maytag washer; some claimed it sounded as if the motor was missing altogether.[204] Meanwhile, the *Stuka*'s fame disappeared as quickly as it had come. As early as the Sicilian campaign, the GIs found that the dive bomber sounded like "a ground vehicle with a loud exhaust." In skies that had come to be dominated by Allied fighters, the once so frightening *Stuka* suddenly appeared to be slow, outdated, and "something of a laugh."[205]

By the end of the war, the German falcons looked more like scared sparrows. So rare did German air attacks become that they were guaranteed to be a topic of conversation in letters home whenever they took place. During the last months of battle, the GIs spotted so few German planes that they began to have problems recognizing them when they did appear in the skies. A company of the 95th Infantry Division, clearing Rheinhausen in March 1945, was strafed by ME 109s right after the aircraft identification officer had confidently put the men at ease by identifying the series of approaching black specks as Spitfires.[206]

What astounded the American soldiers at least as much as the demise of the *Luftwaffe* was the lack of motorization in the German ground forces. The GIs had come to envision those forces as "a great mechanized juggernaut" that transported all of its soldiers either in trucks or in half-tracks.[207] Great was the consternation of soldiers of the 36th Infantry Division, for instance, when they overran a German unit at Bracciano, just north of Rome, that turned out to be the 20th Bicycle Regiment. Even more profound, however, was the amazement of the Americans when it dawned on them to what extent the Germans were still making use of horses as a means of transportation. Unsuspecting GIs were puzzled by the wagon loads of harnesses and saddles near Sainte-Mère-Eglise and the horse trenches at Utah beach.[208] In a field near Carentan, an intrigued paratrooper examined horse-drawn wagons that belonged to the German army, noting that some were still "canvas covered like the ones our ancestors are pictured in while crossing the western plains."[209] But, as they advanced across Europe, the Americans grew used to finding more German bicycles and mounts than trucks and half-tracks, and to hearing the clop of horses' hoofs in the quiet of night when the enemy was being resupplied. And they saw in this an unmistakable indication that the Germans were losing the war. "[Y]ou don't use them unless you're out of gasoline," concluded a GI upon hearing the sounds of German horses during a November night in Lorraine. "And if you're out of gas, you're finished."[210] Eventually, the depleted German army even ran out of horses. In 1944 the German army infantry division was reorganized into a unit with a strength of only 12,352 men instead of 17,200. While the number of horses it harnessed was reduced from 5,375 to 4,656, the number of horse-drawn vehicles increased from 1,133 to 1,466. During the last months of the war, the GIs came across German units that were using sick horses they had hurriedly taken from army veterinary hospitals.[211]

It was not only the offensive means of the German army that were disintegrating. Once they started crumbling under Allied pressure, the famed defensive walls of the Third Reich also proved to be less daunting than the GIs had imagined. The Atlantic Wall that shielded Western Europe was immediately shown not to be impenetrable in June 1944. In Normandy, only 18 per cent of the planned defenses turned out to have been completed on D-Day. The West Wall or Siegfried Line that blocked the entrance to Germany itself eventually also collapsed, albeit only after persistent hammering. With 68,000 battle and 72,000 nonbattle casualties, the Siegfried Line campaign proved tremendously costly for the American forces.[212] Yet, when the GIs had a chance to inspect the conquered defensive line from up close, they were not always impressed. "I was for some unaccountable reason surprised," admitted a private who saw the dragon's teeth of the Siegfried Line near

Rimling, "to find that it was an actual line."[213] German propaganda had exaggerated the strength of the West Wall and, as a result, the Americans expected to find a massive, towering, uninterrupted wall with an intricate underground bunker system. In reality, the West Wall turned out to be a band of many small, mutually supporting pillboxes that had been neglected since 1940. Surprised, somewhat disappointed even, the GIs discovered that the Siegfried Line often consisted of no more than "just columns of concrete" and "a bunch of holes in the ground."[214] What baffled the Americans most was that the efficient Germans had been so careless as to intersperse the defensive line with roads. In other places, German farmers had been allowed to build fills of stone and earth across those dragon's teeth that ran through their fields, and American tankers gratefully used them to enter the lion's den unhindered. The total collapse of the famed German military system appeared imminent.[215]

As the GIs witnessed the erosion of Germany's military power, confidence in the might of their own war machine thrived. They became especially awed by the tremendous firepower it was increasingly generating. The air force sowed death and destruction among the German troops without as much as being challenged. Men of the 29th Infantry Division watched incredulously from a rest area near Les Foulons the way endless, gigantic waves of aircraft pounded Saint-Lô during the Normandy breakout. They noticed how the concussion "pressed gently against shirts and trousers and shook the leaves on the trees." "What the Germans must have thought," wrote a sergeant of the 35th Infantry Division who had watched the same fury, "is beyond comprehension." The grimaces of the Germans who were captured while the dust was settling frightened the GIs. Most of them were "pale white" with "glassy stares;" others had gone "stark raving mad" and surrendered as "blubbering idiotic creatures."[216]

American artillery achieved the same pulverizing effect. A private of the 99th Infantry Division observed how a barrage cratered the hillsides and splintered the woods across the Wied River in Germany in 1945. The spectacle convinced the GI that the accuracy and power of the American guns placed them "among the most nerve-racking, most venomous, most deadly weapons of war." When phosphorous shells created "a gaudy pyrotechnic display" at Brest, soldiers of the 8th Infantry Division "wondered what Jerry thought of the might of *our* artillery."[217] In fact, the Germans could not but admit that they were stunned by the American artillery's firepower. During the last months of the North African campaign, German POWs were telling the GIs that American artillery fire was becoming "the worst hell on the front." So fierce was the massive barrage of the Ninth Army on targets across the Ruhr during Operation Grenade late in February 1945 that German soldiers were captured "dazed and muttering to themselves while others cried and screamed for days afterward." "It was not easy to sympathize with anyone who had dealt us so much misery in the past," said a shaken private who watched the inferno's red glare across the Ruhr, "but we couldn't help feeling sorry for anyone who was out there in the middle of that shattering fire storm."[218]

After having been intimidated by German tanks for so long, nothing encouraged the GIs more than the new Pershing tanks that appeared in Europe toward the end of the war. They arrived only in very small numbers, but the heavy tanks with their 90 mm guns left those GIs who caught a glimpse of them no doubt about what lay in store for the Germans. "As these monsters clattered by," wrote a soldier who saw Pershings for the first time near Kempen in March 1945, "we amused ourselves by throwing German helmets in front of them which they flattened out like egg shells."[219]

As the conflict crawled to its climax, the GIs noticed that the war was swallowing Germany's troops as greedily as its matériel. Those soldiers who did not perish in the Allied firestorms surrendered in ever greater numbers. The Allied victory in North Africa had produced the first huge wave of German POWs to inundate American ranks. There had been so many of them – 275,000 in the last week of fighting alone – that the GIs had allowed the Germans to drive their own trucks to the prison stockades. While the Americans marched across the European continent from Salerno and Normandy, however, the number of German POWs was reduced from a wave to a trickle. During the Battle of the Bulge, the news that a German soldier had been captured spread like wildfire among the men of a company of the 87th Infantry Division who were dug in at the Saint-Hubert-Tillet line. Droves of curious GIs descended on the command post to have a look at the prisoner. Their unit had entered the front line only two weeks before the start of the Ardennes counter-offensive, and they had not yet seen a single German prisoner from up close. Yet, the novelty of seeing German POWs would soon wear off for them, as it would for many other GIs. Within a few months after the failed German offensive, the American combat soldiers were drowning in a deluge of German POWs. When resistance in the Ruhr pocket collapsed on 18 April 1945, for instance, no less than 317,000 Germans were rounded up in a matter of days. In its three-week drive to the Elbe, the 84th Infantry Division alone captured more than 60,000 POWs. Erecting prison pens became so time-consuming for the division that engineers came up with the idea of driving around the POWs while dropping barbed wire and posts at intervals and then supervising the Germans as they fenced themselves in.[220] Elsewhere, the POWs were simply waved to the rear, barely escorted. Paratroopers of the 101st Airborne Division who were rolling toward the Alps over the *Autobahn* in April 1945 saw "more field gray uniforms than anyone could have imagined existed." They witnessed how German soldiers marched to the rear over the median strip in blocks of several thousands like sheep, each batch guarded by no more than a few lightly armed Americans.[221] The 42nd Infantry Division at Haar had to set POWs free on armistice day because the prisoner cages were filled to overflowing. They told some to hide in the weeds and to surrender again the next day; others were simply advised to put on civilian clothes and go home.[222]

The swelling tide of defeated German soldiers washed away the last lingering suspicions about the enemy's military superiority. The GIs' scrutiny of captured German soldiers revealed that they were neither the valiant nor the fiendish enemy they had pictured. The Americans were shocked to find how washed-up and burned-out the formidable German foe turned out to be. "The alleged magnificent heroism of the German people," concluded a relieved corporal of the 84th Infantry Division in a letter to his parents in Seattle, "is refuted by the number of prisoners taken and the manner in which they were taken in these last few months."[223]

The American soldiers arrived in Europe with clear preconceived notions of how German soldiers looked. Their mental picture had partly been shaped by what were supposed to be the traits of the typical Prussian officer. During the drive on Randazzo, Sicily, for instance, a combat artist with the 9th Infantry Division characterized a dead enemy soldier as "very German" because his face was "very austere, but quite beautiful" with "a fine, sharply pinched, rather cruel German nose and thin ascetic lips."[224] In addition, the GIs attributed several "classic Teutonic features" to the Germans. A combat artist who was sketching for *Parade* near Saint-Lô selected a dead German soldier with eyes of the "lightest blue" and hair that was "yellow-blond" as a subject because he represented "the ideal young Werther type of German."[225] Some Americans were convinced that a European with blue eyes and blond hair was German by definition. Near Saint-Dié in the Vosges, a sergeant of the 3rd Infantry Division opened fire on a civilian vehicle, badly wounding a member of the French resistance. It turned out the NCO had panicked upon noticing a man with blond hair in the car and had instinctively suspected a German ruse.[226] Such stereotypical expectations had been fueled by the Nazi portrait of the ideal German as an Aryan. When a wounded German captain was brought into a command post of the 29th Infantry Division in Normandy, one of the American officers instantly thought he "looked the part of a German war poster: handsome, blond, and tall."[227]

The Germans who were captured in North Africa in May 1943 at first seemed to confirm the stereotypes. According to one GI, all of Rommel's soldiers were "young & big & husky fellows." Moreover, several of them turned out to be "overbearing mean ones" who "took defeat bitterly."[228] But by the time of the Sicilian campaign, the GIs observed that most German POWs were very different from those in the Tunisian prison pens. They were "[l]ess arrogant and surly," looked "meek and innocent" instead, and became embarrassingly "anxious to please." "The Germans fought hard until they knew they were beaten," photographer Capa said disparagingly, "afterwards they all have cousins in Philadelphia." A surgeon who treated German casualties in the Italian Gustav Line in February 1944 noticed that several of them openly swore at Hitler; "a thing," he pointed out in his diary, "I never heard in Africa at any time."[229] The German soldiers also stopped being the mirror image of the Nazi posters' ideal Aryan. Late in the war, US Army reports indicated that the German soldier the GIs were most likely to face would be either a veteran who was a seasoned but "prematurely aged, war weary cynic" or a new recruit who was "too young or too old and often in poor health."[230] The GIs' own experiences increasingly confirmed this. An American who scrutinized German POWs during the Saint-Lô breakthrough was amazed by how different the enemy looked from the newsreels he had seen at home of Germans goose-stepping victoriously across Poland and France. "For the most part," he noticed, "they were little men who, when captured, were anything but erect or cocky." More and more GIs observed that the Germans were not at all "like the described supermen." Instead, they looked "very human," "unimpressive," even "crummy" and "seedy."[231] The classic Teutonic features became harder to discern. A combat engineer who saw his first batch of German POWs at Vierville in Normandy described them in his journal as "lousy & undersized & scurvy & dirty, with greasy hair & flat mouths & short necks." The GIs also imprisoned fewer and fewer impeccably groomed soldiers. The Germans became "unmilitary looking." They surrendered helmetless and unkempt. Their bulky overcoats seemed "cut to fit the brawny ideal Aryan" and made them look "small and delicate."[232] Their uniforms more often than not were a mixture of worn-out garments, beat-up boots, and unauthorized articles. German soldiers who surrendered at the Siegfried Line near Dillingen hurried to remove their boots; the GIs noticed that they were not wearing socks and instead had rags wrapped around their tortured feet.[233] "The sight of these captives," a combat doctor wrote in his diary after his unit had captured several ragged Germans near Castelforte, Italy, in March 1944, "boosts everyone's morale."[234]

Not only did the German soldiers appear increasingly ragged, they also smelled. On patrols, GIs sometimes claimed they were guided by the "distinct odor of the Germans."[235] They disagreed on what caused that odor. Some insisted it was the sweat-soaked leather; others blamed the vile-tasting German cigarettes that smelled like a combination of burning feathers, mildewed hay, and horse manure.[236] Whatever it was, the Americans often turned down German clothing and equipment (even blankets when the weather was piercing) because it was "indescribably filthy and smelled to high heaven." A similar smell usually pervaded the places that had sheltered German soldiers. In the sweltering Italian heat, filthy German hide-outs were so infested with lice and fleas that the GIs claimed the Germans attracted vermin "like the sun draws water." Americans who examined the pillboxes in the Siegfried Line were overcome by "a sour smell" of "foreign food and of unwashed bodies" and of "sweat & urine & old dirty clothing."[237] In dugouts, houses, and bunkers formerly occupied by Germans, GIs not infrequently traced the foul odor to piles of feces. They should have known that most German soldiers resorted to such unsanitary behavior because they had no choice. American combat soldiers lived in similar conditions when under heavy fire. Stuck in foxholes, GIs defecated in their helmets and urinated in the waxed ration containers, if not on the bottom of the pits; trapped in houses, infantrymen used butter churns, vases, drawers, and unoccupied rooms as toilets; buttoned up in tanks, soldiers relieved themselves in shell cases.[238] But the GIs chose to ignore the fact that the enemy – always under fire, often on the run, chronically exhausted and plagued by dysentery – was forced to lie in his own excrements because of the fortunes of war. Instead, they interpreted the enemy's uncleanliness as evidence of "his lack of training in simple sanitation and field discipline," a failure that seemed to imply a degenerateness characteristic of German soldiers if not of Germans. "It is well known among us," a sergeant wrote in his journal while stationed near the Siegfried Line, "that the common Kraut soldier lives like a pig. He doesn't bathe, he doesn't keep his clothing clean. They nearly all have lice & don't seem to mind it."[239]

Apart from being ragged and dirty, many of the captured German soldiers were famished too. Although the GIs learned to appreciate some of the German rations, especially the cans of fish and the tubes of cheese, they agreed that the German military cuisine left much more to be desired than their own. They deemed the German rations to be filling but unbalanced and lacking in vitamins. Moreover, the war had forced many ersatz products on the enemy that possessed an artificial and inferior flavor. According to the GIs, German coffee "tasted like hell," for example, while the black bread "appeared to be made of saw dust."[240] So poor did they rate the overall quality of the enemy's food that they believed it was responsible for the particular greenish color of many of the German dead. Ignoring that perhaps the enemy bodies turned a sickly green more often than the American dead because they were left unburied much longer, the GIs attributed it to deficiencies in the German diet.[241] When the Allied air force commenced systematically interdicting the German lines of supply, food also stopped arriving in sufficient quantities. Soldiers of the 36th Infantry Division, for instance, who at the outset of the Italian campaign observed that there were few "thin Jack Spratts" among the German soldiers, from 1944 on indicated that more and more of them appeared somewhat undernourished.[242] In those circumstances, German POWs could not help being impressed by the field rations the GIs had grown tired of long ago. Nothing amazed the enemy more than the presence in those rations of such luxuries as genuine chocolate. When a wounded German captain complimented the field ration he had been given after having been captured at the Vire River in August 1944, an American officer retorted "that if he found that palatable, his army was in worse shape than he realized."[243]

The American disappointment with the demeanor, look, and condition of the captured opponent gradually became tinged with contempt. Perhaps it was because the GIs interpreted defeat as a failure of manliness that they were overly sensitive to what they thought were effeminate traits in the appearance and manner of the German prisoners.[244] If the yellow-blond and red-golden color of some of the enemies' hair did not already look effeminate itself, the way most Germans wore their locks certainly did. The fact that the German soldiers were allowed to have their hair long never ceased to amaze the Americans. "It seemed only in America," said a surprised private of the 87th Infantry Division, "that men wore the Prussian crew cut." To the GIs, the long hair seemed unmanly and incongruous with true soldiers. "Some of them," a Japanese–American soldier in the Alsace wrote to his parents, "are real dandies with long, well-kept hair, and it's not strange to see freshly caught prisoners combing their hair unconcernedly in the prison camps."[245] The GIs also resented other subtle signs of effeminacy among the defeated. One American, for instance, wrote to his parents that the Germans were a "conceited bunch" because all of them treasured "at least a million photos, mostly of themselves." But that was not all the enemy soldiers carried with them. An infantryman in the

Alsace claimed that most Germans had "a small mirror, fingernail file, nail clips, comb (sometimes even a hairbrush), tweezers, and similar items in their pockets." In contrast with their own more spartan attitude, this self-pampering seemed proof of an unbecoming delicacy among the German soldiers. In Brittany, an annoyed lieutenant of the 8th Infantry Division observed that while his own men were "stripped to bare essentials," the Germans surrendered "loaded with items we would not have thought of carrying" such as "knives, razors, and scissors of all sizes, shapes, and purposes."[246] It was as if the American soldiers sensed some kind of moral corruption behind the German face of defeat and were eager to uncover it. A soldier of the 3rd Armored Division was so irritated by the long hair of an SS officer who was captured in the vicinity of Bastogne that he grabbed a pair of scissors and "hacked him all up."[247]

Apart from the general degeneration of the German soldier, the GIs pointed out several specific abuses within the ranks of the enemy that they thought exposed most clearly the exhaustion and corruption of their army. The American soldiers especially disliked the officers of the German military. They could not deny that the ones they met in the field were often very capable. "Whenever there was an officer," said a private of the 90th Infantry Division, "we could count on a fight, even if it was hopeless from the Kraut's point of view."[248] Yet it seemed to the Americans that the German officers had an excessively high opinion of their own worth and expected to be treated as a separate class that was far removed from the ordinary soldier. This was something the American enlisted men in particular were very touchy about, since all of them had, at one time or another in their army career, encountered officers with similar tendencies. Nevertheless, such officers were common mostly in training camps and at the rear. American officers who shared the hardships and dangers of the front lines were generally well liked by their men. By the end of the war in the European theater, 71 per cent of the privates in line infantry companies claimed that all or most of the officers in their unit were willing to go through anything they asked their men to go through.[249] This proved to the GIs that, when push came to shove, American strength lay in democratic unity. They had a hard time, however, believing that such an attitude could also thrive in the ranks of the German army. Not in the first place because of its Prussian roots or Nazi leadership, but rather because it was European. A lieutenant of the 9th Infantry Division pointed out that, after all, Old World armies had traditionally been run by a system in which the officers gave the orders and "the fighting was done principally by the enlisted men."[250]

The GIs automatically assumed that, as in most other Old World armies, the German military hierarchy still mirrored strict social stratifications and that its officers were aristocrats in uniform. To be sure, the German officer corps had traditionally been able to attract the highest social classes. Although the middle and lower-middle class had gained access to the German military caste with the rise of the mass conscript army after 1870, as late as 1932 33 per cent of the generals and almost 24 per cent of the officers still came from the nobility. But with the start of World War II, the rapid growth of the German army had caused the share of the nobility to shrink and had transformed the small professional officer corps into a large *Volksoffizierkorps*. By 1943, less than 18 per cent of the field marshals and generals were nobles.[251] The GIs, however, remained unaware of that change. That many of the German officers behaved and looked the way Americans imagined aristocrats only strengthened the existing stereotype. What made the GIs at the front furious, for instance, was that German officers had the nerve to insist on surrendering only to officers of equal rank. "Such formalities had to be dispensed with," an African-American lieutenant commented dryly, "we didn't have time to be scooting all around the country looking for a general as a matter of protocol."[252] Moreover, in sharp contrast to the increasingly ragged condition of the ordinary German soldiers, many high-ranking German officers were captured in impeccable uniforms until the last days of the war. "I do know that we never captured a German officer," insisted one GI, "who wasn't spick and span and looked ready for inspection." In August 1944, a soldier of the 30th Infantry Division at Domfront witnessed the surrender of a group of German soldiers who were "commanded by an Esquire-looking pink and white officer who carried a cane." Some German officers looked the part of nothing less than military royalty. On 4 April 1945, men of the 101st Airborne Division at Berchtesgaden captured general Theodor Tolsdorf, commander of the LXXXII Corps, whose "convoy was loaded with personal baggage, liquor, cigars and cigarettes, along with plenty of accompanying girlfriends."[253] That these men often were not officers from frontline units did not matter. The GIs had made up their mind that all German officers were "smug," "egotistical," and "arrogantly grand."[254]

Although American intelligence was well aware that the Nazis encouraged the officer's personal interest in his men as well as the social mingling off-duty, the GIs in the front lines were convinced that the haughty German officers were not close to their subordinates at all and could not care less about their well-being.[255] An American in North Africa wrote to his parents that his unit had caught a German general while he was trying to escape. "He was more worried about his baggage," the soldier fumed, "than his division of 12,000 men." That same suspicion bothered a corporal, who observed a captain and scores of enlisted men in a German POW cage in Luxembourg. The GI not only noticed how perversely the officer's "lean, clean-shaven, sullenly handsome face contrasted with the unhealthy look of his troops," he also sensed the officer's "arrogance and ruthlessness and his men's respect for it, even in defeat."[256] The American soldiers, whether enlisted men or officers, refused to accept such Old World anomalies. In a German cemetery near Cherbourg, a medic was struck by the fact that the grave-markers of the enlisted men were nothing more than weather-beaten boards that had been nailed together, whereas that of an officer had been meticulously carved and painted. "Why was he," asked the incensed GI, "even in death, so much better than the enlisted men killed with him?" A company commander of the 2nd Infantry Division, on the other hand, who was approached for help by a wounded German officer after the crossing of the Weser River, felt "revolted at his appeal to me as a member of the 'officer class.'" The American officer decided simply to ignore him.[257]

If the attitude of the German officers irked the Americans, the presence of foreign troops in the German army puzzled them. Tankers of the 4th Armored Division, on their way to the Blavet River in Brittany in the summer of 1944, were stunned when they ran into a cavalry unit made up of Russians. Thinking they were allies who had arrived on the scene to hook up with them, the Americans held their fire. Even when the order came to engage the force, they hesitated for fear of instigating an international incident. Only when the order was repeated more forcefully, with the explanation that these Russians were mercenaries, did the armored force at last wipe out the cavalry.[258] The GIs in Normandy similarly could not comprehend what Japanese troops were doing in Europe. "We didn't have to go to Japan to get our first Japs," a paratrooper wrote to his family. "We found 'em in trees here and properly disposed same." In the vicinity of Carentan, rumors spread that these soldiers had been sent "on lend-lease from Japan to teach the Krauts how to camouflage." It took some time before the GIs realized that the "Japanese" were in fact former Soviet soldiers from the Asiatic republics who had joined the German ranks.[259]

Foreign troops formed an intricate patchwork in the German army. They came from all over and even from outside Europe. Some formed separate forces, others were part of German units. Some had volunteered, others had been forced to join. Some were *Hilfswillige*, others wore the *Wehrmacht* uniform, still others displayed *Waffen SS* insignia. By March 1945, even the *Waffen SS* with its strict racial selection had turned into a multinational force in which only 40 per cent of the soldiers were German nationals.[260] The GIs were unable to distinguish between the myriad subtleties of nationality and status the foreigners represented within the German army. What was more, they were unwilling to make that distinction. The American soldiers knew next to nothing about the political realities and ethnic intricacies of Europe that had determined why foreigners wanted or had to fight on the side of the Germans. They often, therefore, could feel nothing but contempt for POWs who appealed to them for better treatment on the basis of their non-German nationality. The Americans simply regarded all of them as mercenaries or traitors and refused to believe the Germans had been able to force foreigners to fight for them.[261] In the front lines, such distinctions were academic anyway. If some of the foreigners were really fighting with the Germans against their will, a private in the Alsace asked his parents,

> why don't they shoot over our heads? Yeah, as we always say, if it's in a Heinie uniform shoot the hell out of it. The whole thing is a mess so why stop to think about the circumstances. They kill us so we do the same.[262]

One thing about Germany's foreign troops, however, was unmistakably clear to the Americans. The Poles, the Russians, and the Mongols were, a surprised tank operator wrote home from Normandy, "[d]efinitely not the fanatical young Nazis" they had been expecting.[263] Whether volunteers or conscripts, the non-German units proved to be among the least dependable elements of the enemy's army; often they surrendered as soon as the German officers and NCOs failed to prevent it. As time went on, the GIs stopped asking why foreigners were willing to fight for the Germans. Instead, they started wondering what shape the Germans were in that they found it necessary to lean on men they considered racially inferior and knew were militarily unreliable.[264]

No questions remained about the shape of the German army when frightened children in ragtag uniforms began appearing in the front lines in increasing numbers. Armies have always relied on the stamina of the young. During World War II, heavy loads, long miles, sucking mud and sloping mountains often proved too rigorous physically for infantrymen who were only thirtysomething. In an American infantry unit, anyone over 30 was quickly known as "the old man."[265] That armies had to sacrifice men who were in the prime of life unavoidably added to war's painfulness. "The fact that death's chief victims in war are young men or youths who are just becoming men," wrote an American officer, "contributes greatly to the general mood." But even in the eyes of the young American combat soldiers, there was a world of difference between the waste of men who had just reached their prime and the perversion of sacrificing "kids who'd never really had a chance to live."[266]

Battle was eager for the stamina of the young, but impatient with the innocence of children. Many of the German teenagers who were rushed to the front had not even experienced simulated warfare in a training camp. It pained American soldiers to encounter boys-in-arms who simply did not know what they were supposed to do. When a platoon of the 2nd Infantry Division in Czechoslovakia brought in three young prisoners early in May 1945, the captors learned that the boys were barely 14, had been forced into the army only two weeks earlier, and had never seen action before. They had dutifully followed the advice of their worried mothers to surrender to the Americans at the first opportunity.[267] Maternal advice, however, could not save all of the German boys who were thrown into the jaws of battle. While crossing some fields in the Rhineland, soldiers of the 9th Infantry Division suddenly found themselves face-to-face with "a bunch of kids." The youngsters were armed with nothing more than antiquated rifles and stood in foxholes that were only waist deep, but they did not have enough sense to surrender. Infantrymen pointed the boys out to tankers who just "blew them away." "We felt like butchers," a distressed private admitted after having partaken in the slaughter of several young boys who had manned defenses at the Czechoslovakian border during the last days of the war.[268]

Although bullets fired by boys were capable of leaving the GIs "as dead as those of any SS soldier," the Americans were more furious at the regime that had put the guns in their hands than at the children who pulled the triggers.[269] It was upsetting to the GIs to have to take boys who had managed to survive the slaughter of the front lines to prison pens as if they were as guilty and dangerous as the men who had sent them to war. An embarrassed tank operator of the 13th Armored Division confessed to his diary that he had been obliged to console a "scared and hysterical family" in the vicinity of Cologne after their 13-year-old child had been captured in uniform and taken to a prison cage nearby.[270] Some GIs refused outright to lock up children in uniform. Men of the 44th Infantry Division in Austria were pleased when their platoon sergeant took a German boy over his knee and administered a serious spanking as a more appropriate punishment for a soldier his age. During the last weeks of the war, many GIs took the guns away from scared and crying boys and simply told them to go home. The German army that had once been the pinnacle of military power in Europe had been reduced to a force the American soldiers could no longer take seriously.[271]

On the eve of battle, the Americans did not feel intimidated at all by the prospect of having to fight the Italian armed forces. In the front lines, the GIs found their estimation of the Italian army as a farce rather than a force largely confirmed. From the outset of the war, the Latin soldiers vanished almost completely in the shadow of their formidable Nordic ally. With the Great War slaughter and a string of Nazi victories in mind, the GIs went to war with the German army in an atmosphere heavy with insecurity and apprehension. It took much time and a series of Allied victories to convince the Americans that the German foe was not all valiance and fiendishness and that he was indeed as human and vulnerable as his opponents. But once the erosion of the image of German superiority was set in motion, the process took a furious and irreversible course, making it increasingly evident to the GIs that even this strongest of Old World countries lacked the military muscle needed to establish global power. The world war exposed shortcomings in the German army similar to those the Americans identified in the other European armies: the rigidity of mind, the limitations of industrial production, the division of class, and the reliance on vassal forces to compensate for the shortage of manpower. By the end of the war, nothing remained of the German superman image but the stark reality of a foe burned-out as completely as any had ever been. Together with their Soviet comrades, the American soldiers emerged from Europe's second great war in the twentieth century as the indisputable victors.

To the GIs, the spectacular erosion of Germany's military force was not only proof of the decisiveness of the Allied victory over the Axis enemy. It was also the most poignant illustration of the demise of the Old World's power. The American soldiers had seen with their own eyes that the Old World armies had been by far the weakest links in the Allied coalition. After 1940, it had been only the German army, with its daring, efficiency, and technology, that had appeared to be upholding the age-old reputation of Europe as a daunting military power to be reckoned with around the world. From the American perspective, the humiliating crash of the formidable German army therefore also symbolized the final collapse of the Old World's hegemony. When the American and Soviet troops at last linked up in the middle of Germany, it was obvious to the GIs that Europe was no longer the military epicenter of the globe. By that time, it had also become glaringly clear to America's combat soldiers that Europe's society had stopped being the throbbing heart of western civilization.

Part III
The Civilians

5   The Civilians – Introduction

The war first and foremost forced the American combat soldiers to pay attention to Europe's natural surroundings and to focus on its fighting men. It was difficult for the GIs to discern the Old World's civilians clearly through the fog of battle. Where resistance was weak, they merely rushed past the curious bystanders in hot pursuit of the enemy. In combat areas, either communities had been erased or the inhabitants had largely vanished. Only in the rear did normal European life restore itself more or less, but the opportunities for the Americans to get out of the line were scarce and brief.

At the front itself, the GIs barely had a chance to get to know the Europeans at all. Battle often erupted in places where not many people had lived to begin with. It preferred to rage not in densely populated areas, but in isolated forests, fields, and mountains. It had a knack for anchoring itself not on urban centers or historical capitals, but on hamlets and obscure villages. The men of the 9th Infantry Division, for instance, were so tired of fighting in the Roetgen, Hürtgen, and Monschau Forests and skirting Europe's urban areas that they complainingly baptized their unit the "Country Division."[1] Some of the places the GIs fought for were so lonely that they were not always convinced these were worth their sacrifices. A private wrote to his parents after weeks of action in the Belgian Ardennes:

> Personally, I can't see any reason for anybody to fight over this country, it's a mess. Here, we're in the hilly country with mile after mile of pine trees planted in straight rows. Not many roads, a few little villages of stone houses with the barns on one end.[2]

Fighting one's way into cities with resounding names seemed much more rewarding than suffering for Podunks. "I had always wondered about the taking of a large city," gasped a medic upon nearing Metz after months of liberating countryside.[3] The capture of Europe's capitals promised to be the ultimate experience for the American soldiers. Unfortunately, many of those capitals lay in the path of their allies, and even Paris had to be left largely to French troops. Rome, however, was open to the GIs. Not only was it the first Axis capital to be conquered by the Allies, the GIs' guidebooks also reminded them that it was "one of the most important of the world's capitals" as well as "the capital of Christendom."[4] With such credentials, the Eternal City could not fail to impress the American soldiers. Upon entering its gates, GIs who had been stuck in the Anzio beachhead and the Cassino mountains for months were instantly seized with "the intense nervous excitement of great moments, in which even the dullest of us were conscious of participating in historical events of overawing importance."[5] Soldiers fought for survival, but if they had to die, it somehow seemed to make more sense to fall near a place that would linger in the memory of many. "I can't help but think," wrote a tank operator who witnessed a badly wounded American in the tiny French place of La Haye-Pesnel in the summer of 1944, "it's more dignified to be buried at Waterloo than in Kookamonga somewhere."[6]

Most combat soldiers, however, did not spend much time battling for the metropolises of Europe. Instead, they soon learned to appreciate a mere house or barn that could serve as a shelter in their sector. In the mountains of Italy and the forests of Western Europe, the few houses that were captured intact in the small villages were reserved for company headquarters and aid stations; the platoons remained in their foxholes and dugouts. Even in cold and wet weather, officers could only allow small groups of men from rifle platoons that occupied foxholes throughout the night to thaw and dry out in barns and houses for a few hours during the day. When the command post of E Company, 506th Regiment, 101st Airborne Division was set up in a convent at Rachamps during the Battle of the Bulge, it had been a month since even the company headquarters had been in a building.[7]

No matter whether a European community was large or small, when combat soldiers had to enter it fighting they were hardly given a chance to experience how it normally looked. Warfare proved to be even more vicious in built environments than in natural ones, and battle dictated from beginning to end what the GIs would see of a village, town, or city. In the nasty business of street-to-street and house-to-house fighting, picturesque squares, romantic parks, elegant avenues, and stately homes vanished in the dust and smoke. As a matter of fact, the very first place that often attracted the American soldiers' attention in a European town was the cemetery. It happened to be one of the safest havens in any built environment: the soft soil allowed the digging of foxholes amidst cobble and brick, the solid walls offered excellent protection, and the sturdy buildings and towers at the entrance formed veritable bulwarks. Even the tombs themselves provided good cover. After entering Saint-Lô, for instance, soldiers of the 115th Infantry Regiment immediately established a command post in one of the cemetery's most imposing mausoleums. The place had thick marble walls, a heavy door, and an underground crypt, and it turned out to have been used by the Germans before them.[8] The irony of this introduction to urban Europe was not lost on the American soldiers. This is how a paratrooper remembered a Dutch town during Operation Market-Garden:

> Beside a Church we dug our holes,
> By tombstone and by cross.
> They were too shallow for our souls
> When the ground began to toss.
> Which were the new, which the old dead
> It was a sight to ask.[9]

Those combat soldiers who were not exiled to the towns' cemeteries during the fury of battle were most often restricted to their cavernous underground. When soldiers moved into houses, they refused to stay in what they called "the open" and instinctively hurried into cellars to avoid flying glass or direct hits. The GIs soon learned to select houses on the basis of their cellars' quality. If they had not yet been claimed by command posts or aid stations, they often rushed into the basements of hotels because these had been built large and sturdy for the storage of food and wine. They even preferred the cellars of buildings that had already been pounded into ruins because the rubble on top offered excellent protection against incoming shells. During prolonged city fights, soldiers settled down in the basements for the long haul. They heated them with stoves they removed from the upstairs rooms, their pipes protruding from windows, doors, and holes in the walls. They scrounged wax for light and could be seen marching with candles sticking out of their pockets, packs, and gas mask carriers. From time to time the GIs urged their families, sometimes in wax-stained letters, to send them more candles. Others bought them from civilians with money or cigarettes. Only in Germany did the quest for candles end because there the civilians had stocked their cellars with plenty of them as a result of years of air war. GIs who lacked candles fashioned "bottle-lamps," bottles filled with fuel from trucks or tanks and with a rag stuffed in the neck. Because blacked-out cellar windows prevented ventilation and candles and especially gasoline lamps gave off dirty streams of smoke, life in the cellars blackened the soldiers all over. Men of the 26th Infantry Division who spent weeks in the cellars of Saarlautern in the winter of 1945 were still spitting up black soot months after they had left the area.[10]

It did not matter that war perverted the GIs' view of Europe's built environment. Towns that were caught up in the fury of battle became unrecognizable anyway. What the enemy did not wreck, the American soldiers often had no choice but to destroy themselves. Before it could be liberated, Monte Cassino was ruined, Saint-Lô ravaged, and Saint-Vith wiped off the earth. Many towns had been reduced to ruins and rubble by the time the GIs established control. Villages became disemboweled, cities took on the appearance of empty shells, and homes everywhere were transformed into skull-like buildings. At times the extent of the damage was mind-boggling. A city as large as Aachen was 85 per cent destroyed. In Jülich, a city lying on the right bank of the Ruhr, the physical destruction was estimated to be 100 per cent. Infantrymen descended upon what was left of the towns like parasites. They ripped shutters from windows to serve as litters. They tore down curtains to use as bandages. They turned billiard tables into operating surfaces. They smashed up furniture for firewood. They unhinged doors and gates and placed them over dugouts as roofs. They dragged mattresses into foxholes and cellars. Amidst all this, the dying European communities gave off a sickening odor. It was composed of the smell of cordite, charred wood, dust, musty walls, blasted manure piles, and gasoline fumes as well as the stench of burned flesh.[11]

If battle completely distorted the picture of Europe's urban environment, it made its inhabitants disappear from sight altogether. Civilians fled before the thundering approach of war, leaving entire towns deserted and eerie-looking. More than once, these reminded the GIs of the ghost towns of the American frontier. One paratrooper even thought of Pompeii when he entered a small town near the Volturno River where people and animals had vanished and plates with half-eaten food were still on the tables. Both in the mountain villages of Italy and in the Vosges, the only people the GIs sometimes encountered were the very old, who had either refused to leave their homes or had simply been left behind. A sergeant of the 26th Infantry Division saw his first civilians near Albestroff late in November 1944; he had then been at the Lorraine front for over a month. When the Allies entered Germany in September 1944, they found vast areas depopulated because the Nazi authorities had ordered the civilians to evacuate to the east. In the German communities that the Americans occupied during all of 1944, only about a third of the people had stayed behind. In the rubble of Aachen, the first major German city the GIs captured, only some 14,000 of the 160,000 inhabitants had not fled. When the Ninth Army crossed the Ruhr late in February 1945, it encountered scarcely a soul in a zone that stretched some ten miles east of the river. Only when the Allies approached the Rhine did they encounter ever larger numbers of German civilians as the Nazi leadership had by that time started encouraging them to stay put for fear of a collision between the wave of refugees from the west and that from the east.[12]

Sometimes the civilians had disappeared because the military authorities had warned them of impending attacks. In Normandy, the Allies dropped leaflets on towns to inform the people they lived in danger zones and to urge them to hide in the countryside with their families for several days. In German towns across the Wied River, American pamphlets told civilians they would soon be under siege and advised them to go to their cellars and not to loiter in the streets. Most often, however, the civilians left on their own initiative. They developed a remarkable sense for detecting and predicting battle danger. Even the combat soldiers respected their judgment and learned that where they could see civilians there would usually be no enemy opposition.[13]

Until the front had passed, civilians lived in cellars or steered clear of the towns altogether. They hid in the surrounding fields, hills, and woods. In Italy, they fled the lowlands and mountain villages to seek refuge in ravines and caves where they sometimes lived with entire communities for weeks. Only after the fury of battle had subsided did civilians dare return to their streets and houses. GIs who watched civilians at Bitche in the Vosges enjoy the sun and fresh air after days of heavy street fighting noticed that they all looked pallid and wan from the long hiding in cellars. Some of the civilians in the Eupen-Malmédy region had lived in basements for almost two months when they finally ventured out at the end of the Battle of the Bulge. Often the combat soldiers had already moved on by the time the civilians decided to leave their underground hideouts. A lieutenant of the 320th Infantry Regiment helped liberate village after village in the Alsace during the fall of 1944 without encountering a soul. Bermering too seemed totally deserted when his regiment took it. This time, however, the officer was forced to stay behind while his unit moved out. The combat troops had barely left when droves of French civilians started appearing from nowhere. "I saw more of them in the last 30 minutes there," the stunned lieutenant wrote in his journal, "than I had in all the previous time."[14] German civilians not infrequently stayed in their cellars for several days after the Americans had captured their town, until hunger and thirst finally gave them the courage to face the occupiers. Likewise, civilians all over Europe returned to their homes from the surrounding countryside only when they somehow sensed that the war would leave them alone again. Some returnees were lightly packed, others returned with carts loaded with chairs, beds, mattresses, and household items, pulled by anything except the horses that had been confiscated by the retreating German army. They could be back in no time, startling the exhausted GIs who had crawled into their beds for a quick nap. The moment the battle of Roccagorga ended, soldiers of the 350th Infantry Regiment witnessed how Italian peasants, who had been totally invisible throughout the fighting, appeared on the roads with their carts – as if by a miracle. Elsewhere, refugees reappeared in their old communities only days or weeks after the battle. Some had nothing to return to at all. The areas the Americans occupied in the West Wall sector in 1944, for instance, were barely able to support a third of the original populace.[15]

When battle had finally moved on, civilians eagerly started rebuilding their lives and their communities as soon and as much as possible. Where the front lines had changed into the rear, a semblance of normality thus gradually returned. The American combat soldiers longingly referred to that world outside the combat area as "civilization."[16] It was there that they could get to know the European people in more or less natural circumstances.

Unfortunately, America's combat soldiers had few opportunities to get away from the front lines in Europe. The critical situation with respect to manpower left the US Army not much room for allowing the GIs rest periods, passes, leaves, or furloughs. If at all possible, units that had run out of steam were relieved and withdrawn to rest areas for short periods. Those areas that were operated by divisions or higher units were located in large communities. They offered billets in hotels and in buildings with canvas cots and blankets. They also provided hot bathing facilities, mess halls, American Red Cross clubs, movie theaters, and postal and financial facilities. The other rest areas were organized in smaller towns. They were limited to warm billets and facilities for clothing exchange, hot baths, and warm meals. But combat soldiers usually spent no more than 72 hours in a rest area. Moreover, rest areas were never situated far from the front lines and soldiers were always sent to them on duty status.[17]

Even more rarely did smaller units or individual soldiers obtain passes, leaves, or furloughs to leave centers or recreational areas. Before the invasion of Normandy, passes in Great Britain could not exceed 48 hours and hard-to-get leaves or furloughs were never valid for more than ten days. Not until September 1944 could troops on the Continent receive passes of 48 hours to various towns and cities. Only in January 1945 were they increased to 72 hours. The largest leave center for GIs in the ETO, Paris, was established on 22 October 1944. Brussels, the second largest, opened on 28 January 1945. That same month, a recreational area became operational at the French Riviera, where officers were billeted in Cannes and enlisted personnel in Nice.[18]

Passes for combat soldiers remained scant throughout the war. Only a few men from one company could receive them at a time in order not to weaken the unit at the front. Company commanders and platoon leaders often selected the most deserving men to fill the quotas from higher headquarters, taking into account the length and intensity of combat duty, wounds, and bravery. On other occasions, companies organized draws to determine who would get the available passes. In February 1945, for instance, a company of the 100th Infantry Division near Bitche had each platoon draw two men. They in turn were ordered to the company command post, where yet another draw singled out the two lucky ones who would be sent to Paris. Leaves and furloughs that lasted a whole week were even harder to come by on the Continent. The first ones, to Great Britain, were granted no earlier than January 1945.[19]

Even when soldiers did receive permission to leave the front lines for a few days, they still had to make it to the rear. The unit's own trucks and jeeps had to take care of transport and the trips could be quite an ordeal. Two lieutenants of the 3rd Infantry Division who were fighting in the German Hohe Rhön Hills, for example, were granted a week's furlough for Brussels early in April 1945. They took off in a jeep for a long and arduous trip that led them through Darmstadt, Mainz, Koblenz, and Bonn. In the Ardennes they got lost and had to spend a night in Malmédy before finally reaching the Belgian capital. The return trip was not an easy undertaking either as their vehicle had to wind through the rubble of Reims, Metz, Worms, Darmstadt, Würzburg, Schweinfurt, and Bamberg before finally reaching the front again. Traveling to leave centers in the rear sometimes proved so exhausting, especially in the winter, that it nullified the effect of the rest and forced units to give returning soldiers up to 48 hours of recuperation before sending them into combat again. Only on 1 March 1945 did rail transportation for recreational purposes become possible, first between Luxembourg City and Paris, gradually also to all other large leave centers and recreational areas.[20]

For the Americans who refused to go AWOL and did not desert, getting wounded was often the only way out of the combat zone for more than one week. The men who eventually made it from the field and evacuation hospitals near the front to the general hospitals of the large cities in the rear were the only combat soldiers able to observe Europe's society without interruption for weeks and months. But they enjoyed that privilege at a price most GIs were unwilling to pay.

The war did not allow the American combat soldiers to catch more than glimpses of Europe's civilians: while racing through their towns, while seeking shelter in their cellars, while catching their breath in rest areas, while visiting towns and cities on brief passes, while recovering in hospitals. Nevertheless, from these fragments the GIs did manage to piece together a mental image of the European people. That image was molded by the particular conditions of war, of course, but it was also influenced by their American background. As soldiers, the Americans saw a European society that had reached the point of disintegration. As Americans, the soldiers believed that this was the result not only of World War II, but also of the more deep-seated deficiencies that had been eroding the Old World for ages.

6 The Labyrinth of Nations

It was easy for Americans who had never left their side of the Atlantic Ocean to imagine Europe from that far shore as a monolithic culture. Similarly, it was tempting for American soldiers to view the European war from a distance as a clear-cut conflict between two sharply delineated camps: the victimized Allied countries on the one hand and the evil Axis nations on the other. The GIs' bewilderment was therefore considerable when they crossed the ocean to find that nothing was the way it looked in a Europe that seemed to relish political intricacy. To begin with, the very manner in which the different European peoples received the American soldiers proved to be confusing. The GIs had, of course, expected to be cheered in the countries they were liberating and to be shunned in the ones they were conquering. Instead, the enthusiasm greatly differed not only between the different Allied countries but even within them, while some of the enemy behaved as if they were the ones being liberated. Furthermore, as the GIs became better acquainted with country after country, they were aghast at the diversity, division, and discord that appeared to rule Europe.

GREAT BRITAIN

On 26 January 1942, the GIs who walked down the gangplank at Belfast were the first American troops to arrive in Great Britain officially. They were treated to a festive welcome with speeches and a band. Although the novelty of disembarking GIs would soon wear off, the British made a point of cordially receiving the desperately needed American reinforcements throughout the war. This was much appreciated by the GIs, who greeted their first sight of warring Europe with nervous apprehension. As late as August 1944, a batch of replacements that arrived at Liverpool was welcomed by the British with a band playing "The Star-Spangled Banner." "It was a touching sight to see the British there to greet us," admitted a private. "It made chills go up and down my spine."[1] As the war dragged on, the British civilians in general did not shy away from expressing gratitude to their overseas allies. All over the islands, GIs who were training enjoyed being given the V-sign or "thumbs up" by grinning Brits. "Hospitality engulfed us on all sides," observed a chaplain of the 1st Infantry Division.[2]

Many of the British communities whose lives had been intertwined with those of particular American units for extended periods found it hard to part when the time had come. When the Rangers left Dundee for Glasgow by train after three weeks of practicing attacks on coastal defenses in 1942, so many of the city's inhabitants packed the station that the commander had to allow his men an extra 15 minutes to say good-bye.[3] American troops who pushed off for combat could face even more emotional farewells. For security reasons, men of the 101st Airborne Division pretended they were leaving Aldbourne for yet another maneuver instead of the invasion of the Continent. But the civilians could not be fooled. "Leaving Aldbourne was a tough job," said a touched paratrooper, "... it got me to see them cry and take it as they did."[4] GIs on their way to Holland for Operation Market-Garden could see from their low-flying planes that the English were waving at them from fields, streets, and roofs. During the war on the Continent, many American soldiers further strengthened the ties with civilians they had befriended in Britain by keeping up a steady correspondence. More than a quarter of the letters the GIs sent from France during the first four weeks of the invasion were addressed to places in Great Britain. British friends in turn mailed packages to the American soldiers across the Channel that contained anything from "boiled sweets" to more personal gifts.[5] While in France in August 1944, the chaplain of the 1128th Engineer Combat Group mentioned in his diary that he had received "a small but fine book on English architecture" from an old judge he had acquainted in the little English town where his unit had been stationed.[6]

Those GIs who were fortunate enough to return to England from the battlefields received even more heartfelt receptions. A wounded paratrooper who arrived in England by LST from Utah beach late in June 1944 was overwhelmed:

> English people, military and civilian alike, lined the water's edge. They waved to us, said encouraging things and some had tears streaming down their cheeks.[7]

Returning Americans who had escaped combat unharmed were welcomed less solemnly. At Newbury, for instance, the civilians were out in full force with a band and they gave the men of the 501st Parachute Regiment a rousing welcome on arrival at their old camp from the battle of Normandy. The feelings were mutual. When the 1st Infantry Division returned from Sicily in the fall of 1943, one of its chaplains noticed that the soldiers were most impatient to use their furlough time to visit the families they had befriended in Britain prior to Operation Torch in November 1942.[8]

The American combat soldiers were able, of course, to get to know the British under conditions that would not be found elsewhere in Europe. Although the GIs in Britain were stationed in a war theater and lived in anticipation of combat, the country had not turned into a battlefield as scarred as the rest of Europe. Since the purpose of the Americans' presence in Britain was the build-up and training for the invasions of Europe, it was also the only country where time was on their side to form actual friendships. The parting of the paratroopers at Aldbourne, for instance, was emotional because they had been living side by side with the people of that small Wiltshire village for about nine months when they finally took off for Normandy. Time allowed the GIs to get to know the British civilians more intimately than any other Europeans. Most of the people who were present at Dundee station when the Rangers pulled out, for example, were volunteers who had housed the Americans in their own homes for weeks. Moreover, in spite of their busy training schedules, the GIs in Britain got time off now and then, which enabled them to venture out into the country from their camps. The 90th Infantry Division, for instance, was stationed at a camp near Birmingham from the beginning of April 1944 to D-Day. For two months, trucks drove soldiers to the nearest town of Kidderminster (some 14 miles away) and to the city of Birmingham (about 25 miles away) every evening and on Sundays. The others could always visit Bewdley, the nearby village.[9] Most places like Bewdley had not much entertainment to offer beyond the pubs, but it did not take long for the GIs to discover that the pubs were the "hearts of each British hamlet." This surprised many Americans who had imagined them as bars for lonely drinkers, tended by shady figures. Instead, they found that running a pub was "a very respectable profession" in Britain and that such an establishment resembled a neighborhood meeting place or social club more than a bar. The pub thus proved to be an excellent place for making friends among the civilians.[10] All in all, US Army surveys confirmed that the longer a GI stayed in Britain, the more likely he was to appreciate the people. In November 1943, for instance, 63 per cent of the enlisted men who had been in Britain less than three months said they liked the British, 22 per cent felt somewhat irritated by them, and 15 per cent disliked them. For those, however, who at that time had already lived in the country for a year or more, the numbers respectively were 78 per cent, 15 per cent, and 7 per cent.[11]

The GIs liked the country as much as the people. The British landscape enchanted the Americans. "The architecture and formal landscaping," an enthralled corporal wrote to his family in Seattle, "are unmatched by anything I've ever seen."[12] The cozy little villages appeared quaint yet at the same time familiar as the Americans knew them from Christmas cards and the nursery rhymes of Mother Goose.[13] Spring and summer were fragile but elegant seasons in Britain. "Some day," a chaplain promised in a letter written from Cornwall in July 1943, "I shall write an essay on the fragrance of summertime in England: hay, lilac, rose, box; damp air, dry air, sea air, mountain air. All mixtures and blends." The Americans who left England early in June 1944 never forgot the charms of its spring which, observed a lieutenant, "were even more appealing for battle-bound soldiers who knew not what their fate would be."[14]

Although the British people struck the GIs as very different, they never seemed entirely foreign. No matter how far the British and American branches of the Anglo-Saxon tree had grown apart, they still sprang from the same roots. "The most evident truth of all," taught the Army guide to Britain, "is that in their major ways of life the British and American people are much alike." Common law, the lecture continued, as well as representative government, political liberties, and religious freedom had all been imported from Britain.[15] All this probably helps to explain why American soldiers could suffer the shock of déjà vu when exploring the country. A GI who visited the British capital for the first time in his life in October 1944 was overcome by the weirdest sensation:

In London I walked in a glorious trance. Every signpost and street marking seemed to designate an old, familiar place ... The whole experience gave me the ridiculous feeling that I was visiting a place that I'd been a thousand times before for the first time.[16]

What facilitated the understanding between both peoples even more, of course, was that they shared not only historical roots but also a common language. "More than once," claimed a chaplain of the 1st Infantry Division in England in 1944, "I have heard a soldier say that he could live there the remainder of his life and be happy."[17]

Even some of what the Americans had imagined to be British vices pleasantly surprised them by turning out to be virtues. This was particularly true of the proverbial British reservedness, which contained many seeds of potential friction with the GIs. Americans tended to be much less restrained in words and deeds. "It seems," noticed one GI in England, "that as a people we have a nervous reputation."[18] The Americans, on the other hand, were liable to interpret their hosts' restraint as haughtiness. That is probably why their Army guidebook was quick to warn that although the British were "shy about showing their affections" and were "not given to back-slapping," this did not mean that they were unfriendly.[19] The GIs eventually agreed. They learned to value the sincerity of the friendship the British meted out so sparingly. Shaking hands, wishing luck, saying good-bye, explained a sergeant in a letter to his family in Delaware, was not "just the custom." The British, the pleased NCO ascertained, "honestly mean it."[20] The rumor that the stiff Brits had no sense of humor was also proven false to those Americans who got to know them better. "[W]e found they had a reserved but acute sense of humor," noted a GI who had been stationed in England for nearly half a year. "We were brash with our kidding, but they very subtle and thorough."[21] What the Americans came to admire most in the British, however, was that the restraint which seemed to pervade their whole being made them carry the many burdens of war with an unbending will and perfect dignity. Over and over again, GIs described the British civilians as uncomplaining, patient, disciplined, persevering, stouthearted, and brave. They thought British imperturbability beyond description and agreed it was their gift for understatement, more than anything else, that made them both an amazing breed and a great people.[22] "I am glad that I have a little bit of English blood in me," an American platoon leader wrote to his family in July 1942. "And after seeing and hearing these English people, knowing what they have gone through, I am sure you would feel the same."[23]

The era of good feelings became somewhat threatened, however, when the stream of GIs swelled into a tidal wave. At the beginning of the American influx, the exotic allies aroused the interest of British civilians everywhere. In Northern Ireland, for instance, the Americans drew a great deal of curiosity and country folk in particular gazed at them with undying fascination.[24] In 1942, many English people had never before met Americans either. "Indeed, we were a bit of a curiosity when we went to the towns," observed a chaplain of the 1st Infantry Division when his unit arrived in England early in August 1942. A sergeant who visited Bournemouth that same month wrote to his family: "I had a dozen people stop me on the street and ask what kind of a uniform I was wearing. It was the first time they had seen an American." When hundreds of thousands of Americans kept pouring into Britain, however, "the novelty and the first fine flush of enthusiasm" gradually wore off, as one lieutenant put it.[25] On the eve of D-Day, more than a million and a half GIs were stationed in Britain, and they crowded roads, buses, trains, hotels, restaurants, theaters, and pubs. Even the American soldiers who had been in England before the deluge resented the hordes of countrymen that upset the carefully cultivated relationship with the British. Some of them could not help sympathizing with the civilians' "longing for the quiet calm of English life." Others lamented that to the British their presence was now degenerating into "a wartime necessity – like rationing."[26] As the number of GIs increased, so did the danger of friction. Moreover, hardened American veterans tended to be less considerate of the civilian population when returning from overseas campaigns. In April 1944, the 504th Parachute Regiment returned to Stoughton from Italy. During visits to nearby Leicester, the paratroopers behaved as if combat "had dissolved most of the thin veneer that civilization spreads over the instincts." They drank too much, chased women, got into fights, and generally made a lot of noise. One of them readily admitted they behaved "like uncouth barbarians."[27] The 101st Airborne Division came back from Normandy a month after the invasion. With seven-day passes in hand and all the back pay in their pockets, the veterans descended on London "to tear the city apart." One British newspaper later compared the havoc they had created to that of the Blitz.[28]

As the GIs were packed tighter and combat loomed larger, the irritations with the British were bound to multiply. The War Department had anticipated such problems from the outset and issued a stern warning in its GI guide to Great Britain:

> It is always impolite to criticize your hosts; it is militarily stupid to criticize your allies.[29]

But ill feelings could, of course, not be avoided entirely. Nothing less than history saw to that in the first place. In reference to the persecution of the Irish, the redcoats of the American Revolution, and the War of 1812, the Army guide informed the GIs: "there is no time today to fight old wars over again and bring up old grievances."[30] Yet the memory of the Americans could prove to be as tenacious as that of the Europeans. While recovering from jaundice in a hospital in Northern Ireland in June 1942, a GI was disgusted by the hostile remarks some of his comrades were hurling at friendly British soldiers passing by. "Many patients are anti-British," he wrote in his diary, "prejudiced by stories from ill-informed parents about winning England's wars."[31] It was not only the taste that World War I had left that was bitter; the memory of wars from the more distant past could cause uncomfortable sensations too. Training marches of the 29th Infantry Division in Devon, for instance, took the men more than once past the high granite walls of Dartmoor Prison. One of the unit's officers refused to forget that this was where the British ally had held thousands of American prisoners "in disease and hunger" during the War of 1812. When he crossed into Germany late in 1944, a private from Maine could not help recalling how the British had fought against his people and with the Hessians some 150 years ago.[32]

A few of the traits of the contemporary British also proved too peculiar for the Americans to get accustomed to. Above all, the GIs remained puzzled by how leisurely the British appeared to be even in a time of national emergency. They did not accuse them of being lazy, but they certainly diagnosed them with a certain dullness and slowness. The Army guide zealously summed up evidence in an attempt to convince the GIs that the British were "not really slow:"

> Their crack trains held world speed records. A British ship held the trans-Atlantic record. A British car and a British driver set world's speed records in America.[33]

The GIs, however, only had to compare cricket with baseball to undermine that evidence. They were amazed by the slowness of the game and even more so by the subdued behavior of the players. That the teams laid down their equipment for afternoon tea simply stunned the Americans. Those rituals of tea, more than anything else, strengthened the impression of British leisureliness.[34] "The subject of tea is a fascinating one here," an intrigued GI wrote to his parents. The Americans just could not get used to the fact that in Britain tea occurred at ten, noon, three, five, and at night "as inclination suggests." Especially so, a lieutenant told his mother, because "tea" each time meant "about an hour's break in the day's routine!"[35]

The GIs could not always avoid thinking that this leisureliness implied a kind of cunning; as if the British people had grown used to sitting back while letting others pull the chestnuts out of the fire for them. There was, after all, more evidence that seemed to point in this direction. The fact that Britain had accepted Lend-Lease aid, for instance, while still not having repaid the debts incurred during World War I, was one of the most important things American public opinion held against its ally. That is probably why the GIs reacted so sensitively to any suspicion of being manipulated by the British into paying the bills of their war yet again. It angered the GIs, for example, that often only the American claims officers were able to calm the tempers of civilians who suffered damage during the build-up and training which, after all, was also aimed at rescuing their own nation.[36] Disdainful of the Old World's class system, the GIs were least willing to accept this kind of attitude from the British aristocracy. When men of the 9th Infantry Division damaged a large tree on the estate in Wales where they were stationed, a young man in riding breeches was quick to pull over his car and demand compensation. "Evidently that was his job in the war effort," fumed a lieutenant, "keeping the Americans up to accounts." The lady of an estate at Newbury instantly regretted her insensitivity when she complained about the destruction new camp construction was causing. The paratroopers responsible for the damage had just returned from Normandy, their ranks decimated. A red-hot Texan officer barked at her that she should complain to "the men who died to save your damn estate."[37]

Yet, despite the unmistakable irritations, one American soldier thought it safe to conclude that, in general, the GIs and the British civilians got along "about as well as can be expected of any two peoples who are as much alike as they are unlike." Indeed, US Army surveys showed that the GIs had "a uniformly favorable attitude" toward the English people throughout the war. In November 1943, January 1944, and April 1945, for instance, respectively 73 per cent, 74 per cent, and 72 per cent of the American soldiers in the ETO held a very or fairly favorable opinion of the English people.[38] And because Britain was the safest as well as the least foreign place in the European war theater, the GIs increasingly looked at it as a home away from home. A chaplain who arrived in England late in 1943, after having lived in Iceland with a combat engineer unit for nearly a year and a half, was overcome by emotion when he noticed the similarity between his America and a Britain that looked "'civilized,' with trees and grass and English-speaking people." Those who returned to England from the campaigns in North Africa and Sicily felt no less fortunate. "I am in England and glad of it," a lieutenant of the 2nd Armored Division wrote to his mother in December 1943, "which is quite an admission from an old Anglophobe!"[39] The GIs who left England for the bitter fighting on the Continent soon longed intensely for the European island of security. When correspondent Martha Gellhorn accompanied wounded GIs aboard a hospital ship on 8 June 1944, she noticed that as the coast came into sight "the green of England looked quite different from the way it had looked only two days ago; it looked cooler and cleaner and wonderfully safe." To a GI who arrived in England after having been badly wounded near Aachen in the fall of 1944, the country looked "gray, misty, and good – next best to home." That is how many of the Americans who lived in the front lines remembered the old island. "We talk about England nowadays," a nostalgic Kentuckian wrote in his journal near Mortain in August 1944, "as if it was the States."[40]

FRENCH NORTH AFRICA

The GIs who landed on the shores of French North Africa on 8 November 1942 had been told they would be securing "the springboard to the reconquest of Europe."[41] The American soldiers, however, were more impressed by North Africa's strangeness than by its strategic importance. They had conjured up images of endless deserts and lush jungles; instead, they stumbled onto large, modern cities like Algiers and Casablanca with cafés out on the sidewalks. They had expected an African way of life and found the French colonies to be curiously oriental in atmosphere. Although the Army guides had informed them that about one-tenth of the 17 million people living in North Africa were Europeans, the large number of French people in cities like Oran still managed to take some GIs by surprise.[42]

Their first campaign in the European war theater did not make the American soldiers feel much like liberators. The signals the civilian population sent were confusing and disheartening. The first encounters with the colonies' European inhabitants were not of the kind to boost the GIs' confidence. The French populace seemed paralyzed by the military and political shock wave the Anglo-American invasion had brought about. As the 1st Infantry Division moved through Arzew and Oran during the first days of the campaign, French civilians just stared at them "stoically," betraying "neither happiness nor hatred, just a mild interest."[43] Moreover, the GIs had been warned that the Moslems' experience with European colonists had given them a "natural inclination ... to regard any invading force with suspicion."[44] And indeed, when the campaign carried the GIs further inland, the only thing that seemed to matter to the predominantly Arab population in the desolate countryside was that the soldiers were white, not what uniform they were wearing, and so they largely kept to themselves. Only when they reached the coast of Tunisia in the spring of 1943 were the American soldiers able to breathe a sigh of relief: not only were the Axis forces in North Africa close to defeat by this time, but the French populace had now also clearly joined the camp of the Allies and was cheering them on without restraint. A surprised tank operator who took part in mopping up pockets of resistance in Bizerte noticed that the French civilians suddenly proved so happy that they refused to leave the sidewalks even when artillery shook the plaster from the buildings around them.[45] That kind of reception brought the encouragement the GIs desperately needed after a winter in which morale had sagged more than once. When the 1st Armored Division liberated Ferryville on 7 May 1943, French inhabitants lined the streets cheering, waving, and kissing. A soldier who had been among the first of his division to enter the town admitted the reception had given him and his comrades a "tremendous lift." "I dare say there were very few G.I.s that day who didn't have a lump in their throats," the American scribbled in his diary. "[I]t's rather nice," he continued in a letter to his family, "to feel that they appreciate your being there."[46]

Some of America's combat troops spent more than half a year in French North Africa. It gave them ample time and opportunity to form a picture of the region's various population groups. "Ay-rabs" is what the GIs called the Arabic-speaking people of North Africa.[47] And it appeared as if the forceful emphasis on the first syllable served to vent the loathing with which they filled most Americans. The Arabs' wretchedness was a prime cause of revulsion in the GIs. "Such poverty most of us had never seen before," remarked a combat engineer who waded ashore in French Morocco. The GIs thought the huts of the natives looked "[n]ot even as good as Indian tepees." Although an Army pamphlet had assured the American soldiers on the eve of the landings that the natives were "fully clothed," it had not prepared them for the oddness of that clothing. One GI's disrespectful summary of the native dress as "mostly white sheet affairs" was typical. The Arabs' fascination with American textiles was cause for much hilarity among the soldiers. It was not long before natives could be seen wearing parts of uniforms as well as garments made from army mattress covers and canvas jeep tops.[48] But the Arabs not only looked ragged, they also appeared to be disgustingly dirty. "You haven't smelled anything," a medic from Iowa claimed, "until you've gone through an Arab village in the summer time." The inhabitants, a paratrooper elaborated, "look as if they had shied from baths all their lives."[49]

Moral standards too seemed to be totally lacking. The GIs were appalled, for instance, by the Arabs' habit of overloading their pack animals and whipping them without mercy. According to war correspondent Helen Kirkpatrick, the brutal treatment of horses in particular was "a subject of extreme criticism" among the Americans.[50] The GIs were quick to ascribe such behavior to the innate cruelty of the natives. "They treat their burros and camels kind of awful," one private concluded, "and probably their families the same." Scenes of Arab women performing hard labor while their husbands looked on did much to strengthen that opinion. "The Arabs pray," a lieutenant sneered, "and the women do all the work."[51] Moreover, the stubborn Arab pleas for cigarettes and chocolate – or any other GI item – gave the people the reputation of beggars, whereas their knack for bargaining at the same time made them look cunning. In addition, the GIs considered most Arabs to be thieves. Pilferage did pose a serious problem from the moment Allied landing craft were being unloaded on the beaches. A surgeon at a bivouac near Oran claimed that the area had to be "guarded like the devil" against natives who had been "trained for generations in thieving."[52] Worse, however, was that the Arabs did not seem to place much value on human life either. Rumors soon circulated about GIs who had been murdered for their shoes; some were said to have been found with their testicles stuffed in their mouths.[53] Alarmed GIs took increasing care to avoid the native sections of towns and cities. "People have literally disappeared in the Casbah," a fidgety sergeant reported from Algiers to his family in Ohio, "never to be seen again, dead or alive."[54] The Americans did not think that people who resigned themselves to such wretchedness had the right to show much self-esteem. Mauldin, for instance, noticed that

> there was often a powerful streak of pride, too, which our people chose to interpret as sly malice, because an American finds it hard to imagine a proud man who doesn't even have a decent pair of shoes to his name.[55]

Neither did white Americans find it easy to accept pride from a people that was dark-skinned. The Army guide to North Africa warned the GIs to avoid any expression of racial prejudice regarding the Moslems. It explained that they were "a fair-skinned people" and that only a few had "the swarthiness which is commonly associated with a near-tropical climate."[56] Nevertheless, to the GIs most North Africans looked suspiciously dark. A private asked his family in Arizona:

> Did you ever see an Arab? You haven't missed anything. You don't believe it? Let's prove it: Take a cork and black your face, hands, and feet very, very black.

"The natives," a surgeon in a bivouac area near Oran confessed to his diary, were "a dirty race; dark, something like Mexicans."[57] The inferiority the Americans assigned to this colored race led to abuses and even to a disregard for lives. GIs charged with guarding a training camp at Magenta, Algeria, for instance, were told that no Arab should be trusted and that they could fire on "[a]nything dressed in white and not promptly responding to the password;" the order soon caused some of the guards to become trigger-happy. As time went by, the natives stopped looking like human beings to some GIs. "Here Arabs live all over," a soldier wrote home matter-of-factly in 1943, "some we shoot on sight, some we search and some we make a deal with to buy eggs and chickens."[58] By the time the American soldiers reached the coastal region of Tunisia, they were "thrilled to see white people again." The Army guide to Africa had advised the GIs to "[a]ccept with reserve what local Europeans tell you about North Africans." As it turned out, the opinion the Americans formed of the natives by themselves was hardly more flattering than the one the Europeans held.[59]

That probably helps to explain why the American soldiers were not particularly critical of the fact that the natives were forced to live under French colonial rule. Their lack of criticism is surprising because America had traditionally been most disdainful of Europe's imperialism. Even the US Army guide to North Africa, for instance, made a point of telling the GIs that the native population had never accepted French rule and continued to resist and fight it throughout the entire region.[60] Moreover, the GIs could see for themselves the glaring inequalities between the French colonists and the natives. The vast grainfields and rich vineyards of the French in northern Morocco and Algeria contrasted sharply with the small Moslem farms farther south. In most towns, "pinkish colonial buildings" overshadowed "poor white plaster Arab houses." In larger cities, Moslem slums had literally been separated from modern French downtowns by imposing walls.[61] Whereas Arab children were "ragged and naked," a chaplain noticed, French children were "usually clean and dressed neatly."[62] The American soldiers were dismayed by the number of natives who suffered from running sores. During the winter of 1942–43, GIs in Oran witnessed how Moslems who had died in the cold streets at night were hurriedly thrown onto carts early in the morning. In the spring of 1943, the Arab section of Meknès had to be put off-limits because of the high incidence of leprosy.[63] "At first this thieving was perplexing to us Americans," admitted a paratrooper,

> but less and less difficult to understand when we appreciated the poverty of most Arabs. The poorest Negro in our Southern states is wealthy compared with them.[64]

There were plenty of indications that pointed to French oppression and exploitation as causes of the dispirited attitude of the Moslems and their poor living conditions. GIs witnessed how French authorities responded to the Arab looting of Gafsa by executing natives without a trial and on the basis of the flimsiest evidence. When the 760th Tank Battalion commenced training French troops at Magenta near the Sahara desert in the summer of 1943, an inexplicable number of Arab casualties poured into the aid posts. A hurried American investigation revealed that the French "seemed to delight in shooting up the Arabs' huts and running over them with the tanks." A chaplain who visited a French-run factory at Cherchell, Algeria, encountered only Arab girls of between six and twelve years old who, for ten cents a day, were feverishly tying the knots of rugs sold at $15 a square yard.[65] Yet, all the evidence to the contrary notwithstanding, the GIs preferred to blame the "lazy, indolent customs" of the Arabs for their predicament.[66] Despite the glaring French oppression, the autochthons' lethargy remained so incomprehensible to the Americans that they were willing to believe even the most outlandish explanations for it. Since the GIs had been warned not to buy native cigarettes because they might contain a substance called keef or marihuana – which was said to make the smoker "careless" and to cause "rapid moral deterioration" – some soldiers concluded that "the entire nation was hooked on marihuana." Still others believed that the people's languor was a result of "damaged and enlarged spleens from chronic malaria."[67] By the time he left North Africa for Sicily, a sergeant of the 45th Infantry Division had become convinced that it was the natives' indolence that made continued foreign occupation of their land possible:

> The donkeys had more personality than the Arabs. From the look in their lucid brown eyes, one would guess that these, and not the people, would some day revolt against oppression.

As long as the Arabs did not have the will to throw off the French yoke, another GI asserted, they deserved to be "peons to conquerors."[68]

In fact, the Americans came to appreciate the need for a white presence in North Africa. "You should see this country," an indignant soldier wrote to his girlfriend. "The guy who named it 'The Dark Continent' wasn't mistaken."[69] The GIs were pleasantly surprised to find that there were some Americans among the white missionaries they liberated. They deemed the work of these people much called for, so much so that they could not refrain from displaying a missionary zeal themselves. It was obvious to the GIs that the natives had failed to bring out the full potential of North Africa. The region begged to be further cultivated, developed, and civilized, and only whites seemed able to shoulder that burden. With the Germans and Italians on their way out and the French not yet fully back in control, American soldiers for the time being undertook the job with enthusiasm. They felt the dark continent first of all needed a thorough cleaning. The US Quartermaster Corps soon could not keep up with the demand for mops, brooms, brushes, and soap in North Africa. And in more than one village, GIs could be seen scrubbing reluctant Arab children in improvised baths.[70] Despite the war, American soldiers did not lose sight of the business opportunities that beckoned in the region either. A paratrooper, for instance, viewed the rapid growth of the airfield at Youks-les-Bains, Tunisia, with contentment. Allied activity had turned the nearby village into a boomtown and the American could not help feeling "like a real estate agent who is developing a fast-selling piece of property." Even during the hectic first week of the invasion, a tank operator managed to inform his parents in Philadelphia that North Africa was a perfect market for five-and-dime stores because the Arabs stampeded for trinkets.[71] All in all, the GIs considered it a blessing for the natives to have the opportunity to be recreated in the image of the white benefactors. "Give the women fine clothes and they will cast away veils and robes," a self-assured GI wrote. "And give an Arab a truck and you'll think he never had seen a camel."[72]

In the meantime, the GIs would not allow themselves to be run over by native hordes who did not know any better. At Les Trembles, an outpost of the 1st Infantry Division in southern Algeria, a lieutenant solved the problem of chronic theft by hiring a few Arab boys whom he fed well in return for chasing away the others with entrenching shovels. "The system worked perfectly," the American officer concluded self-congratulatory. "An example of the old principle of 'divide and rule.'"[73] The imperialist urge proved to be dangerously contagious among white peoples in dark continents.

SICILY AND ITALY

In the spring of 1943, even before the campaign in North Africa had ended, American soldiers could be seen raising one finger instead of the two symbolizing V for Victory. It signified I for Invasion. The GIs believed that the indirect approach of North Africa was merely prolonging the war and they were impatiently awaiting the direct assault on the European continent. None of them looked forward to the dangers of that campaign, but all knew it was the only one that could win the war and take them home again.[74]

When in the early morning of 10 July 1943 the first American soldiers set foot in Sicily, the sensation was a chilling one. The GIs realized that this time they would not only be facing enemy armies, but would also be surrounded by a hostile population. A sergeant of the 45th Infantry Division never forgot the first moments after the landing: "Gradually the thought struck each of us ... 'Now I'm on Axis territory – Axis home territory!' We wondered what came next."[75] The Army guide to Italy warned the GIs that operations in enemy territory demanded "special precautions."[76] Nevertheless, the American soldiers were hardly prepared for the reception they received from the enemy populace in Sicily and Italy during the next 22 months. In most Sicilian communities, white flags were hanging from the windows and civilians were clapping and cheering in the streets only minutes after the Italian and German troops had disappeared from sight. "A queer race these Italians," an amazed lieutenant wrote to his mother. "You'd think we were their deliverers instead of their captors." Two months later, when Italy surrendered, the officer was even more baffled when the Sicilians rushed into the streets crying "Finito!," rang the church bells, and started candle-light processions.[77] The celebrations only grew in excitement on the peninsula. "Their exuberant welcome appears very sincere," a combat doctor admitted incredulously during the riotous reception in Rome. That air of caution and disbelief stayed with the GIs all the way to the Po Valley, but it could not dampen the Italians' fervor. "Contrary to our anticipated conception," noted a weary officer of the 88th Infantry Division on 3 May 1945, "the natives in the valley received us in a relieved spirit of reverent happiness and glory."[78]

Even before the invasion and the enthusiastic reception, the US Army had anticipated that it would be impossible for its men – who, after all, had found it hard to fear and hate even the soldiers of Italy – to dread and detest the civilians of that enemy country. It had worried that this would compromise the security of soldiers who were expected to play the role of occupiers in a conquered land. That helps to explain why it exerted itself in warning the GIs – in a guide prepared before Italy's surrender – not to fraternize with the civilians. The Army booklet acknowledged that "citizens of Italian blood compose a large and patriotic portion of our American population," that Italians were "a naturally hospitable people," and that not all of them were pro-Axis or pro-fascist. Nevertheless, it also urged the GIs to bear in mind that Italy was "the cradle of the Fascist idea," that the Italian army had "spray[ed] mustard gas on the naked warriors of Ethiopia," and that Mussolini would not have accomplished much without help from the people. Therefore, the guide insisted, it would be "mistaken kindness to wipe the slate clean of their outrageous acts" and to "treat them at once as honest members of the human race."[79]

When in September 1943 Italy transformed overnight from an enemy country into an associated power, the relationship between what had at first been conquerors and conquered became even more complex. With the earlier misgivings and warnings in mind, the GIs never managed to shake off their distrust of the Italians entirely, despite the fact that they had now technically become allies and seemed most likeable. It bothered the GIs to see that American flags were covering walls that had once yelled "DUCE!" "Also," noticed Mauldin, "they get awfully tired of hearing everybody – Fascists, ex-Fascists or non-Fascists – wail about how Mussolini made them do it."[80] How sincere could the sympathies and feelings of such a people ever be? Somewhere north of Rome a lieutenant cynically asked himself: "The hysterically happy Italians place everything at our service – what else could they do?" The suspicion that the Italian civilians were opportunistic turncoats rather than sincere well-wishers thus remained throughout the campaign.[81]

If the reception itself was confusing, so were the impressions of Italy's different regions. Those GIs who had been glad to leave behind the strangeness of Africa experienced a tremendous shock upon arrival in Sicily. The European island failed to offer the more familiar surroundings they had hoped for. The Army guide had made sure to warn the GIs that on Sicily they would meet "the poorest, most neglected, and most miserable of Italian citizens."[82] Still, the pitiable living conditions in the Old World's insular outpost horrified the Americans. It seemed to be North Africa all over again. A Jewish paratrooper wrote to his family: "they're as poor and dirty as anything I ever hope to see in my life." Soldiers gazed in disbelief at mud-and-straw farms and at dwellings "no bigger than woodsheds back home." The people themselves were "ragged" and "tubercular-looking." At Caltanissetta, a surgeon noticed that the bystanders were "combing lice out of one another's hair on the sidewalks." All over the island hung "a smell like Africa."[83] The invasion of the Italian mainland did not seem to lead to more civilized surroundings either. In the scorched and impoverished south the people were "just like the Sicilians." One GI thought southern Italy not worth "one turnip patch in Tennessee."[84] Northern Italians condescendingly labeled their fellow citizens south of Rome "Africans," and the Americans soon understood why. Nearing Rome was like crossing into a new country with different people. A combat engineer described the Eternal City to his parents in Pennsylvania as up-to-date enough to offer "a few of the comforts of civilians such as electric lights, buildings, wash bowls & latrines." "Rome," he concluded, "is just like another part of the world compared with the rest of Italy." This was true of the entire northern region, which, according to a corporal in the Po Valley, was "the best part of Italy by a long ways."[85] The GIs found it to be much more urbanized and industrialized than the rural south. The people seemed cleaner, better educated, and more civilized. They looked refined and dressed well; in stores in larger cities many even spoke some English. The countryside too was more appealing: the people were industrious, the farms substantial and well organized, the fields rich with wheat, tomatoes, and grapes.[86]

Still, the favorable impression of northern Italy failed to dissipate entirely the negative connotations the south had given rise to. Neither could it erase the prejudices that had tenaciously stuck in the American mind since the days when masses of poor, illiterate peasants from Sicily and southern Italy had arrived in the New World. Although the Army guide claimed that "Americans and Italians have always gotten along very well," it nevertheless felt the need to remind the GIs not to use "any of the offensive terms which some ill-bred Americans occasionally apply to natives of that country." It also told them to be aware of the fact that fascist propaganda had tried to convince the Italians that Americans viewed them "as a race of hand-organ men and banana peddlers."[87] But the offensive terms were as hard to dispel as the negative stereotypes, some of which found a new breeding ground in the war-torn country. Italian thievery, for instance, acquired notoriety among the GIs, especially in the south. Tregaskis reported from Sicily that looting was the inhabitants' favorite pastime. Of the Neapolitans the GIs said they could "whip the gold out of your eyeteeth while you're yawning." Rumors soon claimed that it was not safe to go to Naples on a pass without a gun because bars, brothels, and the black market were run by Italian gangsters who did not shrink from murder. The American soldiers did not find this banditry entirely surprising. After all, they knew the Italians in America had already proved – never more so than during the Prohibition – to possess a remarkable gift for molding illegal activities into thriving businesses. Across Italy, GIs ran into civilians who had lived and worked in the US, and not a few insisted on entertaining the Americans with proud, nostalgic stories of their careers as gambling-joint operators in New Jersey or bootleggers in New York.[88]

"It seemed that all these Dagos had been deported from Chicago and were Al Capone's crooks," a lieutenant from Indiana observed wryly.[89]

No matter what ingenuity the Italian people displayed in illegality, Italy's war record made clear to the GIs that as a nation they lacked the strength and efficiency to be taken seriously as a first-rate power in international affairs. Mauldin's belittling analogy said it all:

> Italy reminds a guy of a dog hit by an automobile because it ran out and tried to bite the tires. You can't just leave the critter there to die, but you remember that you wouldn't have run over it if it had stayed on the sidewalk.[90]

Italy would have done itself a favor by having remained a spectator in international affairs. Not because its size or location necessarily precluded it from being a world power, but because its people did not possess the kind of character capable of sustaining global commitments and long-term responsibilities. In the eyes of the American soldiers, Italy was the "land of Romeo and Juliet."[91] It was a mecca for artists. It was the home of fashion designers. Paratroopers noticed that even coarse peasants took their time to admire the quality of their silk invasion maps before giving the urgently needed directions.[92] Italy was also the country where men had "the mincing movement of a girl" and seemed irresistibly drawn to the occupation of hairdresser. Italian barbers invariably looked "sleek and polished" and would "powder and fluff until you look like a Don Juan." They appeared to multiply whenever GIs liberated a town. "Roving barbers" even gave haircuts and shaves to men of the 760th Tank Battalion while they were waiting for the order to enter Rome on 4 June 1944.[93] More than anything else, however, the Italians were born singers. In the spring of 1944, an enraptured lieutenant of the 36th Infantry Division listened to the song of an Italian peasant who returned from his work in the valley of Avellino. Although his voice had never been trained, the officer thought it "more moving than any of Verdi's great arias."[94] Despite the war, the Americans had plenty of opportunities to attend operas in Italy. Naples had performances every day; Rome even opened its *Teatro reale dell'Opera* to the soldiers; GIs who rested at Caserta during the battle of Cassino in the spring of 1944 listened to Mascagni's *Cavalleria Rusticana* while guns boomed in the distance.[95] Italy exuded sensitivity and spontaneity, it breathed passion and emotion. But the Americans were convinced that the Latin temperament lacked the matter-of-factness and steadfastness required for any enterprise of vast size and long duration.

Such a people could not but trigger a patronizing reflex in the Americans. When Tregaskis arrived at the harbor of Licata in July 1943, he noticed that the GIs had lost no time putting Sicilian civilians to work at the docks unloading ammunition. While the Sicilians "chattered genially, regarding their plight as a huge joke," a big American sergeant took shepherding them quite seriously and had "already assumed the proper imperial attitude."[96] Of course, not even the Sicilians and southern Italians had sunk to such a state that the GIs thought them in need of direct colonial control like the North Africans. After all, they were weather-beaten but not swarthy,

Latin but not Arab, Catholic but not Moslem.[97] What would suffice in their case was some kind of tutelage, not unlike that given to children deprived of their parents. A sergeant of the 45th Infantry Division trusted that with that kind of guidance there was still hope even for the southernmost Italians:

> The Sicilians, by the world's standards, are a simple people. They are a peasant people generally, living close to the earth and finding pleasure in simple things. But they are educated quickly.[98]

FRANCE

Two days after the liberation of Rome, American soldiers left England to storm the beaches of Normandy. Some two months later, GIs from the Mediterranean theater arrived at the Riviera and joined the campaign in France. Weary veterans and scared newcomers alike realized that the fighting ahead would be ferocious, but all of them understood that only the second front in Western Europe would help seal Germany's fate. After months of arduous training and rigorous preparation, the Americans set foot on French soil with grim relief: they were at last on their way to do what had to be done before they could go home.

If the GIs had a general idea of what the war held in store for them in France, they were less certain about what to expect from the country's inhabitants. Throughout history, the Americans had regarded the French with a "combination of skepticism and sentimentality." The stunning collapse of France in 1940 and the subsequent collaboration of the Vichy government with the Nazis had clearly tipped the balance in favor of skepticism.[99] The ambiguous attitude of the French during the North African campaign had done nothing to change this and was still fresh in the memory of many American soldiers. The US Army guide to France did its best to reassure the GIs:

> You will probably get a big welcome from the French. Americans are popular in France. Your father or uncles who were in the A.E.F. may have told you about that.[100]

But to learn that they would "probably" be welcome in a country where they were about to risk their lives to liberate a people from years of oppression must have raised not a few eyebrows among the GIs.

The reception by the Normans raised even more eyebrows. In the early hours of 6 June 1944, paratroopers – surrounded by the enemy and disoriented by the dark – turned to the civilians for help. To their dismay, however, they often found the French in the coastal area "too frightened and excited to be of any assistance." At more than one village, airborne troops had to retreat into the dark without directions because farmers refused to open their doors or slammed them shut upon seeing who the visitors were. The civilians, of course, had plenty of reasons to be scared. The arrival of the paratroopers was a total surprise that rudely aroused them from a deep sleep. The foreign-tongued soldiers looked demonic: uniforms stained with mud, faces black with charcoal, noses and foreheads streaked with green paint, heads shaved or sporting Mohawk cuts. Moreover, the French had been conditioned by years of living in a police state; they knew how the Germans punished individuals and communities that aided the enemy. On top of that, the French had no certainty about the nature and size of the operation that was unfolding, and the failure of a raid like the one at Dieppe had not yet been forgotten. Nevertheless, the faltering response of the French did not sit well with American paratroopers to whom the war was not exactly without risks either.[101]

The American troops who moved inland from the beaches later that day also ran into apathy and antipathy from French civilians. A captain of the 29th Infantry Division encountered his first liberated Norman on the road inland from Omaha beach near Saint-Laurent. The elderly farmer was pacing up and down so agitatedly in front of his cottage that the officer decided to offer the man some of his soggy invasion money to patch things up. To the irritation of the American, however, this gesture did not seem to make the Frenchman any happier than the liberation. A chaplain of the 1st Infantry Division noticed that the French started to warm to the advancing Americans only when the beachhead seemed secure and they believed that the Allies were in France to stay.[102] When on 11 June troops of the 18th Infantry Regiment entered Balleroy, a relieved sergeant scribbled in his diary: "The people are friendly & called us Libirators. They are the first people that are not pro Nazie."[103]

Still, even after the Allies had established a large foothold, the GIs did not feel that they were being hailed everywhere they went in Normandy. Many Normans, of course, had little reason to cheer. They paid a high price for their freedom. Endless bombing and shelling as well as furious ground battles wreaked terrible havoc in the region, and civilians who mourned the death of relatives and neighbors and worried over the destruction of farms and orchards did not experience the Allied invasion as much of a liberation. But the American combat soldiers did not always take that into full consideration; instead, they were often discouraged to find the people "unemotional" in the many ravaged parts of Normandy. Carentan had been battered during the first week of the invasion, but as late as July a combat engineer lamented that its inhabitants refused to pay any attention to the GIs:

> S & S has had a lot of stories about how delighted the French people have been to be liberated and what a great welcome they have given us. Personally, I haven't seen it.

Months after Saint-Lô had been devastated, the Americans still sensed that the civilians were giving them the cold shoulder. A private of the 84th Infantry Division passed the town on his way to the front in November 1944:

> In St. Lô most of the people trudged along with their heads down or glared sourly if they looked at all. Their attitude was understandable but it gave us an

uncomfortable feeling and we wanted to tell them that we had no desire to be there either.[104]

The relationship with the Norman people was further spoiled by the phenomenon of civilian sniping. The countryside had been infested with German marksmen from the beginning of the campaign. Within weeks, however, rumors circulated that French civilians too were taking potshots at the Americans. Although some GIs claimed that these people were German soldiers in civilian disguise, others maintained that they had seen with their own eyes how French female snipers had been taken to the rear as POWs. The most stubborn rumors focused on the women, some of whom were also said to have directed German artillery fire on American lines with the help of walkie-talkies. The GIs believed that these women were driven to such acts because they had consorted with German soldiers. Whether there was substance to these stories or not, the ease with which they made the round among the American soldiers proved that the Norman populace had not gained much of their trust.[105]

The GIs were convinced that there was more to the lack of enthusiasm among the Normans than the invasion's havoc. After all, how could a people reject suffering as the price for freedom? The Americans groped for other explanations. It was rumored that the Normans had gotten along very well with the enemy and that many local girls had married German soldiers. Some GIs surmised that the Germans had favored the region in order to ensure supplies from the rich dairy country and to win the people's support in case of an invasion.[106] But still other Americans interpreted Norman apathy as just another manifestation of French defeatism. After having stared into the blank faces of French civilians at Lessay, a lieutenant wrote to his wife in August 1944: "I suppose if President Roosevelt had sold out to Hitler and Generals Marshall and MacArthur and Eisenhower proved incompetent, we might look the same."[107]

Yet American suspicions concerning the French reception dwindled as fast as they had sprung to life when the Allies finally broke out of Normandy's hedgerow shackles and rushed inland. Only with this breakout and pursuit came the commencement of what would become known among the GIs as "the liberation campaign" or "the good campaign."[108] When he arrived in the relative peace south of Le Mans on 15 August, after the inferno of Mortain, a lieutenant of the 35th Infantry Division recorded in his journal:

> from the stench of the battlefield to the fragrance of flower gardens along the roads; from the feelings of fear and hate, grief and despair, to that of victory, cheer and triumph, was, and is yet, almost more than I can realize.[109]

In those parts of France that had escaped the full fury of battle, the French spirit proved not to be broken. There the people unleashed without restraint their feelings of relief and joy upon seeing the liberators. The Americans who raced into a much less scarred Brittany, for example, saw the civilians transfigure from indifferent to so enthusiastic that they became "almost a nuisance." Those who rushed to the north and east of France had similar experiences. A private of the 30th Infantry Division, on his way to Condé-sur-Vire at the start of the breakthrough that followed the Saint-Lô bombardment, was so touched by the first sight of civilians next to the road offering water and flowers that he had "difficulty in holding back the tears of welling emotion."[110] What followed was a "triumphal procession" across France that made the American soldiers feel "like royalty." Even after having seen countless US troops pass, the Bretons continued to cheer on the GIs in droves. The Americans who hastened to the north and east encountered civilians who were "delirious" and "going mad with joy." Mauldin, who landed with the 45th Infantry Division in southern France in August 1944, also found the people "honestly and sincerely glad to see the Americans."[111] All over the country, the French were now throwing apples, roses, and crocheted tricolors at the GIs. They thronged the squares, listened to fiery speeches, and chanted the national anthem. The Americans had to shake so many hands that their fingers turned numb, and it was hard for the soldiers to hide their embarrassment when people fell to their knees to kiss the liberators' shoes. By April 1945, 74 per cent of the GIs in Europe believed that most French people sincerely liked the Americans.[112]

The French celebration ended abruptly, however, for those American troops who bogged down in Alsace-Lorraine in the autumn of 1944. In this region, the proximity of Germany cast shadows over the liberators darker than those of the gloomy season. French civilians no longer lined the roads but watched the American columns from their doorways. There was little joy and the people seemed less friendly. The GIs were warned to watch out for German sympathizers when dealing with the Alsatians. They found it increasingly hard to tell whether they were still in France or already in Germany. Even when maps confirmed that they were in friendly territory it remained hard to believe. To the Americans, the northeastern part of France for all practical purposes looked like "Swastika Land." Place names sounded German. Shopkeepers accepted marks. GIs were baffled to hear the "so-called French" converse in a guttural rather than melodic language. Most children listened to German names and appeared to have a much harder time understanding French than their parents.[113] Americans who listened to French hymns during church services were taken by surprise by sermons delivered in German. "It sounded like a political pep talk," an upset soldier wrote to his parents.[114] The divided sympathies of a region that had been torn between two different countries and cultures for centuries confused the Americans. They talked with parents who had sons in German uniforms and daughters in the French resistance. They met families who had children in the German army but spoke in disgust about neighbors who sympathized with the Nazis. "They seem to be indifferent to principles," a bewildered medic concluded in a letter to his wife. And so American doubts about the sympathies of the French, which had been smoldering since North Africa and Normandy, flared up again. A discouraged Japanese-American soldier in the Vosges asked his parents:

Do you suppose it makes much difference to them which side of the line they are on? Anyway, to the average American foot soldier who watches his buddies die and dig for his life on this lousy French soil these little things make him ask "Why the hell don't the French fight their own wars?" It's a small viewpoint but you get that way when you run out of strength and expect principles to take you over these hills.[115]

In addition to the conflicting images of the reception, there appeared through the fog of war a picture of French life that was not the most flattering either. If the political intricacies of France had baffled the American people ever since the Declaration of Independence, the internal wrangles of the war years had created an even stronger impression in the US of "a virtuoso French talent for intrigue and vendetta".[116] The American soldiers who encountered the French in North Africa certainly did not find the puzzling military and political climate of the Mediterranean colonies conducive to a better understanding of the Gallic people. Neither did the society and culture of continental France hold the kind of familiarity that so struck the GIs in Britain. The US Army did what it could to help unravel the mysteries of the French people in order to avoid them giving rise to misunderstandings and frictions. A lieutenant of the 2nd Armored Division, who was a staunch Francophile and had traveled the country extensively before the war, diligently organized orientation lectures for several companies in the months before D-Day. He wrote to his mother: "I gave the French as much of a build up as I could to counteract the running down they get from the British."[117] But the GIs did not really need the British to remind them of what was peculiar about the French. They took plenty of stereotypes and prejudices with them from America. The US Army's guide to France needed over 20 pages more than the most voluminous publication on any of the other peoples in the European war theater to convince the GIs that the French were "very much like a lot of the people you knew back home."[118]

   To most GIs, however, it certainly did not seem that way when they finally saw France with their own eyes. "From the moment we hit the beaches, you could tell it was a different country," a private wrote to his parents. "The air even smelled different." In a journal entry of early July 1944, a combat engineer agreed with the private: "From what I've seen of France so far I don't think I would much like it even in peacetime. England was a little like home but France is really a foreign country."[119] France was never given a fair chance, of course, to show itself from its best side during the liberation. It was the war that dictated where and how the GIs would see the country. The Army guide, for instance, was aware that to most Americans France meant Paris, but it was quick to point out that as soldiers they should count on spending most of their time in "the provinces." "Paris," the booklet said, "can come later." For America's combat soldiers, Paris came much later indeed – if at all – and when it came, it was merely in the form of a short, blurred interruption between battles. And this hurried, superficial introduction to the French capital often only served to create an impression of the Parisians as "rapacious, cunning, indifferent to whether they were cheating Germans or Americans."[120] Instead of acquainting them with the City of Lights, the war offered the soldiers the grand tour of Normandy. There, for weeks, the GIs gazed at piles of rubble where once villages had stood, at craters where orchards should have been blooming, and at stinking carcasses where cows used to graze. The sights moved one GI to describe the once charming dairy country as the "mud hole of Hell."[121] When the GIs finally catapulted out of Normandy, the speed of the pursuit blinded them to much of the beauty elsewhere in France. Then the war capriciously called a halt again and forced the Americans to become thoroughly acquainted with Alsace-Lorraine. In the dreariest weather imaginable, the bog down allowed the GIs ample opportunity to take in the backwardness that characterized much of this region's countryside. The Army guide had predicted that farms would not look their best anywhere in France because the Germans had imprisoned many men and confiscated the horses. It had therefore cautioned the GIs to keep in mind that the French farmers were "among the best there are" and had proved to be "shrewd, hard-headed, successful and conservative."[122] To label the rural people of Alsace-Lorraine conservative, however, struck the GIs as an immense understatement. In northeastern France, the soldiers more than once thought they had stepped back in time. In the many tiny villages and hamlets, homes often had none of the comforts that most of the Americans took for granted: no radio, no telephone, no central heating; not even electricity, indoor toilets, bathtubs, or running water. The GIs were shocked to find that families were willing to live under the same roof as their animals – either next to the barn or over it – and had no qualms about keeping manure piles in front of their homes and almost out on the streets. The appalling living conditions in Alsace-Lorraine certainly managed to convince the GIs that the French farmers were hard-headed, but not at all that they were successful.[123]

In its summary of the Gallic people's main traits, the US Army guide described them as if they were model adherents of the Protestant ethic. They were said to receive "a sensible education, without frills," to possess "hard common sense," to be industrious and frugal, and to prefer "looking ahead."[124] The GIs, however, were convinced that their guide had it wrong: they clearly recognized the stereotypical characteristics of a Latin people. The French talked rapidly and eagerly, using hands and feet, but their information never led to a conclusion and rarely proved reliable. Skittish French refugees in Germany, for instance, warned men of the 2nd Infantry Division so often about nearby SS troops, who always turned out to be second-rate *Wehrmacht* soldiers, that by the end of the war the Americans just laughed away their alarms.[125] Even French males seemed to possess some of the volubility and excitability that the GIs ascribed to women. In a country where men could be christened Marcel – a name that sounded, according to one American, like "something a woman gets in a beauty parlor" – this did not come as a complete surprise. A lieutenant told his wife:

all the manly French men must be prisoners in Germany because I see none, or almost none. I remember receiving the same impression in 1937 in Paris and elsewhere.[126]

No American could deny that emotion and imagination had served the French well in many ways. They were excellent wine makers and magnificent cooks who amazed the GIs time and again with the dishes they managed to create from the little food they had. They were veritable artists who found an elegant design for everything from propaganda posters to bank notes.[127] On the other hand, however, the French seemed incapable of dealing efficiently with practical matters. From Casablanca to Strasbourg, the Americans complained, for instance, about the clumsiness of French paper money. They said it looked like "wallpaper" and claimed that the largest notes had "the size of an eight-by-ten diploma." "You have to carry around a lot of paper even if you don't have much money," a private told his parents. To make matters worse, the bills varied in size according to their value, turning money into "a very unmanageable roll of paper."[128] French communication systems proved to be as frustrating as the means of payment. A paratrooper who tried to employ the civilian telephone system of Tébessa for military purposes in 1942 Algeria, discovered that only shouts and insults could prod the indifferent French personnel into action. "I never knew such a bloodheat of rage to rise over so common an operation," the frustrated American commented.[129] The GIs were particularly harsh in their opinion of French technical abilities. They became convinced that the French were unable to operate anything that worked with an engine. On their way from Carentan to Le Mans in an American freight train in the fall of 1944, men of the 3rd Infantry Division thought it hilarious that the US engineers who oversaw the careless French crews had become "frustrated to the point of insanity." But the French gained special notoriety with their reckless driving. "All a Frenchman knows about a truck," Mauldin claimed, "is the general location of the foot throttle." Some GIs were transported from Normandy to the front in American trucks with civilian chauffeurs. After a tumultuous ride with a string of accidents, they concluded that the French "couldn't have driven a wheelbarrow properly." A lieutenant of the 8th Infantry Division watched in amazement as an old fire truck rushed out at Dinard in Brittany:

> In spite of ourselves, we had to laugh at the Frenchmen going about the task. It was like an old Keystone Kops comedy. The amount of chattery, screams, and gestures that apparently went with putting out a fire would have quenched all the flames easily had words been water.[130]

The impression of French impracticality would have been merely funny had it not strengthened the belief in the general incompetence of the nation. That belief had become widespread among the Americans since France's early collapse in the war. The Army guide therefore pleaded with the GIs not to talk of France as if it was "a pushover" and to keep in mind that the explanation for the defeat was much more complicated than they imagined.[131] But the connection between French ineptitude and the country's humiliating predicament during the war was not easily dispelled. On New Year's Eve of 1944, a private of the 100th Infantry Division told his parents that he was writing them a letter from the fourth floor of a hotel in a rest area in France. He clarified that what the French called the fourth floor was really the fifth floor. "If that was the only mistake the French ever made," he added resignedly, "we wouldn't be here today." Of the enlisted returnees surveyed in the US from March through May 1945, 35 per cent of those who had gotten to know at least some French civilians fairly well claimed that France had not done its share in helping to win the war. Among the better educated GIs (those who had graduated from high school) that percentage was as high as 45 per cent.[132]

THE LOW COUNTRIES

Belgium

The American troops who came into view of the Belgian border early in September 1944 had grown used to passing wave upon wave of overjoyed French. Nevertheless, the ecstatic reception that erupted when they set foot on Belgian soil boggled their minds. "The French had given us some fine welcomes as we passed but you could tell the difference when we got into Belguim [sic]," noted a soldier who entered the country with the 1st Infantry Division on 3 September. Many GIs agreed the civilian enthusiasm "greatly increased" in Belgium. A soldier of the 3rd Armored Division claimed that, despite the pouring and chilling rain, the reception in Charleroi "exceeded that of the many jubilant welcomings" in France. The Belgians exhausted themselves thinking of ways to please the liberators. "Everyone should have a chance to live the life of a movie star sometime," said a lieutenant of the 9th Infantry Division who helped capture Binche, "and I had mine then and there."[133] The Belgians handed out beer, food, and even ice-cream cones. They strung flowers on tanks and trucks, waved American and Belgian flags, displayed large welcome signs, and adorned shop windows with portraits of Roosevelt, Churchill, and Stalin. Whenever the Americans halted, people dragged them into their homes, offering refreshments or warm water to wash and shave. The civilians gazed at the GIs with awe and admiration, some even asked for their autographs. The excitement of the liberated civilians at times bordered on hysteria. Youngsters desperately tried to clasp the hands and fingers of American soldiers passing by in vehicles, parents held up their babies and begged the GIs to kiss or touch them, elderly people wept.[134] Engineers who reached Charleroi on 12 September were "so mobbed by welcoming Belgians that the gendarmes had to be called out."[135]

Perhaps it was less difficult for the people of a tiny country to show gratitude to foreign liberators. Belgium had been at the mercy of major rival powers for ages: it had been occupied by the Romans, the Spanish, the Austrians, the French, and the Dutch, and it had already lived under German terror for four years during World War I. In Europe, small countries often had to swallow their pride. The Belgians had come to accept long ago that their freedom depended on guarantees from great powers and they had learned from Waterloo and Passendale that it could often only be regained by foreign armies battling on their land. 1944 was no different, and the people were not ashamed to thank foreigners squarely for what they knew they could not have accomplished on their own. Moreover, America was remembered in Belgium as one of its main benefactors in the Great War. All this may explain why a soldier of the 2nd Armored Division, who had fought his way from North Africa to the Elbe, could conclude after the war that "the trust of the Belgians" had left one of the most vivid impressions of his overseas experience.[136] But the happiness of the Belgians was also undoubtedly heightened by the fact that their freedom was won in the fall of 1944 without the large-scale destruction they had learned to dread. German resistance was so flimsy in the American sector that it allowed the GIs to accomplish the liberation in a matter of weeks and without much havoc. The soldiers themselves were struck by the extent to which the Belgians had been spared from ravage and disruption during the American advance. A lieutenant of the 9th Infantry Division had already fought in North Africa, Sicily, France, and Germany when he observed in November 1944 that Belgium "seemed least touched of any by the war." The GIs found most of the small country's towns and cities largely intact. They also noticed that the Belgians did not look starved and were not poorly dressed. "[O]ne would hardly think they were having a war," a surprised GI exclaimed.[137]

Whatever the precise explanation for the Belgian reception, the GIs were impressed as well as touched by the warm welcome. "I can't get over how nice the people are here," a GI wrote to his parents when passing through Belgium on his way to the front in November 1944. Another soldier told his wife: "They're wonderful people – the friendliest I've ever met, can't do enough for us. They say we have 'le grand coeur' or something."[138] In Belgium, the Americans did not experience much of the skepticism that had often irritated them in France. Even amidst the cheering crowds, the GIs had not always been able to escape the impression that the French were happy to welcome them only because they needed them, not because they honestly liked them and genuinely appreciated their efforts. "The French were always glad to see us," noted a GI, "but I always got the feeling that they felt it was our duty to come."[139] The GIs were convinced, however, that the Belgians were "much warmer" and, most of all, that they were "sincere." They seemed to welcome them "with their hearts" and to radiate "a distinct, unsurpassed feeling of good fellowship and gratitude."[140]

The Americans who moved on to eastern Belgium could, therefore, not have been more dumbfounded. They had barely left the riotous celebrations at Verviers and Liège behind when they suddenly found themselves in the eerie silence of Eupen, where white flags replaced the Belgian colors, streets were deserted, and shutters closed.[141] Most GIs did not realize that what they had entered was the German-speaking part of the country. Belgium had acquired it as compensation for the

German damages of World War I and the Nazis had annexed it again in 1940. All the GIs knew for sure was that the area was "more German than the Kaiser" and that its inhabitants were "no good." The army warned them not to associate with the civilians and rumors soon spread that they sniped at the soldiers and signaled the location of troops to German planes. It proved hard for the GIs to understand how the same people who had greeted them only hours ago like liberators could suddenly regard them as "Attila's Huns."[142] Some Americans simply assumed they had already left Belgium and prematurely started letters home with "Somewhere in Germany." A combat engineer who was sent from Salmchâteau in the Walloons to a field hospital in Eupen was convinced that he had arrived in Aachen.[143]

Another shock lay in store for the GIs in the eastern part of Belgium. On 16 December 1944, the Germans thunderstruck the American troops with a counteroffensive that tore through the German- and French-speaking communities of Belgium that bordered Germany and Luxembourg. In one of war's cruel ironies, the fury of battle returned to the unsuspecting Belgians with a vengeance. Within a matter of days there was nothing to remind the American soldiers of the happy people they had seen only weeks ago. Civilians who had once crowded the sidewalks cheering, now blocked the roads, ashen-faced, in a desperate attempt to flee with carts piled high with belongings. Instead of inviting the GIs into their homes for celebrations, the Belgians now begged the soldiers not to abandon them. The memories of the debacle of 1940 were still fresh, and the people did not need reminding that it had led to more than four years of German terror. Men of the 84th Infantry Division, who had been withdrawn from the Ruhr River to help stem the counteroffensive, arrived at Serinchamps on 21 December to the great joy of the Belgian villagers. When they lined up, however, to withdraw to Baillonville in order to protect the divisional headquarters, they had all the trouble in the world to calm down the panic-stricken mayor and priest who tried to prevent them from leaving.[144] Yet American soldiers and Belgian civilians eventually managed to weather the German fury in the Ardennes, and in many places the shared suffering forged an even greater mutual liking. Perhaps no stronger bond developed than that between the 101st Airborne Division, which defended Bastogne, and the town's inhabitants, who according to the paratroopers did "whatever they could" to support them. But elsewhere too Americans and Belgians had grown closer together by the time the storm abated. A private from the battered 99th Infantry Division asserted in a letter to his parents on 3 January 1945: "the people have been wonderful to us except those that speak German."[145]

The GIs not only appreciated the way they were welcomed by the Belgians, they also liked their way of life. Most Americans knew next to nothing about the tiny country when they first entered it. Only few were aware that it was a trilingual nation; some had no idea at all of what language to expect and were surprised to hear French when they crossed the border. Apart from the German-speaking community in the east and a small Dutch-speaking area in the Flemish province of Limburg, American troops liberated only French-speaking Belgians. As a result, the Belgians at first sight simply appeared to be Frenchmen who spoke yet another dialect. Even when the GIs were cooperating with the resistance in the Walloons, they sometimes continued to refer to the beret-wearing fighters as the FFI.[146] Gradually, however, the Americans became keenly aware of the difference between the two countries. Not a few GIs became convinced that Belgium was "far more advanced than France." Men of the 3rd Armored Division, a unit that had arrived in Normandy on 23 June 1944, saw their first European trolley cars only some three months later at the Belgian city of Charleroi. Not only did they consider this "a spectacle which brought civilization back again," it also instantly reminded them of "cities across the Atlantic." Similarly, soldiers of the 26th Infantry Division, on their way to the Belgian–Luxembourg border from Metz late in December 1944, could not believe that Arlon was decorated with Christmas trees and other Yuletide ornaments. Here too, an American remarked that it was "the first city that reminded us of home since we had left the States."[147]

It did not seem to occur to the GIs that Belgium perhaps appeared to be more developed than France because it had suffered less during the liberation than its big neighbor. They believed instead that Belgium's more prosperous condition had to be ascribed to the character of its people. The Belgians seemed to be more down-to-earth and thrifty than their southern neighbors. This manifested itself nowhere better than in their cleanliness. Despite the wet and muddy fall of 1944, GIs described the inside of many of the houses in Belgium as spotless. They noticed that people normally took off their shoes before they went inside and that the women quite often followed the American soldiers with broom and mop to clean up after them. Soldiers of the 87th Infantry Division who were assigned to a house at Tillet during the Battle of the Bulge found the entrance blocked by a woman and her daughter. They explained that the Germans had slept on straw inside and had left lice behind. Only after both women had scrubbed the place with scalding water and strong disinfectant did they allow the Americans in.[148] "I do not believe that many houses in America could compare in cleanliness," a private of the 79th Infantry Division recorded in his diary. In the middle of autumn, a GI claimed that the entire country looked "wind swept and clean just like a fresh April shower." Even the natural surroundings appeared to be affected by the Belgians' love for neatness. GIs who halted south of Brussels on the evening of 7 September 1944 were surprised by how "well-kept" the forest was in which they bedded down:

> The grooming was so good that all the leaves were carefully stacked in uniform piles, and few, if any, shrubs could be seen on the floor of the woods.

A correspondent for *Yank* could only ascribe the contrast between the "rows of carefully spaced firs" in the Belgian Ardennes and the trees he had seen planted "helter-skelter" in France to "the well-ordered minds of the Belgians."[149]

The Netherlands

It had seemed unlikely, but Holland managed to surpass everything the Americans had appreciated in Belgium. To begin with, the reception by the Dutch was, according to one GI, "just unbelievable." The 30th Infantry Division, for instance, crossed into Holland from Belgium around the middle of September 1944. When the first GIs entered Spekholzerheide, "a tremendous roar went up from the town as from a football stadium" and people "surged across lots" to welcome their liberators. Some even insisted that the soldiers take a rest while they dug their foxholes for them.[150] During the descent for Operation Market-Garden on 17 September, airborne troops noticed that the Dutch were already waving at them from the rooftops. Citizens of Heeswijk ran out with milk and sandwiches while the paratroopers were still dangling in the air. At Son en Breugel, Americans described the people as "ecstatic." At Eindhoven, the applause was so deafening that the GIs had to shout to one another. The Dutch risked their lives to get a good look at the liberators. At Sint-Oedenrode, they packed the streets while firing could be heard not far away. At Schijndel, Americans told the inhabitants not to welcome them because they were not certain about how long they would stay in their town. Despite the warning, citizens handed cookies and other food out of doors and windows to soldiers resting against their houses. The GIs soon felt like movie stars and some were almost embarrassed by the reception they received. American soldiers who tried to put up defensive positions near Nijmegen were overwhelmed by the crowds and had to interrupt their activities to shake hands with civilians who lined up to greet them. What impressed the Americans even more was the active support well-organized resistance groups offered wherever they went in the Netherlands. Many GIs considered the Dutch resistance to be the best and bravest of Europe.[151] Throughout their operations in the small country, Americans described the Dutch people as "charming," "disarmingly lovable," "sincere" and, above all, as "overwhelmingly grateful."[152] The 101st Airborne Division was pulled out of Holland late in November 1944 for rest and reorganization in France. When trucks transported the troops down "Hell's Highway" through Nijmegen, Uden, Veghel, and Eindhoven, people instantly recognized the "Screaming Eagles" shoulder patches of their liberators and frantically started waving American and Dutch flags all over again. "September 17!" they yelled at the touched paratroopers at the tops of their voices.[153]

The Americans learned to respect the miniature country even more as they got to know it better. The Army guide taught the GIs that the Dutch had figured prominently in world history as well as in the rise of America. It told them that many famous explorers had come from or had been financed by Holland, among them no one less than Henry Hudson. It pointed out that the Dutch had been go-getters in the East Indies, South Africa, and Brazil, and reminded them that New York City had once been called New Amsterdam. It also emphasized that this was the country where people had been able to "argue freely on religious questions" at a time when even England had not allowed it, and the booklet asked the GIs not to forget that Holland had been a safe haven for many of the Pilgrim Fathers before they had set sail to the New World.[154]

The GIs who had a chance to meet the Dutch in person observed many qualities they admired. The people turned out to be not only grateful and brave, but also enterprising, hard-working, and amazingly clean. A lieutenant wrote to his wife in California: "Wholesomeness and a good democratic air of independence shine from everyone you meet." The officer considered the Dutch "the most up-and-coming people I've met over here." In March 1945 he used a pass to visit a Dutch family he had become acquainted with in Heerlen half a year earlier. To the American's astonishment, his friends, who had known no English during the first meeting, had already mastered his language quite well.[155] Idleness seemed unknown to the Dutch. Paratroopers who returned to France by truck late in November 1944, for instance, noticed that the civilians had already filled in foxholes in lawns and gardens and were feverishly repairing destroyed buildings. The Dutch also appeared to be a thorough and resourceful people, and the GIs were particularly impressed by their architecture and engineering. At Heteren, they witnessed how a factory made of bricks proved to be so well built that even Typhoon attacks failed to destroy it.[156] At Veghel, the hospital in which the aid station of the 501st Parachute Regiment was housed looked "magnificent and up-to-the-minute." At Nijmegen, GIs marveled at the giant steel bridge across the Waal River. "It had five spans, including the approaches, and must have been six hundred yards long," observed a stupefied soldier from New York. Even many of the ordinary homes had the appearance of "doll houses" and were "very modern in style."[157]

But what was beyond comprehension to the GIs was the Dutch people's "astounding dedication to sanitation." "Almost all Americans could take lessons from them in that respect," claimed an officer who was stationed near Maastricht. The GIs found it almost impossible to describe how spotless Holland was. The homes were "wondrously clean" and "sparkling," and even Limburg's mining towns looked "immaculate." An American at Veghel claimed that he "would not have hesitated to eat off the brick street." Most of all, the GIs were flabbergasted by the daily ritual of Dutch women sitting on their knees, scrubbing floors, steps, and sidewalks with hard brushes and patient determination. An officer of the 95th Infantry Division at Venray "couldn't help reflecting that in the U.S. even paid servants considered it demeaning to get on their knees and scrub."[158] Like many other Americans, a chaplain of the 101st Airborne Division came to regard Holland as a veritable model country:

> They are far ahead of England or any place else in Europe. I would even say that the standard of living for the average person seemed to be above that of the United States.[159]

GERMANY

In Alsace-Lorraine and eastern Belgium, the Americans received an early taste of how awkward it felt to be conquerors rather than liberators. They experienced a similar uneasiness in Luxembourg, where the people generally seemed friendly and happy to see them, but where the widespread use of German nevertheless gave them "a crawly feeling" and the impression that the country was "fairly well riddled with collaborationists."[160] Nothing, however, distressed the GIs more than the prospect of campaigning in Germany proper. When their army first penetrated Germany on 11 September 1944, it was a widely-held belief that they would face "a fanatical resistance movement" and would encounter among the civilians "a truculent, hostile attitude." The GIs came to fear the country's civilians as much as its soldiers. They were convinced that they too would "fight like devils for every inch of German soil."[161] Rumors whispered that the entire populace had been trained in sniping, sabotaging, and booby-trapping. No German was to be trusted: innocent-looking children would toss grenades, charming girls would knife and castrate, respectable grandfathers would launch *Panzerfauste*.[162] To one American infantry soldier, who was about to enter Germany early in 1945, the country stood for "[e]ighty million people – each ready to kill me."[163]

Apprehension soared as the German border came closer. Nazi slogans on walls cried "SEE GERMANY AND DIE!" Large signboards next to roads screamed "DEATH IS AHEAD!" US Army signs added to the ominous atmosphere by warning its soldiers to be on the alert even more now that they were about to enter an enemy country. Anxiety reached a climax when troops actually crossed the border. After the 94th Infantry Division had entered Germany in the early hours of 8 January 1945, one of the unit's shaken soldiers wrote to his parents: "The war was so big to all of us that morning."[164] The GIs developed rituals to relieve the tension. Some stopped to spit on the ground ostentatiously before moving on; many halted to urinate on German soil with exaggerated ceremony. Such acts of defiance, however, could not allay the Americans' fear of entering "the monster's smoking den," not even when thousands of comrades had already preceded them. A combat engineer who crossed the border at Walheim in February 1945 recorded in his journal: "This is the part of the war I have dreaded the most – being in Germany."[165]

The surprise – and relief – of the GIs was great therefore when they found the German civilians to be anything but belligerent. Not a single serious act of resistance against the US Army was reported in the first three weeks of the occupation, and sniping remained limited to sporadic incidents. It would take until the last weeks of the war before American troops encountered a few isolated instances of German civilians fighting at the side of soldiers to defend their town.[166] In general, however, the German communities were already draped in white by the time the GIs arrived in the outskirts. Most civilians appeared too weary to resist the occupation. Many also turned out to be too afraid of the Americans to contemplate resistance. In some places, the first sight of them caused people to panic. When soldiers of an advance task force of the 3rd Armored Division, who were searching for water, kicked open the wooden fence of a house somewhere between the Weser and the Mulde River in April 1945, two elderly people begged the embarrassed GIs to kill them but to spare the life of the small boy who was with them. Nazi propaganda had not only ranted against Jews and Bolsheviks, it had also instilled a fair amount of fear of the Americans. From 1943 on, it had been citing the heavy air raids as clear proof of American *Gangstertum*. When US troops occupied their first German territory in the autumn of 1944, the Nazis started bombarding the population with news of American enslavement decrees, of GIs who forced civilians to clear rubble under fire, and of drunk black soldiers who murdered children. Moreover, people were deluded into believing that the men would be sent to Siberia and that the women would be systematically violated.[167] A combat surgeon who fought his way across Germany with the 12th Armored Division noticed that

> in any newly captured German city there was always a gush of civic relief when people discovered they weren't really going to be raped or gutted by the Jewish American Bolsheviks.[168]

Still, the German fear of the GIs did not always turn out to be completely unfounded. Like all combat soldiers, the Americans too could bring down their wrath on civilians in the heat of battle. They used inhabitants as shields when fearing an ambush, enfiladed homes that did not display surrender flags, trained massive amounts of fire on the slightest suspicious movement anywhere, or raked streets "just for the hell of shooting." Nothing could move the GIs more to take their anger out on the populace than the death of comrades. While filing through the center of Deggendorf in April 1945, for instance, a platoon of the 26th Infantry Division furiously smashed the plate glass windows of store after store in retribution for the killing of a popular lieutenant during the capture of the town.[169]

But in those German communities where not too many incidents occurred during the American takeover, curiosity soon replaced apprehension and civilians began to peek cautiously from behind curtains and to line the streets hesitantly. Although the GIs occasionally crossed "the shamed, darting eyes of the defeated," they most often encountered merely apathetic stares. Here and there the German people actually smiled or waved at the occupiers. In some places they even gave the GIs a liberators' welcome as war's end caused joy that temporarily superseded all their worries about foreign occupation. In the Hanau-Frankfurt area, for instance, women embraced the Americans. Cheering and flowers awaited the GIs in Limburg and Leipzig. It was the wrecked city of Cologne, however, that surprised the Americans with the most enthusiastic reception: delirious civilians handed out beer and wine in a welcome that the soldiers could only describe as "terrific."[170] A corporal of the 76th Infantry Division, who was smiled at by Germans in the Rhineland, confessed: "I am sometimes ashamed for them. For a people who are the Master Race, their attitude is distinctly a disappointment."[171]

Most American combat soldiers refused to accord much credence to the Germans' meekness and hospitality. The Army guide reminded them that the Germans had already misled their fathers with their friendly behavior after the armistice of 1918.[172] The GIs preferred to interpret the enemy's submissiveness as "an outward manifestation of a very guilty conscience" and the laughs on the German faces as "Hitler smiles," full of deceit and treachery. A medic wrote to his wife in March 1945:

> We don't say a word to the German people ... Many smile, but we don't know what lurks behind the smile and we look straight through them.[173]

Those who would have felt like reciprocating the German greetings were not allowed to anyway. The US Army announced a nonfraternization policy on 12 September 1944, the day after its troops had crossed the German border. It was primarily a security decision, to prevent attacks against unsuspecting soldiers, as well as a counterintelligence measure to avoid the leakage of information. At the same time, however, it was intended to show the Germans that their support of Nazism, racism, and aggression had "earned for them the contempt and distrust of the civilized world."[174] The policy rules were first communicated to the GIs in the *Pocket Guide to Germany*, which was distributed when the soldiers approached the border in 1944. In January 1945, the rules were listed in even greater detail in special folders, which the Americans were supposed to carry inside their helmet liners at all times. Nonfraternization only allowed the GIs to have contact with Germans in matters of official business. They were not permitted to converse with the civilians, to shake hands with them, to accompany them in the streets, to visit their homes, to drink with them, to give or accept gifts, to engage in games or sports with them, or to take part in their social events. Only the attendance of German church services was condoned, provided the GIs were seated separately. Violators ran the risk of being fined or court-martialed.[175]

Army policy also prohibited the billeting of GIs with German families. As conquerors, American troops enjoyed the right to commandeer the houses of enemy civilians as they saw fit and, as a result of the nonfraternization directives, the Germans had to abandon their homes whenever GIs decided to move in. It gradually became a matter of routine to the GIs to enter a German town in the evening or night and order the inhabitants out of their homes. The exhausted soldiers often only granted the civilians a few minutes to grab the most essential items, such as blankets, before putting them out on the street. They forced them to stay with neighbors or herded them into the houses of a particular section of town or into large buildings such as schools. Sometimes these last measures caused panic among the Germans, who feared being rounded up for execution. In March 1945, for instance, soldiers of the 99th Infantry Division had to drag hysterical women and children from their homes at Bergheim in an attempt to house them in another part of the town.[176]

Most American combat soldiers had seen too much German inhumanity by the time they started chasing enemy civilians out of their homes to have compunctions about the policy. After having taken over a house at Schollbrunn in April 1945, a sergeant of the 44th Infantry Division justified the act in a letter to his mother by pointing out that the German civilians too were the enemy because they constituted "the backbone of the whole Nazi system."[177] The US Army warned its soldiers to maintain a firm but correct attitude and not to mistake nonfraternization for "rough, undignified, or aggressive conduct." Nevertheless, although some GIs tried to put the civilians at ease when they moved into their houses and even violated orders by allowing old and sick people to stay, others could not resist using such occasions to intimidate families and to harass women. The civilians were allowed to return to their homes only when the soldiers had moved on. In the meantime, the GIs did not take great pains to protect the possessions of the German households. Those houses that contained incriminating evidence, such as Hitler portraits or family albums with photographs of people in Nazi uniforms, the American soldiers quite often wrecked purposely. It was their small way of making the German people pay for the suffering they had allowed to be inflicted on so many others.[178]

Contrary to the rear echelon and headquarter troops, the policy of nonfraternization was generally well observed by the American frontline units. To begin with, the rapid movements of these troops in Germany made the development of intensive local relationships nearly impossible. Moreover, combat soldiers did not need to be reminded that avoiding contacts with Germans increased their security. Nor did they need to be convinced that the Germans had earned their contempt: a dislike for anything that was German came naturally to many frontline soldiers. In April 1945, a US Army survey showed that only 21 per cent of the GIs in the ETO did not harbor strong feelings against the German common people. It was therefore not surprising that, also in April 1945, 68 per cent of the American soldiers in Germany claimed that few or almost none of them had developed friendly contacts with German girls, and 82 per cent of them claimed that few had developed such contacts with older German civilians.[179]

Yet, despite their ill feelings toward the German people, many American combat soldiers could not but admit they were impressed by the enemy's country as they got to see more of it. To begin with, Germany's natural surroundings could be breathtaking. After the mud in Alsace-Lorraine and the slush in the Ardennes, for many Americans the offensive in Germany was "a march toward spring." The gentle season bathed the Third Reich in soft shades, and blossoms turned it into a colorful country. From the vicinity of Munich a sergeant wrote to his wife in April 1945: "Germany is a beautiful [country] much more so than France, though I hate to say so."[180]

But Germany at the same time was much more than bucolic valleys and pastoral villages. The Army guide pointed out that this European power was ranked among the leading industrial nations of the world, and the GIs had plenty of opportunities to verify that Germany was indeed a major producer of iron, coal, machines, textiles, optical instruments, and chemical products. They saw with their own eyes how places that had once produced sewing machines were now manufacturing military goods as diverse as saddle cinches and radio antennas. Most of all, they were fascinated by some of the new products the German industries had developed during the war. Soldiers of the 71st Infantry Division who rummaged through an IG Farben plant near Ludwigshafen, for instance, were much intrigued by its reserves of synthetic gasoline and rubber and by its stocks of electric wire insulated with vinyl plastic.[181] Germany's architecture and engineering also impressed the Americans as very solid and advanced, and nothing excited them more than the German *Reichsautobahne*. To the fellow citizens of Henry Ford, the German highways looked like "real dream roads." In lengthy letters home GIs described that they had two lanes in each direction, were divided by grass median strips, used bridges and underpasses for crossroads, and boasted a surface "as smooth as a highly polished floor." The Americans agreed that these roads were "a marvel of engineering." Not only did they consider the "superhighway" a drastic improvement over "the narrow, winding roads of France and Belgium," many GIs also had to admit they had not seen anything like it in their own country.[182]

What contributed most to the impression of the enemy's high standard of living, however, was the fact that in Germany the American combat soldiers were able, whenever time permitted, to enjoy the comforts of civilian life more fully than anywhere else in Europe. From the moment they had arrived in Great Britain, they had rarely been allowed to experience the luxury of living in private homes. But in Germany they could select the very best houses still available in a town after their battalion headquarters had moved in. Although many big German cities as well as key infrastructure had been devastated by the Allied air offensive, numerous towns and villages had remained largely untouched. Also, the advance of the ground troops often was so rapid in Germany that many regions had escaped massive destruction. After months and years of living in barracks, tents, and – mostly – foxholes, American combat soldiers found the pleasures of hot water, big stoves, electricity, toilets with seats and running water, and beds with bulky feather covers nearly indescribable. Moreover, they were automatically drawn to the well-to-do neighborhoods of the German towns and as a result often stayed in houses they could not even have afforded to live in at home. Life on the right side of the tracks inevitably created the impression that radios and telephones, hardwood floors and pianos, satin sheets and electric razors, libraries and wine cellars were standard in any German home.[183] In those circumstances, the Germans soon appeared to be "the wealthiest people in Europe" in comparison to whom the French in particular seemed "truly paupers." A puzzled lieutenant wrote to his family in the last weeks of the war: "Germany is a lot like the U.S. particularly N.Y. & I can't see why they wanted to take over France."[184] In some regards the German standard of living even seemed to surpass the American. GIs wrote home that the German houses were better and more modern, that the plumbing and heating devices were more advanced, and that "shanties and poor sections" did not seem to exist. As early as December 1944, a corporal had the impression that "Adolf Hitler had housed his *Volk* very well."

By March 1945, there was no doubt left in his mind that Germany had "an unusually high standard of living – guns or butter, or no guns or butter."[185]

The GIs were completely baffled by Germany. With such assets, asked a soldier from Seattle, how could it have become "a disease as well as a country?" He saw plenty of indications that Germany had been a wealthy nation long before it had started exploiting and plundering the rest of Europe:

> Their old cry that they were a 'have-not' nation certainly collapses when one sees their homes and the clues to what must have been their standard of living. Germany was infinitely better off than Merrie Olde England.[186]

Whence then, the American soldiers demanded to know, had come the Germans' greed for world power? What had moved them to bleed the rest of Europe white and to concentrate even more wealth in their country by means of looting and slave labor? GIs who had seen the hungry look on children's faces elsewhere in Europe were outraged to find Germans who were well-nourished and women who were still wearing silk stockings, a luxury item that was not even available anymore in America.[187] A disgusted private wrote to his parents in April 1945: "It'll be at least 100 years before they can use up all the stuff they drained from Europe in the past six years."[188]

Another question that burned on the lips of many GIs was succinctly formulated by a soldier of the 99th Infantry Division: "How was it possible for a madman such as Hitler to have hypnotized so intelligent a nation?"[189] The American soldiers could not deny that the German people possessed an impressive array of qualities. They described them as hardworking, efficient, clean, and "more ambitious than either the English or the French." They interpreted their neat brick homes as evidence of discipline, thrift, and industry. Even the fields and woods looked "orderly." Forest floors were amazingly clean and trees had been planted "in staggering symmetrical rows." It was obvious too that German industriousness could barely wait to apply itself to erasing the ravages of war. While combat troops were still filing by, civilians were already filling up the antitank trenches that had been dug in their fields. In towns where the guns had barely been silenced, uniform piles of salvageable bricks and cobblestones already lined the streets. But the Americans asked themselves why the Germans had allowed their ambition to be channeled into warfare in the first place.[190] The scientific achievements of the Germans were brought to mind throughout the country: at the renowned universities, in the technological hobby rooms of private homes, by the many first-rate radios, watches, and cameras. But the American soldiers wondered why such a progressive nation had decided to use its creative powers for the destruction of humanity. Germany had produced not only famous scientists; it had also given birth to great writers, philosophers, artists, and musicians. Moreover, many of its ordinary citizens were well educated and cultivated too. Yet, though German homes boasted excellent libraries, Shakespeare and art critics shared shelves with Goebbels and Ley. And while many German families owned pianos, Brahms' scores had been blasted into the streets and in Bonn

Beethoven's statue stood forlornly amidst twisted benches and splintered trees. Why, the GIs wanted to know, had the German people been willing to betray the many contributions they had made to civilized life in the past?[191]

Instead of answers, the Americans only found new questions as they examined German society more closely. The religiousness of the German civilians, for instance, proved as inexplicable to the GIs as that of the German soldiers. They read in their Army guides about "the pagan ideologies of the Nazis" and their persecution of the Church in the occupied countries. They learned from their chaplains about Hitler's intentions to replace the cross by the swastika. They saw with their own eyes that the enemy had some kind of "pseudo-religious obsession" with Hitler.[192] Yet, all this notwithstanding, the GIs discovered that traditional religion had remained a potent force among the people in Germany. In the predominantly Catholic districts of the Rhineland and Upper Bavaria, for instance, the Americans had to conclude that the Germans were "religious in the same way as those people who observed in France, Belgium, and Luxembourg." Every crossroad was adorned with a crucifix or a shrine to the Virgin Mary. The tiniest village had a church. Homes abounded with rosaries, Madonna busts, and reproductions of *The Last Supper.* The GIs could hear families praying upstairs when they hammered on the doors of houses they were about to commandeer. At Steinach, early in April 1945, soldiers of the 3rd Infantry Division had to drag away nuns who held up tanks by kneeling in the streets with upraised crucifixes.[193] The religiousness of the enemy people presented yet another paradox to the Americans. Although Germany seemed to display "the greatest number of physical representations of Christ" in Europe, the people's behavior under the Nazi regime clearly indicated that they had "no conception of real Christianity." Some GIs simply suspected the Germans of hypocrisy; others were at a loss and could only decide that "Germans have strange minds about religion as everything else."[194]

How could a hardworking, intelligent, cultured, and religious people so have disgraced itself? It looked like such a tremendous waste of talent and potential to the Americans. "A shame that such a race should be exterminated," a disappointed medic of the 1st Infantry Division wrote to his family in October 1944. "Would that their warped ideas could somehow be surgically removed without killing the patient."[195] The GIs grappled with the question of what exactly had contaminated the German mind. There was no doubt that Nazism was to blame to a large extent. The Americans could not but conclude that Hitler's following had been large. The Army guide advised them to be on their guard against German youth in particular, since it had been taught in school to sacrifice everything for Hitler and the Nazi party and thus had become "the victim of the greatest educational crime in the history of the world." In April 1945, 89 per cent of the enlisted men in the ETO thought that the United Nations should closely supervise and inspect the German schools and colleges for some years to come.[196] But it did not take long for the GIs to become convinced that the older generation was no less tainted. An officer of the 35th Infantry Division somberly assessed the situation in April 1945:

I think the truth of the matter is that many of those [Germans] with respect for the decencies of mankind, met one of three fates, the concentration camp, death, or exile, and all those remaining acquiesced or supported the inhuman policies of the Nazis.

That same month, most GIs in the ETO appeared to agree with the officer's view as 71 per cent of them said they believed that most or almost all of the ordinary Germans were to blame for the war.[197]

The GIs did not accept, however, that the Germans had been led astray by Nazism alone. They thought the roots of their corruption went much deeper and reached all the way back to Prussian militarism. That explanation was suggested to them by, among others, the US Army guide to Germany. It pointed out that the Germans "follow Hitler as they followed the Kaiser in 1914, and as they obeyed the will of Bismarck in the 19th century." World War II was therefore just "a cruel new version of an old story – the story of how Germany, throughout history, organized her people time and again to become conquerors." As a result of that past, the German people had become "dedicated to a policy of war-making and aggression and brutality and hatred of democracy."[198] Militarism indeed appeared to have conditioned the German people. General Bradley's special orders on German–American relations, issued to the men of his Twelfth Army Group, emphasized that the Germans held "all things military in deep respect," and GIs everywhere saw with their own eyes how the Germans "shied away from anyone in uniform." According to a private of the 87th Infantry Division, even a nun at a hospital in Koblenz proved to have "an inborn high regard for Army officers." More remarkably still, the civilians themselves seemed to be prototypes of soldiers. The GIs noticed that they had "a willingness to obey" and knew "how to take orders." They soon learned that firmness and exploiting the authority of the uniform was the best way to get things done in Germany. They discovered, for instance, that shouting harsh commands and threatening to call in "the Military Police" was guaranteed to bring about an immediate exodus of Germans from any house they wanted for themselves.[199] It gradually dawned on the American soldiers that this blind obedience to authority might actually be the key to understanding "the German schizophrenia" that so puzzled them. Perhaps it was precisely this kind of mental makeup that made it possible for the Germans "to be admirable individually and collectively the most vicious people in modern history."[200] If that was so, a majority of the GIs did not think that Germany could be trusted in the future either, because in April 1945 only 46 per cent of them believed that almost all or most of the German people could be "educated away from Nazism and taught to really think and act like democratic people." That is probably why 56 per cent of the enlisted men considered it safer to break up Germany "into small states" after the war.[201]

Since obeying orders had been the sacred credo of German society, the collapse of Nazi leadership and military authority seemed to effect a mental shutdown. Suddenly the German people looked "like addicts without their opiate," their minds "a huge vacuum."[202] Nothing angered the GIs more than that the German common people interpreted the Allied removal of the Nazi leadership as the absolution of their own guilt. All the rank and file of the Nazi party appeared to have evaporated overnight. The frustrated counterintelligence officer of an infantry division wrote to a friend in the spring of 1945:

> I have declared that if I ever find one who will say: "I am, I was, and will remain a National Socialist and you can like it or not," I will clasp his hand and cry: "At last I have found a brave and honest, if an evil, man."[203]

And there was yet another disturbing way in which the German people refused to accept responsibility for the hideous crimes of the Nazi regime. The Twelfth Army Group's pamphlet on nonfraternization lectured: "Except for such losses of life and property suffered by them, the Germans have no regrets for the havoc they have wrought in the world."[204] The American soldiers could not have agreed with that observation more. They were well aware that pleas had not prevented the German forces from invading most of Europe. It therefore upset them that whenever American troops were about to enter a German community, its inhabitants supposed that showing the white flag or sending out a delegation of local notabilities was all that was needed to make the war leave them alone. The GIs had seen the scale of the destruction the Germans had caused elsewhere. They were therefore stunned by the unperturbed manner in which the Germans dared to ask for consideration for their own property. In March 1945, the concerned mayor of a town at the Niers Canal visited a company command post of the 84th Infantry Division. He wanted help to keep the town's only factory operational to ensure employment. The German's audacity struck the Americans as even more insulting when they learned that the factory had been producing nose-cone assemblies for 88 mm shells. That very month, the same division was visited by a German at Hüls who begged the Americans to remove the German soldiers who were sleeping in his chicken farm before his business became a military target. Battalion headquarters ordered the company commander to take care of it. The lieutenant flatly refused and told his men to stay put. Nothing confirmed the schizophrenia of the German people more to the American soldiers than their pathetic scramble to safeguard what was left of their own neat brick homes in the middle of a war they had allowed to ruin most of Europe. In April 1945, 75 per cent of the enlisted men in Europe thought the United Nations should force German labor to rebuild the devastated areas in other countries at POW wages.[205]

At Heidelberg, shops and banks continued to conduct business while the GIs occupied the city late in March 1945. At Göttingen, the famed university was still holding classes when American troops entered the town on 9 April. But, with the disruption of the liberated countries burning in their minds, the American soldiers felt stung by any German attempt at preserving even a semblance of normality in their own society. A captain of the 95th Infantry Division was so irritated by the clouds of steam and smoke Duisburg's industry was spewing out, even as enemy troops were on the edge of the city, that he immediately radioed battalion to bring down a barrage on the factories.[206] The GIs had seen the Germans bring about so much pain in the rest of Europe that the sight of suffering among the perpetrators themselves caused them nothing but the satisfaction of justice. While men of the 2nd Infantry Division were engaged in combat at Ellershausen, an elderly couple was crying hysterically in front of a burning farm. All a company commander could think of was: "What right had they to stand their sobbing and blaming us for this terror? What right did they and their kind have to any emotions at all?"[207]

AUSTRIA

During the last days of the war in Europe, American troops burst out of Germany and poured into Austria and Czechoslovakia. Both countries had been gobbled up by Germany in the late 1930s and it seemed obvious that by crossing their borders the GIs would relive the satisfaction of being liberators. Once again, however, things turned out to be more complicated in the political and ethnic maze of the Old World.

Austria had been annexed by Germany in March 1938 and subjected to such systematic nazification that the country had lost much of its national identity. There was no government in exile for the Allies to maintain contact with, for instance, and captured German and Austrian soldiers were simply held in the same POW camps. It took the Allies until the fall of 1943 to decide that Austria would be treated as a liberated rather than an occupied country. They warned Austria, however, that it would still be held responsible for its participation in the war on the side of Nazi Germany. These political decisions had to be translated to the American troops in the field. The basic directive on nonfraternization originally applied to Germany only. In April 1944 it was decided that "some degree" of fraternization was allowed in Austria and that the relationship with the Austrian people had to be "more friendly than in Germany." But the policy was changed again before the troops entered the country and SHAEF announced that nonfraternization would be the rule in Austria after all, albeit only as a temporary order. The US Army's guide to Austria reflected the confusion surrounding the status of the Austrian people. Although it emphasized that fraternization was not allowed, it nevertheless told the GIs that they were going into Austria "both as victors and liberators." The guide stated that the Austrians were not Germans and that they had been deeply disappointed by them after the *Anschluss*. As a people, they were more hostile to the Germans than to the Americans, and there was little doubt that they would, on the whole, welcome the GIs as liberators. But the booklet hastened to remind the soldiers that the Austrians partly had themselves to blame for the German annexation and that many of those who would cheer the Americans had also greeted the Germans enthusiastically in 1938. Not only were the GIs not to forget that Austrian Nazis had committed crimes as revolting as those of the Germans, they were also cautioned that "Austrians are quick to change their political convictions."[208]

When the GIs at last entered Austria, they found that they were indeed welcomed by the people "as conquering heroes." Austrian flags fluttered everywhere together with American ones made out of every kind of red, white, and blue fabric imaginable. At Steyr, the celebrations were "unrestrained and very difficult to describe." So many civilians crowded the streets at Linz that they brought the American vehicles to a standstill. The spontaneity and warmth of the Austrian reception overwhelmed the Americans soldiers almost instantly. Before they realized it, GIs were shaking hands and kissing girls, throwing caution to the wind and ignoring orders. The Austrians were so happy to see the GIs and so much resented being treated as if they were Germans that the American combat units never enforced nonfraternization as seriously in Austria as in Germany.[209]

CZECHOSLOVAKIA

There was never any doubt among US policy makers about Czechoslovakia's status as a liberated country. For American troops in the field, however, matters were not all that simple. When the Third Army pushed its way into Czechoslovakia, American soldiers at first predominantly encountered ethnic Germans on their way to the Karlsbad-Pilsen-Budweis line. To the GIs, who had looked forward to being liberators again and whose battle cry in Germany had become "On to Czechoslovakia and Fraternization," it seemed as if they would never succeed in leaving enemy territory behind. To their regret, they found the people in the forested border regions of Bohemia "German in speech, customs and sympathy." Their towns were draped with white flags and shrouded in an atmosphere of "fear and silence."[210] It was left to the individual units to decide if and how the nonfraternization rules would be applied. As a result, different units adopted different measures. Some allowed fraternization with everyone from the beginning, others eased the nonfraternization prohibitions somewhat, and still others forbade fraternization with the local Germans only.[211]

Confusion reigned until the Americans moved deeper into Bohemia and encountered the Czechs. A surgeon of the 90th Infantry Division compared the advance from Unterreichenstein to Sušice to "going from night to day." The euphoria that erupted in the small country was matched only by the wild joy the GIs had witnessed in the Low Countries. Suddenly, the white flags made way for a sea of national colors, while the guilty silence exploded into a relieved roar. The civilians were "deliriously happy" and the country looked like "a continuous carnival:" women and children proudly wore their gay traditional costumes, adults cheered and cried, people blocked the streets and danced in the squares. The Czechs had not known with certainty which of the Allies would be first to bring them liberation. Red flags with hammer and sickle could therefore also be seen among the crowds, and towns and villages had erected victory arches across roads with the words of welcome both in Russian and English. But the nationality of the deliverers did not matter to these ecstatic people. The GIs were practically mobbed. Civilians put small Czechoslovakian flags in the muzzles of the soldiers' rifles and bouquets of wild flowers in their hands. Before long, girls were running around with the shoulder patches of American divisions sewn to their sweaters. The GIs no longer needed to requisition houses: the last Europeans to be liberated by the American soldiers practically fought each other for the privilege of housing them.[212]

The American combat soldiers found Europe's political and ethnic diversity to be complex and bewildering. Nevertheless, their world view helped them to bring some order to the confusing array of countries and peoples. Historian Michael Hunt has demonstrated how "race as an essential category for understanding other peoples and as a fundamental basis for judging them" had become a core element in the American world view by the end of the nineteenth century. And he has shown how it was passed on "as a well-nigh irresistible legacy." The GIs in Europe certainly shared in that legacy. The large majority of combat soldiers were Americans of light skin, and they employed a clear racial hierarchy. The native peoples of France's North African colonies belonged to the lowest rung. Next came the Latin peoples of Europe, including the Italians as well as the French. Farther up ranked the Nordic people of the Low Countries. Although the Germans traditionally shared the Nordic peg, of course, they had clearly fallen from grace as a result of their brutal behavior during the war. The Anglo-Saxons, however, steadfastly topped the racial pyramid.[213]

If the GIs managed to bring a semblance of order to Europe's diversity, they never succeeded in making head or tail of its boundless division and discord. Melting pot or not, in America different races and nationalities were at least able to live together more or less peacefully. In Europe, races and nations, and even regions and localities, appeared to be in constant strife. To the American soldiers, the Old World was a volatile feudal patchwork in which war could hardly be called surprising.

Fittingly, it was war that would eventually determine the GIs' overriding impression of Europe. Beyond the fleeting glimpses of different countries and peoples, the limited communication that combat allowed the Americans with the Europeans thoroughly blurred the picture of their world, while the total character of the war colored that picture even darker. As a result, the GIs returned from overseas not so much with impressions of particular European countries and their contrasts as with the perception of Europe as one and the same Old World, a world so aged and crippled that it appeared to have collapsed under the weight of its latest war.

7   The Limits of Communication

During their torturous march across Europe, America's combat soldiers initially obtained merely a series of superficial impressions of different countries and peoples. Nevertheless, there were a number of circumstances in which the frontline soldiers were able to get to know the European people better through close personal encounters. These encounters, however, remained very restricted in scope. To begin with, the language barrier most often precluded any thorough understanding of the people and their situation. Developing a well-informed picture of European society was also not likely when combat soldiers tended to seek contact with civilians mainly to satisfy the most basic needs such as food, alcohol, and sex. Moreover, the GIs were destined to get acquainted with only limited segments of the population. Since most of Europe's able-bodied men had disappeared as soldiers, resistance fighters, forced laborers, or prisoners, the Americans encountered disproportionate numbers of the Old World's weak and aged, its children, and its women.

THE LANGUAGE BARRIER

To the GIs, Europe represented a linguistic confusion reminiscent of the days when God's wrath had descended on the infamous Tower of Babel. Not even American polyglots were adequately prepared to make sense out of the mixture of languages, dialects, and patois that rapidly succeeded each other as the troops marched across the Old World. "French, Spanish, Portuguese, English, Italian, German, Russian, Polish and Indian are tongues that I'm sure can be spoken," remarked a surgeon in an evacuation hospital near Florence late in April 1945.

> A Yugoslav and a Niese (Jap-American) whom we even took care of along with Indians at previous set-ups in Italy and you can imagine what a linguist I should have become – not to mention the Arabic and Yiddish we heard in Africa which was predominantly French.[1]

A basic knowledge of the foreign languages commonly taught at American schools was bound to fall short in the European war zone.

Few soldiers could have been prepared for the first language the US Army encountered in Europe in August 1941. After having been in Iceland for more than a year, the frustrated chaplain of the 5th Engineer Combat Regiment admitted that he, his driver, and the unit's doctor together still had not managed to learn more than 25 words of the country's language, a Germanic tongue that had evolved from Old Norse.[2] Great Britain in turn introduced the Americans to disquieting variations of their own language. The Army guide warned the GIs that in Ireland there was "a brogue for every county." Scotland, not to mention Wales, offered its own linguistic intricacies. But even in the home of the King's English itself, people spoke a language quite different from the American interpretation of English. Many GIs found the English accent – and the "cultured" one of the BBC news broadcasters in particular – hilarious, although their guide had warned them they sounded "just as funny" to the English. On top of that, not only did spelling differ slightly, but many familiar words carried different meanings in England and many common objects different names. The GI guide to Britain's basic glossary alone listed more than 200 words and phrases likely to cause confusion or embarrassment in daily conversations. An intelligible conversation between Americans and Brits about cars, for instance, seemed well-nigh impossible: in Britain, the top of the car was a hood, the hood of the engine a bonnet, the battery an accumulator, the generator a dynamo, the fenders wings, the muffler a silencer, a wrench a spanner, and gas petrol. It "raises the question," said one GI, "of which is the English language."[3] Much linguistic confusion reigned in French North Africa, where even in movie theaters only French or Spanish could be heard. The Italian language and its many regional variations at times baffled even Italian-Americans. Those with roots on the Italian mainland could barely make sense of the Sicilian dialects, for example, whereas descendants of Neapolitans were at a loss in Tuscany. In France, communication proved no less frustrating to the GIs. Their high-school French soon turned out to be inadequate. Mere place names seemed designed to discourage foreigners. The GIs captured places like Ecoquenéauville, Saint-Hilaire-du-Harcouët, Châteauneuf-d'Ille-et-Vilaine, and Blénod-lès-Pont-à-Mousson, but they never mastered their names.[4] Moreover, the French appeared to be permanently excited as they spoke "with the intensity of machine gun fire." This all too often resulted in "volleys of gibberish" that prevented untrained American ears even from following conversations in standard French, let alone discussions in the dialects of Brittany, the Provence, or the Alsace.[5] But perhaps Belgium more than any other country revealed the full dimension of Europe's linguistic jumble. The GI guide to the tiny nation hastened to set straight any Americans who expected Belgians to speak Belgian: they would run into French in the south, Flemish in the north, and bilingualism in Brussels. In the field, the GIs further learned that Belgian French was really a Walloon dialect, that Flemish was a form of Dutch, and that thousands of Belgians in the east spoke German.[6] In the Netherlands, the people simply spoke Dutch, although some GIs mistook the rather obscure language for German, confusing Dutch with *Deutsch*.[7] In their guides to lilliputian Luxembourg, American soldiers read that French was the official language of the grand duchy, that German was generally understood, but that the people commonly spoke the Luxembourg tongue or *Letzeburgesch*, a Frankish dialect, which sounded, according to one GI, like a combination of "bastard French, German, and Flemish."[8] The GI guides tried their best to demonstrate that many of the words used in Germany were similar to English since both languages had evolved from the same root. Nonfraternization, however, allowed little practice and local pronunciations obscured most similarities. Instead, the guttural sounds made German appear "terribly harsh and difficult." "Sounds to me," commented a combat engineer, "as if they just grunt & cough."[9] To complicate matters, signs and texts changed "from readable Belgian-French to the illegible German script." So unfamiliar were the Gothic characters to the Americans that medics who transcribed onto hospital tags the identification booklets of German wounded had to limit themselves to "an approximation" of their names.[10]

The hopelessly complicated communication with the European population formed a handicap even in the front lines. Paratroopers who landed in Normandy the night before D-Day, for instance, were often unsuccessful in obtaining assistance from the civilians not only because the locals were scared, but also because the GIs' knowledge and pronunciation of French was miserable. "No matter how hard I tried," said an exasperated paratrooper who asked for help from a farmer's wife at Foucarville, "I could not get her to understand that I wanted the direction to St. Come-du-Mont." The commander of the 506th Regiment unsuccessfully tried to convince a French family at a farm near Hiesville to let him in by yelling *Fermez la porte*!, while men of the 502nd Regiment who urgently needed horses and carts to transport their equipment asked a dumbfounded farmer for *chapeaux*.[11]

Language problems also added to the difficulties of combat soldiers who had to cooperate with the resistance. When the 378th Infantry Regiment started its drive on Metz in November 1944, the 3rd Battalion was joined by an FFI officer from the area. The Frenchman spoke no English, however, and it was only because one of the American officers happened to know French fairly well that the battalion was able to profit from the Frenchman's detailed knowledge of the terrain, which often influenced its plans of action. Units that lacked the appropriate linguistic talents were less fortunate. On approaching Saint-Malo, for instance, a battalion of the 329th Infantry Regiment hurriedly attempted to coordinate its activities with those of a local FFI unit. None of the allies, however, spoke the other's language. "We could each point at the map," remembered the battalion commander, "but that was all anyone could understand." Both units at last entered battle after an Italian-American officer had tried his best to ensure that both sides got things right. But language problems sometimes left soldiers and resistance fighters completely in the dark about each other's intentions. During a briefing on a dangerous attack toward the Siegfried Line in March 1945, most of the questions came from the anxious officers of a French unit. They were to cooperate with the 3rd Battalion of the 274th Infantry Regiment but had understood close to nothing of the arrangements, which had been made in English.[12] No wonder that language obstacles often prevented American soldiers and European resistance fighters from developing close ties and becoming true comrades-in-arms. A lieutenant of the 8th Infantry Division who fought side by side with an FFI unit in Brittany deplored this:

We regretted that language differences kept us from becoming genuinely acquainted with these men. We could indicate our friendship only by gestures, supplemented on occasion by a French word or phrase we had picked up.[13]

The GIs resorted to any means possible to communicate with the Europeans. Pretending to understand them was, of course, the easiest way. A corporal who was housed by a Dutch family in November 1944 wrote to his parents: "It takes all my prowess as an actor to seem to be listening intelligently, laughing wildly when a joke seems to be afoot."[14] Some tried to compensate the lack of foreign vocabulary by volume and liked to imagine they were conveying meaning by shouting in English.[15] Talking with hands and feet was another option. Soldiers of the 36th Infantry Division tried to obtain a mule from an old Italian woman in the vicinity of Monte Maggiore by clasping their hands and wiggling their fingers like the animal's ears, but they noticed that the grandmother only stared at them "as if she were suddenly facing escaped lunatics." The wordless mode of communication was more successful in Paris. Although the performances of the Folies-Bergère girls contained French dialogue, the GIs who visited the music hall enjoyed themselves tremendously. Many numbers, noticed a pleased officer, were "easy to understand" because they offered "a great deal of pantomime."[16] Still other soldiers literally had to make drawings to convey their intentions to the locals. A medic in Normandy, who was badly wounded and cut off from his unit, tried in vain to tell a nearby family to take a message to an American aid station. In desperation, he grabbed a medical tag and drew ambulances and tents with crosses; the sketch probably saved his life. More than anything else, however, music proved to be the universal language of nations. Soldiers of the 87th Infantry Division, quartered in Tillet right after the Battle of the Bulge, deeply regretted not being able to converse with the local girls. They decided to sing to each other in turn, and when they discovered there were songs they shared, the mood quickly improved as "Way Down upon the Swanee River" and "Alouette" resounded throughout the Belgian village. Likewise, a Kentuckian officer could hardly believe his ears when he heard children at Kerkrade sing "My Old Kentucky Home" in Dutch. Hymns too were shared on both sides of the ocean. Americans and Europeans hummed "Silent Night" in brotherly unison at Christmas, and throughout the year soldiers and civilians attended each other's services, singing the familiar religious songs in different languages to the same God.[17]

Americans who did not speak the language of the area they were operating in could only hope that communication would be facilitated by civilians who knew some English. And they were surprised to find that the knowledge of English was fairly widespread on the Continent. The Army guide told the soldiers that many Italians spoke English "in one degree or another," especially in urban areas and tourist centers. But even in the rural areas, particularly those of Sicily and southern Italy, so many locals had once lived in America that, at least according to Mauldin, "[e]very group of two or more had a member who spoke English, more or less."[18] In France, the Army guide predicted, large cities like Paris would have English-speaking storekeepers and government officials. Moreover, most French youngsters would know "a smattering of English" that they had learned in high school or picked up from American movies. In the Germanic parts of Europe, the inhabitants' knowledge of English increased noticeably. The Army booklet on Belgium mentioned that in most Flemish cities people understood English "fairly well." According to the soldiers, a surprising number of Luxembourgers had a good command of English, while in the Netherlands younger people spoke it "better in some cases than the G.I.'s." Many Germans too knew at least some English. So did the Austrians who, the Army guide pointed out, could learn the language in all of their secondary schools as well as in numerous commercial and language institutions.[19] The GIs noticed that many of the officers and the younger soldiers of the German army spoke English fluently. In fact, the English of some of them was so impeccable that they managed to lure Americans into ambushes with it. Line officers warned replacements who arrived at the front in northeastern France in September 1944 to check whether soldiers who had forgotten the password were truly Americans by listening whether they pronounced a w like a v, but veterans conceded that some enemy soldiers would not even make that mistake.[20]

On the other hand, American combat soldiers had become acquainted with non-English European languages at high school, some even in college. Yet the typical shortcomings of the often largely theoretical knowledge manifested themselves the moment the GIs set foot on the Continent. An officer of the 29th Infantry Division, for instance, who made determined efforts to gather information on German forces from an inhabitant at Louvières on 7 June 1944, discovered that this was all but impossible in an exchange of "mutually baffling Tennessee high school French and Norman country dialect."[21] Still more disappointing was the fact that even a thorough knowledge of one or more foreign languages did not guarantee communication in Europe. A college-educated sergeant from Pennsylvania, who spoke German fluently and French fairly well, had been looking forward to improving his language skills in the Old World; fate unfortunately sent him to Italy.

But the American troops possessed one important linguistic advantage: they came from a multi-ethnic society in which almost every imaginable language on earth was represented more or less. No matter what country the GIs found themselves in, therefore, they could almost always fall back on at least a few comrades within their unit who spoke the native language. In North Africa, for instance, and to an extent even in Italy and France, the Hispanics acted as interpreters for their comrades. The many Italian-Americans remembered their families' native tongue in varying degrees (in some units, recent immigrants barely spoke English) and were often instrumental in easing relations with the former enemies. GIs from the bayou lands of Louisiana or the New England regions bordering Quebec proved invaluable in the French-speaking parts of Europe, where the Dumas, Maunoirs, Parenteaus and LaVoies led the way for their buddies, albeit often in archaic speech. Americans managed to communicate with German POWs and civilians in Milwaukee dialects, New York Yiddish, or Pennsylvania Dutch. In addition, recent German immigrants who had fled the Nazi regime served in several American combat units. That they knew their native language better than English could at times lead to absurd situations. When on the night of 5 June 1944 a paratrooper challenged his sergeant in Normandy, the NCO – who was a refugee Austrian Jew – froze and instinctively yelled *Kamerad!* rather than the password. More often, however, the language skills of recent immigrants were put to good use. American soldiers of German, Polish, and Russian origin cajoled the enemy into surrendering, lured him into ambushes, or extracted valuable information before sending him to the rear. The interpreters also smoothed relations with the civilian population, and GIs often were fortunate enough to find a comrade who spoke not only the language of the country but even the dialect of a specific region.[22]

The knowledge of languages was one of the few status symbols left to the combat soldiers. Rank did not buy safety up front, and money no luxuries, but being able to converse with the local population made for easier access to food, alcohol and, most importantly, women. Soldiers who spoke the language of the area therefore inevitably became the mouthpieces of their unit. Comrades constantly besieged them with requests that ranged from asking directions to translating the obscene jokes and lewd propositions that were shouted at female bystanders. The interpreters' aid was rewarded with popularity as well as alcohol and cigarettes.[23] When their linguistic skills became useless in a new country, however, their status plummeted as if they had suddenly lost a magical power. "[W]e've been riding him about losing his touch since we got into territory where his French doesn't count," a combat engineer said gleefully of a Cajun comrade. "He knows about ten words of German just like the rest of us."[24]

Some GIs literally saved themselves from potential death or mutilation at the front with their language talents. The 141st Infantry Regiment, for instance, nominated one of its lieutenants for the position of aide-de-camp to Robert I. Stack, brigadier general of the 36th Infantry Division in Italy. The lieutenant had just lived through the battle of Cassino and prayed that he would get the job. The interview did not go well, however, until he mentioned to Stack that he spoke French. Since the division was slated to be sent to France soon, Stack gave him the job and the relieved lieutenant spent the remainder of the war in relative safety. Divisions normally arrived at the front with interpreters,[25] but as casualties rose and needs increased, linguistic replacements and reinforcements sometimes had to be sought among the frontline men. So it could happen that in the middle of the furious battle of Mortain in August 1944, a German-born private of the 30th Infantry Division was withdrawn from the front because he was urgently needed as a battalion interpreter for the POWs. In the European war zone, the gift of tongues could mean the gift of life.[26]

The GIs en masse awoke to the importance of knowing languages. Some wrote to former teachers to thank them for their linguistic skills. Others blamed themselves for having neglected foreign languages and made resolutions to attend classes after the war while encouraging family and friends in America to take up linguistic study without further delay.[27] A few even envisioned ambitious plans for the future in which languages played a key role. One corporal put his hopes on the kind of internationalism taught by an educational system "that would require at least one language other than his own as the minimum for a responsible adult." Likewise, after having discovered in France that language was "such an important factor in mixing with people," a medic wanted "to see a universal language taught in every school in every country, along with the native language."[28]

Meanwhile, the GIs in Europe took to studying languages diligently whenever time permitted. Several soldiers had looked ahead and carried pocket dictionaries with them on their trip to Europe, sometimes French ones that had already been thumbed by veterans of the Great War. Soldiers took basic lessons in French on board some of the ships heading for North Africa. Here and there, GIs in England reviewed some French in the weeks before the invasion; paratroopers of the 101st Airborne Division learned certain French phrases by heart before jumping into Normandy. From countries where common languages like French and German were spoken, GIs sent requests to their families for pocket-sized dictionaries and textbooks. Others searched houses for such linguistic aids, although in Germany they rarely proved useful since they were printed in Gothic type. Many also studied vocabulary and phrases from the US Army guides to the different countries of Europe. Enterprising civilians, on the other hand, sensed a new market and offered language courses to eager GIs. They ranged from evening classes at 20 cents an hour by French locals in North Africa to basic introductions to Italian by young camp followers at replacement depots near Naples.[29]

Gradually, foreign words and expressions seeped into the GIs' speech and writing. Each country added new words to the soldiers' vocabulary. Letters from England commenced or closed with "Cheerio." Among the first French words the Americans picked up in North Africa were "allay," used to chase away obtrusive beggars, and "to parleyvoo," which meant: to speak French (by extension, a Frenchman was sometimes called "a Parleyvoo"). In continental France, *C'est la guerre* became the universal expression of GI resignedness. The Americans also snapped up *Boche*, the favorite French slang term for German. For some inexplicable reason, however, mundane *beaucoup* became the most fashionable French word among the American soldiers. It caught on early in the war. A soldier of the 1st Armored Division, who had fought in French North Africa, wrote to his parents from the Anzio beachhead early in 1944: "We lost Bou Coup!"[30] In the course of the French campaign, the GIs all but lost the ability to construct an English sentence without the word. A lieutenant who arrived as a replacement for a rifle company of the 9th Infantry Division late in July 1944 described his first briefing:

> This meeting was my first exposure to the word "BEAUCOUP." There were beaucoup Germans, beaucoup planes, beaucoup artillery, beaucoup tanks, and beaucoup miles. I got the drift that it meant many but I was not about to ask for a definition.[31]

Dealings with enemy soldiers and nonfraternization with the civilians limited the active usage of German among the combat soldiers to a few words and a series of commands. "About the only German we know," a sergeant noted in his journal in April 1945, "is *Ja, Hande Hoche, Raus* & we've kidded around with *Verboten & Achtung.*"[32] Other favorite borrowed shouts were *Waffen Nieder!*, *Kommen Sie Hier!*, and *Macht Schnell!* Yet *Kaput* became by far the most popular German word, no doubt because the GIs thought it best captured the essence of Europe's condition. Soldiers learned key German phrases from instructors during training in England, from army publications such as *Stars and Stripes* and *Yank*, and, late in the war, from pamphlets issued on board troopships. Pronunciation, however, often remained unpolished. Soldiers of the 90th Infantry Division who were engaged in street fighting at Dillingen kicked in doors yelling "Handy-ho!," their best approximation of *Hände Hoch!* [33] Toward the end of the war, the GIs' knowledge of foreign words became a rather exotic mélange. American soldiers used dialectic phrases and regional accents that betrayed where they had campaigned. For some concepts they had learned the entire European terminology. They referred to women, for example, as colleens, lassies, *mademoiselles*, and *Fräuleins*. The GIs ended up combining different languages indiscriminately. A medic in the Bitche sector, who had spent months in the Vosges, caught himself mixing French and German when he realized civilians were laughing at expressions of his such as "tres goot." On 8 May 1945, a huge headline in the newssheet of the 5th Infantry Division announced the end of the European war. It exclaimed: "BOCHE KAPUT!"[34]

The GIs loved to show off at home with the foreign languages they picked up, no matter how meager their vocabulary. They opened letters with "En France" or "Dear Mooter unt Fatter." They ended them with "à plus tard" or "c'est tout." In Lorraine, a private concluded a letter to his parents by signing "Franksois" instead of Franklin.[35] With some help from the Luxembourg family he was staying with at Bettembourg, a medic from Chicago told his wife: "Je vais acheter cadeau pour ma femme er me petite fille." "A little more of this," he added jokingly, "and I shall become a cosmopolitan European."[36]

THE QUEST FOR FOOD

Most American combat soldiers were not attracted to the Europeans because of their cosmopolitanism; they sought contact with them merely to satisfy primary needs. Food was the first concern that drove them to the civilians. Living outdoors and performing hard physical labor almost constantly, young soldiers burned calories at a furious pace. Moreover, eating was one of the few pleasures left to the men at the front. Sharing meals with buddies took their minds off the horror for a while and relieved some of the tension. "It was funny how big a deal chow was up here – even K-rations," observed a private who arrived at the Maginot front as a replacement in September 1944. "Eating was something you looked forward to, the big events of the day." When danger did not preoccupy the soldiers, food was always on their minds. "It was like traveling with your thirty children," a lieutenant said of the constant complaints of hunger from his platoon.[37] Even in their dreams, GIs were plagued by culinary cravings. Early in January 1945, a corporal wrote from Belgium to his parents that although it was unusual for him to remember a dream, a recent one remained before his eyes all too vividly:

> hundreds of guests in an unparalleled hall of utter magnificence, and food such as I (nor anyone) has ever seen. Steaks as large as door mats on silver platters at every place. White capped cooks beaming as they carried trays with four foot lobsters on them and stewards pouring fine, chilled wines.[38]

On the eve of battle, American combat soldiers often received excellent meals, as if they were "being fattened for the slaughter." During the last days before the invasion of Normandy, paratroopers in England could choose from luxuries such as steak, fried chicken, white bread and butter, fruit cocktail, ice cream, and coffee in unlimited quantities. Photographer Robert Capa noticed how mess boys on the USS *Chase* served tasty hot breakfasts "with unusual zest and politeness" to soldiers of the 1st Infantry Division who were about to land on Omaha beach as the first wave.[39] Soldiers quickly learned that an attack was in the wind when food improved substantially and that exceptional meals were often followed by new field orders. "And the condemned man," wrote a paratrooper of the last hours before takeoff for Operation Market-Garden, "ate a hearty meal."[40]

The whirlwind of combat, however, did not always allow the army to continue supplying the men in the front lines with food that was comparable in quality and quantity to that offered to the GIs in the rear. The availability in the European war zone of brand-name delicacies like Coca-Cola was much publicized, but the bottles were rarities in the front lines. The army prided itself on providing all troops overseas with traditional Thanksgiving dinners in November, but from North Africa to the Alsace combat soldiers complained they did not see proof of that. The army made earnest efforts to offer kitchen-prepared meals to all soldiers as regularly as possible. B rations were issued by field kitchens behind the combat lines and sometimes even at the front, but even these did not contain fresh foodstuffs: meats and fruits were canned; vegetables, eggs, and milk were dehydrated.[41]

Much worse was, of course, that frontline conditions often forced the soldiers to do without any B rations whatsoever and to live on packaged operational rations for extended periods. The GIs utterly detested the British ones, on which they relied heavily in North Africa (and the paratroopers again during Operation Market-Garden). A medic of the 34th Infantry Division, who had been eating them for a month in the French colonies, summed up what was wrong with them:

> Breakfast, stewed steak, tea and kidney pudding. Dinner, cold corned beef or salmon or sardines. Supper, vegetable stew and tea. With all these meals we have what the British call biscuits, but what is in plain words hard tack.

It "will support life," grumbled a paratrooper in Holland, "but not morale."[42] The US Army spent a considerable amount of time and energy on the development of its own packaged rations to ensure that they would be both healthy and tasty. The ten-in-one ration was intended for group feeding in combat situations that allowed a minimum of food preparation. The GIs liked them better than any other rations because they contained such frontline delicacies as canned milk, sweet corn, bacon, and sausages. But their weight – 45 pounds per cardboard box – often prevented the infantrymen from carrying these rations, while the tank crews gratefully hoarded them. The C ration was issued as an individual ration in the combat zone. One of its two units contained a 12-ounce can with meat and vegetables. It could be any of four varieties: beef stew, pork and beans, meat hash, or spaghetti. The other unit offered biscuits, coffee, and sweets. The C ration was not to be issued for more than 72 hours in a row. In reality, however, the GIs at the front often lived on them for drawn-out periods, sometimes as long as three months. As a result, many combat soldiers complained about the lack of variety (they especially disliked the hash, stew, and biscuits). In some cases, the prolonged diets of C rations led to vitamin deficiency and nausea. During actual fighting, the Americans subsisted on K rations. They were composed of flat cans with meat, eggs, and cheese as well as biscuits, fruit and chocolate bars, bouillon, coffee, and sugar. All troops disliked the K rations and many GIs upset the nutritional balance of the packages by consuming only what they liked, which was mostly the coffee, the chocolate, and the crackers. Finally, for stopgap use in emergency situations, the soldiers could fall back on D rations. They were nothing more than chocolate bars enriched with vitamin B1 and most soldiers preferred to eat them in between regular rations. They tended to make the men thirsty, however, and in some cases also caused nausea.[43]

The field rations had been developed with the express purpose of preventing the GIs from living off the land. Both in the MTO and ETO the US Army therefore admonished its soldiers in stern terms not to forage among the civilians. It told them that the Europeans could not afford this, and that additional strains on military supply lines as well as epidemics would result, eventually endangering the American troops themselves. But, after months of campaigning, the combat soldiers often craved more and better food than that of the field rations. In a survey of the infantrymen of four divisions in Italy in April 1945, over half the men claimed they had not eaten as much as they needed the last time they had been on active combat duty. Twenty-two per cent stated the reason was that they had not been able to obtain the food, another 30 per cent that they had not liked the available food. As a result, combat soldiers generally ignored the prohibitions on foraging, while their company officers looked the other way.[44]

Mostly, the GIs were driven to foraging among the civilians to obtain the kinds of food they lacked in their diet. One of the foods the combat soldiers soon craved, for instance, was chewy meat instead of the greasy, glue-like substances of the C and K rations that to some looked like "dog food." It was not easy to find because the German soldiers craved it too and in many cases had taken cows and pigs from the farms before retreating. But American combat soldiers were nothing if not resourceful. They fished in streams and ponds with hand grenades and TNT. They hunted deer. They combed fields and abandoned farms for cows, pigs, chickens, and goats. Former butchers, cooks, and farmboys performed the slaughtering and dressing. Soldiers tied skinned carcasses to tree branches and covered them with ponchos, roasted slabs of meat over open fires in foxholes, stewed them in helmets, or fried them in shaving cream for lack of butter. The GIs became willing to take culinary risks to taste chunky meat again. Americans, many of whom at first thought it strange that Europeans ate rabbit meat, were soon plundering the cages and hunting the animals themselves.[45] Some lost all qualms about cutting steaks from cows that had already been dead for a while. "[A]s long as they don't stink," argued a sergeant near Carentan, "I don't mind. It's still beef."[46] In the Hürtgen Forest, GIs even resorted to eating meat from dead horses. At times, the American appetite for meat was responsible for friction with the Europeans. GIs at a bivouac near Newcastle all but caused a diplomatic incident when they ate the Royal Swans of the king's summer palace. Livestock had become extremely precious to the people on the Continent, and the GIs tended to forget that the civilians craved meat even more than they did. Despite the excellent relations between the paratroopers and the Dutch during Operation Market-Garden, the inhabitants of Nijmegen were forced to complain to the American military authorities because the looting of chickens, pigs, and cows was getting out of hand.[47]

More and more, fresh foodstuffs were like "nectar and ambrosia" to the frontline men.[48] Starved of fresh vegetables, GIs invaded fields to pluck ears of corn and occupied gardens to harvest carrots and tomatoes. Without paying much attention to the stunned French bystanders, Japanese-American soldiers who emerged from the Vosges forests to liberate Biffontaine rushed into the fields, where they dug up fresh cabbages and began to munch them greedily. Americans scoured the countryside for onions and potatoes in particular, because the former added much needed flavor to the rations, the latter substance. At the Maginot Line in September 1944, combat soldiers scouted fields for them on their bellies, digging them up with entrenching shovels, using their helmets as baskets. Fresh fruit became another delicacy. Although the Germans had a habit of booby-trapping orchards, American soldiers could not resist the temptation of picking fruit that was often only destined to rot. They gorged themselves with oranges in North Africa, lemons and melons in Sicily, grapes and figs in Italy. In the Mediterranean, the incidence of diarrhea among the GIs each year rose sharply during the fresh fruit season. In June of 1944, the soldiers in Normandy regretted that the innumerable apples were still too green to add taste to the rations. But a few months later, shell blasts shook ripe fruit from trees all over Western Europe. The GIs descended on it like locusts. They made sauce from the small, sour cider apples of France and stuffed themselves with the large, sweet table fruit of the Low Countries. During the wintertime, soldiers searched cellars for jars with preserves and saturated themselves with sweet and sour cherries. Men of the 1st Infantry Division who took a jam factory at Aachen shot holes in the juice barrels and drank all they could. Only an outbreak of diarrhea was able to halt the orgy.[49]

Fresh bread also was rare up front. Early in February 1945, the newssheet of the 399th Infantry Regiment proudly announced that the unit's bakeshop had turned out 2,690 breadrolls, 3,090 sugar cookies, 1,324 apple turnovers, 1,930 chocolate cakes, and 800 chocolate drops for the men in the foxholes. "All of which sounds fine indeed except that we haven't tasted any yet," one of the regiment's privates told his parents with indignation.

> It's like the ARC [American Red Cross] gals who turn out endless lines of delicious doughfeet doughnuts which are intercepted at Division HQ and used to plumpen up white collar boys in the rear.[50]

Most of the time, the combat soldiers were condemned to chewing on "poison-tasting" crackers and biscuits that were not "fit to feed the A-rabs." When a loaf of white bread did reach the men now and then, they thought it tasted "like cake."[51] The GIs were eager to barter with the civilians for any kind of freshly baked bread, from baguettes to pumpernickel. They did not even mind that some of the local ersatz bread tasted as if it was made with sawdust. When the 760th Tank Battalion was withdrawn from the Cassino front in February 1944 for a few days of rest and maintenance near Monte Porchia, the men scrounged several sacks of flour and implored some civilians to prepare for them the rare treat of fresh bread.[52]

The US Army also failed to satisfy the American appetite for eggs with its powdered variety. "Right now," a soldier wrote from Italy in the fall of 1944, "I'd give $10.00 for just one." Throughout the European campaign, the GIs bought, bartered, and stole eggs at a furious pace. A sergeant jotted in his journal in September 1944: "We know about a dozen words of French between us, but 'erfs' is one we learned very early."[53] While on the move, Americans punctured eggs with their trench knives and drank them raw or stuffed them in pockets and hid them under helmets until they had time to prepare them. Once they had entered Germany, the GIs could search for eggs unabashedly. They plundered crocks with brine, forced German civilians to fry eggs for immediate consumption, or ordered them to boil them so that they could be transported. In one German town in April 1945, men of the 87th Infantry Division broke into chicken coops, banged on doors with rifle butts, and demanded eggs at gunpoint.[54]

After months and years of powdered or, at best, canned milk, combat soldiers griped that they could hardly remember the taste of fresh milk. "I would give a month's pay for a glass of milk," a private in Italy complained in the winter of 1945.[55] The US Army warned its soldiers not to drink milk obtained from civilians without at least boiling it or adding purifying pills.[56] But the men did not always heed that warning in their eagerness to drink "real" milk. A private of the 26th Infantry Division who found a pail of milk "of unknown age" in a German farmhouse, simply brushed away the yellow scum and gulped down the rest. "I felt the possible nutrition was more important than the sour taste," he explained.[57] GIs cornered cows ·

at each opportunity and farmboys who knew how to milk them – using helmets as buckets – became popular members in each unit. At the front near Cassino, a lonely cow was unfortunate enough to wander into the zone of the 34th Infantry Division. "[T]he poor thing," a soldier observed, "was milked five times between noon and supper time."[58]

The Americans had a particular passion for ice cream. At the front, even a GI who had never much cared about it admitted he craved some "because we get so little in the way of sweet things."[59] In many parts of Europe, however, the luxury had disappeared. On 4 June 1944, paratroopers of the 506th Regiment received an outstanding meal that included ice cream. The men were so surprised – they had not seen the delicacy since they had arrived in England nine months earlier – that the word quickly spread: "When you get ice cream for supper, you know that's the night."[60] Strange as it seemed, on the Continent the treat sometimes was still available, albeit only as watered-down "pseudo ice-cream." The Italians, for instance, had invented ice cream, and it showed. "If there was a place that was open, they would have some kind of ice cream," one GI remembered fondly. For the 4th Ranger Battalion it was "the morale clincher of the Sicilian campaign" when some of its men returned from Palermo with a truckload of the sugared cream.[61] Belgium was another country where the production of ice cream had not slowed down, a fact that added much to the overall impression of the people's hospitality. Cheerful civilians handed cones and sandwiches to the GIs while they raced through their country in September 1944, and even in the tiniest villages there were ice cream parlors that attracted lines of olive drab during rest periods.[62] In the wintertime, soldiers concocted ice cream by mixing snow with sugar and cocoa or lemon powder from their rations or, when they were lucky, with canned milk and vanilla extract from the mess tent.[63]

When the GIs moved out of a town, they took as much of the foraged food with them as they could carry. They packed boiled eggs, for instance, or rabbit meat they had smoked. Soldiers of the 84th Infantry Division, readying themselves at Grandmenil for the Allied counteroffensive early in January 1945, took time out to butcher and clean a Belgian pig and roped the hindquarters to their packs before jumping off. But these reserves of fresh food never lasted long, and time and again the GIs had to turn to the civilians to replenish them.[64]

The Europeans quickly understood that the best way to show their gratitude to the liberators was to give them food as they marched or drove by. While in pursuit of the enemy, the GIs thus received apples, eggs, onions, sugar, waffles, and even baked chickens from exuberant civilians. In the outskirts of Rome early in June 1944, soldiers of the 88th Infantry Division, about to take the city, passed through a group of some 40 women who silently and hurriedly labored to provide as many GIs as possible with wine, bread, and spaghetti without forcing them to slow down for even one minute. Only in Germany did the Americans sometimes refuse to accept gifts of food for fear of poisoning.[65]

But food had become too precious in wartime Europe for people to give away in large quantities. Here and there, civilians decided to sell food to the GIs for money. In Italy, for instance, poor farmers erected crude stands on the main roads leading to the front and peddled sugared almonds and walnut fig bars for small change. More often, however, the Europeans were not interested in money and preferred to barter. The American authorities in Great Britain, for instance, issued "hospitality rations" to GIs who accepted civilian invitations for meals. The system permitted the soldiers to enjoy homemade dinners in family circles without putting a strain on British food reserves, while it allowed their hosts to taste wartime delicacies, such as coffee, sugar, and canned fruit. Barter continued unabated at the front. GIs in North Africa traded the hated British rations for eggs, chickens, dates, and tangerines with the Arabs. The Europeans gladly accepted the American C and K rations that the soldiers were equally glad to trade for fresh food whenever possible. GIs on their way from Brittany to the Belgian front in September 1944 even used train stops to barter rations for eggs, bread, and wine.[66] "It's funny," Mauldin said, "to watch a civilian, sick of his potato soup, brown bread, and red wine, wolf one of those horrible K rations as eagerly as the soldier tears into the soup and bread and wine."[67] The Europeans gobbled the rations' beef stew and meat hash, savored the chewing gum and candy, and were fascinated by the instant coffee, dried bouillon, and lemon powder.[68] But, apart from cigarettes, nothing represented more buying power in the wrecked European economies than the rations' chocolate. One private claimed that in the Old World a chocolate bar was "like a fur coat in America."[69] As time went by, however, the civilians too lost their appetite for the army rations. Fortunately, the well-equipped American soldiers had dozens of other items to offer to the impoverished Europeans in exchange for more and better food. Cigarettes constituted the combat soldiers' new currency and could be used to buy almost anything that was available in the Old World. After the Battle of the Bulge, for instance, men of the 84th Infantry Division worked out an exchange rate with Belgian housewives during a rest period at Nonceveux: one warm apple pie, without sugar, for one pack of cigarettes. US Army clothing also was a prized item. In North Africa, Arabs fought over olive drabs, and an old pair of army shoes could fetch as much as 40 eggs. But from Normandy too a lieutenant wrote to his mother that a farmboy brought him fresh milk every day in return for K rations and a discarded pair of shoes. Medics in an ambulance platoon of the 1st Armored Division thought nothing of bartering blankets for food with Italians during the winter of 1945.[70] "In a war-torn country nobody refuses anything offered," noted a GI in a training camp near Naples. "Even G.I. contraceptives have become a shameless medium of exchange."[71]

The American soldiers discovered, however, that the Europeans often simply did not have enough food either to sell or barter. The Army guides warned the GIs not to be fooled by British hospitality when invited to the dinner table. They told them not to accept "too many helpings" in Northern Ireland, to "go easy" on food in England, and always to keep in mind that what British housewives seemingly casually offered as a meal could well be the family's ration for an entire week.[72]

On the Continent, local requisition of most foodstuffs was prohibited by the US Army and the purchase of food in restaurants expressly forbidden. Hunger was most prevalent in the cities because wrecked railroads and shortages of coal and gasoline prevented the shipment of foodstuffs from areas of surplus. But in the countryside too the food situation could be precarious as farmers had often not been able to sow or harvest. Children across Italy waited patiently, with small pails in hand, for GIs to finish their meals and give them the scraps. They never touched the food they received, but carefully took it home for their families. In France, the memory of the famous Parisian chefs soon faded among the GIs. The Army guide informed the soldiers that the average French adult had lost 40 pounds as a result of the Nazi occupation. During the liberation, food shortages overshadowed all others in a country that had been nearly 90 per cent self-sufficient before the war. French children too gathered around garbage pits to beg the Americans for their leftovers, and officers quite often had to stop their men from giving them entire meals instead of scraps. Lack of transportation had made food shortages particularly acute in some areas of France. In the Riviera, for instance, the GIs were told in no uncertain terms to live on their rations only. Americans in the Vosges claimed that the locals were actually willing to pay for army rations.[73] "In Marseille they ate only bread & grapes," observed a private. "Here they haven't seen bread in 4 years."[74] Although the GIs found the people of Belgium and Luxembourg comparatively well off in terms of food, they noticed that the civilians there were not ashamed either of lining up for mess-kit scraps after years of rationing, ersatz products, and black-market prices.[75] Most of the Netherlands remained occupied by the Germans until the end of the war, and the Americans could not see past the effects of the atrocious Dutch "hunger winter" of 1944–45 in the liberated southern parts of the country either. The GI guide to Holland reminded the soldiers that the Dutch people had eaten "excellent food and a great deal of it" before the war, and it listed some of their delicious gastronomical specialties such as crêpes or pea soup with sausage. But in December 1944 a corporal noted that there were "only two things in plenty – hard, black bread and apples." By March 1945, an officer in Venlo witnessed how both Dutch adults and children rushed at GI containers with leftovers "like I used to see the hogs run for the garbage when I was back on the farm."[76]

European deprivation eventually forced many GIs to turn to the home front for more and better food than they could find in their rations. Because of chronic shipping shortages, American postal services required evidence of a serviceman's request for a package. As a result, the GIs regularly put postscripts in their letters with detailed descriptions of the kinds of food they wanted their families to mail to them. They stressed they should send only small packages because they had to throw away what they could not carry or immediately eat, and asked them to include only food that did not spoil easily such as canned products, dried fruits, and hard candy. They begged their families to be sure not to mail anything that resembled what was in the rations: no crackers, no Spam, not even Life Savers. Although restrained by rationing practices themselves, relatives and friends in America were able to ship tons of food products to their boys in the front lines of the kind to make European mouths water: from sausage and fried chicken to sardines, from tomato juice to soups, from apricots and grapefruit juice to honey and jellies, and from doughnuts and fruitcakes to Aunt Jemima pancake flour. The combat soldiers craved sweets more than anything else and so their families also sent them Three Musketeers, Babe Ruths, marshmallows, Hershey silver bells, and chocolate-covered peanuts.[77] When reminded of the endless stores of goods at home, the GIs could afford to become choosers again. "I prefer Alice Marks to Schrafft's," a corporal hinted when petitioning his family for more candy.[78] Some of the American food parcels that arrived amidst European want contained nothing less than delicacies such as canned oysters, lobster paste, and caviar.[79]

THE NEED FOR TOBACCO AND ALCOHOL

Smoking had been very popular in America before the war. The average family had spent no less than $70 a year on cigarettes in the 1930s. Lack of recreational opportunities as well as emotional stress made smoking an even more widespread and persistent vice among America's combat soldiers, and many of those who had never before tasted a cigarette picked up the habit at the front. American cigarettes soon flooded the European war theaters. Fresh troops who arrived at Le Havre went first to the nearby "Cigarette Camps," large tent areas named after popular American brands such as Chesterfield and Lucky Strike. Cartons were cheap in PX stores across Europe, and cigarettes were a standard item in the GI field rations. To the Europeans, American tobacco proved a godsend after years of inhaling vile-tasting ersatz concoctions. From the outset, the US Army was aware of the value of tobacco in dealing with the civilian population. Soldiers of the 9th Infantry Division, for instance, received two cartons each before wading ashore in Algeria in November 1942 with strict orders not to smoke them but to hand them out to the civilians as a gesture of goodwill.[80] Cigarettes quickly became more valuable in war-torn Europe than money, and the civilians preferred the American ones to those of the British soldiers, which according to GIs who had tried them contained "a small portion of tobacco and an ungodly amount of straw."[81] Whereas the American brand with the minarets and camels was all the rage in French North Africa, in Europe people scrambled for any kind of tobacco the GIs flaunted.[82] Paratroopers who arrived in Belfast in September 1943 threw packs of cigarettes from their ship and watched how Irish dockworkers "were scooping them up as fast as they hit."[83] A year later, an amazed private reported from Marseilles that Frenchmen were willing to pay 50 francs for a pack of cigarettes that Americans could buy from the army for three francs. Across Europe, the GIs witnessed with even more amazement how young and old and both men and women searched the ground for butts and then rolled new cigarettes from the American tobacco leftovers.[84]

If the US Army had to ship its own tobacco to the war theaters because it was so scarce, it regretted that its soldiers were able to find intoxicating substances rather easily in Europe. Apart from the fairly common use of marihuana and the occasional abuse of amobarbital pills (known by the soldiers as "blue 88s" and normally used to treat combat fatigue) or morphine (available, for instance, in medics' first-aid kits), drugs did not constitute much of a problem during World War II. Alcohol, however, was readily available in the Old World and eagerly consumed by the American combat soldiers.[85]

First of all, soldiers quite often resorted to drinking alcohol at the front for the most practical of reasons: potable water was not always available. That was certainly the case in Italy. The Army guide warned the GIs that during the summer water was so scarce in some parts of the country that the peasants did not have enough to drink. In the North African djebels, the Americans had already learned how hard it was to maintain adequate supplies of water, and things did not improve in the mountains of Italy. Water had to be carried up steep slopes on the backs of mules and men and only reached the soldiers in driblets. GIs therefore tried to quench their thirst by catching rain in helmets and shelter halves or by filling their canteens with snow. Mauldin made his famous, disheveled characters – Willie and Joe – stop shaving during the winter of 1943, when the 45th Infantry Division to which he belonged was clinging to the mountains of Cassino, near Venafro, and did not even receive enough water to drink. On the other side of the Alps, water was not always available in abundant quantities either. During the first days of the Norman invasion, it was so scarce that a medic on Utah beach was chewed out for sharing some from his own canteen with a wounded German.[86] After the breakout, troops often moved so fast that water supplies could not catch up with them. In August 1944, for instance, a soldier of the lightning 30th Infantry Division was forced to shave with cider and when, on a particularly hot day, he made the mistake of drinking calvados, the Norman apple brandy, "like water," his thirst was so unbearable the morning after that he "licked the dew off the leaves of the bushes."[87] In ruined cities where underground pipes had been destroyed, water was not easy to get either. During the fighting in Saarlautern in February 1945, men of the 328th Infantry Regiment could count on receiving only one canteen of water a day.[88]

Europe's public sources of water often offered no solution. Pumps, wells, and fountains abounded in the Old World and chic spas boasted mineral springs that had healed the sick for thousands of years. But the Army guides warned the Americans to stay away from that water if they preferred to remain healthy. In Italy they told the GIs to avoid public drinking fountains because "what is potable water to the average Italian citizen is not necessarily so to the American soldier." Still according to the GI guidebooks, water supplies in most other European countries were "generally safe" in the cities, but were "less reliable" in rural areas, largely because of "unsatisfactory" sewage disposal.[89] But even water that had been safe in Europe before the war could sometimes no longer be trusted. So many cities had been disrupted that a soldier of the 28th Infantry Division grew convinced that "a city water system such as ours is practically unheard of on the continent."[90] Moreover, in rural areas German troops occasionally contaminated drinking wells on purpose. The Army guides also instructed the GIs not to drink from Europe's rivers or streams under any circumstance. Giving in to that temptation was always dangerous. Only after they had already been consuming water from a spring at Caumont for quite a while in June 1944, for example, did men from the 26th Infantry Regiment discover two dead Germans up stream.[91]

The GIs were urged to drink only chlorinated water from US Army lister bags or five-gallon cans. When that was not possible, they had to boil the water or at least add purifying halazone tablets to it. Water that was safe thus often acquired a horrible taste. Not only was canteen water tepid to "piss warm" in the summer, it also had a strong chlorine flavor regardless of the season. In some places GIs even resorted to drinking water from canals and sewers that they treated with halazone tablets. The lemonade powder that came with the K rations for the purpose of flavoring water unfortunately proved to be one of the most unpopular ration items of the war, and the GIs soon turned to the home front for other flavoring extracts.[92]

As a result of all this, however, the GIs also turned to other beverages. The GI guides, for instance, advised the soldiers to look for bottled mineral water in the cities. During the battle for Dillingen, in the Saar bridgehead, thirsty Americans resorted to drinking the juice of cherry preserves stored in German cellars. But most GIs found alcohol the more acceptable alternative to water. When paratroopers of the 101st Airborne Division seemed likely to run out of water soon after their landing in Normandy, they simply switched to drinking cider.[93] Throughout the war, water shortages formed the perfect excuse for GIs to justify drinking alcohol. "Couldn't get decent water for awhile," a soldier in Germany told his parents in April 1945, "so wet my whistle with wine and champagne." In the Old World, alcohol thus seemed to be nothing more than a sophisticated form of chlorinated water. Since Parisian water was not very good, for example, even the US Army guide itself guessed that the Americans would "follow the native custom of calling the wine waiter."[94]

Drinking, Bill Mauldin admitted, was "a big thing in a dogface's life."[95] That was, of course, not only so because the quality of Europe's water was questionable. To begin with, a few GIs inevitably brought the habit with them from home. One soldier of the newly arrived 94th Infantry Division at the Lorient front turned out to be such an alcoholic that his comrades had to ration him to one cup of cider a day to prevent him from endangering the squad. But the large majority of combat soldiers took to drinking in Europe under pressure of the harsh conditions of war. During rest periods, men drank because they were bored and homesick. At the front, they drank to suppress fear, to ward off the cold, and to chase away fatigue. Surgeons of the 326th Airborne Medical Company landed in Normandy with 92 quarts of whiskey on the night of 5 June 1944. They claimed that the alcohol kept them operating at Colombières without a rest until the 7th or 8th. In battle, men drank to calm their nerves and to ease the pain. General McAuliffe wanted the wounded in besieged Bastogne to receive "booze for comfort," and he made sure that anything alcoholic, even crème de menthe, was distributed.[96] Most of all, however, combat soldiers drank to forget. And it took more than a few drinks to drown the memories of hunger and trench feet, of close calls and narrow escapes, of murdered friends, mutilated enemies, and butchered civilians. A few days after the capture of Saint-Lô's moonscape, a combat engineer wrote in his journal: "This is not social drinking we do. You belt it down fast & get your jolt fast."[97]

But the American soldiers could not expect much alcoholic solace from their military. Some GIs complained bitterly about the moral crusaders at home who had made it impossible for their army to make the issue of liquor rations at the front official policy. "Drinking, like sex, is not a question of should or shouldn't in the army," Mauldin argued.

> It's here to stay, and it seems to us here that the best way to handle it is to understand and recognize it, and to arrange things so those who have appetites can satisfy them with a minimum of trouble for everybody."

He regretted very much that such an arrangement seemed highly unlikely for the American troops "only because the home folks would scream their heads off at any hint of the clean-cut lads overseas besotting themselves." Mauldin pointed out that the Europeans were much more pragmatic regarding alcohol and made no bones about issuing liquor rations because they had more than once observed "war and armies at first hand."[98] It was indeed quite a sensation for GIs who were attached to British troops in North Africa to line up for the rum ration in the morning or to receive a daily beer allotment in the hospitals. To be sure, as the American troops marched across the Continent and captured ever larger caches of German liquor, their army too started distributing alcohol rations among the line companies. These rations, however, were intended for the units' officers only, and they received no more than about a bottle of liquor per month so that, if they decided to share it with their men, hardly anyone had a chance to get intoxicated. It was rare for enlisted men to receive liquor from army sources. At times, PX rations could contain a few bottles of beer. And around Christmas 1944, for instance, men of the 95th Infantry Division, in reserve at Hargarten, received champagne from a warehouse cache at Metz, compliments of general Patton. But GIs who wanted a more serious consolation from alcohol had to look for liquor elsewhere.[99]

They did not have to look far in an Old World that appeared to be the victim of a conspiracy of wets. "While there are temperance advocates and a few prohibitionists in Ireland," the GI guide to the emerald island commented dryly, "you won't see much of them." Europe's liberal stance on alcohol was a revelation to men from a country that had abolished nationwide prohibition only a decade ago. The guidebooks had to teach the Americans that Europe's pubs, taverns, public houses, and cafés were "much more and much less than a bar:" they were neighborhood gathering places, social centers, and reading rooms. The Army booklets also had to discourage the GIs from trying to compete in consuming alcohol with the English or the French, who were respectively said to drink beer and wine like water.[100] In the Old World, the GIs did not even have to search for alcohol. Wherever they passed on the Continent, Europeans flooded their liberators with liquor. In Normandy, people stood in the streets with pitchers and glasses to serve cider; from Marseilles to the Vosges, wine appeared to be the civilians' chief means of exchange; in the Walloons, Belgians gave away wine and champagne by the bottle; in Holland, bartenders handed out glasses of beer to paratroopers who had landed only hours ago. Such receptions did not always remain without consequences. Both at Ferryville, Tunisia, and Lucca, Italy, a private of the 1st Armored Division mentioned in his diary that men of his unit had become seriously drunk as a result of having been unable to refuse drinks from civilians. Officers tried to keep their men moving. In Algeria, an infuriated company commander of the Big Red One forced a medic to dig a hole in front of his comrades and to empty his bottle of wine in it. A taut major of the 3rd Infantry Division grabbed wine bottles from men who were doing a lot of drinking at Rothau in the Vosges and defiantly smashed them on the street for the civilians to see. Nevertheless, the flow of alcohol from civilians to soldiers continued unabated throughout the war. Even under fire, the sturdiest basement to offer shelter often turned out to be one of Europe's many elaborate wine cellars that offered temptations the GIs could not resist.[101]

"There was just too much booze around," Stephen Ambrose concludes in his study of a company of the 101st Airborne Division. Almost every European village the paratroopers liberated was "full of wine, cognac, brandy, and other fine liquor, of a quality and in a quantity quite unknown to the average enlisted man."[102] The alcoholic variety and the profusion of names, brands, labels, and appellations made the GIs' heads spin. They were warned about poteen in Northern Ireland. They tried to make sense of bitters, stouts, ales, and porters in England. They discovered legbi in North Africa and shared zombi with the Foreign Legion. They praised the Tuscan wines in letters from Italy. They compared the innumerable Alsatian, Belgian, Luxembourg, Dutch, and German beers. They drenched themselves with cider in Normandy, tasted muscatel at Marseilles, drank real champagne at Reims, and were introduced to the wines of the Rhineland. They spoke with awe of calvados and of schnapps made of grain, potatoes, apples, pears, and plums. When the GIs roamed Germany, they uncovered army liquor stores that would have made the prohibitionists at home turn pale. "6 cases of Champagne, 3 cases Cointreau, 1 case Benedictine, 5 cases Cognac (large) and 4 cases Cognac (small)," detailed the inventory in an officer's journal after his unit had captured one such cache.[103] Early in May 1945, men of the 101st Airborne Division discovered no less than 10,000 bottles of liquor with famous brand names in Göring's quarters at Berchtesgaden. The officers decided that "trying to stop the celebration was like trying to stop the tide."[104]

Some GIs learned to distinguish between the different sorts of liquor and came to appreciate the quality of specific kinds. A lieutenant wrote to his wife that the present he had received from the mayor of Mayet in France was not just a bottle of red wine, but a "Grand Vin Rouge, Chateau du Colombier Monselon, Pauillac, Haute-

Médoc!" "Just wait till I get back and some social deb tries to put on the dog with champagne," a teenage private told his parents from Luxembourg. "Boy, will I square her off."[105] Even the Army guides contributed their bit to the cultivation of American oenophiles. The French one listed the Château Lafite, Château Margaux, and Château Latour as the Bordeaux wines to keep in mind. The Italian booklet, on the other hand, found such recommendations arbitrary: "it is better to suit your own taste. And if you like to drink a sweet wine with meat, don't let it bother you."[106] Spoiled taste buds made some GIs picky. Paratroopers who discovered large barrels near Carentan eagerly tasted their contents but left them untouched when they discovered they contained only cider.[107]

Most GIs, however, could not have cared less about the quality of Europe's liquor. "It is almost straight alcohol," admitted a private who resorted to drinking schnapps during the battle for the Metz forts, "but I was hard up like all G.I.'s and would drink anything I could get."[108] Alcoholic potency and quantity were what mattered, because they alone could guarantee the desired effects. Anything that contained alcohol attracted the soldiers, claimed a private in Germany, as long as "it could be drunk without any obvious damage to our internal organs."[109] Mass wine disappeared from churches and at aid stations men eagerly lined up for "GI gin," a cough syrup that was composed of a good deal of alcohol. Soldiers of the 99th Infantry Division in Germany, who thought they were sharing a bottle of particularly powerful cognac, eventually discovered with the help of a dictionary that they had been drinking burning alcohol for lamps. Soldiers also made their own concoctions. They created "stupor juice" in Normandy by diluting calvados with wine or cider, mixed cognac with crème de cacao, and distilled cheap Italian wine into "kickapoo joy juice." During winter, a surgeon of the 88th Infantry Division on Monte Fano tried to brew rubbing alcohol into something potable, while men of the 9th Infantry Division in Germany mixed grapefruit juice with antifreeze. Men even turned careless in their quest for liquor: infantrymen at Saint-Lô were injured by booby-trapped wine bottles; paratroopers at Haguenau were shot at by snipers during a daytime search for booze; tank crews of the 13th Armored Division in Germany threw out camouflage nets and gas masks in order to store wine.[110] What the drinks lacked in alcohol degree, the GIs compensated for by consuming large amounts. In April 1945, an appalled sergeant wrote to his mother, after having sat through a pink-champagne bacchanalia somewhere in Germany:

> It's a shame that all soldiers seem to act the same way. If they have one bottle for 10 men – they drink it. And if they have 20 bottles for 10 men – they drink it. It's really stupid and disgusting but there isn't much you can do about it.[111]

Soldiers did not just sip hard liquor: they guzzled bottles of Remy Martin with long pulls and, according to an officer of the 35th Infantry Division, drank whiskey "like a long lost desert wanderer quenching his thirst at a fresh mountain spring."[112] They replaced the water in their canteens with cider and filled the five-gallon water cans with beer at breweries or wine from huge barrels. Men of the 14th Armored Division stacked so many cartons of liquor in their tanks and half-tracks during the race through Germany that by March 1945 they could afford to breakfast with K rations and champagne.[113]

For some soldiers, getting intoxicated was the sole purpose of drinking. Others, however, were caught off guard by the nastiness of particular liquors. Numerous GIs had little or no experience of alcohol. Soldiers who had been teetotalers because of religious convictions or a lack of interest in alcohol sometimes picked up the habit during the war. Moreover, many GIs had simply been too young to drink at home and were able to experiment with liquor for the first time at the front. When locals in a Lorraine village insisted on giving schnapps to soldiers of the 100th Infantry Division, for instance, the women protested that some were too young.[114] But boys in uniform got their hands on liquor anyway. "You drink whether you like drinking or not," a 20-year-old private wrote to his father, "just for the hell of it, and also your nerves need relaxation, and also you don't want other guys to think that you are a sissy or a mother's boy."[115] Still, even experienced drinkers could be tricked by the unfamiliar substances of Europe. The Army guides warned that British beer could "make a man's tongue wag at both ends," that calvados was meant to be sipped and not to be gulped down "in one swig," and that beginners should approach Dutch gin "with caution" and had to "GO EASY on Schnaps."[116] But thirsty men threw caution to the wind. Perhaps no other drink wreaked more havoc in the American ranks than champagne. All over Europe, the GIs liberated German army and Nazi warehouses stashed with the expensive bottles. In Leipzig alone, men of the 2nd Infantry Division discovered 2,000 cases of champagne that had belonged to the German garrison.[117] Many GIs had never before tasted the chic yet treacherous drink. The sparkling wine tasted "like soda pop or 7-Up" to uninitiated soldiers, who drank it from the bottle and by the bottle with results they most often did not foresee.[118]

The alcoholic escapades of the American combat soldiers did not always remain unnoticed even by those they had left at home. An angry wife reprimanded her husband and lieutenant in a letter she sent to the ETO in December 1944: "I shall tell *you* that some of your letters after a few bottles of Burgundy are quite gay and devilish and unlike the sober man I have known!"[119] Unfortunately, the effects of alcohol abuse were also felt within the combat units. It was disquieting, for instance, that soldiers sometimes took off to the front under the influence. During the nerve-racking waiting that preceded the move-out signal, men liked to calm and encourage themselves with liquor. A company of the 1st Infantry Division started drinking in the last hours before it would be rushed from southern Algeria to the front in Tunisia. By the time the unit departed, it had become "a noisy, drunken mob, shouting, singing and heaving bottles out of the trucks to shatter resoundingly on the sidewalks." Soldiers of the 26th Infantry Division turned to liquor while waiting to cross the Rhine at the Hanau bridgehead in March 1945. When the trucks were delayed, the men fell asleep on the sidewalks, the heavy drinkers in the gutters.[120] But even in the front line, alcohol could make things spin out of control. A surgeon at Anzio, for example, mentioned in his diary that a soldier had died in his ward after having been shot by an NCO "because·of his crazy drunkenness." Not just individuals but entire units could become unruly in battle as a result of alcohol. When Koblenz fell on 15 March 1945, a private of the 87th Infantry Division found himself amidst "the chaotic air of a drunken, end-of-the-world carnival" as he witnessed how inebriated GIs emerged from the cellars and "ran crookedly past, firing anywhere."[121] Intoxicated combat soldiers disgraced themselves and embarrassed their comrades. In July 1943 Mauldin entered Vittoria just in time to see how MPs quickly arrested a pair of infantrymen who were:

> armed to the teeth, draped with bandoleers and grenades, drunk as lords, with their flies open, displaying a brace of limp and rather stringy-looking sex organs to an assortment of young Sicilians of both sexes.[122]

More importantly, however, drunk soldiers also posed security risks to their buddies. That was especially true in the evenings when soldiers who tried to relax with liquor disrupted the vital guard duty. During the critical days of Operation Market-Garden, for instance, a captain who checked the roadblocks at Uden late in the evening found one of them unmanned. He finally traced the missing paratroopers to a Dutch tavern across the street, where he found them "sacked out on the top of the bar."[123] By the time combat soldiers at last moved to the rear for rest and reorganization, they were more than ever ready to unwind. Men from the 88th Infantry Division who were pulled back from the Santerno Valley in the autumn of 1944 started drinking even before they boarded the trucks; many were already drunk when they arrived in the rear. When on 1 December 1944 paratroopers of the 82nd and 101st Division – just back from Operation Market-Garden – were given a pass to Reims, so many fights erupted between drunk soldiers from both units that all passes had to be canceled three days later.[124]

At the end of the war, the judge advocates of the US Army agreed that intoxication had constituted the largest contributing factor to crime in the ETO and that it had fueled violent acts and sex offenses in particular. A US Army study, conducted in the ETO immediately after the war, concluded that liquor control was "an apparently insoluble problem in civil administration as in military operations." It did suggest, however, that stricter discipline, with prompt and severe punishment of drunkenness, could have reduced military offenses. The study also voiced that if unit canteens had been allowed to issue beer and wine, it might have kept the men away from the Old World's hard liquor.[125]

THE AID TO THE SICK

"The medical corps," Mauldin noted, "has probably done more to endear our army to civilians in stricken areas of Europe than the high-powered agencies which came over with that task in mind."[126] As early as the summer of 1941, when American troops landed in Iceland, the medical personnel played an important role in winning over the local population. Some of the US Army's concern with the people's well-being was, of course, motivated by self-interest. The Americans worked with their Icelandic colleagues, for example, to prevent epidemics in the civilian population from spreading to the troops, as in 1942 when an outbreak of mumps was quickly contained. But the GIs also treated large numbers of Icelanders who were injured near army camps or struck by military vehicles, supplied local hospitals with drugs, and participated in consultations concerning civilian patients. American veterinarians even helped to examine and treat livestock.[127]

In those areas of Europe that war was ravaging, the American soldiers found civilians in dire need of medical attention of every imaginable kind. In Italy, for instance, medical personnel who had their hands full with their comrades during the frenzy of battle, at the same time had to concern themselves with civilians who came under fire. The activities of one of the ambulance platoons of the 1st Armored Division's 47th Medical Battalion during the summer and fall of 1944 give an idea of their responsibilities. On 9 July, an ambulance picked up a sick, old woman near Volterra amidst the hysterical wailing of her family. On 13 August, the entire platoon pitched in to help evacuate the aged, invalid patients of a hospital at Pontedera while the town was being pounded by shells. A week later, an ambulance drove 25 miles up a cart track in blackout darkness to pick up a sick farmer and his wife on a hill above Fórcoli. Another long night ride on 10 September led to a wounded civilian in the shelled town of Altopáscio. On 22 October, three ambulances were sent out on dangerous night travel to the shelled town of Riola, where wounded civilians were waiting for help. Two days later, another vehicle climbed to Cavarzano to pick up a girl whose leg had been crushed by a truck that had overturned on a hairpin trail. US Army medical stations normally gave priority to the soldiers, but civilians were admitted for treatment whenever time permitted. Many Italians suffered from war injuries and not infrequently old wounds had already festered into the kind of gangrene that made amputation unavoidable. But the civilians also visited American medics and surgeons with ills and minor ailments. That was especially true in the poor rural and isolated mountain areas, where peasants had not even seen doctors regularly in peacetime. Many stood in line with toothaches or with toes that had become infected because shoes were rare. Grandmothers suffered from heart failure; young fellows had chancroids, buboes, or gonorrhea; babies were brought in with diarrhea, swollen glands, or skin infections. Within a few days of the 760th Tank Battalion's arrival in the front lines at Monte Maggiore, three of its doctors had delivered babies.[128] Quite a few grateful parents named their newborns after American medics and surgeons who, Mauldin noted, had aided them "in their own spare time when they needed rest badly."[129] Appreciative Italian peasants paid the American benefactors with noodle soup, fried rabbit, fruit, and aged wines; some even offered them goats. The Italian population also benefited from the stringent measures the US Army took to protect its soldiers against the country's diseases, especially malaria and typhus. Malaria control ranged from company measures within a one-mile radius of the unit to large-scale engineering projects that drained flooded areas, filled craters, and applied larvicides to water surfaces. When a typhus epidemic threatened to cause disaster in overcrowded and louse-infested Naples in the fall of 1943, it was nipped in the bud only because the Americans rushed massive supplies of methyl bromide and the newly developed DDT to the city and started a systematic delousing campaign.[130]

Across the Alps, Europeans were no less desperate for American medical assistance. There too, the fury of battle mutilated even the most innocent, and busy medics could not but make time to treat civilian victims. On D-Day itself, for instance, some 80 wounded men of the 506th Parachute Regiment were waiting in the church of Saint-Côme-du-Mont for the ground forces to arrive. The medics nevertheless used their limited supplies to help the badly wounded local residents too. One father was so grateful for the treatment of his six-year-old daughter's severe head wound that he offered the embarrassed medic his gold pocket watch. As in Italy, American medical personnel in Western Europe not only played the role of combat doctors for civilians, but also that of general practitioners because the war had caused medical care to be scarce or lacking entirely in many places. Official medical procedures for the ETO allowed the treatment of civilians in army hospitals only when necessary to save lives. Medics and surgeons in the front lines, however, helped the population with whatever they could. On the very day of the invasion, for example, a surgeon of the 502nd Parachute Regiment managed to deliver a baby in an aid station at Sainte-Mère-Eglise. When time allowed, medics even took on veterinary tasks, dressing the shrapnel wounds of priceless cows and horses belonging to poor peasants.[131]

Inside Germany, the biggest concern of the American military was typhus again, which was likely to be introduced from Eastern Europe by German troops and slave laborers. The GIs had been immunized against the disease and the US Army therefore focused on preventing it from turning into a plague among the Europeans. It started its campaign with massive inspections and delousings among the Germans and displaced persons west of the Rhine. In March 1945, it established a cordon sanitaire along the Rhine and Waal Rivers that only Allied military personnel could cross from east to west without being dusted with DDT. The Germans did not only profit from these measures, they also relied on the GIs to solve many other medical problems. In 1944, the Nazi regime had drastically reduced even the gasoline rations for doctors, midwives, and veterinarians. In the cities, some doctors had switched to bicycles to visit patients. In the countryside, however, people had begun suffering from lack of medical help and Nazi officials had been obliged to appeal to army medical officers to care for the civilians when stationed in neglected areas. When American medics entered such areas, they were invariably besieged by German civilians. During lulls in combat, they often treated more local residents than GIs in the small villages and little towns, where retreating German troops had sometimes commandeered the last remaining doctor.[132] "[O]ur civilian practice continues to flourish," a medic of the 100th Infantry Division reported from the French-German border to his wife. "Eggs and schnopps and 'Opple Cookin'' come in as fast as we can eat it."[133] In the war-torn Old World, German civilians were no less grateful than the other Europeans for the American aid to their sick and wounded.

THE ATTRACTION TO CHILDREN

As the war dragged on, a growing number of American fathers were being drafted. To them, the mere sight of wide-eyed European children staring at the passing soldiers could cause painful pangs of homesickness. A 32-year-old medic, who had been married 12 years and had two sons, wrote to his wife during the drive on Bitche in the Vosges early in December 1944: "We've been moving again, Dear, and I've been seeing so many kids Neil's and David's age – it kind of gets to me."[134]

But the sight of children touched not only American fathers, it mellowed almost any GI. In a time of war between races, nations, and ethnic groups, Europe's children woke the soldiers up to the basic truth that people were much the same the world over until the claims of state and culture coated them in different veneers. The Army guide informed the GIs that "British children are much like our own," but the soldiers noticed that this was no less true for the children from Sicily to Holland. "I am amazed to see in how many ways people are *alike*," a chaplain reflected in his diary after having enjoyed watching children in Iceland play tag and hopscotch.[135] Those American soldiers who were able to set aside their dislike for the German people had to admit that even the enemy's children were no exception. A Baptist soldier of the 4th Armored Division asked his wife in March 1945 from the vicinity of Worms to raise their baby daughter in Chicago without hatred: "Never let her forget that the little boys and girls in Germany are like all other little boys and girls all over the world, children to love and be loved."[136]

The GIs adored Europe's children because they seemed to be the only people overseas who had survived the war untainted by hatred and prejudice and could still afford the luxury of spontaneity. A corporal was so charmed by a little girl who jumped up at him to steal a kiss on his way through an Alsatian village in November 1944 that he wrote to his family: "These little children out here are the sweetest things you have ever seen. They are about the only decent people left in the world."[137] Too young still to have chosen sides, they did not have to prove to the GIs that they were innocent. Whereas the Americans could never be entirely sure of the loyalties of the Italian people, for instance, they had no qualms about directing their sympathies to the children. After all, Bill Mauldin pointed out, they "certainly never had much to say about the sacking of Greece and the invasion of Ethiopia."[138]

But if the war had left Europe's children uncorrupted, it had certainly not left them unaffected. Childhood was an endangered stage of life in times of war. A GI who observed children in England, for example, was struck by "how terribly quickly they mature and get old these days."[139] Throughout the conflict, worried parents had tried whatever they could to supply their children with the basic nutrients, and entire communities had joined in by setting apart fresh milk and occasional loads of oranges or lemons for the youngest. Yet, in spite of this, everywhere in Europe the GIs could see how hunger had gnawed at the children. The GIs took so many British children to mess halls that units had to issue orders to stop the practice. In the Italian ports of entry, children begged for food with infant brothers and sisters at their side.[140] French children at Le Havre harbor looked "malnourished with big eyes in drawn faces;" in the Riviera, youngsters suffered from rickets; in the Alsace, they developed open sores. A medic of the 100th Infantry Division in the Bitche sector at the French-German border found most children there "vitamin and mineral starved."[141]

Moreover, soldiers from various armies had served as role models for Europe's children for years and the youngsters had picked up some of the less flattering habits of the uniformed men. As soon as they could walk, for example, toddlers were reaching for the discarded butts troops left in their trail. "Already at the ages of 4, 5, 6 and 7 they were smoking cigarettes like veterans," a corporal of the 743rd Tank Battalion noticed in Normandy. "It is too bad the soldiers give them cigarettes."[142] Furthermore, GI lingo was the first introduction to English for many European children and it often had disastrous effects on their communication skills. "[D]isheartening is the fact," observed a private, "that all the kids know all the worst army terms and they always use them."[143] Soldiers unthinkingly also rendered themselves guilty of initiating children into the facts of life much too prematurely. They thought it great fun, for instance, to blow up condoms and teach kids how to tie a knot in them. One sergeant claimed he had seen hundreds of children repeat this on his way through France and Belgium. Frontline troops in reserve at Bettendorf, Luxembourg, in the fall of 1944 received a visit from an upset priest who had been sent by the villagers to ask the Americans to keep "the balloons" away from the children.[144] But the GIs considered it less amusing to notice that the games of Europe's youngest were changing from tag and hopscotch into imitating battle, not infrequently with weapons abandoned by soldiers. "The most discouraging thing I've seen today," a corporal wrote to his parents in March 1945, "is little German children playing 'war' in their backyards. This experience has meant nothing to them. They will be ready for the great marches of World War Three."[145]

"I really feel sorry for the kids," a platoon leader of the 9th Infantry Division wrote from France to his wife in the summer of 1944. "These GIs sure do have hearts of gold for they give everything they have away."[146] That was not to say the American soldiers found all children equally endearing. The GIs disliked the begging Arab urchins for their boldness, for instance, and considered them a terrible nuisance. The Army guide taught the men Arab phrases for "Scram!" and when those did not do the trick the GIs did not shrink from throwing stones at the kids.[147] Moreover, in Germany nonfraternization applied to the entire population, without exception. Interestingly, SHAEF's wartime conviction that the American soldiers most often tended to disregard those orders in encounters with German children was dismissed by a postwar US Army study as a "curious myth."[148] Some combat soldiers distrusted and disliked the German people enough to fend off children who merely asked for candy. A corporal who had been approached by two blond children for chocolate near Leipzig early in May 1945 described his rebuff with obvious satisfaction in a letter home: "I pushed the child to one side and answered 'Nichts für eine deutsche Kind' and the two little girls shrank away with hurt looks on their pink faces."[149]

Elsewhere in the European war theaters, however, the American soldiers felt irresistibly drawn to the children and spoiled them in any way they could. They responded most generously to their pleas for "gum, chum," "caramelli," and "bon bons" with chewing gum, Life Savers, chocolate, and even with pieces of sugar from their rations and candy from home packages. From the earliest days in Great Britain, the army tried to stop the GIs from taking kids to the mess, but the practice continued and spread to the Continent, where field kitchens regularly helped feed needy children besides the hungry soldiers. During the battle for Metz in the fall of 1944, for example, men of the 11th Infantry Regiment's 1st Battalion repeatedly took more food than they needed so as to distribute it among the French children who were hungrily watching the chow lines. After the GIs had finished, the mess sergeants lined the kids up to feed them the leftovers too. But the American soldiers did much more than share their candy and food. Combat units used lulls in battle to organize Saint Nicholas and Christmas parties for kids from war-torn areas, and individual soldiers asked their families to send vitamins, jars of baby food, and toys for the children of Europe.[150] "I'm not going Sister Kenny or anything," a corporal wrote from Holland to his parents in December 1944,

> but I do have one request and nothing could make me happier. I want the best Vitamin Pills in as large a quantity as possible. Enclosed is my check for them. I won't feel that this trip has been in vain if I can do a little bit for these poor heroic kids, these beautiful children, cheated by fat-bellied war lords even of their very bodies.[151]

Above all, the GIs were horrified by the many European children who were wandering aimlessly because they had lost their families. Not a few combat units adopted boys who hung around the soldiers in search of some affection. The GIs took them in as "a combination son and servant" and gave them all kinds of odd jobs as they towed them along on their travels. Although strict orders were issued against this practice, surprise inspections quite often discovered children in ill-fitting uniforms and oversized helmets among the regular GIs.[152] The American soldiers forgot about the frontline dangers in their eagerness to offer the orphans what Europe could not: a home and perhaps even a future. "We have a very sweet French kid with us here who has become a part of us," a Jewish corporal wrote to his family in September 1944. "Everyone is crazy about him and we are thinking of smuggling him into the United States after the war."[153]

THE LONGING FOR WOMEN

"If we are honest," an infantry officer declared, "most of us who were civilian soldiers in recent wars will confess that we spent incomparably more time in the service of Eros during our military careers than ever before or again in our lives."[154] The overseas women were already on the GIs' minds before they boarded ship. Soldiers purchased diaries that shrewd publishers had provided with a separate section for the names of the girls the men were about to leave behind (subdivided into "blondes", "brunettes," "red heads," and "miscellaneous") and another one for the new women they were bound to meet abroad (with handy divisions for the different countries). Farsighted GIs loaded up on soap before they sailed and packed other presents such as lipstick, stockings, and chocolate in their barracks bags with the purpose of ensuring feminine attention in the war-torn world.[155]

Much to their chagrin, however, the American combat soldiers soon found out that for them the opportunities to encounter women were rather limited. The sea voyage to the European war theater in itself was an early indication of the deprivation to come. Those few troops who traveled with nurses or WACs were the fortunate ones. A lieutenant who sailed to Scotland on the *Queen Mary* with a batch of replacements witnessed how, as more and more days passed, the hundred or so nurses on board turned into "a challenge to every red blooded male on the ship." Most GIs, however, had to satisfy themselves on board ship with the memories of the women they had left behind or the fantasies of those they were to conquer abroad. When a private of a chemical mortar battalion arrived in Naples from Newport News, Virginia, in April 1944, his first reaction was one of relief at seeing "women again for the first time in twenty-eight days."[156]

Once the American soldiers moved up to the front, they discovered that the chance of seeing women, let alone mingling with them, decreased even further. Apart from the wounded and sick, those combat soldiers who landed in French North Africa in 1942 often did not see women for several months; "if you except," clarified a lieutenant of the Big Red One, "the unattractive and unapproachable Arab women."[157] But in Italy and Western Europe too, most women had fled the battle zones if they had not been caught by surprise. Moreover, American soldiers had to stay in the front lines for long periods without receiving passes to the rear. They therefore thought it a cruel joke that the army insisted they carried condoms at all times. At the front, most GIs only used them on their gun barrels to keep out rain and dirt.[158]

Apart from survival, the GIs up front not surprisingly had one overriding concern on their minds as the war dragged on: sex. "In a war sex talk gets to be an obsession with men & we're no different than any other G.I.s," admitted a combat engineer who was stationed near Carentan in July 1944.[159] The preoccupation with sex colored more and more of the soldiers' speech. The GIs eroticized European place names. Béziers in France, for instance, was more appropriately renamed "Brassieres," and Sinzig at the Rhine River was destined to reach fame as "Zig-zig on the Rhine."[160] The soldiers also added ribald verses to perfectly respectable songs and created new ditties they "liberally sprinkled with four-letter words." "Fuck" undoubtedly was the most commonly used word of the GIs' vocabulary. "This word," observed an officer,

> does duty as adjective, adverb, verb, noun, and in any other form it can possibly be used, however inappropriate or ridiculous in application. Many soldiers seem hardly able to utter a sentence without using it at least once.

"Oh, that word," complained a private from Arizona who had arrived in North Africa only days earlier. "If there's one word I could destroy that would be it. Everything, everybody, every place is described by that word."[161] So littered with profanities did the soldiers' language become that when American Red Cross girls entered their sanctuary, the men felt uneasy and constrained and hardly dared to open their mouths for fear of offending the "tender, womanly ears."[162]

But mere talk could not prevent the soldiers from becoming sexually starved at the front. Letters expressed the longing, diaries mentioned the wet dreams, songs advocated masturbation.[163] The men tried to obtain relief in various ways. Pent-up desire occasionally even drove soldiers to sex with animals. Although homosexual contacts were even more taboo in the army than in civilian life, some heterosexual GIs found solace in "a kind of situational bisexuality" in the exclusively male environment.[164] Most men, however, were condemned to an incessant longing for women and they welcomed anything that refreshed their memory of the opposite sex in the front lines. The lucky ones had been able to hold on to pictures of teasing Betty Grable, flirtatious Rita Hayworth, or vampish Jane Russell. Disheveled GIs tried to cheer up comrades who had to live without pinup girls by dressing up in female apparel and posing "with exaggerated hip action and fluttering hand."[165] During looting at Gerolstein by men of the 90th Infantry Division in March 1945, some GIs undressed German mannequin dolls and put them out on the sidewalk. Their comrades gave the naked dolls "appreciative grins" as they filed by. When only moments later a mobile unit of the American Red Cross arrived, the lonesome, girl-crazy men instantly jilted the mannequins to woo the women of flesh and blood. "Their fatigues couldn't hide the fact that they were girls," observed a private, "and we practically drooled, watching their every movement."[166]

The conditions of war intensified the GIs' sexual appetite in several ways. To begin with, the army's masculine environment emphasized virility, while the military simultaneously detached the soldiers from the social controls – home, neighborhood, school, church – that had contained and repressed sexual impulses in more familiar surroundings. "War," noted a GI, "offers us an opportunity to return to nature and to look upon every member of the opposite sex as a possible conquest, to be wooed or forced."[167] Others interpreted the soldiers' sex drive as an even more fundamental biological response. They saw in it an almost instinctive attempt to counteract the massive destruction of the human species. A lieutenant of the 825th Tank Destroyer Battalion arrived in England on 6 June 1944. On 27 June, a few weeks before he would sail to France himself, he wrote to his wife:

War ... enormously heightens the reproductive urge, witness our own. Over here, nearer the front line, it's like a mania. From officers to privates we're obsessed by sex, and much the same seems true of the civilian population. Nature's way of compensating, I suppose, for all the death. The more life is threatened, the more it asserts itself.[168]

More than anything else, however, the young men's obsession with physical love, their fixation on the sexual act, simply stemmed from the prolonged abstinence forced upon them by the abnormal circumstances of war. As distance reduced sweethearts and wives at home to mere memories and as time made even those memories fade, physical needs easily eroded moral restraints. Veterans, for instance, were always more likely than newly arrived soldiers to sleep with women overseas and to show the highest rates of venereal disease. The army's Preventive Medicine Branch conducted an anonymous sex survey among the enlisted men of the MTO in September 1945. It revealed that although almost half of the respondents intended to marry their girlfriend and nearly a third of the repliers had spouses, three quarters of them admitted to having slept with Italian women. Yet the survey also showed that these GIs could hardly be considered oversexed. After all, their average frequency of sexual intercourse overseas of once to twice per month could by no means be called excessive for men with an average age of 26 years.[169] The preoccupation with sex among the GIs at the front was therefore no wonder. During the siege of Brest in August 1944, soldiers of the 8th Infantry Division forgot the war for a few moments when two horses came down a road and the stallion tried to mount the mare:

As the horse whinnied in frustration, we cheered them on. When the male failed again, we groaned in sympathy. It was the best show of the war to a bunch of men who for months had been forced to keep sex well in the back of their minds, and we admired the animal's determination to get on with his pleasure despite the efforts of war to interfere.[170]

When combat soldiers were able to meet the opposite sex at last, most of them merely used women to satisfy physical urges, showing an interest in nothing but the females' sexual qualities. "There was," commented one officer, "an unmistakable similarity in it to eating and drinking, a devouring of the woman as object."[171] Harlots could appease that kind of hunger as well as the next woman and it was therefore no surprise that the demand for females offering sexual relief against payment soared among the GIs. As a result, the US Army in Europe fought a continuous and frustrating battle against prostitution and the venereal diseases that came with it.

The issue already caused quite a bit of tension in Great Britain. The British considered prostitution a most private matter; they did not like to discuss it publicly and their government did not regulate it thoroughly. Yet the business flourished in Britain as elsewhere. The US Army tried to fight VD with the same methods it would employ in continental Europe. Its attempts, however, were seriously hampered by

British law and social custom. American units in the first place emphasized education: the media, special films and posters, lectures by surgeons, chaplains, line officers and NCOs warned against visiting prostitutes. The units also informed the GIs about the prevention of VD, and the army provided prophylactics. Each soldier received six condoms per month and two chemical kits per week. But only after much discussion and pressure did the British allow the Americans to set up prophylactic stations in places frequented by men on pass, although in Northern Ireland local sensitivities demanded that they were renamed "aid stations." The Americans could not count on the civilian authorities to crack down on prostitution because they did not have much control over the phenomenon: if brothels were rare, streetwalkers were all the more plentiful. Moreover, many nonprofessionals joined their ranks to ease temporary economic hardships as women on the home front sang:

> Me no likee English soldier.
> Yankee soldier come ashore.
> Yankee soldier plenty money.
> Me no jigajig for you no more.

To make matters worse, prostitutes who spread VD could not be traced because British law permitted libel action against those who accused women of being infected. British social and legal hurdles notwithstanding, the US Army managed to bring down the rate of new VD cases per 1,000 troops from 58 at the end of 1942 to about 20 by mid-1944, although some warned that the decrease was in large measure due to the great number of recent arrivals who had not yet had time to contract VD.[172]

When units moved to the battle zone, their VD rates showed a predictable pattern: they remained relatively low during periods of combat, but climbed rapidly during lulls allowing rest and reorganization.[173] VD became a veritable scourge in the Mediterranean countries. Mauldin, for instance, was shocked by the region's "unbelievable degeneracy."[174] Sheer hunger forced women who were trying to survive without husbands in a ruined economy to abandon moral principles. Already during the North African campaign, GIs were chanting:

> A can of 'C' ration
> Will whip up a passion
> In Stella, the Belle of Fedela.[175]

As innumerable amateurs joined the ranks of the professional prostitutes, control became almost impossible. Field commanders in French North Africa at first allowed selected brothels with European women to stay open for the GIs. Only when these measures failed to bring the VD rates down and protests from chaplains and medical officers increased did the commanders declare the *maisons tolérées* off-limits in July 1943, in accord with the official policy of the War Department. In Italy, neither placing all brothels off-limits nor inspecting and licensing houses helped.

Patton immediately installed medical teams in the six largest brothels of Palermo, and one month after Naples had been liberated Fifth Army headquarters kept one large brothel outside the city open and placed all the others off-limits to GIs. But such policies failed abjectly because most GIs had clandestine contacts with amateur prostitutes who sold sex to support themselves and their families and were cheaper than the professionals. So many Italian women resorted to prostitution for survival that the problem of VD spiraled out of control. When the 760th Tank Battalion arrived on the peninsula from North Africa in October 1943, for example, some men from B Company asked permission from their sergeant to see the medics for prophylactic treatment within less than an hour of the unit's landing. Naples and Rome, the Italian cities most frequented by soldiers on pass, remained the most notorious centers of infection despite stern warnings and the presence of numerous prophylactic stations. The GIs called Naples the "City of Sin" and joked that it would have been the biggest whorehouse in the world if someone had put a roof over it. Estimates said that by 1944 half the available women in Italy, and in populous areas 95 to 100 per cent of all prostitutes, had some form of VD. Nevertheless, 57 per cent of the GIs in Italy who reported sexual contacts admitted that they did not always use both a condom and a prophylaxis treatment as prescribed by the army. The situation had disastrous effects on several combat units, despite the fact that the line officers had been warned they would take the blame if their units produced disproportionate numbers of VD. The 82nd Airborne Division, for instance, counted 130 VD cases per 1,000 men in November 1943, the 1st Armored Division 192 in December of that year, and the 34th Infantry Division 173 in January 1944. After the war, the US Army conceded that its battery of preventive measures, including education, establishment of prophylactic stations, periodic examination of prostitutes, and policing of clandestine contacts, had been "only moderately successful" throughout the Italian campaign.[176]

American medical planners feared that VD would pose similar problems in Western Europe. Reports indicated that its incidence had increased threefold in France since 1941. In response, the US Army made sure that even its assault troops landed on the Norman beaches with condoms and chemical kits. But the VD threat remained small during the initial stage of the invasion. Few women had stayed behind at the beachhead and in June 1944 there were only 8.5 VD cases per 1,000 men, in July only 4.2. For the troops who landed in southern France in August 1944, opportunities for sexual contact significantly decreased as they advanced northwards into predominantly rural areas. Moreover, the relative rapidity of movement west of the Alps prevented VD from becoming too serious a problem among the combat troops in general. As always, the potential for trouble lurked mainly during rest and recreation in the rear. Whereas prostitution was unorganized and barely tolerated in Britain, Americans learned that on the Continent it was not only a socially accepted, but also a legally sanctioned and regulated institution in which brothels were commonplace. This situation allowed the US Army to envision systematic control over the business in continental Western Europe. The official policy of the War Department had always been the suppression of prostitution. In North Africa and Italy, attempts to regulate and license brothels had been made in the field despite the existing orders, but they had failed because prostitutes could spread VD before showing the symptoms. Medical officers in the ETO therefore vowed to place all brothels off-limits. To begin with, however, their attempts were thwarted by commanders who considered sex necessary recreation for the troops and thus allowed regulated bordellos to continue their business. Patton, for instance, insisted on keeping inspected brothels open for his Third Army. In Paris too, it remained the unofficial policy of local military commanders to keep red-light districts operating, despite orders from the chief surgeon of the US Army. Known of old among Americans as "an easygoing city," the capital honored its reputation by taking the responsibility for more than two-thirds of the venereal infections the GIs contracted in France. But even in places where the GIs were officially barred from all brothels, the plague of VD could not be eradicated. Long lines of American soldiers waiting in front of bordellos in Nancy, for example, evaporated at the first sight of MPs but reassembled as soon as they had disappeared. In Marseilles, all of the 31 licensed houses were placed off-limits, but the girls simply moved their business to hotels, bars, and rooms where they evaded all control. The Army guide to France warned against hard-boiled dames in cafés, prostitutes in clip joints, and tarts in night dancing places. So notorious were the Parisian cabarets of Pigalle among the GIs that they referred to the place as "Pig Alley." Soldiers who found the brothels at Cherbourg off-limits switched to picking up prostitutes in the outskirts of the city, and business simply continued in the open fields. What complicated the control over sexual contacts even more was that the GIs often preferred to pick up freelance prostitutes who offered pleasure for nothing more than cigarettes or rations. American soldiers derisively called such women "Hershey bars" and their services could be had anywhere. Towns and cities were plagued by streetwalkers. GIs soon nicknamed the determined ones "body snatchers" and some of these even managed to administer sexual relief to soldiers during train or truck stops on the way to the front. By March 1945, the VD rate had become so alarming among the Allied troops in Belgium, for instance, that SHAEF hurriedly supplied civilian hospitals with penicillin for the treatment of infected prostitutes. French and Belgian authorities worked closely with the Americans in tracing prostitutes who harbored VD, but their GI customers were of little assistance as they rarely remembered the women's names, let alone their addresses. Not surprisingly, the VD rate in the continental ETO doubled in 1944, although it would remain lower than that in Great Britain throughout the war.[177]

Eventually, VD was brought under control in the European war theaters by means of treatment rather than prevention. In the summer of 1944, a surgeon of the 88th Infantry Division who was in Rome on a pass noticed that the hotel lobbies were jammed with whores. "Everyone has a great time," he confided to his diary. "There's a rumor that soon a new drug will be on the market that will cure gonorrhea in twenty-four hours." Indeed, that same year penicillin at last allowed the American army to cut down on manpower losses due to VD as the new antibiotic spectacularly reduced the days needed to treat gonorrhea and syphilis.[178]

Unfortunately, wartime conditions did not only drive GIs into the arms of prostitutes, they also encouraged some to resort to rape. Rape became a large problem in the ETO only with the invasion of the Continent. A first big wave occurred when the Americans broke out of Normandy and rushed through France in August and September 1944. The second wave was registered in March and April 1945, when American troops were swiftly conquering large parts of Germany. Rape was a serious offense in the US Army and carried severe punishment. Company officers invariably warned their men about the offense before sending them on a pass and dutifully lined them up for identification whenever rapes were reported in a town where they had spent the night. Both rape waves took place at a time when troops were moving rapidly. It may indicate not only that the GIs were driven to rape when speed precluded any normal sexual contact, but also that they felt less inhibited when convinced they could get away with the crime without being apprehended.[179] Still, that does not explain why the problem was much more serious in Germany than in France. Whereas 16 per cent of the complainants in rape cases in the ETO were French, 64 per cent were German.[180] The fact that the GIs in Germany were conquerors who possessed absolute power and consequently felt that they could take whatever they wanted, undoubtedly played a major role. Ironically, nonfraternization itself may also have contributed to the high incidence of rape cases in enemy territory. "Friendly intimacy" was forbidden in public and in private, and the American soldiers were ordered to stay away from German women. But the soldiers' physical needs did not, of course, just vanish upon entering Germany. Many Slavic DPs in Germany offered sexual services in return for food, but most of these women looked so disheveled, and they were so notorious for VD, that the GIs were afraid to run the risk. As a result, and despite the threat of stiff financial penalties (contracting VD inside Germany was considered proof of fraternization until June 1945 and entailed a whopping $65 fine), the vast majority of nonfraternization violations during the war concerned sexual contacts with young German women.[181] It appears, however, that combat soldiers attempted to escape the odium of friendliness with the enemy when socializing with German women by limiting their contacts to sex devoid of emotions. Their motto in Germany, "Copulation without Conversation Is Not Fraternization," certainly points in that direction.[182] Some GIs must have considered intercourse without consent the next logical step for conquerors who wanted to have sex with the defeated. Rape trials showed that combat soldiers in Germany took their chances most often when moving into houses commandeered by their unit and that the offenders had quite often been drinking. They usually threatened the occupants with their weapons and then forced one or more of the women to have sex with them before putting the family out on the street.[183] A private of the 90th Infantry Division, for example, alarmed by muffled voices in the cellar of a house near Gerolstein, caught a GI who was trying to rape a very young girl while pointing his rifle at about 20 adult civilians who stood powerlessly against a wall. The private immediately reported the offender, and although at first he feared that his comrades would hold this against him, he was relieved to learn that they had "all lost respect for [the rapist] and began to talk about him as though he was on the 'other side.'"[184] The reality of war had weakened moral standards enough to make prostitutes very popular women among the American soldiers, but it had not so corrupted ethical principles as to allow the average GI to condone rape.

Although the combat soldiers mostly had physical gratification on their minds, they did sometimes become attracted to a woman because of "her presence itself and not merely her body." In times of war, men tended to consider women "islands of sanity in a world gone mad." Amidst the loneliness and the threats, GIs longed for their "gentleness and affection" as well as for "the protective, orderly existence" they symbolized.[185] In his diary, a surgeon of the 88th Infantry Division described an encounter with an Italian woman during a Red Cross dance in Rome late in June 1944:

> As I dance with her, I forget all about war, politics, and the Army. I shall always recognize her perfume – a blend of lilacs and lilies of the valley, which sends my senses reeling. I have never held a woman such as Maria in my arms and enjoyed it so much.

The officer ended up spending his entire leave with her, but he confided to paper that he had become "too fond of Maria by this time to demand anything that both of us might later regret."[186] His romantic escapade was not an exception. The names and addresses of European women in small GI notebooks, carefully penciled beneath the home addresses of comrades, are silent proof of similar short-lived romances.[187]

Most combat soldiers moved on before love affairs could bloom into more serious relationships. And even when time did permit a better acquaintance, the difference in language often did not. American wooers hopefully consulted the Army guides' vocabulary lists, but those only told the men how to ask for medical help, food, and shelter. Taking along comrades as interpreters on dates, in what a GI in Czechoslovakia called a "Cyrano de Bergerac arrangement," could clarify things, but it did not allow much privacy.[188] Many American soldiers expressed frustration at their inability to develop more meaningful tête-à-têtes with a particular girl because of linguistic shortcomings. A corporal from New York described to his parents how he had danced a slow waltz with a pretty French girl during a town gathering in September 1944:

> we got along pretty nicely. But there's the hitch. I lapse into a slight haze, and make conversation with her. I told you this story before. I talk, she nods, she talks, I nod. She grins, I grin. Then exhausted by our long speeches (3 words) we lapse into silence.[189]

Chaotic times, strange lands, and unfathomable languages caused plenty of misunderstandings that thwarted the growth of more stable liaisons between soldiers and women. On the one hand, it was not always easy for the GIs in wartime Europe to tell who the women they met really were. "The girls dress pretty well considering that war has been here," a private wrote to his parents just after he had arrived at Marseilles from New York in December 1944, "and they overdo their make-up even more than in Hollywood." A week later he told his family that he had found out that the women he had mentioned were in fact prostitutes, not the city's "respectable girls."[190] It also happened, however, that GIs slept with women whom they assumed were prostitutes, but who adamantly refused to receive any kind of payment the morning after, feeling insulted by the mere offer.[191] On the other hand, it was equally hard for the GIs to know what their own feelings were for the women they met abroad. An officer observed that men with uncertain tomorrows tended to cling to "occasional loves" and to pour "all their longing for beauty and gentleness and charm" into them. "Almost of necessity," he added, "there was much illusion in this love." Late in November 1944, the badly mauled 442nd Infantry Regiment was withdrawn to southern France to guard the border with Italy; the unit stayed there until March 1945. During that time, the regimental chaplain had his hands full trying to dissuade several young Japanese-American soldiers from getting married to the "local girls." Most often they had met the girls only a few times and had never understood much of what they had whispered in their ears. Investigations by the chaplain revealed that the women were in fact prostitutes who conducted their business in the local hotel. "So desperate for human affection were they after putting battle behind them," the boys' spiritual guide observed, "they could think only of the moment and not the future."[192] In wartime, how much of supposed love was plain lust, how much mere infatuation, how much just longing?

Yet, despite the confusion of the times, some soldiers did find true love. It was, in the words of philosopher and veteran J. Glenn Gray, the kind of love that transcended physical attraction as well as "the appeals of tenderness and beauty," the kind of love that was "painfully specific and individual."[193] The American army tried hard to discourage soldiers from marrying in the war theaters for fear that family responsibilities would distract them. It warned the men about the uncertainty of future movements and the hazards of war. It also explained the procedural complications in intimidating detail: commanding officers would have to grant their permission, overseas transportation would not be available for dependents until a long time after the soldiers had been discharged, and foreign girls would not automatically become citizens upon marrying an American. Yet, the military's deterring tactics notwithstanding, some 30,000 GIs married British girls during the war, and by January 1946 at least 6,000 women from the Continent were the wives of American soldiers. Undoubtedly, many of those GI husbands were members of service units who had had more time in the rear to get to know Europe's girls better. There were nevertheless also combat soldiers who managed to meet women they would marry. Some had marriage on their minds as early as the Icelandic operation; many more decided to tie the knot before jumping off from England; and no one will ever know exactly how many returned to addresses they had hurriedly jotted down in notebooks on the way to the front or during lulls in battle. There was, however, a ban on marriage with the enemy. When it was lifted for Austrian nationals on 2 January 1946, 300 applications were filed within two weeks. The GIs were only allowed to marry German nationals after 11 December 1946; by the end of that month, 2,500 of them had asked their commanding officer's permission.[194] Almost none of these GIs had seen combat, but even while the war had been raging, some frontline soldiers had not been able to prevent falling in love with German girls, sometimes while retaining a genuine hatred for their people. True love, concluded one officer from his experience in wartime Germany, "is no respecter of persons and frequently chooses archenemies as its unhappy principals."[195]

It should be noted, however, that the American combat soldiers were not only drawn to Europe's women for passionate affairs of the flesh or heart, but also for matters of a much more mundane nature. That is, they often approached women with household problems. GIs who were fed up with army food but had too little kitchen experience to cook up something else, eagerly fished for invitations to home-made meals. Dirty soldiers also routinely called on housewives for hot water and baths. Most often, however, they turned to women with their dirty laundry. Combat soldiers rarely had time to wash their clothes. At best, they soaked them in creeks and canals or boiled them with chunks of soap in helmets over open fires. All over Europe, women were more than willing to lend the GIs a hand, not in the least because the Americans handsomely compensated them for it. Within a week of his arrival at Budareyri in September 1942, for example, the chaplain of a combat engineer unit had managed to make arrangements with an Icelandic family for his laundry.[196] According to one soldier, the GIs in Italy were "solicited day and nite for 'lavare.'" In France, a stanza of the World War II version of "Mademoiselle from Armentières" ran:

> She got the palms and the Croix-de-Guerre
> For washing soldiers' underwear.

Soldiers in Germany complained about nonfraternization because it meant, among other things, that they were now forced "to take up washlady chores." Soon, however, the GIs were violating those rules as women in Germany, like those elsewhere in Europe, were eager to do their laundry for cigarettes, cakes of soap, chocolate, or sugar.[197]

Still, in the liberated countries, women did not only take care of the Americans for reasons of profit; they also did it to show them gratitude and affection. Not a few invited GIs to dinner because the young soldiers bore resemblance to sons who were imprisoned or had been killed, and it happened that American soldiers spent the night in bedrooms where photographs and framed diplomas were the only reminders of lost sons. A couple of soldiers of the 44th Infantry Division were invited to the home of an Alsatian woman whose sons had been drafted by the German army:

> Now she says when she looks at us we remind her of her boys. It must be pretty rough on her because she is crying, not slobbing all over us, but tears just well up in her eyes as she talks.[198]

To young GIs – many had barely left high school – these women in turn became surrogate mothers for the time being. A French woman in the vicinity of Casablanca, who had lost two sons in the French army, insisted that a few GIs had a warm dinner at her house and would spend the night in soft beds. "She calls us her sons," said one of the Americans, "and we call her MaMa." In December 1944, a corporal of the 84th Infantry Division wrote to his parents about Holland:

> I have at least five families in the wonderful little land which will take me in night or day, rain or shine – and make me feel at home. Mama Elizabeth, Mama Herman, Mama Post, Mama Sommers, Mama Decker.[199]

Yet, no matter what void Europe's women filled in the lives of the GIs, the American soldiers' image of the Old World's opposite sex was seriously distorted by the conditions of war. Even before the war, Americans had imagined the women of Europe as much more loose and uninhibited than those at home. The Army guides tried their best to undermine those false assumptions. One of them, for instance, described Ireland as "an Old World country where woman's place is still, to a considerable extent, in the home," and it emphasized that young ladies would have to ask their families' permission to go out with a GI.[200] It was the reputation of the women in the country of French kisses and French letters, however, that seemed particularly frayed. The Army guide regretted that France had been depicted "too often in fiction as a frivolous nation where sly winks and coy pats on the rear are the accepted form of address." As one lieutenant noted, these assumptions were especially common among GIs who were "stuffed with highly colored tales" their fathers had brought back from the Great War. The Army guide's warning that the real Paris was not that of "wild women," for instance, was no doubt aimed at the GIs who had heard veterans of that war rave about "Gay Paree." The guide assured the GIs that France was "full of decent and strict women" and that French girls actually possessed "less freedom than girls back home."[201] Combat soldiers who were able to date girls from respectable European families could confirm the Army guides' exhortations. They reported that Icelandic girls under 18 were not allowed to go out in society, that they could walk Catholic Irish girls to the corner but not to the door, and that army dances in French towns attracted "mamas chaperoning for dear life." GIs with Polish roots who tried to charm DPs from their ancestors' land of origin soon learned that chastity was not an empty word to Catholic peasant girls. A private who became enchanted by "a thorough home girl" at Pössneck claimed that it was "this sheltered quality, this lack of aggressiveness or emancipation on the part of many German girls" that the Americans appreciated so much.[202]

But few combat soldiers ever had the opportunity to acquaint decent European girls in the midst of war. A private of the 87th Infantry Division who stayed behind in a German village somewhere between the Saale and the Weisse Elster River after his unit had moved out, witnessed a remarkable transformation:

A little later, people came out cautiously, eyes lifted up to the sky, and a dignified promenade began. I was struck by the number of pretty girls who appeared, walking sedately, escorted by an older member of the family. There had not been one at large while the troops were in town.[203]

These families, of course, had taken wise precautions to shield their daughters from enemy soldiers in the front lines. Yet even in friendly territory and during rest in the rear, most combat soldiers only met the very women for whom they had practiced such phrases as "coushay avec?" and "zig zig?" Unfortunately, the war made ever increasing numbers of European women susceptible to such solicitations. The professional prostitutes were joined by thousands of women who were willing to sleep with GIs because of poverty and hunger. Moreover, women of all walks of life were easily seduced by the healthy-looking, brazen Americans after years of loneliness and waiting for their friends and husbands. With most young men off to distant training camps or war theaters, for example, the GIs called Britain "a wonderland." A lieutenant, stationed at a camp near Macclesfield with the 825th Tank Destroyer Battalion, complained to his wife in June 1944: "Keeping town girls (almost no young men around here since war began five years ago) out of our men's barracks and beds is a major housekeeping problem."[204] Similar problems occurred in France, where an estimated one and a half million men had been held in Germany as POWs since 1940. Almost all of them were between 20 and 40 years of age and 57 per cent were married. Economic hardship forced wives of French POWs to work outside the home or to take in work like sewing and laundry, and many only managed to survive with financial support from their parents. In Germany, the situation was even more deplorable. Millions of men had been killed or imprisoned, and for years the women had seen only children, old men, and crippled veterans. Economic pressure, combined with the lack of male companionship, drove many into the arms of the former enemy. Unofficial estimates indicated that 10 to 20 per cent of all German women were engaged in some form of prostitution around the end of the war; the VD rate understandably skyrocketed.[205] In those circumstances, the GIs were bound to get the wrong impression of Europe's women and easily concluded, for instance, that Italian women were "wonderfully, disgustingly free," that French women were "easy to get," and that there was "a lack of morals" among the women of Germany.[206] The war years were not the best of times to convince Americans that the women of the Old World were not as loose and uninhibited as legend had it.

Neither did wartime deprivation allow European women to put on their best looks for the American soldiers. Only occasionally did the GIs admit to the existence of a particular European allure among the females. Some caught glimpses, for instance, of the "indescribable French 'chic'" or of the *great* femininity" of the Gallic women. A combat engineer in northern Italy wrote to a friend that even the peasant women "as a rule have poise and a type of charm lacking in our girls."[207] In the towns and cities that served as military rest centers, however, the GIs were more likely to notice and assort with the whores and harlots. These creatures of the street seriously discredited European womanhood, as can be judged from several GI songs. American troops in North Africa loved to chant "Dirty Girtie from Bizerte," a ditty detailing the vices of French women in versions that could reach 200 unflattering stanzas. When the GIs invaded Sicily, they were quick to adapt the song into "Sloppy Lena from Messina," and in Italy they again changed the title into "Filthy Fannie from Trepani."[208] On the other hand, the European women who guarded their reputation more carefully than the Girties, Lenas, and Fannies lacked the means to accentuate their charms the way they had before the war. The Army guide to Britain informed the GIs that soap used to be plentiful, but that the war had made it so scarce that factory girls often could not wash the grease from their hands and hair. The booklet also pointed out that if British women perhaps looked "dowdy and badly dressed," it was not because they were ignorant about fashion, but because clothing had been rationed.[209] Everywhere in Europe the GIs noticed the effects the scarcities had on women. Makeup had become unavailable or unaffordable; silk stockings had disappeared or were replaced by less elegant woolen ones; sandals with wooden soles had replaced high-heeled shoes due to lack of leather. Women had patched and repatched their clothes endlessly during the war, and although they tried to be nonchalant about this, it was nevertheless obvious to the GIs that their dresses were "sat in," their furs "old-fashioned," and their clothes in general "old and worn."[210] When the 2nd Battalion of the 116th Infantry Regiment was withdrawn in September 1944 to Le Conquet near Brest for rest and reorganization, the unit organized a dance in a "war-shabby resort hotel." One of its officers observed the female guests with a critical eye:

> The assembly did not outshine its surroundings. Although the French girls undoubtedly did their best, their frocks showed the effects of four years of occupation-enforced austerity, climaxed by the siege.[211]

"If some of them could dress and paint like American girls," a corporal from Nebraska wrote about the English girls in 1942, "they would be very attractive."[212] In comparison to the rather shop-worn European women, any American female in the war zone had the effect on the GIs of a fresh, healthy breeze. Correspondent Inez Robb reported how it felt to be an American woman among the troops overseas in February 1943:

> You don't have to look like Rita Hayworth or wear a sweater like Lana Turner to be a social success in North Africa. You have only to be an American woman on the sunny side of 80, without a noticeable squint and still be able to navigate under your own steam.[213]

Whenever American Red Cross girls arrived near the front, GIs swarmed to them like bees to honey, and a private on a pass to Florence noticed that the WACs stubbornly stuck together in groups as if for protection. American girls, more than anything else, came to represent home to the young men in uniform, and the spiraling idealization of the absent was enough to guarantee them the GIs' adoration anytime. Correspondent Lee Miller, who was with the 83rd Infantry Division during the battle of Saint-Malo in the summer of 1944, described how homesick infantrymen sought her company, teasing her and asking her "to talk American."[214]

The girls from home made the American soldiers realize even more what war had taken away from the women of Europe. When the 36th Infantry Division was pulled out of San Pietro in December 1943, a sergeant noticed that the American Red Cross girls were "careful to use perfume, powder and rouge, because they knew we got a bang out of it, and *they smelled clean*." A medic who arrived at an American field hospital after having been wounded at the French-German border in October 1944 was suddenly made aware of the more intangible condition that had dulled the beauty of so many of the women he had seen in the Old World:

> As the nurse leaned over me I looked at her clean, innocent-looking face. The eyes glowed softly and warmly, so different from any woman one might see at the front, so different from the staring eyes filled with fear and worry.[215]

The limited contacts that battle allowed the American soldiers with the civilians overseas contributed to a serious distortion of their picture of Europe. The linguistic complexity did not only impede a better understanding of the people and their society, it also strengthened the impression of a hopelessly divided world. More importantly, the exceptional circumstances in which the contacts took place ensured that the GIs saw Europe at its worst. When they looked for food, they only found hunger. When they wanted to quench their thirst, they found alcohol more plentiful than water. When they set up aid stations, suffering people flocked to them for relief. When they took out their rations, hollow-eyed children gazed at them expectantly. When they flaunted their cigarettes, desperate women lined up to sell their bodies. The American soldiers thus emerged from the fog of battle with a picture of Europe as a world of immeasurable oppression, want, and immorality. That the conflict in Europe was a total war did much to strengthen that negative picture.

8   The Totality of War

The war the American combat soldiers encountered overseas proved so total in nature that it appeared to have tainted everyone and to have contaminated even the smallest corner. On the one hand, the GIs witnessed with dismay how Europe's civilians could not be stopped from interfering with the business of warfare. On the other hand, they also watched in frustration how war could not be prevented from engulfing all of Europe's society. As a result, whether the American combat soldiers were fighting in the front lines or resting in the rear, they never had a chance to form a reliable picture of how Europe might have looked under the normal conditions of peace.

THE CIVILIAN INTRUSION

Soldiers had always tried to prevent civilians from complicating their tasks, but the GIs' attempts to screen the battlefield from outsiders were doomed to fail in a conflict that appeared to involve everyone. Throughout the war, Europe's civilians aroused much suspicion among the American soldiers. That was, of course, particularly true in enemy territory, where the Army guides warned the GIs that their lives might be "in more danger than it was during the battles."[1] In October 1944, the V Corps even endeavored to evacuate a five-by-ten-mile area in the Eupen-Malmédy sector completely in order to prevent the German-speaking Belgians from becoming security risks. The experiment proved too cumbersome, however, and the American army decided enemy people would henceforth be controlled at home. This entailed that all enemy communities were to be subjected to a series of security actions immediately after capture. Whenever American soldiers took over a German town, they conducted house-to-house searches to collect explosives, ammunition, guns, even knives. They also confiscated all means of communication, from radio transmitters to pigeons.[2]

As demonstrated in Eupen-Malmédy, the GIs were not permitted to let down their guard against civilian treachery even in those regions of friendly countries that bordered Germany. In Alsace-Lorraine too, the Americans could not help seeing franc-tireurs or informers in almost anyone who spoke German. Troops of the 26th Infantry Division who were sent to Metz for rest and refitting in December 1944 heard so many rumors about pro-German civilians sniping at Allied soldiers that they refused to visit the city without their weapons.[3] But the US Army thought it wise to warn its soldiers not to trust civilians too much anywhere in Europe. The guide to France, for instance, advised the GIs to "become silent as a stone when military subjects come up." The American authorities feared that in formerly occupied territory the Nazis had left behind numerous networks of spies, made up of German plainclothes agents as well as collaborating natives.

Across Europe, soldiers were admonished to heed one particular group of people most likely to have been infiltrated by informers: women. Counterintelligence officers expressed special concern about "the traditional woman spy who, by wiles and stratagems, would extract bits of information from soldiers in their leisure hours." More than anything else, the GIs were told to watch out for females of easy virtue. Officers advised their men to be suspicious of girls in bars who asked too many questions about their units during battle intermezzos. "You probably won't get mixed up with anything as glamorous as Mata Hari," clarified the GI guide to France, "the Germans have wised up and are sending around much less obvious spies these days."[4]

If the American soldiers were sufficiently warned about the Mata Haris of the Old World, they found themselves much less prepared to handle the more open ways in which European civilians interfered with the soldiers' war. Wherever the GIs arrived as liberators, resistance fighters emerged from hiding places and rushed forward to put their courage, idealism, and knowledge of the area at the disposal of the regular troops. But the soldiers in the field harbored many reservations about accepting the services of these volunteers, no matter how fervidly they offered them. Operating in battle with people whose lack of uniform indicated they were amateurs never failed to make the GIs jittery. The Italian partisans, for instance, who were especially active in the Apennines and Alps, impressed the Americans with their numbers. And the GIs admitted that these guerrillas were brave, helpful with information on terrain, enemy gun positions, and troop movements, and effective in certain small unit actions. Still, the unruly character of the partisan bands made the uniformed soldiers shudder. A regimental commander of the 88th Infantry Division felt that the partisans who joined his troops when they entered Rome early in June 1944 were "more of a hindrance than a help," not because they lacked courage, but because they had "no organization or leaders." A month later, the officer became even more convinced of this when he observed guerrillas in the Arno Valley who were "armed with every conceivable type of weapon, and with miscellaneous belts of ammunition draped across them in the fashion of Mexican bandits."[5] American soldiers raised similar objections elsewhere in Europe. The GIs who campaigned in France could not deny that the resistance facilitated their job on many occasions by providing accurate intelligence, harassing German supply lines, and sabotaging key objectives. In southern France, the Maquis sometimes fought side by side with the GIs in regular battles and on occasion liberated towns before the Americans arrived. Nevertheless, the inexperience of the resistance fighters made the trained soldiers cringe. The carelessness with which they, often unknowingly, risked their lives in battle struck the Americans as unjustifiable waste. A lieutenant of the 8th Infantry Division was horrified by the numerous blunders committed by a unit of the FFI that fought with his men on the Crozon peninsula in Brittany. He noted, for instance, that the Frenchmen lacked experience in using the terrain for concealment and that they, rather than edging along the hedgerows, exposed themselves in the open fields with a nonchalance that verged on the suicidal. Scouts of the 94th Infantry Division who received valuable help from a local FFI guide near Lorient were eventually forced to send the man away because he endangered all of them by staying in sight too much.[6] A lieutenant of the Big Red One evaluated the resistance fighters he saw in action both in France and Belgium as "generally brave as lions, untrained and not much help."[7] Many GIs had no doubt the Netherlands possessed the best organized and most helpful underground movement in Europe. Yet, even Dutch resistance fighters could not always convince the Americans that they belonged in the war zone. In October 1944, an African-American soldier ran into a Dutch patrol that was guarding vital installations at the border with Germany near Aachen. Although the sentries wore orange-colored brassards and could show reliable credentials, the GI could not help remaining apprehensive. "Perhaps," he explained, "because they were armed and not in uniform."[8] As their combat experience increased, America's citizen-soldiers became more and more adamant in their conviction that war could not be the business of just anyone.

It was particularly hard for the GIs to accept that war had also become the business of women in Europe. When they first steamed to the British Isles in 1942, "Rosie the Riveter" was not yet a fixture in America's wartime society. In Great Britain, however, war by that time had already forced hundreds of thousands of women to take a job in a factory or to join the military auxiliary forces. It was therefore quite a revelation to the Americans to see women in such large numbers in rather untraditional roles. Men of the 1st Infantry Division had barely arrived at the port of Gourock in August 1942 when they were commenting agitatedly on the fact that Scottish women were working as freight handlers and car cleaners. In letters home, GIs expressed their amazement at British women working as truck drivers, mechanics in dirty overalls, bus conductors, and "postmen." A sergeant who visited a barber shop in August 1942 could hardly believe that the personnel was entirely female and reported to his family in Delaware that he had received his first "woman haircut."[9] Women in military uniform caused even more of a sensation. The US Army guide to Britain spent an entire page on preparing the soldiers for this unfamiliar situation. It assured the GIs that British female officers and NCOs could not only give orders to male soldiers, but that the British men also "obey smartly and know it is no shame." British soldiers respected women in uniform, explained the guide, because not a single one of them had been known to quit her post or to fail her duty under fire. It therefore urged the GIs to remember that British girls who wore ribbons on their tunics had not earned them "for knitting more socks than anyone else in Ipswich."[10] All these preparations notwithstanding, the first encounters with British women in uniform made quite an impression on the Americans. The sergeant from Delaware not only had to reconcile himself to his woman haircut in the summer of 1942, he also had to swallow hard when he saw a female corporal "wear stripes just like the men." Even at the end of the war, uniformed British women managed to impress an American who was visiting Brussels. The 19-year-old private described them in a letter to his parents as "a robust bunch of gals who wear their sleeves rolled up always." He added, not without awe: "No wall flowers in the U.K."[11]

The magnitude of the war had made it impossible for many European women to remain on the sidelines of activities that had traditionally been reserved for men. But nothing bothered the GIs more than the presence of women – still symbols of domesticity – on the battlefield itself. If the slaughter of men stopped being a crime for the duration of the war, to most GIs the killing of women would always feel like murder. A private who shot a sniper at Bergheim in the winter of 1945 and discovered that the culprit was a girl in civilian clothes, vividly remembered that his comrades "ribbed me mercilessly about it and made some rough remarks about my morality in connection with her death."[12] It was fortunate for the GIs' peace of mind that females in uniform remained exceptions in the front lines of the European war theaters. Despite Goebbels' cry for total war, even in Germany none of the 450,000 women in the military auxiliaries were allowed to fire weapons.[13] However, Europe's women were numerous and vital in the front lines of the various resistance movements, and the GIs were impressed by the part they played in the underground. The risks they took and the sacrifices they made as members of the resistance were, a GI of the 35th Infantry Division noted,

> almost incomprehensible to American soldiers who had generally thought that women's contributions to national defense should not go beyond USO shows, the WAC's, or industrial work.[14]

The misery of total war forced Europe's civilians to disturb even the peace of soldiers who were dead. The GIs themselves did not always shrink from robbing enemy dead of their valuables. It was, for instance, a fairly widespread practice to cut off the fingers of German bodies that wore gold rings. Yet, when noncombatants showed disrespect for dead soldiers, they touched a tender string in the GIs. The war degraded civilians to scavenging battlefields, not for money or jewelry, but for clothing. Shoes in particular had become scarce in Europe and the sturdy footgear of the GIs was much sought after. Barely two days after the Allies had landed in Sicily, a chaplain of the 1st Infantry Division claimed he could not find one American body with shoes on. The GIs were even more shocked to find bodies of fellow Americans stripped of every usable piece of clothing by Italian peasants. It was equally common in Italy to come across dead German soldiers without boots or clothes. But the French did not turn away from disrobing dead enemies either. Near Saint-Lô in July 1944, a private of the 3rd Armored Division noticed with dismay how civilians were roaming the battle site for anything salvageable and even stooped to taking shoes and clothes from Germans who had been killed.[15] Although the GIs understood that people who had lost everything could not be blamed for taking clothing that would be buried anyway, they nevertheless resented the civilians for what they construed as acts of irreverence toward men who had made the ultimate sacrifice. And the affront was not considered less when the victims were enemy soldiers. In June 1944, a paratrooper in Normandy felt offended when "it got to the point where after a fight these [French] people would come out and loot the [German] bodies while they were still warm." It upset the GIs in Italy even more that the peasants thought nothing of disinterring the German dead to take their shoes and clothes.[16] But, in a war that was total, nothing could stop the noncombatants from intruding even upon battlefield's inner sanctums.

THE ENCROACHMENT OF BATTLE

The American combat soldiers refused to accept that battlefield and noncombatant world could not be separated. As if by instinct, they attempted to shield both natural environment and civilian society from the fury of battle throughout the war. But in Europe's total war the GIs learned the hard way that preventing the juggernaut of battle from disturbing the life of the noncombatants was even more against the odds than keeping the civilians from meddling in warfare.

The Natural Environment

The butchering of each other was almost easier to endure than the violation of animals, crops, farms, homes, bridges, and all the other things that bind men to his natural environment and help to provide him with a spiritual home.[17]

That was the feeling of an officer who had seen combat in Italy, France, and Germany. It was shared by many of his comrades in the European war theaters. There was something compulsive, for instance, in soldiers' attempts to avoid unnecessary damage to the natural surroundings amidst the ravages of war. A private of the 84th Chemical Mortar Battalion complained about trucks tearing down the trees of beautiful orange and grape orchards during the breakout from the Salerno beachhead; a lieutenant of the 36th Infantry Division regretted trampling the new green wheat during close-order drills in the Italian spring of 1944; a sergeant felt embarrassed about driving his jeep through sections of seedlings in the Ardennes forests during the Battle of the Bulge. On their way to Belgium after the fall of Brest, men of the 29th Infantry Division left the train to stretch their legs during a halt. Suddenly, and without being ordered, the GIs started cleaning up the area, piling up the innumerable empty ration cans that had littered the sides of the tracks for months. It was as if they were trying to erase the traces of all the soldiers who had ever passed.[18]

Combat soldiers could be particularly moved by animals. These creatures were totally innocent and thus represented a world that had disappeared beyond the horizon and a time that had receded into the past. A cock's cry could suffice to trigger a wave of nostalgia. "Strange, strange sound of peace," a lieutenant from Arkansas sighed in his journal after having heard a rooster crow faintly in a brief interval between artillery barrages at the Norman village of Le Neufbourg.[19] Animals symbolized home and a life of peace, and that made it important for the soldiers to have them around and to prevent them from getting harmed. The GIs took pity on Europe's stray pets and made them the units' mascots. Orders were issued from time to time to get rid of the animals, but the men ignored them. Soldiers of the Big Red One smuggled their cats and dogs on board when leaving Sicily and were tremendously saddened when they had to abandon them because of Britain's strict quarantine laws. In April 1945, correspondent Lyn Crost noticed that the men of the Japanese-American 422nd Regimental Combat Team in Germany were accompanied by "everything from pheasants to dogs." She learned that some of the stray pets had been picked up as far back as Italy.[20]

In the front lines, there were numerous instances of soldiers lavishing "unusual care and tenderness" on animals that contrasted sharply with the cruelty around them.[21] Not even the lowliest of species escaped their concern. Even while he was under German fire in the Geilenkirchen salient in November 1944, a mortarman found time to lift a struggling spider from the water in his foxhole and set it free. Almost 50 years later, the private recalled in his memoir: "At this moment his life seemed important." Life was a precious commodity at the front and GIs took good care of the animals that kept them company. A stray cat with a fungus disease visited the men of the 349th Infantry Regiment nightly at Montecatini in the winter of 1944. For ten consecutive nights, a battalion surgeon fed the animal powdered milk and C-ration hash and treated it with tincture of green soap, sulfathiazole, and salicylic acid. When the feline had fully recovered, the pleased doctor confided to his diary: "It looks as though I am of some use after all."[22] GIs from the countryside were especially sensitive to the suffering of farm animals. When men of the 90th Infantry Division arrived at a German village after having been pulled back from heavy fighting in the Saar bridgehead at Dillingen, two Maine farmboys were determined to make the rounds of all the barns to milk and feed the mooing cows, a job that took the exhausted soldiers until long after dark. In the Colmar pocket, a lieutenant from Montana literally risked his life to prevent cows from starving when he slipped into the stalls of bellowing animals at Mittelwihr to cut their ropes, knowing that the Germans were observing the area closely. The energy that soldiers could expend on rescuing an animal betrayed an intense preoccupation with survival. When a cow fell into a deep antitank trench in a German town at the Saar River, several men of the 90th Infantry Division spent more than a day building platform after platform and pushing the animal out of its trap step by step, refusing to give up on the dazed creature.[23]

Nothing, however, softened the American soldiers more than the sight of horses. Many GIs had some experience with the animals and in every unit there were men who had worked with them for a living, whether as breeders in Kentucky or cattlemen in the West. The 83rd Infantry Division, for example, appealed to ranchers and cowboys to round up the many horses that came with the 20,000 Germans who surrendered to the unit south of the Loire River in September 1944. GIs examined the equine species lovingly wherever they went in Europe, from the ponies at the National Horse Race in Iceland to the big farm animals of Brittany.[24] A soldier in

Great Britain wrote to his father: "I can't help but think of you every time I see one of these Clysedale [sic] horses."[25] The Americans were tormented by the vulnerability of the graceful animals in the gruesome, mechanical war. In October 1944, soldiers of the 29th Infantry Division, on shooting practice near Valkenburg, Holland, after the siege of Brest, were caught off guard by four stray horses galloping into the line of fire. An officer noticed that the "beautiful and pathetic sight" caused "an involuntary murmur of dismay" among his men, and he was pleased that they ceased firing instantly. "Anyone seeing them and caring for the great heart and beauty of the animals," the officer commented, "had to be glad that, after so many centuries, the horse was no longer a votive offering to war."[26]

Yet, despite the GIs' desperate attempts to protect the natural environment from senseless harm, battle time and again encroached upon it mercilessly. In Normandy, for instance, battle's fury chased away most of the living creatures and it troubled the GIs that not even birds twittered or chirped in the many hedges and orchards. A disquieted medic wrote to his family: "[T]he tweeting chatter of tiny feathered beings is momentarily drowned out by the twisting, whistling rush of great unseen forces."[27] The GIs soon realized, however, that the creatures that could take to their wings in battle were the fortunate ones. They watched with regret how many other animals were forced to suffer by man-made madness. Precious livestock was decimated under fire. "[D]ead cows," one company commander vividly remembered, "had become for us a sort of symbol of the war in France." In the Norman dairy country, fields were strewn with stiff-legged, bloating cattle. The stench of the decaying animals made soldiers retch. Troops had no time to remove the carcasses, which decomposed in the open until the farmers returned, burned them with kerosene, and covered them with lime. In the meantime, GIs were pained by the grotesque scenes of the cadavers. "Visualizing the fields of dead animals who had no stake in the warfare was a terrible sight to behold," admitted a battalion surgeon of the 29th Infantry Division.[28] No sight, however, was more revulsive to the American soldiers than that of horses suffering. And the increasing dependence of German troops on the noble animals made horrible carnage unavoidable. At Coutances in Normandy, GIs hurried along the roads to escape the sickening stench of dead horses. At Nonant-le-Pin, thousands of animals butchered in the Falaise pocket made the streets impassable. During the attack on the village of Hürtgen in the forest of the same name, GIs had to shake the horses' entrails from their boots.[29] Americans became willing to take risks under fire to end the suffering of wide-eyed, whinnying horses. A paratrooper applauded such an act of mercy during the Battle of the Bulge: "Though man's brutality to one another is tragic enough, to see helpless animals suffer by his actions is even more tragic." "[T]he slaughter of the horses made me sick," confessed a tank operator of the 4th Armored Division who witnessed the annihilation of Russian cavalry at the Blavet River in Brittany.

Animals are so damned innocent of it all! And that innocence inflates the value of their lives. The same animal whose life you would so casually take in lieu of a human being's becomes, in war, a newborn infant who ought to be safely cradled away somewhere.[30]

The Civilian World

That same innocence was what made the civilian world sacrosanct in the eyes of the American combat soldiers. Early in June 1944, men of the 760th Tank Battalion were nervously waiting on the outskirts of Rome for the order to roll into the heart of the city. When, seemingly out of nowhere, a wedding party appeared in the street and solemnly passed the many tanks, a deep, respectful silence immediately descended on the dirty soldiers. Only a few days later, in Normandy, an officer caught sight of a procession of young girls in white communion dresses at the village of Couvains. The disheveled soldier instantly went for his brakes and abruptly stopped his jeep to prevent the children from getting so much as dusty.[31]

It pained the American soldiers, however, that apart from making some symbolic gestures there was nothing they could do but watch how battle contemptuously refused to regard anything as sacred in Europe's total war. No matter how hardened the GIs became against seeing dead soldiers, civilian casualties never failed to make them shudder. Noncombatants seemed more precious than the human beings whose very uniforms were an admission of guilt to the crime of war. That the Allied side too was responsible for the killing of civilians made it only harder to accept, even when the victims were Germans. In the winter of 1944–45, a surgeon stared at the horribly mutilated bodies of a family that had been crushed in the cellar of a ruined house in the Brandscheid area. "I had no love for the Krauts," he confessed, "but such sights of civilian slaughter always sickened me."[32] It was the kind of blood no soldier wanted on his own hands. When men of the 84th Infantry Division entered a village near Brachelen in February 1945, a young girl lying dead in a wheelbarrow inside a barn was the first civilian they laid eyes on in that German community. Although scruples had not hindered the soldiers while blazing their way across the Ruhr River only hours earlier, this startling scene immediately caused them to fetch the local priest to assure him that they had nothing to do with her death.[33]

Yet, in its rage, battle encroached upon the civilian world in more than one treacherous way. The GIs hated fighting for towns while citizens were still around. Tense, scared, angry, the soldiers could not help responding violently to the slightest movement or sound that appeared threatening. In house-to-house fights, for instance, cellars tended to form the last redoubts of cornered enemy soldiers, but nervous GIs sometimes discovered after they had lobbed grenades down the stairways that the suspicious sounds had been only the muffled moans of families jamming the underground shelters.[34] Moreover, whereas battle frightened the most seasoned soldier, it left uninitiated civilians panic-stricken. A German artillery barrage at Veghel during Operation Market-Garden, for example, chased paratroopers into the "very depressing atmosphere" of a basement, where they were forced to listen to Dutch civilians "moan, shriek, sing hymns, and say their prayers."[35] But worse even than the civilians' panic under fire was the inexperience that made them oblivious to danger. Soldiers had become conditioned to respond to the slightest suspicious sound by dropping to the ground. Noncombatants lacked such reflexes and not infrequently went about their business unperturbed while hardened veterans rushed for safety. "[H]ow naive they can be," a sergeant said of the Italian farmers in the Velletri sector. "Can you picture with shells, shrapnel, bombs and everything dropping all around them and they will be all planting, hoeing or working somehow with their crops." It was, noted a private who watched French civilians at Casablanca in November 1942, as if "they thought that since they weren't fighting the shells wouldn't hit them."[36]

Unfortunately, bullets and shells did not avoid civilians. Worse than that, bombs purposely sought them out. Nothing made the cataclysm of the mid-twentieth century more total than the air war. The Army guides tried to prepare the GIs for this aspect of modern warfare. "There are housewives in aprons and youngsters in knee pants in Britain," warned one booklet, "who have lived through more high explosives in air raids than many soldiers saw in first class barrages in the last war." Nevertheless, "the mournful wailing of the English air raid sirens" and the sight of "a London where chapels thirteen centuries old have been blown to fine dust and the limbs of children have been pulled from under smashed stones" had "a sobering effect" on American soldiers who had expected to find the real battlefields across the Channel.[37] The mass destruction on the Continent made total war look even more obscene. The very ports of disembarkation looked as if they had been pulverized by tornadoes. If the ruins of Naples made one GI feel "somewhat uncomfortable," the "giant, decayed corpse" of Le Havre left another American "emotionally and spiritually wounded."[38] But the effects of the air raids were nowhere more visible than in the enemy's homeland. As early as November 1943, the Allies had listed about 40 German cities as either seriously damaged or virtually destroyed by the strategic air offensive.[39] The GIs could see for themselves what this meant: Aachen was "[m]ore incredible than the wildest Dali landscape," Cologne "a city of basements," Hannover "as desolate as a city on the moon," and Munich "pretty well kaput." Even a professional officer of the 95th Infantry Division could only gaze incredulously at how bombs had changed the course of a stream at Dortmund and had made it possible to look across large parts of Bremen from ground level. "Sometimes," an awed paratrooper concluded, "there was an advantage to being in the front lines."[40]

The vicious spiral of total war made the Germans wreak new havoc from the air just when the liberated civilians thought their ordeal had ended. On 12 June 1944, the first of thousands of V-1s was fired against England. The GIs soon referred to the weapons as buzz bombs, robot bombs, or flying bombs. Troops in the front lines at first were not particularly impressed by them. To soldiers of the 2nd Infantry Division at the Siegfried Line in November 1944, for example, the bombs were "merely curious sights to see" and the men were "amazed at the stories of fear of the bombs in the rear areas."[41] But even short visits to the rear quickly convinced frontline men of how destructive and nerve-racking the new weapons really were. London and Antwerp were the preferred targets of the V-weapons. Most American combat soldiers, however, were introduced to the murderous missiles during stays in hospitals and replacement depots at Liège. In their eyes, that Belgian community was "the most buzz-bombed city in the world." Like the civilians, the GIs there became mesmerized by the weapon's baleful sound, which reminded them of "a Model T with leaky gaskets" or "a greyhound bus as it shifts gears." The unpredictability of the bomb forced them to "freeze and sweat it out" each time one appeared in the sky. On the morning of 3 January 1945, a sergeant convalescing in Liège counted 47 bombs in three hours and admitted that the weapons were turning him into "a nervous wreck." The futility of the *Vergeltungswaffen* bothered the American soldiers more than anything else. They realized that this air offensive would not change the course of the war and that it was only adding to the grief of the helpless civilians. "It was enough," said a wounded American at Liège, "to make a soldier want to go back to the company."[42]

The destruction that rained from the air was as heartbreaking to the soldiers as it was devastating to the civilians. More than once, grotesque scenes of mutilated bodies gripped the GIs' stomachs upon entering a town. At Avellino, for instance, Allied bombers had killed so many Italians that they could not be buried and had to be burned in the streets.[43] The survivors too offered a sorry spectacle. An American soldier who saw his first ruined city in England in 1942 could not forget "the very empty look in women's faces as though it didn't matter very much what happened tomorrow." The ceaseless fear made the British people worn-out and high-strung. A lieutenant who went to London on a pass in January 1944 and witnessed two air raids was surprised to see "how generally apprehensive the populace seemed – much more tense than you would expect after all these years."[44] On the Continent, the GIs soaked in much more gruesome pictures of the survivors. Italians at Velletri stared "bewildered and dazed" at the GIs from the ruins of their town. In the eyes of the shell-shocked peasants at Pietramelara nothing was left but "the dull color of earth." Amidst the debris of Mortain, French people "stood crying and rocking back and forth, as though in prayer." In heap after heap of rubble, the GIs encountered European civilians who had gone mad and were screaming and wailing hysterically without end. Helpless medics could comfort them with nothing more than sodium amytal and sugar water before moving on to the next town.[45]

Most of all, however, the American soldiers were tormented by the irony of a war that often left them no other choice than to destroy what they wanted to save. Could they consider themselves true liberators, they wondered, when their Army guides prepared them for encounters with European families that would not understand why Allied bombings had made them homeless or had taken the lives of loved ones? Did they stand a fair chance of offering the German people an alternative to fascism, they asked themselves, when those same guides warned them that the air raids had given Nazi propaganda the opportunity to represent the Americans "as bombing only churches and hospitals and deliberately machine-gunning women and children?"[46] Having sailed to Europe on the premise that they would be helping people, it was not easy for the GIs to become reconciled to the sight of lives that their own military had ruined. Men of the 45th Infantry Division who entered a small village inland from Salerno were suddenly treated to silence and hostility instead of cheers. The soldiers remained puzzled until they saw the horribly mutilated body of a little boy that was laid out in the street. They learned that the child had just been strafed by an Allied fighter. "[A]s far as the village was concerned," brooded Bill Mauldin, "that man had come all the way across the ocean for the express purpose of killing that child." At times, the American liberators were more anxious to be forgiven than eager to be cheered. When Dutch civilians responded enthusiastically to the men of the 101st Airborne Division as they passed through their towns at the end of Operation Market-Garden, one of the paratroopers felt a surge of relief: "It gave us a good feeling to see that we were still welcomed as liberators in spite of the destructive battles that had been fought around their homes."[47]

The GIs readily admitted they hated "the utter hopelessness and futility of total war." A corporal in Germany wrote home sarcastically in December 1944: "Thanks to the Allied Air Forces most of Europe resembles Stone Henge more than anything else." Nevertheless, the American soldiers also realized that they were trapped and had to accept the consequences of this kind of warfare if they wanted to win it. "You may deplore 'total war,' at least in theory," lectured a lieutenant of the 2nd Armored Division, angered by his mother's doubts about the morality of bombing German cities. "But, as long as you are in the midst of one, you won't ever win it except by using total war facilities to the utmost."[48] To most combat soldiers, the matter was not a question of ethics, but of survival. They were guided by their instincts and shunned bothersome philosophical questions. The destruction of the Benedictine monastery of Cassino was a case in point. The religious retreat was one of the most renowned in Christendom and the GIs up front regarded it as "a symbol of much that we thought we were fighting for." But atop its mountain it was also a key point in the towering Gustav Line. Even while Fifth Army orders kept the air force from bombing the abbey, frustrated ground forces did not refrain from causing serious damage to the building with their artillery. When on the morning of 15 February 1944 impatient American infantrymen watched how bombers released the first of 600 tons of high explosive that would at last demolish the fortress, they could only "cry for joy as bomb after bomb crumbled it into dust." Only the men of the 34th Infantry Division showed regret: they resented the Allied commanders for giving the New Zealand and Indian troops the kind of air assistance that had been withheld when their unit had tried to storm Cassino earlier.[49] The iron law of total war applied to all involved, and the GIs could only count themselves lucky that it was not their country that had been dealt its horrible fate. Under the clouds of billowing black smoke from Saint-Dié, a combat engineer wrote in his diary in November 1944: "On this Thanksgiving Day in France we may be truly thankful that if we have to fight a war, it is being done on foreign soil – and not at home."[50]

Apart from the destruction and death caused by the actual fighting, looting was another of the many plagues of war that descended on the civilians, and it did not go away with the arrival of the American troops. The Army guide to enemy Italy warned the GIs: "Pillaging is inexcusable in an American soldier anywhere under any circumstances." Germany was to be no exception. "Respect property rights," repeated the GI guide. "Vandalism is inexcusable." Army regulations allowed the GIs to send home Nazi souvenirs and war trophies, but prohibited the mailing of non-military items. Company officers were expected to check outgoing parcels and their signatures were required before a package could be accepted.[51] In the field, however, these directives proved not to be enforced, although they were repeated again and again until the end of the war. Looting and pillaging continued to be frequent occurrences both in the conquered and the liberated countries and these offences constituted a special disciplinary problem for the US Army. In his study of a company of the 506th Regiment, 101st Airborne Division, Stephen Ambrose concluded:

> Nearly all the men of Easy, like nearly all the men in ETO, participated in the looting. It was a phenomenon of war. Thousands of men who had never before in their lives taken something of value that did not belong to them began taking it for granted that whatever they wanted was theirs. The looting was profitable, fun, low-risk, and completely in accord with the practice of every conquering army since Alexander the Great's time.[52]

The reasons why soldiers looted were numerous. It was indeed fun: rummaging through drawers and closets of abandoned houses in strange countries often provided one of the rare means of relaxation to soldiers in the front lines. Pocketing souvenirs was, of course, a good way for a soldier "to establish in postwar memory his claim 'to having been there.'"[53] But soldiers also had a strange knack for collecting things that were totally out of place on the battlefield. A GI in Italy, for instance, did not think it strange to adorn his foxhole with a clock from a farmhouse mantel. In a ruined house that served as a command post at Saint-Lô, an officer's attention was irresistibly drawn to a toy mouse on a table; when his unit finally moved out, he grabbed the plaything and carried it with him across Europe.[54] The irrelevance of such objects to battle was exactly what made them precious to a soldier. "[T]he point is," said a sergeant who had fought in Italy, "the things that attract him are *not* G.I. issue. For some reason civilian things seem more valuable to him." Such items were more than reminders of the life the GIs had left behind, remarked an officer, they also "appeared to give the soldier some assurance of his future beyond the destructive environment of the present. They represented a promise that he might survive."[55]

Most soldiers, however, were only aware of the material needs that made them loot. Some of what technically could have been called looting was totally innocent. Soldiers searched houses, for instance, for items that served practical purposes at the front. They looked for trinkets such as cigarette lighters and pocketknives or combed houses for stationery, fountain pens, ink bottles, and pencils to ensure the flow of mail home. Some GIs, however, regarded Europe as a giant flea market full of bargains and focused on more specialized items. An officer of the 760th Tank Battalion, for example, narrowed his search to demitasses and saucers for his wife. Not a few Americans grabbed the opportunity to enlarge their collection of firearms at home. One excited connoisseur informed his parents that he had laid hands on "two old cap-lock muzzle load pistols" as well as "a double twelve, made of Krupp steel."[56] Finally, there were soldiers who took to pillaging in an outright attempt to turn the war into a financial profit. Europe was hog heaven, for instance, for a mess sergeant of the 9th Infantry Division who had a gift shop in New Jersey; he systematically ransacked abandoned houses, storing the items in the unit's kitchen trucks. Safes and bank vaults exercised an irresistible attraction on many curious soldiers, who were fortunate to possess enough explosives to force open the most ingenious systems, using anything from bazookas to Teller mines.[57] Mindful of the changing fortunes of war, quite a few GIs opted for the safety of more stable investments than foreign currencies. The soldier with "the most finesse in looting" in a company of the 26th Infantry Division, for example, was known to limit himself to "light, small items such as stamps, jewelry, coins, and precious metal objects."[58] Precious stones and metals were most sought after. GIs who looted stores at Dillingen in December 1944, for instance, greedily filled their gas-mask carriers with jewelry and other small objects. Some American soldiers made a habit of frisking both German POWs and civilians in search of their pocket watches, which were ornate family heirlooms in heavy gold or silver cases.[59]

American military authorities were especially concerned about the embarrassment that looting would cause in friendly countries. The Army guide to France, for instance, urged the GIs to respect the people's belongings and to remember that "[t]he quickest way to get the local French angry with your outfit is for some members to rough-house and destroy any French property." Company officers could count on trouble from their superiors when unable to prevent their men from robbing friendly civilians. To an extent, peer pressure too dissuaded many from breaching the trust of sympathetic populations. "[I]t would not have been considered good form to steal from your allies ...," explained one GI, "and you would have been kidded by your buddies."[60] Nevertheless, even in friendly territory looting could not be prevented entirely. On D-Day itself, for example, soldiers of the 29th Infantry Division were caught ransacking a holiday cottage on Omaha beach. Where civilians had vanished, the temptation to take things from empty houses often proved too strong. In the so-called Island, a five-kilometer-wide area between the Lower Rhine and the Waal River, Dutch civilians were evacuated during the static warfare of October–November 1944. The situation almost invited the paratroopers to pillage and, bit by bit, watches, clocks, jewelry, and pieces of furniture disappeared from the homes. The protection of historic buildings against plunder also posed problems for the US Army. When necessity called for the accommodation of troops in châteaux and monasteries, for instance, objects of great value were invariably damaged or stolen.[61] The more scrupled GIs could only regret the blemish this behavior cast on their army. At the

Belgian-Luxembourg border, a private summed up the dismal record of the 87th
Infantry Division after having been in Europe a month and a half:

> frequently, with a superior officer's connivance and signature, chests of silverware
> were sent home, silver dishes, banquet cloths, mother-of-pearl opera glasses,
> cameras, jewelry, ancient dress sabers – everything from paintings to thimbles –
> and this while we were still in Allied territory.[62]

When the American troops entered Germany, the looting abruptly ended. In
enemy territory, looting became known among the GIs as "liberating," plunder as
"appropriation."[63] Although the military regulations against looting remained valid
in Germany, the GIs could not help regarding the enemy's possessions as rightfully
theirs. "It was a unique feeling," explained a paratroop captain who took part in the
sacking of Berchtesgaden early in May 1945. "You can't imagine such power as
we had. Whatever we wanted, we just took." The march across Germany caused
the kind of exhilaration that had intoxicated victorious armies since the earliest times.
In a letter from the Rhine Valley in March 1945, a lieutenant confessed to his wife
in California: "We've taken over the premises. They belong to us by right of
conquest. It gives you a strange feeling, Janie, rather wild and brutal."[64]

German property was taken at will not only by right of conquest but also by way
of retribution. "After what they did to France & Belgium," a combat engineer
explained to justify the looting near Ahrweiler in March 1945, "most of us feel they
have it coming to them." GIs who befriended a Belgian family at Bilzen in the winter
of 1945 regretted that the young mother still had to do the laundry by hand. Weeks
later, the men returned to the town on a pass from Germany and dropped off a washing
machine. It was, they said, "a present from Hitler."[65] The indignation of the
Americans increased as they penetrated deeper into enemy territory and uncovered
the full extent of Germany's plunder. At Boppard, the 87th Infantry Division came
across a German officers' supply dump that contained delicacies such as sardines
from Sicily, fish from Norway, olives, butter and cheese, and chocolate flavored
with coffee, orange, and vanilla. Men of the 71st Infantry Division explored a
castle at Kulmbach that had served as a lodging for German soldiers:

> We found paintings, museum displays (models) statues, cognac, rum, whiskey,
> and cans of everything from mushrooms to sardines to cocoa, jars of honey, jam,
> cherries, pears, all kinds of vegetables, blueberries by the case, cigarettes, cigars...
> And in the whole lot, there was NOT ONE German label. Mostly French, with
> some Norwegian, Belgian, and other countries.

In April 1945, soldiers of the 90th Infantry Division discovered the largest and most
valuable German treasure in a salt mine at Merkers. Apart from the entire gold reserve
of the *Reichsbank*, it contained piles of suitcases stashed with gold and silver tooth
fillings, watch cases, and wedding rings.[66]

The GIs gradually lost all inhibitions about taking the enemy's belongings.
Officers closed their eyes or participated in what became systematic searches for

the spoils in each newly conquered German town. Advance housing parties ordered the people out of their homes and appropriated the best loot before the battalions arrived. Next, the men from the line companies combed the houses for snipers, booby-traps, and arms, "liberating" anything that caught their fancy in the process. After having settled down in the houses, combat soldiers had time to hunt for more souvenirs from attic to wine cellar. Nothing escaped their scrutiny. Haystacks were searched because rumors claimed they often hid riches. Once the soldiers knew the Germans had also concealed valuables in cellars and had buried them in gardens, they extended their souvenir hunts to tapping on basement walls and sweeping yards with mine detectors. As the troops advanced, pillaging became more and more unbridled. "As far as looting goes," a medic told his wife in March 1945, "I'm beginning to see that the Americans are just as bad as the others."[67] The search for loot could make the soldiers careless. They wandered into houses on their own, for instance, falling prey to snipers or booby traps. Occasionally, looting even complicated unit activities. According to eyewitnesses, the 333rd Infantry Regiment's mop-up at Geilenkirchen in November 1944 was "slow, tedious, and frustrating," partly because "the officers and non-coms were lax in allowing the clean-up operation to turn into a treasure hunt." An officer of the 121st Infantry Regiment admitted that even during the hard fighting in the villages of the Hürtgen Forest it was not always easy to keep the men from looting and delaying the attack.[68] Company officers who tried to stop the practice did not endear themselves to their men. Only the fact that combat soldiers could not carry heavy loads far put an effective brake on their "appropriations" in Germany. "Now the boys are saying," wrote a combat engineer in his journal in the spring of 1945, "'If you can't eat it or drink it or — it, leave it!'" Apart from such practical considerations, the American conquerors continued to "liberate" Germany unabatedly, defying orders until the very end of the hostilities.[69] When the 79th Infantry Division published its combat history while still in Germany right after the war, its preface stated with pride: "Printed on German presses with German ink on German paper."[70]

Battle inevitably encroached upon the civilian world as soldiers in enemy and friendly uniforms killed, destroyed, and looted indiscriminately. There was nothing, however, that the American combat soldiers abhorred more than the carnage the civilians started among themselves. The liberation released years of pent-up anger, which was immediately directed against anyone who was even slightly suspected of collaboration with the fascist oppressor. The GIs soon learned that no war is more total than that in which neighbor turns against neighbor. They were aghast at the frenzied vengeance that erupted in most communities only moments after the inhabitants had been freed. "The big danger was not Germans," said a combat engineer who witnessed the fights between resistance groups and collaborators when entering Lyons in September 1944, "but we were in the middle of a French civil war."[71] Before American civil-affairs or military-government detachments arrived to ensure proper ways of justice, lynch law had already claimed victims in many towns. When soldiers of the 88th Infantry Division entered Vicenza in the Po

Valley, for example, about two dozen suspected collaborators had already been executed by fellow Italians. Appalled GIs watched how stone-faced partisans distributed the victims' shoes among the bystanders. Although he had seen his share of cruelty by that time, one of the unit's combat surgeons was sickened by the sight. "Vicenza," he put in his diary, "is a rough place. I'll never forget it."[72] In the wake of liberation, most European towns became rough places, with scenes of revenge many hardened combat soldiers would never be able to forget. The ritual of shaving the heads of female collaborators caused most disgust. A soldier of the 9th Infantry Division was forced to witness how French women at Laon were disgraced in that manner and then chased into a crowd of frenzied people viciously whipping them with their belts. The GI admitted he felt "uncomfortable being put in a situation where you sympathize with your enemy."[73] Such scenes disappointed American soldiers who had hoped that the long years of war had served as a catharsis for the European soul. "It is perhaps a great error to think, as we all have," feared one officer, "that suffering brings humility and piety." The poisoned atmosphere also made GIs wonder whether Europe's liberation from fascism had really opened the way to a more peaceful existence in the Old World. "Are we creating our own monsters," wondered a sergeant, "who, now that the wine of militarism has titillated their taste buds, will want to continue to fight wars of repression in the name of patriotism?"[74]

THE PERVERSION OF TOURISM

Of old, soldiers had joined the army in part to find adventure and to see the world. But when the Americans sailed to a war in the Old World for the second time in barely 25 years, from the outset the memory of Europe's wastelands guarded most against thinking of themselves as tourists. More importantly, the total nature of the second conflict threw war and society together in such a jumbled mass that it would have prevented the American combat soldiers from obtaining a tourist perception of Europe even if they had felt like trying.

In the front lines, of course, the Americans could not expect to find even a semblance of normal society. All that remained to the combat soldiers up front was the memory of a peacetime civilian existence and they desperately tried to keep that alive by artificial means. Nothing opened the doors to that faraway life faster and wider than music. A lieutenant who heard some popular American tunes amidst the dreary Vosges forests in the autumn of 1944 told his diary: "The music makes me aware that there is indeed another world devoid of death and suffering."[75] The repertoire of GI songs was rather limited. "Roll Me Over in the Clover," "For Me and My Gal," "There's a Long, Long Trail," and "Show Me the Way to Go Home" expressed the soldiers' vacillating moods. But they only adopted two songs as their favorites: "Over There," a ballad that had survived the Great War, and "Bless'em All," a melody borrowed from the British army. If the GIs did not feel much like singing, they loved to be carried away by music. Musical instruments were instantly snapped up at the front. On the very eve of the Ardennes counteroffensive, for instance, men of both the 90th Infantry Division at the Saar River and the 99th Infantry Division in eastern Belgium – totally oblivious to the approaching disaster – were enjoying barn dances with music from violins and harmonicas. But no other instrument was more popular than the piano. They were so sought after among the Americans that when green troops of the 84th Infantry Division entered the Siegfried Line in November 1944, they were warned to watch out for booby-trapped pianos. Hand-cranked Victrolas that had not been crushed by rubble also were the objects of delight at the front. F Company of the 358th Infantry Regiment found one in the bridgehead at Dillingen and wore out the few German records that came with it. Even when the men were withdrawn across the Saar River in a hurry in December 1944, they refused to leave the gramophone behind and lugged it with them during the move to help consolidate the Bulge.

Music broadcasts were very popular too, although the soldiers at the front could only listen to them by means of portable radios and tank-crew sets during lulls in battle. The GIs did not care much for the BBC music, which they called corny. They grew tired of the many SHAEF exhortations about discipline and cleanliness on the Armed Forces Network, but enjoyed its swing music. Often, whether by choice or because the broadcasts came in clearer, they listened to Axis Sally and Lord Haw Haw on the enemy stations. The Germans used female broadcasters with sexy voices and played exactly what the GIs liked to ensure they would get hooked. Axis Sally was known to broadcast the best jazz music as well as the most popular American songs, such as "Sweet Georgia Brown," "Don't Get Around Much Anymore," and a lot of Bing Crosby.[76] The GIs did not only tune in to the American-style propaganda programs, but also to the regular German broadcasts. An American who listened to them on a portable radio at Anzio, for instance, considered the German music "sweeter – more melody and less brass than ours."[77]

The sweetest of the German songs – or any songs for that matter – undoubtedly was "Lili Marlene." It was the biggest hit of the war and transcended armies and nationalities at the front. German radio stations played it incessantly, to the approval of many GIs. Soon it was covered in other languages. A soldier of the 36th Infantry Division in France claimed he had already heard the song in German, Italian, French, and English. In France and Belgium, Americans humming "Lili Marlene" were sometimes scolded by the civilians to whom it was nothing but a loathsome "boche song." But the GIs loved it in all its versions. A combat surgeon concluded his wartime diary with the English words to "Lili Marlene" as copied from *Life*. Beneath it were the words in German, as given to him by a German POW at Anzio.[78] Lili Marlene led soldiers back to the nostalgic times of civilian life, and it did not matter in what language she seduced them to believe that they had really returned there.

With or without music, the yearning for the peacefulness of civilian life kept nagging at the front. American soldiers who watched *Up in Mabel's Room* in a makeshift theater at the Luxembourg-German border in February 1945 did not care about the poor quality of the picture; what fascinated them was the unusual sight of "pretty, well-dressed girls and men in civilian clothes against undamaged interior decorators' backgrounds."[79] In abandoned houses, GIs entertained themselves by poring over the family albums of former occupants. Combat soldiers jumped at chances to reenact domestic scenes. Participants in the two-week battle for Dillingen in the Siegfried Line in December 1944 moved into a house, fixed their K rations, and then "actually set the table from the china cabinet and set down to eat just like a family." Paratroopers of the 101st Airborne Division had their very first taste of living in private houses at the front when they moved into Germany early in April 1945. A private described the luxury of entering one's "own home" after guard duty:

> Beyond the blackout curtains a light glowed and, as we hung our rifles on the hat rack and shed our raincoats, idle chatter drifted from the kitchen and gave us a warm, settled feeling. A pot of coffee would be simmering on the stove – help yourself ... Wash your hands at the sink. This was home.[80]

Combat soldiers found comfort in the make-believe but often did not have as much as a house to use as a stage. Costumes then remained the only props, and men in the front lines were inevitably attracted to dressing up as civilians. Scarves made out of parachute silk, for example, were the ultimate fashion fad among the soldiers in Normandy. At Castelfranco, infantrymen walked out of stores with Italian top hats, canes, and umbrellas in the summer of 1944. Men of the 84th Infantry Division at Palenberg near the Ruhr River, in December 1944, sported homburgs, spats, and vests as if they had stepped "directly out of *Esquire*." Similarly, it took a battalion of the 87th Infantry Division only a few hours to take on "a gaudy, musical-comedy appearance" during a lull in battle at Berdorf. The Ardennes counteroffensive had just been stemmed and there were no civilians left in the Luxembourg town. Soldiers were soon rummaging the stores and in no time decided to play the part of the inhabitants. First, brightly colored scarves became the craze. Then the men turned to outrageous jewelry: rings that fit only on the first knuckle, rhinestone pins that were fastened on khaki lapels, earrings that dangled from just one lobe. When someone suggested that lace would be perfect camouflage in the snow, the figured fabric became the dernier cri and soon covered most helmets. The charade abruptly ended when angry orders came down to get back into uniform without delay.[81]

Life in the civilian world could never be more than wishful thinking for soldiers at the front. But even when combat troops had the opportunity to see Europe in the rear areas, it was impossible for them to pretend that they were tourists strolling through a peacetime society. To begin with, as the Americans normally measured their stays away from the front in mere hours, sheer lack of time prevented them from seeing many of the prewar attractions and enjoying Europe in a culturally and historically acceptable way. The GI guide to Italy's cities, for instance, much regretted this. "You probably won't have the 14 to 16 days," the booklet noted dryly, "which people who know Rome say is the minimum period in which the sights of Rome can be seen hastily."[82] Ironically, the combat soldiers least able to explore

Europe were those in the rear with the most leisure time. A GI who arrived in Paris for treatment, after having been seriously wounded during the Battle of the Bulge, was given "a guided tour" by the ambulance driver, who called out "sights that none of his passengers could see." In the weeks that followed, sight-seeing did not improve for the patient:

> Instead of the Louvre and the Eiffel Tower there were hospitals; in place of the Folies, the operating theater; rather than Parisiennes there were GI medics wearing clean ODs.[83]

Whether resting or recovering in the rear, combat soldiers were not in the right mood to savor the European experience anyway. "If it was only during peace times," a sergeant in Italy told his parents, "I could say that this opportunity to see so many parts of the World has been the greatest thing that has ever happened for me."[84] But it was war, and far greater things obscured the joy of travel. During the long months in Britain, when they were waiting to be committed to the front, the GIs grew bored, impatient, and restless, despite all of the country's cultural attractions. They had sailed to Europe as soldiers and their minds were preoccupied with battle, which they knew was the only course that would end the war and take them home again.[85] On the Continent, during short breaks between battles, worrying about the immediate future came more naturally to the Americans than admiring the grandeur of Europe's past. A GI whose unit halted briefly in Rome in June 1944 testified to that:

> We prowl through Rome like ghosts, finding no satisfaction in anything we see or do. I feel like a man briefly reprieved from death; and there is no joy within me.[86]

Longer rest periods in the rear only provided the soldiers with time to cultivate their homesickness. The Americans had turned nostalgic the moment the New World had disappeared over the horizon. The Army guide to France's cities mentioned to the GIs that they might be interested in visiting Le Conquet near Brest for no other reason than that it was "just about the nearest French town to the United States." Across Europe, the GIs could not help being reminded of home. Twists of the imagination made Bournemouth look like Atlantic City, London like San Antonio, a highway into Florence like the East River Drive in Philadelphia, Paris like Washington, and Jössnitz, Germany like Montclair, New Jersey. Unfortunately, none of the flimsy resemblances could stand up to closer scrutiny, and even Paris was found out to be "a poor substitute for the place they really wanted – home."[87]

In that state of mind, combat soldiers in the rear discovered that "the cultural manifestations of a society offer attractions incomparably inferior to those of the bar and the brothel." That was at least the conclusion of a paratrooper who spent two weeks in Naples with the 82nd Airborne Division before it was shipped to England to prepare for D-Day. Other soldiers readily agreed with his observation. A combat engineer who admired cathedrals and their paintings in the vicinity of Naples was well aware that he was fascinated by "things that only 1 out of a 1000 soldiers care about seeing," as most of the other men went to the rear "to drink & carouse around." To many GIs in Europe, a pass to London meant nothing more than "a nonstop binge," a visit to Paris merely "a tour of the bars."[88] To be sure, there were Americans who would not have been interested in Europe's culture even if given the chance to see it at leisure and out of uniform. Many had just left high school and were, as one veteran admitted, "young and dumb, i.e. not nearly so aware of history and its importance." Others had simply been brought up with different values. They were the ones for whom the Army guides had to avoid sounding too high-brow in singing the praises of Europe. "[D]on't let us frighten you," said one such booklet, after having had the audacity to claim that the real Paris was that of great beauty and culture and not that of night life. "If you're the type who wants to have a gay time, you will undoubtedly find plenty of interesting cafes, restaurants, and places of amusement."[89] But the majority of GIs on combat passes preferred to spend most of their time in soft beds and cozy bars, not because beauty and culture did not appeal to them. "We had left the living hell that was war for the front-line soldier and were going back to it," explained a lieutenant of the 26th Infantry Division, who spent time in Paris on a pass from the Saarlautern sector. "Seeing the sights just did not appeal to us as much as having a bang-up good time."[90]

Combat soldiers not only lacked the time and the right mood to sightsee Europe, they also had to do without the vital attributes of the tourist: money and cameras. The US Army went to great lengths to pay its soldiers as regularly as possible, even if it meant that payment officers had to rush from foxhole to foxhole under fire. But money was totally out of place at the front. GIs quite often lost all of their pay in battle and even Thomas Cook could be of little help up front. A soldier who had lost his traveler's checks in an Alsatian foxhole and could not remember the serial numbers, complained that the form the American Express Company had sent him to fill out was "rather complicated and is supposed to be notarized."[91] There were few opportunities to spend money in the combat zone anyway. In the many desolate areas, like the Apennines or the Vosges, there was nothing whatsoever for the soldiers to buy. "Until we get out of the woods, we might as well be in the jungle," wrote a private who claimed he had not spent more than a few dollars in the two months that he had been in the Belgian Ardennes. In more populated areas, on the other hand, many articles were lacking or reserved for civilians with ration coupons. As a result, the GIs accumulated large amounts of cash in muddy foxholes. "I haven't spent a penny in ages," a private wrote to his parents from the Vosges in November 1944. "At $70 per month I'll be rich by the time we hit Berlin."[92] The GI guides to Europe urged the soldiers to save the money as "a nest egg for getting started in business after the war is over, or buying a home or a little farm." The GIs overwhelmingly followed the advice. By February 1945, between 90 and 95 per cent of the enlisted men overseas had automatic monthly deductions taken out of their pay for family support or savings. On top of the – often substantial – allotments, seven out of ten soldiers were able to send extra money home, generally by postal money order. A combat engineer who had $80 withheld from his $100 monthly pay, for instance, still managed to send additional money home periodically, and it was not unusual for GIs in foxholes to be clinging to receipts of homebound money orders worth up to $150.[93]

The little cash the soldiers did keep for themselves was usually paid in the currency of the country they happened to be in. This further lessened the meaning of money to them. The GIs were bombarded with information on all kinds of foreign currencies and exchange rates, from the farthings, threepences, and half crowns of the British – "your arguments that the American decimal system is better," the Army guide lectured, "won't convince them" – to the 14 different coins and bills of Germany.[94] But combat soldiers never stayed long enough in any of Europe's countries to figure out the intricate currencies. Moreover, the strange designs and shapes of bills and coins gave foreign money an even more unreal character. The Americans called it "playmoney" and loved to send it home for souvenirs. To add to the confusion, it was not always clear to the GIs whether certain kinds of European money were still valid or not. In Austria, for instance, both shillings and German *Reichsmarks* remained legal tender for a while, then the Allies switched to military shillings. Eventually, the combat soldiers stopped bothering about money altogether. Paratroopers of the 101st Division, for example, who took a box from German POWs that turned out to contain a *Wehrmacht* payroll in marks, kept only some for themselves and distributed the rest among civilians after attending Mass in a local church.[95]

The result of all this was that most combat soldiers were practically broke. So little money remained at the front that the stakes in gambling games were reduced to "tokens, souvenirs, booze, or a hundred million dollars."[96] Penniless frontline men resented the Red Cross service units for charging them and preferred the free service of the Salvation Army. Some lived on money they took from German POWs or dead, but most obtained what they needed from each other and civilians through barter, an arrangement in which tobacco became "the 'gold' of the land."[97] Not surprisingly, by the time soldiers were withdrawn from the front, they had often lost touch with society's economic reality. An excited combat medic, about to leave for Paris on a pass from the Bitche sector in February 1945, told his wife that he had seven cartons of cigarettes with which he planned to buy presents for her and their sons. In the rear, however, combat soldiers discovered that storekeepers still preferred hard cash over cigarettes. Moreover, high demand and scarce supplies combined with artificial exchange rates to create prices that caught the frontline men totally unprepared. They found London to be "*fabulously* expensive." A private who received a pass to the English capital near the end of the war, for example, complained that the fees of the prostitutes at Piccadilly Circus "had been inflated from a few shillings to as high as twenty pounds." In Italy, prices shot up too. In June 1944, a soldier claimed he paid $1.30 for a loaf of bread in Rome and $2.10 for a meal of macaroni, fried eggs, and French fries at Salerno. In Paris, prices were simply "outrageous." In the fall of 1944, an "average dinner" was reported to cost about $15; in the winter of 1945, the price of "an ordinary dinner at a mediocre restaurant" was said to have more than doubled. Neither could the GIs believe that plain sweaters and simple dresses were ten times more expensive in the Riviera than in the US.[98] Far from understanding the financial intricacies of the disrupted economies, the GIs blamed their pecuniary woes on the greed of the Europeans. "The natives are growing rich on us!" the Americans groused as early as the Icelandic operation. "We came here to protect them from the Germans," scoffed a private, shocked by the prices in Algeria. "Now we need someone to protect the soldiers from the merchants." The civilians, concluded a soldier in France, "all seem out to do you, if possible." No matter who was to blame, the exasperated combat soldiers lacked the money to buy more than kitsch. "Jewelry," a disappointed lieutenant wrote from Cannes to his mother, "is just out of the question."[99]

Cameras were as rare among the combat soldiers as money. USO entertainer Bob Hope claimed that "every soldier in the Army of the United States carried some kind of camera as standard equipment." But Hope never spent time in the front lines. In some units, soldiers were simply not allowed to carry cameras into combat and had to leave them in storage. Others quickly discovered that in battle a camera was "just something else to carry." Apart from a few pocket models, cameras therefore remained very scarce until the combat soldiers' conquest of Germany.[100] Not only was German photographic equipment the best in the world, from box models to Leicas, but cameras also happened to be on the list of objects enemy civilians had to turn in for security reasons, and that gave frontline men the first pick. Even then, the soldiers often were not able to send pictures home because rolls of film were scarce or could not be developed. In January 1945, a private of the 99th Infantry Division, then in a foxhole in the Belgian Sourbrodt Woods, was still promising his parents that he would forward his pictures, taken in England in October 1944, as soon as possible.[101]

Warring Europe was no ideal environment for snapshot takers. It did not matter that the combat soldiers had few cameras; Europe had squandered its photogenic charm anyway. What the American soldiers encountered across the Atlantic, at the front as in the rear, was not the Old World of tourist fame but a world ablaze. Total war, in some way or another, had affected every acre of Europe's territory and every aspect of its society.

To begin with, physical destruction had brutally scarred much of the face of Europe. The tone of the GI guides to the cities of Europe was ominous. Their introductions drew attention to the fact that the information they contained was "correct as of the outbreak of the war," but they hurried to add: "About the only thing in this booklet that can be guaranteed is the terrain. The rest of it is up to the fortunes or misfortunes of war."[102] The pocket guides were full of sobering warnings: while prewar Naples was simply said to be "gone," they were still uncertain about "just what the war has done to Paris." Moreover, the Army booklets contained painful ironies because they had gone to press while the war was still wreaking terrible havoc. They thus praised the district around Arnhem, for example, as "the most picturesque in the Netherlands" and informed the American soldiers that December and January were excellent months to visit the Belgian Ardennes to "practice your favorite wintersport."[103] The GIs rarely recognized the picture-postcard Europe. The Old World of famed ruins had turned into an infamous, ruined world, where the remains of the past's grandeur were buried by fresh rubble. After a visit to Rome, an American soldier indifferently entered in his diary on 11 June 1944: "See many old ruins, but we now have seen many ruins." The Army booklet on Italy's cities could only attempt to sound light-hearted about Europe's tragedy when setting the GIs straight on what were its old and its new ruins: "You've seen a lot of ruins in Italy; the Colosseum, however, wasn't wrecked by Long Toms. It got that way through the passage of time."[104]

But the war had not only physically maimed Europe, it had also broken its spirit and eroded its *savoir vivre*. Much of its cultural heritage had disappeared from sight. A GI who had visited the National Gallery in London wrote to his parents on 26 September 1943 that it was "rather easy to see these days, as everything is packed away." Indeed, its paintings had been sent to mines in Wales, and the museum displayed only one masterpiece at a time each month. In September 1943 that happened to be a Velasquez, but the American soldier noted that there had also been "a fairly good collection of modern British water colors on the War Effort."[105] The Army guides warned that the art of Rome would be either hidden or stolen, and some GIs were deeply disappointed to find Florence's Uffizi as well as its other renowned museums and art galleries empty and closed. The famous Dutch masterpieces of private and public collections had disappeared underground near Maastricht and were only brought to light again in September 1944. The invaluable art treasures of museums from all over Europe had been relegated from their usual temples to dank caves in the Third Reich. In an iron mine at Siegen, GIs discovered hundreds of paintings and sculptures, many damaged by dampness. In the salt mines of Merkers, Americans counted 393 paintings, 2,091 boxes of prints, 1,214 cases of miscellaneous objects, and 140 textiles. Countless other works of art, taken from occupied countries to enrich the private collections of Nazi leaders, were found in the mines of Altaussee in Austria.[106]

Europe had few means left to entertain. In the summer of 1942, the GIs in Londonderry complained about the fact that dances could only last until nine in the evening because of the curfew. In the wintertime, the lack of heat in Europe's cities made even seeing a movie a disagreeable experience. A corporal described how he watched *Jungle Princess* at Reims in January 1945:

> You can see the breath of the audience in the theatres and you sit there in your overcoat, greatly stamping your feet throughout the performance to keep them from frostbite.

Christmas in the Old World could not enchant either. In mid-December 1944, an American in Marseilles found virtually no cards, no store displays, and no street decorations. "I don't know," he told his parents, "whether France just doesn't make as much of Christmas as we do or whether the war has caused the loss of Christmas spirit."[107] Regardless of the season, it was never easy for the combat troops to catch the original flavor of a European city, if only because in places that were not off-limits to the soldiers, civilians were quickly reduced to a minority. A private who visited Brussels at the end of the war characterized the Belgian capital as the "home of Leopold (III), a few Belgians, and 88 million Joes and Tommies."[108]

Even "Gay Paree" failed to live up to the expectations of many GIs. "I was shocked and surprised both," a lieutenant wrote to his wife in November 1944, "for really Paris has so little to offer now."[109] Because of fuel shortages, there was no heat or hot water in most of Paris. At the Lido, GIs "got a kick out of watching the semi-nude chorus girls shivering with goosebumps plainly visible on their bare skin." The American army advised its soldiers to stay out of the restaurants because the Parisians themselves did not have enough to eat. Instead, the GIs dined at hotels taken over by the American military and supplied with rations. Nothing in Paris was what it had used to be. An infantry officer on a pass from the Siegfried Line in November 1944 found even the Eiffel Tower closed to visitors "because of a rumor that the Germans had weakened it."[110]

Many other of Europe's traditional tourist gathering places acquired a special irony in the shadow of war. The role of the hotel, for example, changed drastically. When paratroopers of the 506th Regiment moved to Torquay for exercises in English countryside that resembled Normandy, they did not check in as sightseers:

> We were billeted in a large hotel overlooking the ocean. Our presence here was supposed to be a secret, and guards were placed on all the doors so we wouldn't go roaming around the city.

On the Continent, hotels in the rear were in great demand as quartering places for mauled units that were withdrawn to rest; up front they became popular among the soldiers because their sturdy basements could withstand much pounding by artillery.[111] Europe's beaches also underwent striking metamorphoses. Where once they had beckoned bathers to the sea, war turned them into potential bridgeheads from which soldiers could be launched inland. As a result, the Axis redesigned many beautiful beaches into death traps. The Norman coast was pretty, observed a medic who landed there late in June 1944,

> but its pure, clean, and beautiful appearance was now treacherous. Its clean, white sand was infested with hidden mines. Beautiful waves hid barbed wire and concrete obstacles.

The idyllic summer cottages on Utah beach were really German pill boxes with painted shutters. At several spots near swanky Nice, minefields simply made it impossible for the GIs to reach the water. When the 85th Infantry Division was withdrawn to a rest and training area at the Tyrrhenian Sea in the summer of 1944, the soldiers were only allowed to take a swim under close supervision from lifeguards after the engineers had cleared a place for them on the heavily mined beach. Even then, the dark-red scars of the many men who had been wounded ensured that no GI would forget he was not on a grand tour of Europe.[112]

The American combat soldiers were never able to think of themselves as tourists in Europe and they resented the people at home for not understanding this. The home front constantly showed that it did not fully comprehend the soldiers' ordeals in the European war theaters. "[P]eople back home had no conception of what combat was like," noted a private in the Alsace, who had not been able to change his clothes or wash in weeks, but received a package from his sister that contained shaving cream and after-shave lotion.[113] GIs had to return money orders to concerned family members with the assurance they did not need more dollars where they were. An American, dug in amidst the forests of the Belgian Ardennes, politely thanked his parents for their check, but regretted to inform them he could not cash it because the matter had to be taken care of in one of the branches of a London bank. Relatives and friends were also chronically curious as to whether the soldiers had already seen this or that place in Europe. "[W]hat the heck makes you think we have time for sight seeing," a medic wrote from the Alsace, irritated by repeated questions from his parents about Paris.[114] From America also came unabashed requests for soldiers in foxholes to send *Chanel No. 5* from the French capital or rosaries – preferably blessed by the Pope – from Rome. Lonely, worried wives were not always the most understanding persons either. "I don't know what you thought I came over here to do," an angry platoon leader in Germany snapped at his wife after she had expressed concern in a letter about him and "the Paris girls." While the 42nd Infantry Division was staving off strong German counterattacks near Strasbourg early in January 1945, one of its sergeants curtly wrote to his spouse: "Shelia there is no chance of getting any pictures made: Where we are now it is all war and no funny business." When snapshots of the sergeant seemed to be out of the question, his wife – and she was not the only one – was seized by the idea of visiting him overseas. Once more, her husband tried to clear up the situation:

> Shelia I would love to have you where I could see you: But one day of it here and you would want to go home and never see the place again. It is not the Europe you read about in travel books.[115]

War was the sole raison d'être of the GIs in Europe. And despite often desperate attempts during rest periods in the rear, war loomed too large for the combat soldiers ever to chase it from their thoughts. One of the practical tips in the GI guide to Paris suggested:

> If you become depressed by viewing the many skeletons and bones in the Anatomical Museum you can pack yourself on a bench in the shady zoo and be amused by the antics of kids and monkeys.[116]

Yet, the American soldiers displayed a morbid curiosity about skeletons and bones even when withdrawn from the front. They were strangely fascinated by Europe's military past and by its legendary battles. Combat soldiers halted at medieval forts during training marches in England, wandered the plains of ancient Carthage while awaiting shipment to Italy, and visited the Great War battlefield when recovering at hospitals near Verdun.[117] The GI booklet on Italian cities emphasized the importance of Leonardo da Vinci in Milan's history, but thought it best to draw the average soldier's attention by describing him as an Ordnance rather than a Renaissance man. It listed hand grenades, shrapnel, the parachute, demountable bridges, a flame thrower, and an armored vehicle among da Vinci's military creations and also pointed out that, while painting *The Last Supper*, the master had "invented the real M.1 models."[118]

Even more interesting to the GIs than Europe's remnants of ancient battlefields and history of weaponry were its memorials to the soldiers of times past. It was as if the combat soldiers were haunted by their vulnerability and insignificance and looked for comfort in the knowledge that those who had died in battle ages ago still lived on in Europe's memory. An American soldier who visited Edinburgh, for example, cast a mere glance at the crags and cliffs and then spent much of his time strolling through military museums, where he particularly enjoyed reading the "tributes to past heroes." After the campaign in Sicily, a GI admired many of the island's catacombs and monuments, yet he became especially impressed by the body of a Roman soldier from the third century that still lay "well preserved in a glass case in an ancient cathedral."[119] But, in England as in France and Belgium, the absolute must for the GIs was a visit to the tomb of the unknown soldier of the Great War. The Army guide to Paris listed it as one of the most important sights, together with the Eiffel Tower and the Parc du Trocadero. The Americans gazed at the tombs of the immortal soldiers in pensive silence. A sergeant from Ohio considered the memorial the most impressive of all the monuments in London. After having taken in the inscription and the beauty of the simple design, the NCO was "almost convinced that the common enlisted man is after all a human being, a rational sensible person." A platoon leader of the 9th Infantry Division, who was being treated at a hospital in Paris, managed to go on a one-day tour of the city in November 1944. The officer first caught the subway to the opera district but then suddenly changed his mind. He ended up at the Arc de Triomphe and there spent most of his time at the last resting place of the unknown soldier, which he described in minute detail to his wife:

> It was pretty yesterday, for there were so many flowers on the tombs of the unknown soldiers. You have seen pictures of the Arch de Triumph, well, under one side is the urn containing a blue flame. The flame is the flame of eternal life of the unknown soldier. The flame is at the head of the unknown soldier's grave. It was so very interesting, wish I could have had a camera.[120]

Even in the rear, the war determined in large part what the American combat soldiers would see of Europe and how they would see it, thus totally overshadowing its traditional peacetime attractions. "Most of us," admitted a paratrooper, "sailed away from Europe with no knowledge of what it really was."[121]

If combat did much to distort the American soldiers' perception of Europe by allowing them only limited contacts with the population in exceptional circumstances, the total character of the war colored their picture of that overseas world even darker. Nothing upset the GIs more in Europe than the fact that warfare and civilian society proved impossible to separate. They were shocked to find that the war had become so demanding that it forced many of the civilians to make it their business. They were still more stunned by the fact that battle had become so ruthless that it refused to regard anyone or anything as inviolable, even among the most innocent noncombatants.

The result was that the war, whether at the front or in the rear, never allowed the American combat soldiers to get a well-informed idea of how Europe had looked under the normal conditions of peace. Instead, the GIs saw a society that appeared to be disintegrating and unlikely ever to recover fully again. What is more, the collapse seemed so utter and complete that the Americans refused to believe that the war alone could have been responsible for it. They sensed that World War II was merely the terminal symptom of a more complicated European disease, and suspected that the crash was in large measure the result of a much longer and more fundamental process of ruin that had been undermining the Old World.

9 The Old World

Early in December 1944, a draftee from Chicago was readying himself for the sea voyage from Boston to Europe. The soldier was married and had two children, and only curiosity could somewhat assuage his grief before he boarded the *Mount Vernon*. "The thought of going to Europe," he wrote, "despite its hazards, awakens my imagination. To me, the Old World will be a new world. A forward-looking spirit consoles me."[1]

But the Chicagoan, like most other American combat soldiers, would soon agree that although Europe was indeed a novel place in many ways, it could by no means be called a new world. Born in a young and impetuous country, the GIs found the weight of Europe's age oppressive; raised in a land of great plains and rocky mountains, they felt ill at ease in the constraints of Europe's space; fighting for republic and democracy, they were appalled by Europe's tradition of tyranny. The overseas experience convinced the American soldiers that the Old World had been suffering from stagnation and decline long before the onset of World War II.

THE WEIGHT OF AGE

Despite its name, the Old World managed to take some GIs by surprise with its age. "The country," a private wrote from Northern Ireland to his mother in March 1942, "is a pretty sort of place but is awfully old." A Texan's letter home betrayed a similar air of revelation after he had visited some cathedrals and catacombs in Sicily: "There is much interesting history back of these places that would take many sheets of paper, in fact many books, to describe." To American soldiers who watched Belgian peasants spin wool, German children play with pig bladders, and Alsatian town criers ring bells or beat drums, it felt as if scenes from the past were being reenacted before their very eyes.[2]

If Europe's ancientness surprised some American soldiers, it impressed almost all of them. The Old World instantly brought to life, for instance, the romantic images of the Middle Ages. The "curious, Methusalak-old towns" of Italy made a lieutenant suspect that they had "probably not much changed from the day the Children's Crusader bands marched through them."[3] Nothing, however, struck the GIs as more medieval in appearance than the English countryside, which exuded "the romance of a millennium" and caused many an American to fantasize about encountering knights in armor in the ancient forests or meeting King Arthur on the narrow, winding roads.[4] In the Mediterranean region, on the other hand, it looked as if biblical times had continued. Arabs wearing flowing robes, carrying staffs, and riding sideways on donkeys reminded GIs of Palm Sunday, while journeys from North Africa to Italy brought to mind the story of Saint Paul's missionary adventures.

Throughout Europe, the remnants of classical times impressed the Americans more than anything else. Men of the 3rd Armored Division in Britain reverently contemplated the wall surrounding their tent camp at Newcastle after having learned it had been built by none other than the Romans. In Sicily, incredulous soldiers of a reconnaissance unit of the 2nd Armored Division discovered a shortcut to Palermo in the form of a small Roman road that was not even marked on their map.[5] Nowhere did the spirit of the ancients fill the air more than in Italy. It was, a surgeon concluded at Atripalda, "a country ancient as any, the birthplace, really, of civilization." The stars shining over Bari reminded an American that they were "the very ones studied by the old Roman scholars," and the sudden storm that shook the invasion fleet in sight of the Sicilian coast did not fail to release in some GIs the memory of Aeolus' wind and Odysseus' fate.[6]

It was hard for the Americans to understand how the inhabitants of the Old World could accept such a towering past as part of their lives with such matter-of-factness. GIs wrote with rapture about German gravestones with seventeenth century names, English churches built eight centuries ago, and Icelandic cemeteries a thousand years old. Comparisons with their own history made the soldiers humblingly aware of their country's extreme youth. The relics of Britain's Roman occupation reduced even the monuments of America's east coast to "things of yesterday" in the eyes of one chaplain, while Italy's mountain towns made a regimental commander realize they had probably been "old when Columbus discovered America." Yet amidst all this, an American noticed, the Europeans – in an almost blasé way – seemed to "wonder why anyone is interested."[7]

To some GIs, the sense of age proved to be an enlightening experience. Whereas America boasted size and newness, Europe could pride itself on the fact that "time lived on unchanged through generations." The Old World's attachment to that past was, according to a chaplain in England, "more of a virtue than a vice:"

> In our worship of the modern we are willing to raze and destroy what we feel stands in the way of the new. The British are not willing to do that. They make progress a little more slowly and save as much as possible which is good from the past.[8]

Some Americans learned that weathered relics from the past could be much more impressive than the newest constructions of steel and glass. The "stone forests of cathedrals," for instance, awed a corporal who was stationed in England:

> That contemporary shrine and highest expression of American religion, Radio City, which houses the radio, movies, and thirty-six chorus girls most resplendently, seems a tawdry, simple, empty spectacle after one has seen something like Salisbury Cathedral.[9]

But there was much more to living with the legacy of ages than met the eye. To the people of the Old World, the past was a deep, knotty root that nourished hearts and minds without interruption. On occasion, the blessing of that European condition could reveal itself in a flash to a GI who allowed himself to be dissolved in history. "I felt again the aching beauty of this incomparable land," exalted an officer who helped capture Rome, "I remembered everything that I had ever been and was. It was painful and glorious."[10]

To most GIs, however, it appeared as if the past was holding the Old World in a suffocating grip rather than a tender embrace. Time had become larger than man in Europe; and man's efforts to change the course of history in this part of the world seemed doomed to be absorbed and neutralized by the vastness of ages. Sometimes the American soldiers could not help feeling as if even their own mighty war machine was being swallowed by the looming shadows of Europe's past. A French noble's estate near Balleroy, for example, was "so huge and austere" that the 1st Infantry Division's artillery was "dwarfed under the avenues of majestic trees," and even the tanks of the 36th Infantry Division that rolled onto Saint Peter's Square during the liberation of Rome suddenly looked "tiny in the face of such grandeur."[11] The past showed a perverse pleasure in slowing down the New World's attempts to free the Europeans from oppression. Thick stone walls, built by "[c]enturies of labor," hampered the advance of infantrymen through the fields of Sicily. Soldiers of the 88th Infantry Division who neared Rome early in June 1944 found the many ancient vineyards around the city "as difficult to get through as barbed wire entanglements." More than once they had no choice but to follow the rows of old, gnarled grapevines on a course that led away from the objective. In Normandy, even the tanks bogged down before the age-old hedgerows that enclosed innumerable "odd geometric shapes left by generations of land division."[12] On top of that, the towns and cities of Europe lacked the checkerboard plans of America's settlements. The GIs, used to long, straight streets with regular intersections, often felt "like someone suddenly dropped on a strange planet" when advancing through the age-old mazes of narrow roads and winding alleys. Bereft of detailed city maps, soldiers of the 350th Infantry Regiment, for instance, tried to enter Rome early in June 1944 by splitting into two columns that intended to march along parallel roads while keeping contact with jeeps; the men soon found themselves hopelessly lost in the twisted bowels of the Eternal City.[13] Many cities also boasted elaborate defensive works built throughout centuries to keep out endless series of marauders and invaders. Now, however, the strongholds of the past were cleverly being used by the enemy to frustrate the advance of troops that had come as liberators. The attack on Brest by men of the 121st Infantry Regiment in August 1944, for example, was stopped by Fort Bougan: a deep moat surrounded the seventeenth-century bulwark and its high walls were so thick that even twentieth-century shells "bounced off like marbles on a floor." Metz and its 37 ancient forts held up American troops for weeks in the autumn of 1944. Storming the French city's "medieval ramparts and conical forts" gave a tank operator of the 4th Armored Division the sensation of a "strange time warp." At Jülich, a German city that had its origins in a Roman camp and had been turned into a bastion with walls and a citadel in the late Middle Ages, American volunteers had to blow up heavy double doors under cover of flamethrowing tanks before yelling and screaming troops were able to swarm across the moat and into the huge courtyard.[14]

The ponderous weight of Europe's past had an oppressive effect on many GIs. "At first sight everything looked dirty," noted a soldier in a Sicilian town, "but then you realized it was just old." The Europeans seemed to value remembrance more than vibrance. Buildings had "the disconsolate look of age," churches appeared to be "dead with age."[15] The past's omnipresence created an almost suffocating atmosphere. During the battle for Cassino, a lieutenant was struck by "the ancient sour smell" of the farmhouses. Likewise, a medic observed that in the old towns near the French-German border "the damp, dark walls were wet and shiny" even on hot, dry days and always "smelled foul." The Americans thought they recognized the smell of decay. After having seen similar places in Northern Ireland, England, and French North Africa, a lieutenant of the Big Red One described Petralia in Sicily as "another typically ancient and decadent town."[16]

THE CONSTRAINTS OF SPACE

Age was not the only disease that stifled the Old World. The Army guides warned the GIs that they would find the countries of Europe rather small. Northern Ireland was "only slightly larger than the state of Connecticut;" the whole of Great Britain was "hardly bigger than Minnesota;" France could be put into Utah and Nevada; and Germany was "not as large as Texas."[17] Despite the warnings, the American soldiers soon felt constrained in the cramped and crowded space of the Old World. Europe was not Lilliput, but it was easily dwarfed by the memory of America's proportions and its nature looked rather timid in comparison to the ruggedness of the home country. The Rock of Gibraltar turned out to be only "impressive in a small way;" the mountains of Cassino proved not to be as high as Mount Rainier or Mount Hood; the Ardennes reminded the Americans more of Seattle's hills than of the grandeur of the Rocky Mountains.[18] The GIs also noticed that many of the streams indicated on European maps as rivers would simply have been called creeks in America. The Army guide to Britain pointed out that England's largest river, the Thames, was "not even as big as the Mississippi when it leaves Minnesota." Both the Meuse and the Moselle reminded one American soldier of "the small rivers you see off the highway as you drive out for a Sunday picnic." And quite a few soldiers were surprised to find that not even the fabled Rhine was as broad and swift as the American "Father of Waters."[19]

In Britain, an American chaplain searched "in vain for a patch of woods that look God made." The limited space and the absence of new frontiers had forced the Europeans to cultivate every available acre. "Each square foot's accounted for," a medic wrote home from England. "Our countryside is wasteland; theirs is pasture." Throughout the Old World, the GIs were astonished to find that the people farmed "clear to the top of the mountains." Not an inch was wasted in the urban environments either. "All the houses are built against one another – no yards at all in the little towns," a sergeant from Pennsylvania reported in a letter home. "Here space is needed for other things besides growing grass."[20] The GIs failed to understand how European farmers managed to make a living on plots of land that looked "almost absurdly small" to people used to "tractors and far horizons." The Army guides informed the Americans that 100 acres was a big farm in France and that in Ireland 5 acres was "respectable," 20 acres "substantial," and more than 40 acres "large-scale farming." A medic who owned a modest 240-acre farm in Iowa told his mother that the Irishmen were impressed by such "an awfully big ranch." Surveying the small, odd-shaped fields and pastures in eastern Belgium, a private from Kansas wrote to his parents in December 1944: "If all of Europe is anything like this, I can see why everyone emigrated to the U.S."[21]

The crowded Old World did not only give the American soldiers a claustrophobic feeling, it even slowed down their attempts to liberate the natives. Europe's narrow, closed spaces frustrated the advance of America's modern, mechanized war machine in many unforeseen ways. Traffic was easily held up in the British countryside, where corkscrew roads were, a chaplain complained, "so narrow two passing cars scrape the hedges."[22] The roads of some villages on the Continent were so small and crooked and the corners so sharp that the big American trucks could not drive through them. When the 9th Infantry Division was preparing for an amphibious assault across the Rhine at Bonn, tank retrievers as well as trailers carrying the boats got stuck in the old villages near the river bank and only managed to break free by knocking off the houses' protruding edges. Small Italian communities, with only one road on which one vehicle could pass at a time, caused traffic jam after traffic jam at the front.[23] While infantrymen complained that the villages formed bottlenecks that slowed down convoys and turned them into easy targets for scattered enemy planes, tank crews considered the disorganized towns veritable death traps. In labyrinthine Avranches, German tanks were hidden "in every nook and cranny," and at Schweinheim, the streets were "so narrow as to augment the already internecine power of the enemy fire." The streets of Rochefort turned out to be so small that tanks could barely participate in the heavy fighting for the town during the Battle of the Bulge.[24]

THE SHACKLES OF TYRANNY

The GIs did not only become aware of the stunting effects of Europe's age and size. Almost intuitively, they sensed the deep and disfiguring mental scars that had been left behind by another of the Old World's plagues: the rule of tyrants. As soldiers from a country that had bade the king farewell at birth and had abolished all aristocratic titles and privileges in writing, the Americans were understandably fascinated by the remnants of the rejected system in the Old World. They wrote home in minute detail, for instance, about the magnificent castles ("relic[s] of feudal might and splendor") and the ritzy cafés of Paris's opera district ("[s]upposed to be for the aristocracy back in the earlier days"). The chaplain of a combat engineer unit in Luxembourg, who had been invited by a local nobleman to participate in a boar hunt, had to admit to his wife that he had "really enjoyed the sports of kings."[25]

However, with their inbred suspicion of monarchy and aristocracy, the GIs refused to be fooled by the outward appearances of the old system. The Army guides tried to explain that although the custom of titles might seem "strange and old-fashioned" to Americans, it gave the Europeans "the same feeling of security and comfort that many of us get from the familiar ritual of a church service."[26] But, the Army lectures notwithstanding, the GIs remained ill at ease in a social environment that bore the stamp of rigid hierarchy and class privilege. They were appalled to learn how much of the Old World was still permeated by the distinctions of class. The guide to Northern Ireland informed the GIs that "the large landowners, professional men, industrialists, tradesmen, farmers, laborers, all accept their allotted places in the social set-up." Paratroopers who organized an exhibition baseball game for a local English school noticed that the boys enjoyed the game, but that they were "shocked beyond words" by the American habit of constantly challenging the authority of the umpire.[27] But Europe's hierarchical rigidity revealed itself most painfully in the Mediterranean region. In Sicily, for instance, the GIs discovered that many of the poor peasants still existed in a state of partial servitude on the latifundia of powerful landowners who lived in splendor on the mainland. Even when they entered France, the country that had once fought so ferociously to obtain égalité, the surprised Americans learned that buses and subways were divided into two classes, passenger trains into no less than three. A lieutenant wrote to his wife in August 1944 that although he was aware he had been prejudiced toward the French aristocracy by hearing *A Tale of Two Cities* read aloud as a child, he remained convinced that all was not right even in republican France: "you keenly feel the degradation of the poor by the rich here. There are not enough wholesome middle-class people."[28]

The privileges of the few had been born out of the oppression of the common people and the American soldiers did not have to look far in Europe to find proof of this. A lieutenant who passed the palace of the Bourbon kings at Caserta while on his way to the front in January 1944 was dazzled by its splendor until he was brusquely reminded of the harsh reality behind it: "Like many of the great palaces of Italy, it stood amidst appalling poverty in the town and countryside. The blood of many a peasant family had gone into its construction and maintenance." Correspondent Ernie Pyle too commented with indignation on the contrast between the "rococo domicile" of an Italian baron somewhere in Sicily and the sheds and caves in which his servants had been forced to live.[29] Worse than being reminded of the social injustice of the Old World's past, however, was the realization that the excesses of privilege still existed in Europe. The American enlisted men never stopped griping about the benefits accorded to the officers in their own army, but the sharp barriers between ranks condoned in the European military made their grudges seem like pettiness. The GIs were introduced to the Old World contrasts of rank as soon as they boarded the European troopships that carried them to the war. The tremendous difference in accommodation between the enlisted men in the hold and the officers on deck was a much discussed subject among the GIs. In fact, the American officers themselves were sometimes embarrassed by the blatant distinction the Europeans created between superiors and subordinates. Etched on the memory of a lieutenant of the 66th Infantry Division was the treatment of his men on the Belgian SS *Leopoldville* during the short trip from Southampton to Cherbourg in December 1944. While the crew, composed of Belgians and natives from the Congo colony, provided the enlisted men in the hold with a green, smelly stew in buckets that were lowered by ropes, the American officers were served good food and a glass of wine in an agreeable mess attended by jacketed waiters. The lieutenant prayed that his platoon would never find out about this: "My thought at the time was that this sort of privilege may work in the British Navy or Belgian Merchant Marine but would never work for more than a couple of minutes in the U.S. Army."[30]

Perhaps the American combat soldiers were particularly sensitive to the distinctions of class because they themselves were confronted by the great divide between two Army castes in the war theater: the privileged in the rear and the commoners at the front. Up front, enlisted men and officers alike became keenly aware of what it meant to belong to the lower rung of an immovable hierarchy. When US troops invaded Italy in the fall of 1943, for instance, it was deemed no more than appropriate for general Mark Clark and his Fifth Army's headquarters to move into the palace of the Bourbon kings at Caserta. The lodgings the US Army reserved for its frontline troops likewise befitted their place on the military ladder. Combat troops pouring into Great Britain, for example, were often sent to large estates owned by wealthy families. There they were most likely either to be stowed away in tent camps erected on private golf courses or to be relegated to servant quarters and old stables converted into billets. A platoon from the 506th Parachute Regiment, stationed on an estate near Swindon in 1943, jokingly tried to facilitate administrative matters by referring to themselves as the men "from stable 13."[31] The move to the Continent did not improve the combat soldiers' housing arrangements. Replacements who arrived at Neufchâteau from Omaha beach in November 1944, for instance, were "dumped unceremoniously into a converted stable yard," where they "slept like tired dray horses." Around that same time, but further to the east in the Geilenkirchen salient, a platoon of the newly arrived 84th Infantry Division was assigned to a cowshed, where the men settled down in the troughs.[32] Battle itself in turn taught the combat soldiers to stay down to earth at all times, while reminding them in the cities that they could never afford to live upstairs and instead had to make the best of life in the basement. It was no wonder the frontline soldiers ended up calling themselves dogfaces.

Neither was it surprising that the frontline men readily identified with the common people of the Old World. Many of the privileged Europeans appeared to have fled before the impending disaster. One of the first things that struck the GIs upon nearing the coast of Northern Ireland in 1942, for example, was that most of the mansions were boarded up. The aristocrats in particular were suspected of having abandoned the sinking ship. Americans recovering in a hospital erected in the grounds of a large English estate learned that the earl of the hundred-room manor house was staying in Australia; soldiers of the 42nd Infantry Division resting in a beautiful German castle at Schwarzenberg found out that the prince had fled to Canada. When correspondent Ernie Pyle came across an empty country house somewhere in Sicily, it took him only a moment to surmise that "the baron had skedaddled, as royalty has been known to do."[33] The common people, on the other hand, had not had the means to escape the danger and destruction and had been left no other choice than to weather the storm. They were the people the dogfaces were destined to meet across Europe. In Great Britain, for instance, the GIs were most likely to make civilian friends in the pub, which they soon dubbed the poor or working man's club. In the front lines, even during the furious battles in Normandy and the Ardennes, the last remaining civilians the soldiers encountered were the simple peasants. They risked their lives by staying behind to care for a few precious milk cows, and GIs sometimes discovered them hiding in the cellars with their animals. At Troina, a lieutenant of the 1st Infantry Division noticed that the Sicilians who owned houses full of fine furniture and china had fled, while the wretched peasants were cowering in their shacks. "It is always the ordinary people who suffer most," a lieutenant of the 29th Infantry Division wrote to his wife early in January 1945. "Perhaps because there are more of them. But not only for that – they are the infantry of life. They bear the brunt."[34]

The Old World's privileged, and most of all its nobles, were suspect in the eyes of many American soldiers. They had been synonymous with oppression in the American consciousness for centuries and, in the minds of the GIs, were therefore also easily linked with the outrages of the fascist regimes. When a company commander of the 760th Tank Battalion set up his command post in a large villa at the Arno River in July 1944, he did not fail to notice that the Italian count tolerated his men but did not exactly welcome them into his residence. "I'm not sure it's true," a lieutenant from the 1st Armored Division wrote home from Italy that same month, "but landholders either can't, or rarely are partisans – some say there's a partisan rule against it."[35] The GIs felt much more at ease with Europe's plain people. A private from Ohio, who had spent several pleasant evenings in the homes of Irish farmers in 1942, told his sister: "American farm folk are invariably 'right folk,' and the same seems to apply to Irishers." The ordinary people appeared to be the ones more likely to have kept faith in the old-fashioned but sound values, even in Germany. Men of the 29th Infantry Division were surprised to run into a group of escaped American POWs who had been given shelter by German villagers near Dannenberg in April 1945. "The German country people," concluded a pleased lieutenant, "are much like country folk anywhere." The dogfaces were convinced that the little people of Europe were their true allies in the war. In the spring of 1944, a sergeant of the 36th Infantry Division praised the Italian farmers in a letter to his girlfriend:

Anything they have is yours and the American soldier helps this along by giving them food, candy and cigarettes. It doesn't hurt to be a Samaritan. After all we are fighting this war for the common people of the U.S. and of the world.[36]

The GIs could even forgive Europe's leftists their anti-capitalist radicalism now that they belonged to the most motivated allies in the fight against fascist oppression. In North Africa, the GIs had already encountered many Spanish and French communists who had fled the Continent and hailed the Americans as liberators and comrades. One GI, who had celebrated Christmas of 1942 with soldiers of various nationalities at the headquarters of the Foreign Legion in Algeria, wrote home excitedly that when the Spanish had started the "Internationale" "we all jumped up and sang it giving the clenched fist salute." At the end of the North African campaign, a private of the 1st Armored Division talked with some German POWs who revealed they were communists and who predicted the defeat of Hitler within months; later, in Italy, he ran into refugees from Turin who proudly claimed that for every two fascists in northern Italy there were eight communists and socialists. "They were," the American private decided, "fine fellows." Many of the groups in Europe that actively resisted fascism held leftist convictions. A partisan leader at Colmar assured a combat surgeon of the 12th Armored Division that the poor were the resistance because nobles, bishops, and millionaires were not likely to hide in cellars with Sten guns. When the Frenchman hinted that he might not understand because he was a physician, the indignant American pointed out that he was a New Deal Democrat. The resistance fighters approved of this, clenched their fists, and shouted: *El frente popular del mundo!* The common people of the New and the Old World appeared to have united to quash tyranny once and forever. Early in November 1944, a Japanese-American medic was assisted in his aid station by an Alsatian woman whose husband was a POW in Germany. On one occasion, the medic returned from the front lines covered in mud:

> Then she did something which I will never forget. She led me to the fire and on her knees she scraped the mud off of my pants with a paring knife, like the humble servant. Who says this isn't the little people's war?[37]

And the coalition of little people seemed to be winning the war at the front. The American sons of Europe's political, religious, and economic refugees found much poetic justice in the unexpected opportunity to get even with the privileged establishment of the Old World. When men of the 82nd Airborne Division captured Castellammare del Golfo, they found the Sicilians hungry and angry. A lieutenant and some of his men rushed off to the surrounding large estates where they forced "some rich Fascist landowners" to sell them their wheat. The GIs simply told those who protested to shut up.[38] It appeared as if this Armageddon was not only sweeping away fascist oppression, but was simultaneously creating the occasion for the American troops to join hands with the Old World's downtrodden in an attempt to erase the last remnants of aristocratic tyranny. In the confusing first days of the

Ardennes counteroffensive, an American sergeant came across a group of Belgian resistance fighters in the Forêt de Freyr. They told him, "with proletarian scorn," that the forest had been the private hunting ground of Flemish counts since medieval times, but that they had claimed it now and had turned it into a guerrilla stronghold against fascist tyranny.[39] The GIs in turn took possession of those other striking symbols of the Old World's feudalism: the châteaux. At Prato, a company of the 1st Armored Division rashly moved into a big mansion on a hill, forcing the Italian landowners to be satisfied with the servants' quarters across the courtyard. On the other side of the Alps, it doubly gratified a lieutenant of the 825th Tank Destroyer Battalion to have his men take up residence in a splendid château at Mayet. Not only had they chased a German general from the castle, but the French owner himself turned out to have moved to the porter's lodge at the gate. The "boys from the hills of Tennessee," noted the satisfied officer, would now sleep in the grand salon where once "the feet of gentlemen and ladies" had danced.[40] While a guest at a Belgian castle during the Battle of the Bulge, a GI wrote to his parents that the old baroness was "laughing about tending the fire herself and recalling the past days of grandeur." The American soldiers could not help feeling that the war was bringing an end to a much longer era of darkness in Europe's history than that of fascist domination. During the siege of Metz, a sergeant of the 4th Armored Division watched with as much awe as contentment how American fire managed to raze the city's formidable ancient forts at last. "Maybe," he ventured, "our twentieth-century guns did blow away the Middle Ages."[41]

STAGNATION ...

The GIs felt a compelling need for a tabula rasa in the Old World because it appeared to have become hopelessly stagnant. Of course, Europe's total war did much to evoke the impression of stagnancy. And so did the fact that it was difficult for the American combat soldiers, most of whom had never seen Europe in peacetime and were now only able to have limited contacts with the civilian population, to distinguish between the circumstances that were attributable to the conflict and the conditions that formed an intrinsic part of the Old World. Nevertheless, in their final analysis the GIs were convinced that the Old World's stagnancy was not only, or even mainly, the result of the war, but rather of a more general and deep-rooted degeneration.

The Army guidebooks did their best to convince the GIs that if the Europeans could not be proud of how their part of the world looked, it had to be blamed on the war. They told the soldiers, for instance, that it was only because of the wartime rationing system that it would be hard to find products in Great Britain "available at any corner store in America." They also warned the GIs that with many of its able-bodied men imprisoned in Germany, France's towns, houses, roads, and farms would not be in good condition, but they urged the men not to forget that before the war "[t]housands of American tourists a year used to flock to France because its beauties and picturesque landscape made it a show place." Yet even the official US Army guides had to admit that the differences with the American standard of living were not solely the result of the recent hostilities. They could not deny, for example, that Sicily's farmers had lived "in primitive conditions" long before the war. Moreover, they had to acknowledge that American wages were "about the highest in the world" and to concede that, in comparison, the people in Northern Ireland were "exceedingly poor" and even the wages in England "much lower."[42]

The GIs themselves came to similar conclusions in their perception of the Old World. To begin with, although they had known a system of rationing at home, the American soldiers were stunned by the shortages that existed in Europe. Late in 1942, a sergeant wrote from French North Africa to his brothers in the Bronx: "When you hear anyone complain about rationing in New York, please laugh for me, because you cannot imagine what rationing is." Another sergeant admitted that the American newcomers in Britain usually made "fun of the English standard of living" until they came to understand better the plight that war had forced upon the country; from then on they could only feel sympathy for the people.[43] Yet the GIs never entirely succeeded in separating wartime shortages from Old World want. Had British food always been so unimaginative, or was the war responsible for its blandness? "Maybe it's the war," a private wrote in his diary in October 1942, "but they should learn to cook." "We wonder, too," voiced another soldier, "if British tea will improve when the war is over?" Similar questions arose elsewhere in Europe. The Americans watched with amazement as Italian peasants spent long hours in groves and forests gathering bundles of twigs and sticks for their fireplaces. They were surprised to learn that glass bottles were in such short supply from Casablanca to the Alsace that they had to turn in old bottles or their canteens to buy wine in French cafés. And all this seemed to say as much about the Old World as it did about war. "My own impressions are quite logical," concluded a sergeant from the 44th Infantry Division in France,

> In America we indeed do live well. Here we see frugality and economy carried to what we'd call extremes. No wonder America is called a country of wasters and spend thrifts.[44]

European clothing also puzzled the GIs. They knew that the British could only buy clothes with coupons and were allowed just one suit a year because there was a war on. They realized that tailors in French North Africa sold no suits whatsoever and kept busy patching and repairing old ones as a result of wartime shortages. They understood that many shoes in Europe were wooden-soled because leather had become scarce since the outbreak of hostilities. But it was hard for many GIs, for instance, to fathom why people in Europe had still been wearing the outdated wooden shoes even before the hardships of the war. The Army guide tried to explain that the French peasants wore these "picturesque" shoes because they insulated their feet much better against damp and mud than leather and because they were "part of his thrift." Nevertheless, the GIs refused to accept that people enjoyed wearing such shoes and could not help staring at them in disbelief. A sergeant from Los Angeles, who noticed many people with wooden shoes on his way from Omaha beach to the front in October 1944, could only conclude that the French people were "really hard up." Those same shoes had convinced a lieutenant two months earlier that the people in France "were definitely on the peasantry side, the same as they are in England." "Would be good," the officer told his wife, "to be back with civilized people once more."[45]

The GIs deemed many of the houses the Europeans lived in substandard too. During the breakout at Anzio, for example, a Pennsylvanian noticed that many houses had been ravaged by battle, but he also observed that the others looked "dirty, and old, and beat" and was convinced "that they would have looked pretty much the same with or without a war." Not even the mansions of the aristocracy managed to impress the Americans. All they did, according to one soldier, was combine "museum furniture, usually, with the drafts of a barn and the plumbing of the Middle Ages."[46] The GIs were particularly sensitive to the fact that many European houses lacked the modern conveniences they had become accustomed to at home. They showed a penchant for evaluating the state of plumbing to determine a country's standard of living. That approach did not lead to a flattering verdict on the Old World. In Northern Ireland, lead pipes gave drinking water "a sickly taste;" in Sicily the plumbing was simply "atrocious." And things did not improve on the Continent. "Don't expect French plumbing in hotels, railway stations or homes to be like modern American plumbing," warned the Army guide, "It isn't."

> The French would appreciate an up-to-date American bathroom, with all the gadgets, but have never been able to afford it. After all, maybe your grandad wasn't brought up in one either and he managed to survive.

After having spent some time in several small villages in the Belgian Ardennes in January 1945, a corporal from Seattle felt safe to conclude that Europe was a "plumbing-less continent."[47] Modern heating systems also seemed to be rather rare in the Old World. The GIs saw few houses with central heating in England and were surprised to learn that outside Paris steam heat was only available in a few French homes. In the Mediterranean, heating devices could be outright primitive. When a combat doctor of the 88th Infantry Division installed his aid station in the house of a peasant family in the village of Gagliano in the winter of 1944, he discovered that there was only one fireplace; but each night the Italian family was so kind to offer him and his medics clay pots with glowing ashes to warm up their beds.[48] Similarly, many kinds of electrical household appliances that the Americans had come to take for granted appeared to be rare luxuries in the Old World. A private from Maine, hospitalized at Verdun, found it strange, for instance, that most French people went out to shop for food every day because they did not own refrigerators. Washing machines too were unaffordable luxuries for many in Europe. Intrigued GIs meticulously recorded how Icelandic women carried the laundry to brooks, how the French beat garments with small wooden paddles, and how the Sicilians washed their clothes in sun-heated water by pounding them with flat rocks.[49]

If European homes struck the GIs as uncomfortable, the average Old World town looked much less exciting than the American one. "There seems to be no obvious commercialization at all," noted an American at Neufchâteau early in January 1945. "I see no department stores, dime stores, or drug stores. The cafes sell only beer and 'schnapps.'" The soldier's disappointing impression of the Belgian town was undoubtedly influenced not only by the fact that the city of Chicago was his home, but also by the fact that Neufchâteau had almost been overrun during the Battle of the Bulge just a few weeks earlier.[50] Yet, even without the war, most Americans would have found mass consumption and entertainment much less developed in the Old World. The GI guide explained that much of Europe was a world "not of big department stores and interlocking organizations, but of little shops, operated by the owner and often his wife." A corporal from Rhode Island wrote home with self-congratulation that when he had described the American "super self-service markets" to an English grocer, the man had had to agree that they were "a marvel."[51] Outside the big cities, nightlife never seemed to have offered much in the Old World either. The Army guide warned, for example, that entertainment was virtually nonexistent in Northern Ireland, where pubs closed early and floor shows and juke joints were unknown. But it was a more serious shock to the GIs to learn that even much of France could be rather dull. An Army booklet informed the American soldiers that French provincial towns

> might have more charm and beauty than some of our small towns, but not necessarily as much entertainment. French provincial towns are about like what your home town was when your father was a boy, before movies, the radio and the family car changed all that. Your father wasn't bored. Neither are the provincial French.[52]

The GIs came from a country where machines had dominated the vast agricultural expanse for more than half a century. It was therefore no wonder they proved especially critical of the European way of farming. That the war had silenced the tractors on the fields and removed the horses from the farms was not taken into account as much of a mitigating circumstance by the American soldiers. In their judgment, the Old World's agricultural business was generally outdated. The GIs had already come to that conclusion in Britain. Whereas an Iowan was surprised to learn that Irish farmers did not vaccinate their pigs against hog cholera, a Kansan told his parents: "You can tell how backward England is by this – the Fordson tractor is still a big hit there & they're still made in England."[53] The backwardness of farming in the Mediterranean region simply stunned the Americans. Sicilians had the grain threshed out by horses and mules wheeling in circles, then tossed the chaff with wooden pitchforks "in the immemorial pattern of their ancient pagan world." Southern Italians were judged to be "a century behind time" as they still used sickles, scythes, flails, oxen and "wooden plow shares that didn't look much older than farming itself." But even north of Rome, the Americans witnessed how the natives were still relying on hands and oxen for most of the harvesting.[54] French agriculture too appeared to be far removed from the American cutting edge of technology. The guide to France told the GIs that it would be a mistake to suppose that French farmers were "not smart" just because they were still plowing with horses and oxen:

> Lots of families have been farming the same ground for over a thousand years. Pep talks about labor saving devices or electrical gadgets are also not likely to interest the French farmer. He knows his own business and has prospered on it in place.

Yet, upon seeing oxen plow the land during the race through northern France in August 1944, a soldier could not be dissuaded from thinking that the French "were years behind us in their farming," even though he did realize that this was "in part caused by the war."[55]

Mobility was another aspect of society the GIs observed with a keen eye. And the soldiers from the land of transcontinental railroads and Model Ts were greatly disappointed by what they saw in the Old World. Only the subways managed to impress quite a few Americans. The London underground was rated "excellent" by a sergeant from New England, and a corporal from Houston devoted no less than half a letter to a detailed description of its ticket slot machines, long winding tunnels, fast trains, and quick stops, calling it "really an adventure." In Paris too, the subway was considered "efficient and simple."[56] The European railways, on the other hand, found no favor whatsoever in American eyes. The Army guide had warned the GIs that they would probably be shocked by French railroad equipment because the Nazis had taken their best rolling stock. But the GIs did not think the British railways fared much better. Locomotives were "about half the size of U.S. rail transport" and pulled "dinky freight cars," while traveling in a British passenger wagon reminded some of sitting in a stagecoach. Moreover, European trains in general seemed "almost toylike" in comparison to their American counterparts.[57]

But it was even more of a shock to the GIs to find that automobiles had almost vanished from the streets of Europe. When they arrived in Northern Ireland in 1942, traffic was "almost nil" and, apart from the streetcars, there was "just an armada of bicycles and pedestrians on the road." Bicycles had taken over most of the Old World's streets. In the summer, the fair English girls' legs were sunburned from riding the contraptions day after day. GIs who wanted to view the surroundings in French North Africa during rest periods had to rent bicycles. Everywhere on the Continent bicycles turned out to be "the most common means of transportation" and the Americans saw how some even rode on the rims because rubber had become scarce.[58] The GIs realized that the war was responsible for these unusual scenes and that the few vehicles that were still around had gas tanks moored to their roofs or coke stoves attached to the sides because of wartime gasoline shortages. Yet the fact remained that, to them, even the European-made cars from the prewar period did not compare favorably to the ones produced in America. The Army guide tried to explain that European automobiles were "little and low-powered" because fuel had to be imported from far away. But it proved impossible for a private from Wisconsin to get used to seeing people in Holland drive cars that were "about half way between an Austin and a baby Willis." Even American cars that had been made for the European market looked like inferior variations of the standard models, and GIs jokingly called the Fords and Opels in Germany "schnapps-burners."[59] It proved still more amazing to them that many Europeans appeared to have lived without automobiles before the war. Irish farmers had been going into town in horse-drawn carts as long as people could remember, and Italian peasants fled the front lines in huge canvas-covered wagons that reminded at least one GI of the "American pioneers in the nineteenth century."[60] In many parts of the Old World, people simply seemed unprepared for life in the fast lane. A chaplain of the 1st Infantry Division wondered whether the British built roads for vehicles or pedestrians, but a paratrooper from South Dakota knew for sure that what they called roads in France were mere cow paths at home. In the countryside especially, Europeans appeared totally oblivious to the demands and dangers of modern traffic. Funeral processions, with priests holding large crosses and mourners carrying the casket, frustrated American truck chauffeurs, while decrepit peasant carts, creeping along in the middle of the road, infuriated GI jeep drivers. Heavy military through traffic almost inevitably exacted a painful toll from many civilian communities, but an American correspondent attached to an infantry unit in Sicily merely attributed those casualties to the fact that the natives were "not automobile minded, any more than dogs and pigs and chickens."[61]

The GIs became convinced that Europe's stagnation transcended the temporary paralysis caused by the war and that, instead, it characterized the Old World's natural antithesis to the New World's dynamic and progressive spirit. That antithesis was nowhere more visible to them than in America's practicalness, which in turn found expression in its knack for engineering, its feel for technology, and its machine-mindedness. Even a British Army pamphlet admitted as much when it gave this advice to its soldiers in an attempt to acquaint them with the GIs:

> Respect for American achievement is one of the ways by which we shall discover the Americans. Look, for example, what they've done to refrigerators and combustion engines and acknowledge them as the world's inventive wizards.[62]

The American soldiers enjoyed picturing themselves as men who were showing the Old World the benefits of frontier resourcefulness. "They do not complain because they are without facilities," a sergeant wrote to his sister about the GIs, "they make their own." The GIs boasted in letters home that the troops repaired their shoes with nails made from carpet tacks; that they patched up captured motorcycles, cars, and trucks in no time; that they replaced destroyed bridges by sturdy steel ones in just a few hours; and that they transformed deserted buildings into livable places with electricity by means "of every conceivable odd and end and gadget." And they were quick to contrast the American on-the-spot-improvements with the age-old backwardness of entire regions in Europe. "Never underestimate American ingenuity," a medic wrote from the Bitche sector to his wife in January 1945.

> In this little country town we have telephones for inter-contact with our Bn. units, electricity which consists of a lamp (similar to car lights) connected to a battery of a truck radio – but we still use the back shed for a toilet.[63]

The GIs were no less proud of the factory-like efficiency that American ingenuity had been perfecting ever since the start of mass industrialization. They clearly saw that large-scale efficiency reflected in the equipment and organization of their army. Correspondent Lee Miller, for example, reported from Normandy with a certain pride that the ruins of Isigny were "being scraped away by machinery I'd thought only existed on the covers of *Popular Mechanics*." To a soldier from Chicago, home of the giant meatpacking factories, the likeness of the US Army to the great American temples of production was even more striking:

> Our troops are part of a gigantic transmission belt, a line of vehicles of every sort: peeps, jeeps, trucks, ambulances, tanks, half-tracks, staff cars, self-propelled weaponry, mess trucks, and more trucks, functional to the needs of the troops.

In a letter from Germany, a lieutenant told his wife with obvious satisfaction that the people were impressed by the number of vehicles in the American army and that they knew the GIs had gained control of their town when they smelled the gasoline.[64] But American ingenuity and efficiency had accomplished much more than providing the edge in warfare: they had improved an entire way of life when compared to the fate of the Old World. A sergeant from Los Angeles summed up his impression, and that of many of his countrymen, in a letter to his family in December 1944:

> We have a country that is 100 years ahead of anything they have here, including what I've seen of Germany, France, Belgium, Luxemburg, and yes even and especially England. None of them have modern electricity, or toilets, or bathrooms, or modern transportation; and they never heard of drive-ins, or hot dog stands, or ice cream parlors, or big department stores, or any of the 101 things we take for granted in America. It is like a different world, a world which existed 100 years ago, and then became stagnant. It is a world in a nightmare, where everyone is afraid, not just of war and destruction, but afraid of new ideas, of improving one's lot, of going forward.[65]

... AND DECLINE

In the long run, stagnation inevitably brought decline. And nowhere was decline easier to measure than in the Old World, where the remnants of the past allowed ready and revealing comparisons. GIs who complained about the substandard contemporary housing of Europe marveled at the remarkable condition of the ancient Roman buildings at Téboursouk and Thélepte in North Africa. Europe lagged behind in modern plumbing, but the GIs inspected ingenious public rest rooms from antiquity at Dougga. A chaplain who in Britain had only seen private bathrooms with cold-water faucets was impressed when in one English city he happened upon a Roman building that had once offered cold, hot, and steam baths. Even more astonishing was that the soldiers were still able to use the baths the Romans had built thousands of years ago at Gafsa and Cherchell. Europe's methods of warming houses looked hopelessly outdated, yet in the Roman ruins at Sbeïtla GIs could see the underground rooms and pipes of central heating plants. Late in May 1944, columns of the 88th Infantry Division used part of an ancient Roman road on their way to Italy's capital. The GIs were vexed by its abominable condition and blamed it on Italian incompetence. An upset comrade tried to make them see that they were walking on a road that was 2,000 years old, but he quickly realized he was wasting his breath: Americans were not impressed by an ancient road that had survived the ravages of time; they just wondered why a new one had not been built.[66]

While Europe appeared to focus on looking back and preserving the grandeur of the past, it was importing much that was modern from America. Many GIs clearly had not been aware of the extent to which their country's products had penetrated the Old World's market before the war. They were surprised by the Texaco and Singer signs in Belgium; tickled by the Fords, Chevrolets, and Plymouths in Holland; and amused by Coca-Cola slogans in the German language. A chaplain from Dayton, Ohio, refused to believe his eyes when he opened an electric refrigerator in a French home in Tunisia that said it had been manufactured in his hometown. So "incongruous" did Ernie Pyle consider the fact that at a French farm near Bizerte he had come across a windmill made in Indiana, his home state, that he devoted two entire paragraphs to it in his article on the Allied victory in North Africa. And the GIs found many other indications of their economy's impact on Europe's way of life. Infantrymen who were digging up valuables hidden in the backyards of houses at Gerolstein, for example, discovered that several Germans had provided against a postwar rainy day by stashing US dollars in containers.[67]

American mass entertainment had swept even more of the Old World. It had constituted a tremendous cultural influence ever since the 1920s and movie stars had conquered Europe long before the GIs. They had added Americanisms like "okay," "guy," and "scram" to the Irish language and had taught most continental youngsters a smattering of American slang. In an abandoned German command post on the northern flank of the Bulge, GIs found that German girls shared the walls with Hedy Lamarr and Lana Turner.[68] American swing outblasted waltz music in most European cities. An amazed corporal from Long Island discovered that Liverpool was a center for hepcats and zoot-suiters and billed jazz bands "just about as good as ours." The Third Reich rejected jazz as "nigger music" from a decadent country and banned the sale of its recordings. Nevertheless, American music remained popular in Germany throughout the war, even in Nazi circles, and military stations were forced to broadcast jazz because the troops loved it and were tuning in to Allied stations. In large cities across Germany, youth bands with names like "Ohio Club," "Harlem Club," and "Navajo Pirates" challenged the Nazi authorities by ostentatiously displaying their love for American hot, scat, and jive.[69]

Much more of the overseas lifestyle was introduced to Europe in the wake of the American armies. "[W]e went out ahead of our lines & stop at some peoples home that had never seen yanks before," a GI scribbled in his diary during a march from Mortain to Ambrières on 8 August 1944. Such people were becoming exceedingly rare, however, as the GI invasion wave swept over Europe. The American troops who landed in France on 6 June 1944 immediately renamed the beaches of Normandy into those of Omaha and Utah. By early August, correspondent Lee Miller noted, "totem poles of arrows" had overshadowed French road signs and unit codes such as Missouri Charlie and Vermont Red had mixed with the names of ancient Norman villages.[70] America was the only country that could still afford to sell dreams during the war and thus its movies monopolized Europe, offering its citizens a crash course on the mores of the New World. A lieutenant of the 825th Tank Destroyer Battalion wrote to his wife from Mayet early in September 1944: "We are showing two runnings of Bing Crosby in *Going My Way*, at 3:30 and at 6:30 – for everybody, soldiers and girls, fathers and mothers, the whole town." Audiences across Europe eagerly took in every detail, while teenagers hastily copied them. A GI who arrived in Marseilles in October 1944 thought the girls looked "more American than the Americans."[71] The rhythms of America's urban music failed to sway the Old World's rural regions so easily. Irish country folk continued to prefer their jigs and reels to jive, and the Alsatian farmers insisted they liked Strauss waltzes better than the jitterbug. But the Americans were persuasive salesmen. In March 1945, the 71st Infantry Division organized a dance at Limésy for no less than 400 GIs and an equal number of French civilians. An American and a local orchestra took turns playing music in a large building. The French girls remained nailed to their seats when the American dance band opened the evening with its unfamiliar, shrill sound. Yet, when the GIs asked the French accordionists and fiddlers to take over, the girls rushed to the dance floor and the soldiers soon found themselves hopping along with them to the native tunes. A few hours later, however, the determined soldiers switched to American music again and, although many French people indiscriminately continued the Polka-like hopping, the GIs now found girls willing to be taught the steps to the lively rhythm of swing. Only days after the German surrender in Europe, a GI who visited Brussels on a pass could see for himself how American music was sweeping Europe. He peevishly told his parents in Massachusetts that almost all the Belgian girls knew how to jitterbug while he did not.[72]

Living amidst fear, hunger, and ruins, the American way of life had never looked more attractive to the Europeans. "I guess I'm getting like most of the foreigners – the Irish, the English and French," a medic wrote home in the spring of 1943, "and am starting to regard the U.S. as a sort of Utopia, paradise or something."[73] The

Europeans were impressed by the equipment, food, clothing, and health of the GIs and even more dazzled by the America portrayed in the movies from Hollywood. It was as if the Old World had never heard of America's sharecroppers, labor riots, dumbbell tenements, or breadlines. "We've got everything," a private wrote to his family in New Jersey. "Or at least these people here think so." The French regarded the GIs as "the rich, fat kids on the block;" many Germans believed the US was "mostly full of cowboys and Indians and rich uncles;" and all over Europe there were people who thought Americans owned oil wells as a rule. "[I]t is hard to believe," a GI admitted to his father, "that we are just Americans and not actually the super-race the Germans think they are."[74]

There seemed to be no doubt that America would be the new mecca of the West after the war. Across Europe, people were dreaming aloud of seeing with their own eyes the "rushing land of big things across the sea."[75] Some flattered GIs felt generous enough to welcome them all. "I have invited a major portion of the surviving population over here to visit me in Seattle," a corporal wrote to his parents in February 1945,

> and given them my correct address with that fool-hardy and rash honesty that you all know so well. I have particularly invited the Baroness of Gran Han, Father Francois Binet of Regne, Belgium, with his old mother and father, Mademoiselle Denise of Durbuy, Belgium, the Hermanns of Waubach, Holland, and the Kosters of Herleen and the Posts of Spekelsrade.[76]

But some Europeans were too impatient to wait for an invitation and tried alternative ways to obtain a ticket to the New World. The GIs were convinced, for example, that not all European girls were driven to marriage with an American soldier by love. "Everybody here wants to come to America," a private noted in French North Africa. "The play some of these girls are making for American soldiers is really terrific." French women, a captain of the 30th Infantry Division claimed, would marry any GI "regardless of what he looks like or is," as long as he promised to take them to America.[77] The swelling enthusiasm in the Old World about the New World's boundless opportunities made some GIs worry. A lieutenant told his wife in July 1944 that America was going to be "pretty crowded after the war, for all the English people say they are going to the U.S." Parents talking wistfully of a better future for their children across the ocean revived the image of impoverished hordes flooding Ellis Island for at least one GI. "[U]nfortunately, too many have the same idea," he lamented in a letter home,

> and wouldn't we be in a fine state of affairs if they would be permitted to rush to our shores. I only wish they could get settled over here and develop a type of civilization similar to ours.[78]

But it appeared most unlikely to the GIs that Europe would ever equal or surpass America again. In their final analysis, the most convincing proof of the Old World's decline lay in the infection of its morals. Europe's lack of sanitation, for instance, was the favorite object of GI scorn. The Army guides warned the soldiers that this had been a feature of the Old World even before the war. They claimed that, in comparison to America, the sanitary standards had not been "as strict" in Italy and "somewhat lower" in France, and that, although in the German-speaking countries health conditions had been "comparatively good for Europe," even there disease rates had been "slightly higher" than in the US.[79]

The American soldiers believed that their guides understated matters. They were appalled, for example, that in rural areas Europeans literally lived side by side with their animals. "One of the paradoxes of this country," a chaplain wrote home from Iceland in November 1942,

> is that they will be so apparently dirty as to slaughter animals on the front lawn, leaving the "left overs" to rot or to be dragged around by dogs, and yet a tiny village of a few hundred supports a bookseller.

In Italian villages, farmers and cattle often lived under the same roof, and sometimes people and animals were not even separated by a wall in houses that "smelled strongly of the farmyard."[80] But what most offended the GIs' sense of hygiene was the widespread European custom of keeping manure piles near, and often in front of, the farm. "Almost like a status symbol," a medic in France derisively told his wife. Some thought this so noteworthy that they took pictures of it to send home. By the time they entered Germany, American soldiers were joking that in the Old World a civilian's wealth was measured by the height of his manure pile.[81] Some Americans could not resist the urge to clean up Europe's mess. A company of the 1st Infantry Division in Algeria was terribly annoyed by a manure pile so mountainous that one of the unit's lieutenants estimated it had been "founded by a discharged Roman legionary and added to during each successive century." The GIs decided to contact the local French authorities to have it removed. Unfortunately, their attempt made the stench only worse. As the pile gave off "the stored-up effluvium of ages," the American muckrakers realized that perhaps Old World dirt was best left unstirred.[82]

The Europeans seemed uninformed about the basics of hygiene. American soldiers in Italy were instructed not to eat uncooked vegetables because farmers frequently irrigated crops with sewage and country people were "extremely careless about the disposal of human wastes." In letters from Western Europe too, disgusted GIs described in shocking detail that farmers used human feces as fertilizer on their fields.[83] Toilet accommodation also was deplorable. When the 90th Infantry Division arrived at a camp near Birmingham in 1944, the sanitary officer, used to the standard US Army deep-pit latrines, found seats with holes in them and overflowing buckets infested by flies under them. The shocked American surgeon condemned the British sanitary arrangement as inexcusable and disgraceful. Things did not improve as the GIs marched on. Sicily's sewage disposal system often was no more than "a depression in the middle of each street," and on the Italian mainland soldiers were warned to display "the utmost care" when using public toilets. Across Europe,

American soldiers time and again disapproved of open-ditch sewers, while staring incredulously at toilets with footrests but without either bowls or seats.[84]

Moreover, whereas Europe's pissoirs – public urinals offering little privacy – embarrassed many an American soldier, Europeans proved to be incredibly nonchalant about such matters. A GI who had just arrived in Marseilles from New York was shocked to find that some women thought nothing of trading wine for cigarettes next to the soldiers' latrines. And even when columns briefly halted for "piss calls" on the way to the front, women and children flocked around the men to sell wine without the least bit of discomfiture.[85] The natives themselves showed an amazing lack of modesty in answering the call of nature. A lieutenant of the 9th Infantry Division noted:

> Europeans, especially in the boondocks, would haul out anywhere – in the midst of the whole village on the way to church or any outdoor location when the urge struck them.

In public places, streets, and at ball games, a captain of the 30th Infantry Division corroborated, they would "let go with complete equanimity and aplomb" and with the unconcerned air of a "dog sniffing a telephone pole." GIs witnessed more than once how Sicilian mothers sent their children to the public square to take care of nature's needs, how French males relieved themselves at roadside ditches and against walls without apparently offending their countrymen, and how even women answered the call of nature in public and in broad daylight.[86] "No one cared particularly," noticed a private who was forced to use a latrine in full view of Belgian civilians during the Battle of the Bulge. "Europeans, I used to figure, are closer to the soil anyway."[87]

In the eyes of the American soldiers, who often arrived in the Old World laden with puritanical prejudice, Europeans certainly seemed less bothered by sexual inhibitions. In the autumn of 1944, a lieutenant, recovering from hepatitis at the 186th General Hospital, undertook a visit to Pompeii. The remnants not only offered him a glimpse of the Roman empire, but also of "a wicked city devoted to satisfying the erotic pleasures of visitors." "Some people believe," the officer remarked, "that the catastrophe of Pompeii was the will of God in just punishment for their evil ways."[88] But the American soldiers who visited Paris, for instance, noticed that God's warning to the Old World had not made a lasting impression. "One of the first ideas that you should get out of your head," the Army guide insisted, "is that Paris is a city of wicked and frivolous people." But the Parisians never really allowed the GIs a fair chance to form a more balanced picture of the French capital. Men of the 328th Infantry Regiment who arrived in Paris on a pass from the Saarlautern front in February 1945, for example, had barely jumped from the trucks when street peddlers approached them to sell "vulgar pictures and naked rubber dolls." The maelstrom of the city's nightlife sucked most GIs into the Place Pigalle, into the Moulin Rouge and the Lido, and into the arms of prostitutes. The chaplain of the 501st Parachute Regiment concluded in despair that the morals of Paris were "candidly pagan."[89]

Licentiousness, however, was not just a Parisian, nor a French, eccentricity. The Old World appeared to flaunt its lack of sexual restraint with perverse pleasure. When the 501st Parachute Regiment returned from Operation Market-Garden and arrived at an old French army camp at Mourmelon, the unit's chaplains found the paintings on the walls "obscene beyond description," and both the Protestant and the Catholic officer hurried to cover them with blankets. But the US Army could not possibly have procured enough blankets to hide all of the Old World's morally corrupted art. And so, revealing sculptures facing churches and nude statues bathing in the shadows of cathedrals made GIs frown on both sides of the Alps.[90]

The war had forced many European women to lower their moral standards, but in America their reputation of being uninhibited had been established long before the outbreak of hostilities. The Army guides informed the GIs that "easy women" had been common in Italy even in peacetime and warned about the more liberal point of view in France on sex. Stunned GIs could see for themselves how uninhibited European women really were when they did not even object to dating black soldiers. By February 1945, a sergeant of the 102nd Infantry Division had concluded that the moral standards of the women of most European countries were much lower than those of America. The NCO realized that the war had something to do with it, but he nevertheless remained convinced that in much of the Old World "no high value was placed on chastity anyway."[91] The reputed unrestrainedness of Europe's women caused quite a few GIs to feel uncomfortable in their presence. Two GIs, about to take one of the famous Belgian bubble baths at Spa at the end of the Battle of the Bulge, had second thoughts when they feared – wrongly – that the women attendants who were cleaning the copper tubs would remain in the room even after the bathers had undressed. At Marseilles, a private from California who had just arrived in Europe, marched to a public bath for a relaxing shower. He was forced, however, to spend several fidgety minutes in the waiting room because a pretty girl joined him and it dawned on him that men and women might well think it normal to shower together in France. To his relief, the GI found out that there was a separate shower room for women after all, but he reported to his sister on the incident: "Knowing the French one could expect anything."[92]

Nowhere did the moral corruption prove more widespread, however, than in the enemy's homeland. When the GIs emptied the pockets of POWs and took over houses as conquerors, they had an excellent opportunity to examine the most intimate secrets of their nemesis. That way the Americans managed to produce enough evidence to establish a pattern of depravity in Germany transcending the moral retrogression of other European countries by far and confirming the enemy's wickedness. Paratroopers who captured general Theodor Tolsdorf at Berchtesgaden, for example, claimed they found in his briefcase a few military decorations and no less than 500 pornographic photographs.[93] But what the soldiers dug up in Germany's private homes revealed much more about the nature of its people. Combat engineers had never been so absorbed by a book on Greek art than in a house at Remagen. "The screwy thing about it is," a sergeant noted in his journal, "all the pictures are of statues

& carvings & every last one of them is of people having sexual intercourse."
Curious GIs came across more than works on the classical interpretations of coitus.
A castle near Hesselbach became a magnet for souvenir hunters of the 14th Armored
Division when word spread that it contained a veritable library of pornographic works.
When their comrades of the 12th Armored Division set up a command post in a
mansion on the Danube that had been owned by a lieutenant general of the *Luftwaffe*
and his wife, they uncovered an impressive assortment of whips as well as books
on sodomy, sadomasochism, bestiality, and necrophilia. "We meet the enemy," spat
the unit's surgeon, "and they are pigs." The degeneration had not been confined to
the inner sanctums of a few perverts but had also infected larger parts of the German
population. In a luxurious house in Bremen, owned by a couple with two children,
an officer of the 95th Infantry Division wondered who the photographer could have
been of a series of explicit pictures of the husband and wife. The American's
amazement only grew when he discovered on his march through the Third Reich
that "this kind of family pornography was rather extensive among the wealthy
Germans."[94] At the end of 1944, a private of the 100th Infantry Division wrote a
letter from Germany to his parents in Massachusetts that was simply dated: "Last
Days of Pompeii."[95] Once more, the catastrophe that had descended on the Old World
appeared to be God's just punishment for a people's evil ways.

   The Old World's moral corruption became even more inconceivable to the GIs
when they realized it had been able to take place in spite of the powerful presence
of the Church. The Church's omnipresence in Europe never ceased to amaze the
American soldiers. It took them a while, for example, to get accustomed to the daily
rhythm imposed by the Old World's innumerable church bells. They learned that
the village bells rang each noon and that the striking of the clock in church steeples
could be used to time guard duty at night. Church bells served many other practical
purposes in wartime Europe. In Italy the chiming signaled the approach of the Allied
troops from one community to another, and in Germany the mayor often received
the occupiers while the bells were urging the civilians to leave the cellars and
assemble in the square. But it was not only the bells that were constant reminders
of the importance of the Church in the Old World. On his way to Brest with the 8th
Infantry Division in August 1944, there was one aspect of the countryside that never
changed nor stopped intriguing a lieutenant:

   the incredible number of religious symbols at various spots along the road. One
   came upon them in all parts of France, at road junctions, along forgotten country
   lanes, on main highways, on private farms. Some were rather impressive statues
   of angels or of one of the saints, sometimes of Jesus himself, while others were
   more simple, like the cross.[96]

Moreover, the places of worship themselves were very imposing and often the
best architecture a town or village possessed. "Every village has about 5 churches,"
a private wrote home from Lorraine, "all of them very beautiful." A sergeant from
Wisconsin was impressed by the magnificent interior of a fifteenth-century church

in the tiny village of La Petite Pierre in the Vosges: "The elaborate paintings, the gold leaf and all this art was breathtaking. You wondered how these poor farm people could afford this luxury."[97] Even in battle, Europe's many churches inevitably became focal points for soldiers and civilians alike. In the morning of 6 June 1944, spires were the most important landmarks for paratroopers who had landed in Normandy at night and were trying to determine their exact location. Men of the 3rd Battalion, 501st Parachute Regiment, for example, managed to find out where they were with certainty only after noticing the distinctive spire of Sainte-Marie-du-Mont at dawn. Later that day they continued their journey, first by orienting themselves on the church steeple of Appeville, then by reading a compass bearing on that of Liesville. It happened regularly, on the other hand, that American artillery had to bring down steeples because the enemy liked to use them as observation posts or to hide snipers. The GIs were also forced to violate the sacred places by requisitioning candles from them or by transforming the thick-walled buildings into medical sanctuaries. The civilians in turn quite often sought refuge in the large and sturdy basements of churches when battle struck their community. Just south of the Arno River, a village near Paláia was totally lifeless when the Americans captured it in July 1944; eventually, all its inhabitants were discovered huddling in the church cellar. In the ruined town of Recouvrance, pale civilians emerged from the church after having lived in its basement for over a month during the siege of Brest.[98]

A church, an officer in Holland concluded in February 1945, was not only "indispensable to any European village," it also dominated it "just as its influence controls, to a great extent, the lives of those who live in the dwellings."[99] The American soldiers were perplexed by the Church's authority in the Old World, as if they had expected the waning of Christianity to have preceded the moral decline they perceived. Priests were often the only people who had remained in the villages during battle; they were the ones who rang the bells to inform the others of the arrival of the liberators. Elsewhere, inhabitants not infrequently returned from hiding places in woods or caves led by their spiritual shepherds.[100] The GIs were particularly impressed by the high rate of church attendance in Europe. The Army guide informed them that in Northern Ireland church affiliation was "a serious thing" and that the people had "devout church-going habits," while it pointed out that the English too tended to "make much of Sunday." On Sundays and Saints' days, said another guide, the French churches were filled to overflowing, "from the great cathedrals down to the smallest parish chapels."[101] In the Alsace, a GI could see for himself that Sunday was "a big day" as he watched how parents scrubbed their children and brushed off their best clothes on Saturday night. "All over Europe, war or no war," a medic reported from Germany, "everyone dresses up in their 'Sunday best.'" An American chaplain who held a service in a Belgian church for soldiers and civilians alike in September 1944 was moved when afterwards devout villagers came up to him to ask whether he would sign their hymnals.[102]

The American combat soldiers too found solace in Europe's churches. In the middle of battle's horrors the houses of prayer were sanctuaries that seemed to protect against attack and capture. "The mere fact of being quartered in a church made me feel peaceful and happy," a soldier wrote while resting in a small Catholic church near the Siegfried Line. But the predominantly Catholic churches the Americans encountered in their path not only offered consolation, they also served as sources of inspiration to GIs of various denominations. An officer who visited his "first pure Gothic cathedral" near Lyons described the experience as "a refreshment to the spirit like nothing else." The splendor of Rome's religious monuments enthralled even Protestant soldiers. "Whatever one's religious affiliation," wrote an enraptured tank operator, "entering St. Peter's, one must experience a deep religious feeling."[103]

But all this only made it harder for the Americans to understand how the Old World's moral infection had been able to fester amidst so much saving grace. A Protestant soldier, moved by the paintings adorning an Italian cathedral, wrote to his family in Pennsylvania: "How easy it must be for the catholic people to have a feeling of religious goodness upon worshipping in such splendor. I'm convinced that only good can come of such a religion." How disappointing it was then for the GIs to discover that Italy was "a country where little kids sell dirty pictures on the steps of churches." How perverse to find crucifixes on the walls of taverns across Europe, with Jesus looking down on those who preferred to seek solace in drink.[104] And there was much more to ponder for the American soldiers regarding Europe's religiousness. The Old World had made a travesty of the tolerance and forgiveness preached by Christianity. It had become the scene of revolts and revolutions, of coups and overthrows, of saber rattling and warmongering. Multitudes of saints watched over every nook and cranny in Europe, but they proved glaringly unsuccessful at convincing people to call a halt to bloodshed. The GIs fought furious battles from San Pietro Infine to Saint-Lô and from Santa Maria Infante to Saint-Vith. They witnessed horrible carnage at places like Monte San Fratello, San Nicola Rock, San Gennaro Hill, San Biagio Canal, Saint-Malo Citadel, and Saint-Hubert Farm. "[W]hy," a GI asked himself after having admired a Belgian church at Neufchâteau during the Battle of the Bulge, "with so great a saturation of Christian symbolism is there so much that is war-like in Europe?"[105]

In the Old World, time had hardened long-standing prejudices and hatreds into ugly scars, while a tenacious memory could not keep itself from reopening ancient wounds again and again. That the English invited the GIs into their churches, even when the soldiers belonged to a different denomination, was heartwarming to the chaplain of an armored division. "Surely the lesson that all men are brothers must begin in our churches," the American remarked. "How else can our Christianity unite nations and establish peace upon the earth?" Yet, that basic premise appeared to be far from self-evident in much of the Old World, where even religion itself proved to be a source of endless strife. The Army guide was quick to caution the GIs, for instance, about the Catholic–Protestant question in Northern Ireland:

In America – as you know – we usually take it for granted that some people go to one church and some to another. The Irish, where religion is concerned, take nothing for granted.[106]

The GIs soon learned that Europe was divided on much more than the worship of God. The Old World was wasting away under the nationalisms, regionalisms, and localisms that history had solidly molded. The Americans received their first sobering introduction to Europe's political realities from the British. A private who observed the Tommies in North Africa, for example, had a strong sense that there was "no love lost" between the English, the Irish, and the Scots. Moreover, the GIs in Britain noticed how the Welshmen stubbornly continued to speak of going "into England," while in Northern Ireland the US Army guide did not have an easy task explaining why Eire had protested against the first landings of American troops in Ulster and refused to allow Allied troops to cross its border. "This may strike you as strange – as it is strange – when the grave issues at stake in this war are considered," conceded the Army booklet. Yet it hastened to add:

We Americans don't worry about which side our grandfathers fought on in the Civil War, because it doesn't matter now. But these things still matter in Ireland and it is only sensible to be forewarned.

As if these divisions were not forbidding enough, the GIs were informed not to worry if they experienced difficulties with the local English dialects, because very often a villager from Cornwall could not even understand a farmer from Yorkshire or Lancashire.[107]

It looked to the American soldiers as if the Old World was suffering from outright tribalism. Sicilians told an American in August 1943 that their people had been "ground between two millstones" during the war and considered the Italians to be even worse than the Germans. Some claimed they wanted to join the US and swore they would clamor for independence should that prove impractical. While working with an FFI unit at Vannes in the summer of 1944, a tank operator of the 4th Armored Division acquired a revealing insight into what it was that drove one of the local French resistance fighters: "He spoke Breton and fought for Brittany. Hitler could keep Normandy for all he cared." Even among the slave laborers who were liberated in the German camps, the shared fate of years of humiliation and suffering under a common enemy appeared to have forged neither unity nor a better understanding. "Language differences and ancient national animosities," noticed a weary and disappointed officer in April 1945, "seemed to run as deeply between them as against their masters."[108]

Reason had been doomed to fail in solving the strange twists of the corrupted European mind. "Wars are an old story to the people here," commented the Army guide to the cities of France when it explained that Dreux had been captured and burned by the English in 1188. To the GIs, the Old World appeared to be a giant patchwork of battlefields, ancient and new. The Army guide pointed out to the soldiers, for example, that the archaeological monuments of Sicily would tell them the story of invasions by none less than the Phoenicians, Greeks, Carthaginians, Romans, Saracens, Normans, Spaniards, Germans, and French.[109] When trucks of the 30th Infantry Division ran out of gas in the vicinity of Brussels in September 1944, the Americans realized with a shock that they had come to a standstill near the battlefield of Waterloo. In such a climate, it was easy for the GIs to imagine that the war they had joined in the Old World was merely part of an age-old continuum. During the attack on Volterra, a city northwest of Rome, the commander of the 350th Infantry Regiment remembered that the place had successfully withstood a long siege 2,000 years ago, and he could not help musing whether "the ghosts of those ancient armorclad legions were looking down on our denim-clothed ranks from the lofty heights of Valhalla." An officer who had participated in the capture of Rome itself admitted that he had actually "felt like one of the soldiers who took the city thousands of years before."[110] Worse was that Europe's brutal sequence of wars seemed unstoppable. When a private of the 87th Infantry Division entered the Saar Valley in December 1944, he sensed that the Old World's atmosphere, so heavy with violent memories, bode ill for the future:

> We seemed dwarfed. The sky was so vast and the hills so brooding at that time of the year. One felt it was such an ancient battleground. *Omnia Gallia* was again divided, and, despite all brave hopes and ringing statements to the contrary, I could not believe we would be the last army ever to come there.[111]

The Europeans behaved as if they had put up with the bane of war all their lives. It struck the GIs, for example, that some civilians already referred to the European war of 1939–40 laconically as "the last war" and considered the liberation merely the newest conflict in a row. By that count, older natives had already lived through three major wars when they met the GIs.[112] It was no wonder the American soldiers believed that the Europeans had learned to accept warfare as an inevitable part of their existence. Relatives in America wrote to a captain who was stationed in Northern Ireland in 1942 that a friend in England had complained that nobody of the family had visited him "this war." The officer realized that one of his uncles had probably contacted the man during the Great War. "It seems a bit sad," he replied to his family in the US, "the old family friend dating his visitors by wars. One war, one generation, one visit."[113]

The Europeans had not only resigned themselves to war as the milestone of time, they had also learned to arm themselves mentally against its spasmodic occurrences. Mauldin, for example, thought it only natural that armies foraged now and then, and he assumed the Old World farmers had grown used to it anyway. After all, he reasoned, "Europeans have been hardened by centuries of war and invasion and they seem to know what to expect from soldiers." Somewhere in Germany in April 1945, a similar feeling gripped a private who stared at farmers working on their fields imperturbably while guns boomed in the distance:

Watching these people plowing the fields, they did this for thousands of years, and armies came back and forth, millions of times, it didn't mean a thing. Amazing, amazing![114]

The GIs became convinced that even the physical surroundings of the Old World had adapted to the ceaseless warfare. Houses seemed to have been built to resist waves of aggressors. In comparison to the more common frame houses of America, Europe's dwelling places of brick and concrete looked like pillboxes. At the front in Italy, German troops often turned solidly built houses into the command centers of strongpoints. Casa del Monte, near the trail to Monte delle Formiche, weathered a series of violent attacks before being taken by men of the 85th Infantry Division, while the 34th Infantry Division had to call in tank support to take Villa Crocetta on the crest of Hill 209 in the Caesar Line. Sturdy dwellings in the Belgian Ardennes formed nearly impregnable sniper and machine-gun positions, and American tanks quite often hid behind the old stone buildings to survive the wrath of the German 88s. The solid wall of an aid station at Saarbrücken saved a medic's life by absorbing most of the blast from a direct hit. "Had the same shell hit the house in which you are staying," the GI wrote to his wife in Minnesota, "it would be almost completely demolished."[115] Farms in particular seemed designed to function as strongholds in battle. More than 1,500 hand grenades failed to dislodge German soldiers from Albaneta Farm on the northern edge of the Cassino massif, for instance. During the Lorraine campaign, German troops transformed at least a dozen farms into formidable defensive positions. With high stone walls two-and-a-half-feet thick and interspersed with firing ports, they became pivots in combat, and American soldiers fought bloody battles for places like Berange Farm, Fourasse Farm, Frémecourt Farm, Moscou Farm, and Renaissance Farm. Even villages and towns constituted natural fortresses with their brick houses, narrow streets, and sturdy walls imbedded with broken glass.[116] Moreover, parts of the Old World had imposed spartan living conditions on their inhabitants as if to enable them to endure the recurring pestilence of war. A replacement who had just arrived in Lorraine in November 1944 surveyed a small village in the front line:

> There had been no power plant to be destroyed by our guns, no gas service ... There never had been plumbing facilities in this house, the occupants relieving themselves in the adjoining barns with the animals. But it occurred to me, that for a country that was destined to be a battleground, it was better that way.[117]

The American soldiers could not escape the impression that centuries of intrigue and warfare had also fostered a tremendous slyness among the natives of the Old World. The GIs never managed to dismiss the uneasy feeling that they were innocents abroad who had been lured into a foreign conflict by cunning Europeans. America had traditionally regarded the Old World as a continent where kings and tyrants connived. It was America's disillusionment with its participation in the Great War, however, that was the darkest cloud hanging over the cooperation with the

European allies during World War II. The Army guide had to convince the GIs, for example, that in neither of the two world wars had the French fooled the Americans into doing the fighting for them. The booklet on Germany in turn warned the soldiers not to listen to enemy propaganda that claimed they were "suckers" who had been tricked into shedding blood for Albion's imperialism and Soviet communism; it emphasized that Americans fought for America because its interests were inevitably tied up with those of the British and the Russians. The unpaid European debts of World War I had created another bitter memory in America. The GI guide insisted that the war debts were "dead issues" and told the Americans that it was not necessary to remind the British of the Lend-Lease help they were receiving from the US. "They know about it," the booklet said tersely, "and appreciate it."[118]

Still, American distrust of the Old World's intentions could never be taken away entirely. Bill Mauldin charged that even Europe's mud did not have "an honest color like ordinary mud." A platoon leader of the 103rd Division was impressed by the defensive war the Germans were fighting in the Alsace. "Lacking our lavish means," he observed, "they compensated by patience and shrewdness." This, however, the officer did not identify merely as another indication of German thoroughness, but rather as an example "of the cunning ways of Europe versus the blunter ways of the New World." The GIs never even managed to convince themselves that their European brothers-in-arms were wholly trustworthy. When during Operation Market-Garden paratroopers of the 101st Division undertook a mission to rescue British troops and American pilots on the other side of the Lower Rhine, a corporal sketched his interpretation of the plan: "We would furnish the personnel, the British would furnish the idea and, I suppose, the Band-Aids. A fair swap, by British standards." The civilian population of Europe likewise appeared to have become unscrupulously shrewd after weathering centuries of wars, invasions, and occupations. Mauldin witnessed how the people in the Mediterranean

> more than made up for their losses of fruit, vegetables, and livestock by stealing every piece of equipment that wasn't nailed down, so they usually got the better end of the deal, as Europeans always seem to do.

Stung by the attempts of a Nazi to flatter the GIs who had moved into his house near Stuttgart in April 1945, a medic complained to his wife: "[W]e Americans by European standards are naive."[119]

But if worldly wisdom had to be gained at the cost of sacrificing all values and principles, the American soldiers preferred to cling to innocence. In November 1944, a corporal of the 84th Infantry Division wrote from Germany to his parents:

> Ever since my childish, New World feet touched the continent I have felt the "European disease" – a penetrating malady consisting of hate, hunger, false traditions, myriad divisions of language and religion, "race" suspicion and over-sophistication. I thank God for America.[120]

That stark contrast between the two worlds made some GIs realize that their expedition to the Old World might well be in the best interest of America after all, if only by containing the plague within its overseas breeding ground. A few weeks before the surrender of the German troops in North Africa, a sergeant entreated his sister to look at the GI as her "personal saviour." "He," her brother warned, "is the last barrier between you and a foreign brutal way of life." Still others became convinced that America had the power to do much more than protect its own cherished lifestyle. "This war is not just a defense against Hitler and Tojo," a GI predicted in a letter home. "It is a catalyst for a world in the molten state."[121] Perhaps benevolent innocents were the perfect crusaders in an Old World. It was for fun, of course, that Americans of the 111th Engineer Combat Battalion passed through Rome wearing medieval armor they had picked up in a movie studio south of the city. And it was undoubtedly the imagination sparked by the many châteaux that caused some GIs to refer to themselves in letters home as "your knight." But to a chaplain's assistant who was caught up in the Battle of the Bulge, America's mission had nothing to do with make-believe:

> The Church has such a lot of work to do! One task it must share eventually, I feel, is in restoring these poor, hungry, terrorized children of Europe to bodily and spiritual normalcy. This ravaged continent is crying for missionaries, although it has had so-called Christian civilization for centuries.[122]

When the crash of the Old World's ruin resounded louder than ever upon the discovery of the concentration camps in April 1945, a lieutenant of the 116th Infantry Regiment – a unit with its origins in Thomas Jefferson's guard at Monticello – was convinced that history had come full circle:

> You feel our great army in your heart, in your bones, moving forward, thrusting deep into decadent, corrupt, tyrannical, enslaved old Europe, letting out the poison, letting in the health. We are the great westward emigration to America coming back on itself, renewing the source.[123]

At first, the American combat soldiers were overwhelmed by the cultural, national, ethnic, and linguistic diversity of Europe. Yet, gradually, they came to realize that there was more that united this overseas world than that divided it. What tied all of it together in the minds of the GIs more than anything else was its stagnation and decline. This was, of course, to a large extent the perception they formed as soldiers under the particular conditions of World War II. As Americans, however, they were led to believe that Europe's breakdown and disintegration were not just the result of the war, but also of the Old World's tradition of political cynicism, economic entropy, and cultural decadence, which had been proverbial in the New World for centuries. And even if the American soldiers were not always sure where the ruins of World War II ended and the ruin of the Old World began, it did not really matter to them because they considered warfare to be an integral part of Europe's decline.

But the war did not just confirm the existing prejudices against the Old World among the GIs, it also considerably strengthened them. If the American combat soldiers believed that the Old World had already been wasting away under a process of ruin for ages, the ferocity of World War II now convinced them that they were witnessing this crippled world's final downfall. That conviction was never stronger than during the last apocalyptic weeks of the war.

Part IV
The Apocalypse

10   The Apocalypse

The last weeks of the war in Europe formed a distinct period in the experience of the GIs. The speed of conquest and the chaos of defeat blurred the impressions of Europe's nature, its soldiers, and its civilians into one surrealist picture. Moreover, the discovery of the horrors of genocide in the heart of the Continent amplified the crash of the Old World's ruin tremendously. When the American soldiers at last shook hands with their Soviet comrades amidst the rubble of the Old World, they were well aware that their encounter heralded new times dominated by new powers.

THE STRANGE

"Then there was the strange," an infantry officer recalled when looking back on battle in Italy, France, and Germany. "I think every soldier must have felt at times that this or that happening fitted into nothing that had gone before; it was incomprehensible, either absurd or mysterious or both."[1] Much of the war in Europe proved to have a surrealist quality that made soldiers lose their bearings on the normal world. "[O]utlandish forms of death, atrocities, awesome destruction were the norm," observed one GI, "but unassimilable."[2] No experience, however, was more dislocating to the American soldiers than the conquest of Germany during the last weeks of the war.

The sheer speed of the race across the enemy's homeland made it virtually impossible for the combat soldiers to process the shocking impressions of collapse. As spring warmed the air and cleared the sky, the Allies launched the final offensives into German-held territory. Opposition now crumbled rapidly and enemy soldiers surrendered by the thousands. American infantry units competed with armored outfits in covering ground. The 83rd Infantry Division, for example, traversed 280 miles in 13 days. Foot soldiers hitched rides on jeeps, trucks, and tanks; they drove sports cars and school buses taken from the enemy; some hopped on bicycles in an attempt to keep up with the advance. The front lines were more fluid than ever, confusion reigned, soldiers became disoriented. In his memoirs, a company commander of the 2nd Infantry Division remembered having participated in capturing no less than 48 German places between 12 March and 1 May 1945. Some of them were no more than clusters of a few houses on unpaved roads; the others ranged from villages to metropolises. Many of the objectives were taken with little or no resistance at all. For other places, such as Leipzig, his men had to fight hard. With the end in sight, his unit suddenly found itself surrounded at Böhlitz-Ehrenberg and several men were captured, only to be liberated again the day after.[3]

The race simultaneously invigorated and exhausted the soldiers; it exhilarated and frightened them. The Old World now appeared to have surrendered itself entirely to madness. "I love every word of your letters," an officer of the 116th Infantry Regiment wrote from Dortmund to his wife in Santa Barbara, California. "Receiving them where I do is a little unbelievable but also the only firm reality in this convulsion, this death struggle of a monster."[4] In those last weeks of the war, the combat soldiers' dulled senses only managed to retain the most incongruous images. At Bendorf in March 1945, an officer of the 2nd Infantry Division watched dumbfounded how an old German woman calmly led a blindfolded horse into a burning barn and then resignedly entered her flaming house, closing the door. "I was convinced," the American soldier commented, "that the war would end soon from sheer insanity."[5]

THE GENOCIDE

If the degree of insanity could have determined the end of the war in Europe, the GIs should have known by early April 1945 that the fighting would not last much longer. That was the time when they began uncovering the system that Nazi Germany had designed for the purpose of eliminating anyone who dared stand in its way.

Throughout the war, the media brought enough reports on repression, pogroms, and atrocities for the American people to realize that the Nazis were dealing ruthlessly with their political and racial enemies. In November 1944, Gallup asked the Americans whether they believed the stories that said the Germans had murdered "many people in concentration camps." Three out of four were convinced they were true. The American soldiers in Europe shared in that knowledge and their Army guides repeated that the Germans had "herded hundreds of thousands of innocent people into concentration camps."[6] Some Jewish-American soldiers were so afraid of being tortured and killed if captured by the Germans that they decided to carry dogtags with a "P" or "C" rather than the "H" for Hebrew.[7]

Once the GIs were marching through the Old World, they could see for themselves how the Jewish people in particular had been terrorized. In the Jewish quarters of North Africa's large towns, American soldiers were almost mobbed by hysterically happy people and as early as 1942 were learning firsthand about anti-Semitic laws, the closing of synagogues, and the confiscation of possessions. In Italy, they encountered Jewish refugees who had been roaming from country to country for years and who had been in hiding for months.[8] The effects of fascist terror visibly increased as the GIs approached the borders of Germany. A letter from a Jewish captain to his family in Brooklyn described a discovery in Liège, Belgium, that was typical of what his comrades were finding in most cities of Western Europe:

Our Jews suffered terribly over here. There were atrocities, unbelievable things committed upon these unfortunates. I don't want to repeat these incidents, because they don't make pleasant reading. Out of a population of four thousand Jews there were only some 100 left.[9]

The problem was, however, that neither the Americans at home nor the GIs at the front were able to imagine the full extent of the horror. Thirty-six per cent of those in America who believed in November 1944 that people were being killed in the camps estimated deaths at 100,000 or less, and just over 50 per cent guessed there were a million casualties or less. Only 16 per cent suspected that between two and six million or more people had been murdered. The Army guide to Germany told the GIs that "hundreds of thousands" of innocents had been imprisoned, but it never used the word extermination.[10] The American people remained uninformed about the systematic mass slaughter of Jews until the end of 1944 and later. The media failed to publicize the Holocaust earlier for fear of spreading rumors similar to the fabricated atrocity stories about German behavior in Belgium during World War I. Moreover, publishers and broadcasters regarded the reports that hinted at the true nature of the slaughter with disbelief, for annihilation of an entire people was "a concept that went well beyond previous experience." Until right before their own army's discovery of German concentration camps, GIs could be found discounting stories about extermination as Allied "propaganda."[11]

But the American people were not only uninformed about what was really happening with the Jews. Strong currents of anti-Semitism in American society were also responsible for a certain indifference regarding their fate. Those feelings of anti-Semitism did not just vanish in the front lines. Some gentile GIs suspected the Jews, for instance, of using their alleged shrewdness to steer clear of the combat units, and they deridingly referred to both the Finance Corps and the Quartermaster Corps as the "Jewish infantry."[12] The Jewish combat soldiers themselves regularly voiced complaints about anti-Semitic behavior from both enlisted men and officers. An upset corporal wrote from Luxembourg to his parents in October 1944:

> What is our country doing to stop this persecution? ... Let our government fight a battle against the Fascists at home while we fight over here ... I'm just one of thousands of boys who want to come home and see the things that they fought for materialized completely, and not just half done.[13]

As late as April 1945, 11 per cent of the GIs in the ETO maintained that the Jews had taken selfish advantage of the war, while 8 per cent confessed they personally disliked them.[14]

When the American troops at last penetrated into the heart of Germany, however, much of their skepticism and indifference soon evaporated. New and unimaginable atrocities began to be uncovered in such rapid succession that even men hardened to combat became unable to process the facts and their implications. Amidst the confusion, it took the unprepared GIs until well into April 1945 before the true nature of Nazi Germany's crimes against humanity fully dawned on them.

The deeper the GIs advanced into Germany, the more POWs and DPs they freed. Prior to VE-Day, the Americans repatriated some 441,000 DPs to Western and Eastern Europe from the 12th and 6th Army Group areas. Nevertheless, on 8 May 1945 about 2,320,000 DPs from more than a dozen different countries still remained in those sectors. During the last weeks of the war, the chaos was so complete that even American combat units had to be utilized to help control the DPs when the military situation allowed it. The GIs were stunned by the sheer number of people they were liberating in the enemy's heartland. "Everywhere we have gone we have found the slave laborers by the hundreds and the thousands," an officer wrote to the newspaper of his home county in Arkansas. "I never dreamed there were so many in Germany."[15]

The GIs also found it hard to distinguish between the different categories of the Third Reich's prisoners. There were the Allied POWs, for example, some of whom had lived in military camps, others of whom had been employed as workers in agriculture or industry. Then there were the innumerable foreign workers, who had been recruited by means as various as enticement, indirect compulsion, and open conscription.[16] Moreover, it proved impossible to draw general conclusions about the treatment of these people. The liberated POWs, for instance, were malnourished and had "the wary, hard look of captivity," but on the whole they appeared to have been treated decently.[17] During the last weeks of the war, however, the POW treatment declined significantly and many were found pale, listless, emaciated, and sick. In a POW hospital at Verona, GIs freed 200 Allied soldiers who looked as if they had been treated by "medieval medicine;" they offered "a frightful, horrible sight."[18] Other POWs had been forced by their captors to march hundreds of miles in attempts to evade the Allied troops. Near Witten at the Ruhr River, Americans came across some 1,100 POWs who had survived such marches, and their blood began boiling when they saw that many of them were "unable to rise lying in their own filth."[19] Nothing, however, enraged the GIs more than the crimes committed against captive airmen. American authorities received reports on no less than 800 cases in which airmen had been killed or maltreated by German civilians.[20] In addition, the soldiers noticed that the Allied POWs from the East had been treated much more harshly during their imprisonment in Germany than those from the West. Stories of the "extremely cruel treatment" these POWs had suffered were already circulating among the Americans in the winter of 1944–45. When the 3rd Infantry Division crossed the Main River near Eschau in March 1945, a lieutenant wrote in his diary:

> Here we liberate some wierd looking Mongolians who had been fighting with the Russian Army. These Mongols are starving. They wrestle around in the ditch for some rotten apples.[21]

American reports indicated that the treatment of the foreign workers in Germany had also differed greatly. Those from Western Europe had received virtually the same pay and treatment as German laborers. The Poles had been paid little and had been subjected to many restrictions in public places. The Soviets in turn had been treated as if they were slaves and had been allowed almost no freedom of movement.[22]

In this jumbled mass of human suffering, the exceptional fate of the so-called persecutees did not immediately become clear to the GIs. SHAEF applied the term to those people who had been victimized by the enemy because of race, religion, political beliefs, and/or resistance activities.[23] But the American soldiers often did not realize that they were dealing with an entirely different category of Nazi victims when they came across the first persecutees. By the time the GIs uncovered the first concentration camps in Germany, they had already liberated a bewildering assortment of Oflags, Stalags, transit camps, and labor camps where conditions had varied greatly. Nothing had prepared the soldiers for the monstrous nature of the concentration camps. Some GIs simply assumed they were entering yet another POW stockade. A private expressed his surprise upon seeing the inmates of Buchenwald:

> In the camp ... we noticed that all of the prisoners there were not American soldiers or any kind of soldiers. They were civilians, and there were many, many Jews there.[24]

Others thought they were liberating more labor camps. "We had heard about camps, period, but not of particular camps or of what was taking place in these camps," remembered a medic of the 63rd Infantry Division, who had walked into Dachau totally oblivious of what he was going to find. "As far as we knew, they were forced labor camps, we had no idea as to what was taking place inside."[25]

What the American soldiers discovered in Germany's concentration camps shocked them more than anything else they had encountered during the war. A GI described the nightmarish sensation of walking through Dachau:

> Everyone was strictly horrified. We were sick to our stomachs! And we were pretty callous people. You know, we had gone through a war, for many, many months we were in battle, and we had seen a lot of things, we had seen a lot of hands and heads blown off, and buildings shattered, and people killed, and so on and so forth. But something like this, we had never seen, we could never imagine anything like this.[26]

Genocide was no longer taking place when the Allies started liberating the camps, for Himmler had ordered its end in November 1944. Nevertheless, in the six months between that order and the end of the war, tens of thousands of Jews and other inmates had died from overwork, hunger, disease, and guard brutality. Moreover, in the chaos of the last weeks, epidemics had swept rapidly through the barracks and piles of bodies had been left unburied.[27] The conditions in the camps moved many hardened combat men to tears. African-American soldiers of the 761st Tank Battalion, who were among the first to arrive at Buchenwald, were soon "crying like babies." Veterans became sick to their stomachs and were unable to eat for days. A soldier of the 4th Armored Division saw comrades at Ohrdruf who walked about "wild-eyed," digging their fingernails into their palms until they bled. "There are times," an infantry captain wrote to his sister after having seen emaciated corpses strewn about at Gardelegen, "when I have thought I was going insane from seeing too much and being so close – too close to it." Some simply distanced themselves from the horror through a psychic closing-off and kept functioning only by repressing all emotion.[28]

The Americans tried to describe in letters home what they were uncovering in the concentration camps, but they found it could not be put into words. They had even more difficulty trying to comprehend what they were witnessing. "I couldn't understand this. I just couldn't," said an African-American combat engineer who helped victims at Buchenwald. "So I walked around the camp; I wanted to see more. To understand more."[29] Many a GI at first responded with disbelief to what he was seeing with his own eyes. The stubborn refusal to accept the cruel reality could take irrational forms. A private of the 8th Infantry Division, for example, arrived at the concentration camp of Wöbbelin, near Ludwigslust, early in May 1945. He walked between piles of dead and stared at dying skeletons in dark barracks. Yet, when an inmate told him that some people had been beaten to death for not working hard enough, the GI found this hard to believe and was careful in a letter home to mention that he had not seen any bruises on the prisoners. The same letter also showed that the soldier still did not understand that the persecutees were fundamentally different from the traditional POWs:

> I have no proof of course, that the old man told us the exact truth, but I have listened to the British and American soldiers who have been released. They were not treated so royally in some respects either.[30]

Too many aspects of the hideous Nazi crime of genocide remained beyond comprehension. That the victims were all defenseless civilians made their death look "unfair" and outright "sadistic" to the combat soldiers. Then also, liberating camp after camp and seeing maltreated people as well as corpses by the thousands, there was "the enormity of the evil" that was impossible to fathom.[31] Nothing, however, was harder for the GIs to understand than the systematic nature of the crime. They had grown used to the kind of death randomly dispensed by the chaos and fury of battle, but they failed to grasp how death could have been administered in well-ordered camps by cold-blooded functionaries. The American soldiers were dumbfounded to find that the horror camps had often been operated in the midst of normal communities as if they had been mere factories. They discovered Ohrdruf in countryside that was "a vista of beauty," while the camp itself had been erected near "a most magnificent modern castle." Buchenwald lay in "a suburban-type community" where "the grass was well manicured and cared for." Although the GIs said they could smell the sickening stench of death when they were still 15 miles away from Nordhausen, the people in the town maintained they had never known what was going on in the camp.[32] Most mind-boggling was how the perpetrators of such crimes could have lived with themselves. "And over and over again," wrote a private who was desperately searching for answers, there was the question: where did the German High Command find the large numbers of people to run the concentration camps? To claim they put the criminally insane in charge did not strike me as the truth. Insane people can't run vast camps over a period of years.[33]

Insanity indeed could not serve as an explanation for organized evil. But immorality could. Misconduct by enemy soldiers together with certain civilian aberrations had made the GIs suspect all along that the German people were suffering from degeneration. The horror of the concentration camps did more than confirm what the soldiers had sensed almost intuitively from the beginning: the rot they now uncovered brusquely showed that Germany's moral infection had progressed beyond any cure. The scenes at Gardelegen convinced a soldier of the 84th Infantry Division that the Germans had "degenerated into a state lower than animals."[34]

What was more, the endless repetition of such scenes in Germany also implicated the rest of Europe. In the cellars of Nordhausen, a medic of the 104th Infantry Division came upon diseased and filthy people who were being eaten away by malnutrition and diarrhea. The disgusted American could only compare walking into those dank rooms to "stepping into the Dark Ages."[35] In the minds of the GIs, the medieval times that had descended on Germany threw a dark shadow over all of the Old World. For was not the horror of the concentration camps as much a reflection of Europe's ills as it was a culmination of Germany's decay? To be sure, the American soldiers were enraged at the Germans for having perpetrated the crime of genocide. Yet, at the same time, they realized that similar horrors had been lurking beneath most of the Old World's surface and could have erupted in any of its countries. The GIs had learned about Europe's age-old scars firsthand and had seen its innumerable festering wounds from up close. Perhaps the scale of Germany's crime was unspeakable, but amidst the deep-seated hatreds and intricate resentments of Europe its nature had not been unthinkable. That this crime had been allowed to take place in the very heart of the Continent seemed to say as much about the Old World as it did about Germany. Before the discovery of the Third Reich's concentration camps, some GIs had still been able to hope that their army could regenerate the Old World by letting out the poison. The camps shattered even that last hope. Europe's diseases appeared to have become terminal. The crash of its ruin seemed total and irrevocable. The vacuum it left beckoned new powers to take over.

THE HORSEMEN OF THE APOCALYPSE

It was not uncommon for American soldiers, many of whom knew their Bible well, to interpret what was happening in Europe in apocalyptic terms. The war took on such devastating proportions that it came to look like a cosmic cataclysm designed to punish the Old World for its perseverance in sin. A lieutenant who complained to his wife in August 1944 that a solid middle class did not exist in France and that a few rich degraded the many poor, remarked in the same letter: "God might do worse than send a flood and let the French start over. Maybe the war was the flood." In the last weeks of the war especially, it appeared as if a biblical deluge was washing away Europe's evil. Upon hearing the news of Hitler's suicide, a soldier of the 4th Armored Division was convinced that the Führer's death was God's answer to the challenge the Nazis had offered Him. With the words of Isaiah, the GI exclaimed: "How art thou fallen from heaven, O Lucifer."[36]

Similarly, after the discovery of the unspeakable evil in the camps, the war cannot but have recalled in some GIs the image of the righteous soldiers riding on white horses in the prophetic vision of the Apocalypse. As the American and Soviet troops advanced toward each other across the ruins of the Old World, the GIs certainly believed that both armies were about to establish a new earth.

The American Victors

A poll among white enlisted men in the US in August 1942 showed they completely agreed that the war was a matter of defensive necessity, as nine out of ten believed it was being fought for America's survival. That same poll revealed, however, that 65 per cent of the GIs also agreed that their country was in the war for a much more idealistic reason, namely to "guarantee democratic liberties to all peoples of the world."[37]

Army surveys demonstrated that 18 per cent of the troops in the US in July 1943 did sometimes or very often feel that the war was not worth fighting for. That proportion changed to 35 per cent among troops in the British Isles in January 1944. Being away from home and living with the fear of combat evidently sufficed to effect that jump. Remarkably enough, however, the level of doubt about the war did not rise any further once the soldiers were involved in actual combat. In April 1945, ten months of battle had not been able to increase the number of doubters in the ETO to more than 35 per cent. Similarly, in that same month research among line infantrymen in Italy revealed that those who had been in combat a very long time had not become more likely to doubt the war than newcomers.[38]

It has been suggested that this was so because most GIs thought they had to fight the war if America wanted to survive and that therefore they did not see any alternative course, no matter how tough the combat experience. But why then did doubts about the war increase simply upon arriving overseas and not during the tremendous hardships of battle? In combat, loyalty to one's buddies as well as pride in one's outfit undoubtedly helped to strengthen motivation. It should not be overlooked, however, that during battle the GIs' motivation was also cemented by an increase in the more idealistic orientation to the war. By April 1945, for instance, there were as many American soldiers in the ETO who believed that the principal reason why they had become involved in the war was the destruction of Nazism and fascism (38 per cent) as there were who claimed that it was nationalistic self-defense (37 per cent).[39]

The belief that the American army had come to Europe to help liberate the natives from oppression certainly gained ground among the combat soldiers. After all, the true nature of the enemy's evil as well as the full extent of the victims' anguish was nowhere more obvious than in the front lines. Long before the discovery of the concentration camps, the combat soldiers became disgusted by the misery the Germans had brought upon the Europeans. An officer who saw starved Dutch people fight for garbage at Venlo in the winter of 1945, for instance, "cursed the Germans with deep and bitter feeling." "What untold suffering," he wrote in his journal, "those dumb, non-thinking, egotistical, goose-stepping klouts have inflicted needlessly on untold innocent thousands."[40] But swelling pride probably influenced the American combat soldiers' motivation as much as growing hatred. The enthusiastic receptions by victims of the German aggression all over Europe woke them up to the fact that they were not fighting merely for America's sake. The GIs appeared to have spent remarkably little thought on what it would mean to the Europeans to be freed from foreign occupation by liberators who had come from another world for that express purpose. That is probably why they responded to the first outbursts of European gratitude with a mixture of surprise and embarrassment.[41] Increasingly, however, the GIs came to look upon those receptions as an important motivating force. A soldier of the 3rd Armored Division, for example, claimed that the overwhelming Belgian welcome at Charleroi was "of extreme significance to us because it tended to reemphasize that our efforts – our goal – were directed toward a worthy cause."[42] For the soldiers at the front, the war turned more and more from a matter of practical necessity into one of moral obligation.

When they finally uncovered the concentration camps, many of the Americans who might still have harbored doubts must have understood for sure that they had not crossed the ocean just to keep what they had at home, but also to give back what had been taken from the people in Europe. Soldiers who inspected the insides of the camps burned with anger. Liberated prisoners killed almost 80 guards at Buchenwald, often with the aid and encouragement of GIs. American revenge peaked when a squad killed 122 Germans who had been arrested in the Dachau camp.[43] The GIs left the camps more determined than ever to liberate Europe from domination by the Germans. "We had just mopped them up before," claimed a company commander of the 761st Tank Battalion, "but we stomped the shit out of them after the camps."[44] Still, the appalling discoveries did not only emphasize what the GIs were fighting against. A medic who came across slave laborers for the first time in the Hardt Mountains was moved to tears because the victims made him understand "just what we're fighting for – the right to be free."[45] A soldier of the 84th Infantry Division summarized the effect the last weeks of the war had on him and his comrades:

> If anyone sailed combat-clad to this continent, which is darker by far than Africa, with misgivings as to just why he came, all doubts must have been dispelled if he traveled along the roads of Germany with spear-heading armies.[46]

The horrendous scenes also shocked the GIs into realizing how grave their country's responsibility would be after the war. "Several times I've thought when witnessing such scenes," a private of the 76th Infantry Division wrote to his family in April 1945, "God help our country if it fails to do its share in maintaining and establishing a world peace at the end of the war."[47] A survey, held among American soldiers in Europe in the last two weeks of April 1945, showed that there was a clear majority for a policy of internationalism after the war. Seventy-three per cent of the GIs believed that the best way for the US to keep out of war in the future was not to steer clear of world affairs but to join in a strong organization of nations. More importantly, 65 per cent of the soldiers agreed that there should be an international police force that could be sent any place the permanent organization decided it was needed. The war experience made clear to the GIs that a return to isolationism was unrealistic for a country that had reached the unmistakable status of superpower.[48] "I think of Plato," a lieutenant wrote to his wife in April 1945, "saying the best public officials are those who serve against their will, from a sense of duty."[49]

The Soviet Victors

During the 1930s, most Americans had regarded the Soviet Union as "backward, strange, and unimportant."[50] At the outset of World War II, the American people did not realize that the conflict would bring the crash of ruin for the Old World and the ascendance to global power for the New World. Much less did they suspect that the revolutionary nation in the East would become the dominant power on the Eurasian landmass and play a primary role in the world shaped by the war. As a matter of fact, following the German invasion of the Soviet Union in June 1941, it looked for a long time as if the country would go under in World War II.

But the Soviet Union did not only survive the German blows, it gradually developed into the most important ally of America in the effort to set Europe's house in order. In November 1938, pollsters asked Americans what kind of government they would prefer to live under if they had to choose between the German and the Russian one. Fifty-nine per cent of the respondents favored Germany, only 41 per cent chose Russia. Yet, by July 1941, Americans were hoping by an overwhelming margin of eighteen to one that the Soviet Union would defeat Nazi Germany. In a survey held in America just after the Moscow Conference, some 82 per cent of the respondents believed that "Russia ought to have as much to say as the United States about the peace that is made with Germany."[51]

During the war, the more favorable image of the Soviet Union gained ground in America "among people of all economic and social positions and of all political and religious persuasions."[52] No Americans, however, could have been more favorably disposed toward the Soviet Union than the combat soldiers in Europe. Whereas the British and French allies looked less and less impressive to the GIs as the war dragged on, the Soviet soldiers grew in stature until they appeared to be giants. More and more the American soldiers felt as if the western allies were merely inching forward while the Soviet troops were steamrolling the Germans. It was the battle of Stalingrad that established the Red Army's fame more than any other event. The American soldiers continued to refer to it with awe throughout the war. "Anzio it's been said, is as rugged as Stalingrad," a worn-out private of the 1st Armored Division nervously scribbled in his diary while dug in on the Italian beachhead. The GIs who passed the battlefield of Verdun called it more than once "the Stalingrad of World War I."[53] After that crucial turning point at the Eastern Front, the American combat soldiers never again lost sight of the Soviet advance. "The Doughfeet are worse than U.S. Armchair Strategists when it comes to figuring all the angles of the Red Drive," a private from the 100th Infantry Division told his parents. GIs clung to the few available radios to hear "the wonderfully good news from the Russian front, and the programs of music from the USA" and asked their families to send detailed maps showing Germany with both fronts so that they could also follow the Russian gains.[54] Whenever the advance in the West slowed down, the GIs turned to the Eastern Front for encouragement. A private of the 1st Armored Division wrote in his diary on 22 October 1943:

In Italy, the Germans are falling back slowly above Naples, but not as fast as we would have liked. They are still being hammered in Russia, however.

On 23 June 1944 the same soldier jotted down:

BBC says the Russians have started another big offensive in the mid-Dnieper sec. In France the Allies are stalled at Caen & St. Lo.[55]

Even when hit by the German counteroffensive in the Ardennes, some GIs put more faith in the distant Soviet comrades than in the exhausted European allies on their very flanks. A medic wrote to his wife on Christmas Day of 1944: "We're hoping and waiting for a Russian drive, and some help from the British."[56] To the American soldiers it was becoming increasingly obvious that the armies of the US and the Soviet Union, not those of the weakened European allies, were deciding the issues in the once so powerful Old World. "Every one now knows," a GI wrote in his diary in March 1945, "that the European war must end this year due to Russian and Patton advances."[57]

It was not only the British and the French soldiers who rapidly shrank in size in comparison with the Soviet comrades. GIs of the 87th Infantry Division who learned during the Battle of the Bulge that a German had been captured by their unit, hurried to the command post because they had never seen an enemy soldier from up close. The POW happened to be a tall man of about six feet five. "Those who had seen the German were astonished at his size," admitted a private, "he looked more the way we pictured the Russians."[58] Although the GIs' confidence in their own army steadily grew as the war progressed, they were awed by what the Soviet war machine was doing to the German troops and must have grinned rather sheepishly when POWs assured them they had been sent to the Western Front to rest. No German soldiers looked more burned-out to the GIs than those who had been transferred to the West from the hell of the East. Americans shuddered each time they captured Germans who had lost lips end eyelids to the Siberian cold. And they were embarrassed to see how the famed German soldiers cowered from the mere thought of the Soviets. GI interrogating teams, for example, made POWs talk in no time merely by hinting that the cooperative ones would be sent to America, the others handed over to the Red Army.[59] Increasingly, the Soviet war machine became a standard by which the GIs measured military prowess. After having talked to German POWs in Sicily, a captain wrote home with pride: "Some have actually stated that they prefer the Russian front, to the First Division Sector." When a Polish deserter told soldiers of the 7th Infantry Regiment in Italy that the morale of the Germans they were facing in the Winter Line was low, the GIs regarded this as particularly good news because they believed the enemy there belonged to a crack unit that had survived nothing less than the battle of Stalingrad.[60]

As far as the American combat soldiers were concerned, the Soviets could not move into Europe fast enough. "God speed the Red Army," an officer at Saint-Lô jotted in his journal when news reached him that it was bridging the Vistula.[61] GIs prayed that the Soviets would occupy the German capital soon and as much territory west of it as they could. "Stars & Stripes says a town 67 miles from Berlin fell," a private informed his parents on 2 February 1945. "Hope by the time you get this letter the Rooshians are 67 miles this side of said site."[62] The front was not a place where one could afford distrust of one's most formidable ally. In the last two weeks of April 1945, US Army pollsters asked soldiers in Europe what they thought of the statement: "Russia is more interested in dominating or controlling the world than she is in building a truly democratic world." Seventy-two per cent of the GIs refused to agree with that opinion.[63]

When American soldiers were able at last to shake hands with their Russian comrades in the heart of the Old World, they experienced it as "a thrill" that brought "a feeling of tremendous relief."[64] The first encounter between both armies was nevertheless somewhat awkward. To many GIs the Russian people remained as strange as they had been in the 1930s. "They were clad according to the best tradition," a corporal wrote home from the Elbe, "with flared Cossack coats and those Persian wool-looking hats that go with them."[65] Their language was more puzzling than any the Americans had come across in Europe. The Allied soldiers could communicate only with the help of a few interpreters, signs, and enthusiastic demonstrations of their weapons. The Russians still appeared somewhat backward too. GIs were surprised, for instance, by the number of horses in the Soviet army and noticed that its soldiers were intrigued by cameras.[66]

Contrary to the American opinion of the 1930s, however, the Soviets were now anything but unimportant. No one realized this better than the American soldiers who had monitored and analyzed the Soviet advance hopefully day after day. The GIs had witnessed the demise of the Old World armies: the British had been bled white, the French crushed, the Italians brushed aside, the Germans broken. In the period of March through May 1945, a US Army survey asked recent enlisted returnees from overseas service to rate the war effort of their allies. As many as 31.5 and 30 per cent of those GIs who had had contacts respectively with the soldiers of England and of France claimed that these countries had not done their share. Only one American soldier in a hundred, however, felt that the Soviets had not made their proper contribution to victory.[67] When the American soldiers finally laid eyes on the Soviet army early in May 1945, it looked as formidable as they had imagined. The 8th Infantry Division prepared itself at the Elbe for a first meeting with the Soviets by putting only GIs who were six feet or taller in the welcome teams.[68] And the Soviet soldiers did not fail to live up to the American expectations. They looked physically impressive. GIs noticed they were stocky, had close-cropped hair, and faces like quarterbacks. The Red troops welcomed their American friends with a "strong Russian paw" and a "rib-cracking bear hug." They drank the kind of vodka only "asbestos-lined stomachs" could endure and chewed impressive slabs of bacon with it.[69] Their war machine looked menacing and efficient. Infantry soldiers all seemed to carry submachine guns, while the Soviet tanks dwarfed even the German Tigers. But what astounded the GIs most were the numerous "burly Russian women in uniform," who served even in frontline units. With consternation, the Americans stared at "lady tankers" and at female soldiers who wore no make-up or perfume but instead carried map-cases over their shoulders and pistols on their hips. The armed women made the GIs acutely aware of how far the Soviets were willing to go to eradicate the scourge that had spread from the Old World once too often.[70]

The Germans watched with regret how the two foreign powers they had challenged now managed to link up in the very heart of Europe. They were particularly pained by the thought that the Soviet Union would participate in the new global partnership. Instead of exorcising the communist demon from the Old World, they had awakened the Soviet giant who would now help control it. During the last weeks of the war, the Germans pleaded with the American soldiers to consider forming a front with Europe against the Soviet Union. Road signs and slogans on walls mocked the GIs as "Slaves of Moscow." Propaganda broadcasts in English tried to sow distrust and fear of the Soviets in hysterical tones. Enemy soldiers assured the GIs that the Russians were uncivilized. Civilians in turn appealed to the cultural and racial similarities between Germans and Americans.[71]

But the attempts were in vain. When the Germans claimed the Russians were "pigs," the GIs retorted that their allies "were only returning in kind what the Krauts had been vesting on Russian soldiers and civilians." When the Germans predicted that the US would soon be fighting against the Soviet Union, the Americans disregarded the warning as "the wishful thinking of the defeated."[72] The GIs had witnessed the Old World's crash of ruin firsthand. The war years had convinced them that the epicenters of world power had now irrevocably shifted to Washington and Moscow. Moreover, they believed that America and Russia had shown to be perfect partners for the future containment of the Old World's diseases. When late in April 1945 the Germans attempted to offer unconditional surrender to America and Great Britain only, the American combat soldiers feared for a moment that these cunning Europeans would manage to drive a wedge between them and the Soviets after all. Great was their relief therefore when the German overtures were rejected. "It did my heart good to know we'd do nothing without Russia," a combat medic told his wife in response to the news.

> Unquestionably, we are and should be a trio never to be divided. I assure you the boys on the front line will always fight for this combination – particularly U.S. and Russia.[73]

In the American mind, wars were endemic to the Old World and had come to be interpreted as symptoms of the chronic diseases under which it was wasting away. From the moment the GIs set foot in the Old World, they too had the feeling that they were witnessing not just a continent at war, but a world in decline. World War II merely appeared to be speeding up the collapse of a world that had long before suffered ruin from within. Nothing confirmed the GIs' interpretation of the war more than the combat experience of the last weeks.

The crash reverberated loudest when Germany finally collapsed in a chaos of surrealistic dimensions. The mad rush that followed the crossing of the Rhine late in March 1945 gave a lieutenant of the 3rd Infantry Division the impression that he was witnessing "a great nation deliberately committing suicide."[74] Yet, the war had drained so much power from Europe's military and society that the American soldiers were convinced that not only Germany but the entire Old World had lost, if not its will to live, its ability to lead. Moreover, when the GIs uncovered the horror of the camps, they believed that they had revealed not only the true nature of Germany's evil, but also the full extent of Europe's moral ruin. It irrefutably proved to them that the Old World had lost not only the power to rule, but also the right.

There was therefore no doubt in the minds of America's combat soldiers that World War II was a turning point in history and the beginning of a new world order. More importantly, by the end of the war it also was obvious to them how that new order would operate. Henceforth, the American Republic from the West and the Soviet Union from the East would form a revolutionary partnership to quarantine the Old World's diseases. Little could the GIs suspect that, instead, their country would soon be working together closely for half a century with the infected Old World so as to contain the pest threatening to spread from the assumed new ally.

Epilogue

The American combat soldiers formed their perception of Europe under the exceptional conditions of war. These conditions seriously distorted their mental image of the overseas continent. The violence and destruction prevented the soldiers from seeing much of Europe's scenic splendor and perverted most of its natural beauty. After years of merciless fighting, the mauled European armies the GIs watched in action were only faint reflections of their former selves. The society the Americans discerned through the fog of battle and the shadow of total war looked as if it had reached the point of total disintegration.

The GIs were well aware, of course, that they were not seeing Europe in normal circumstances. Nevertheless, the Americans were convinced that what they were witnessing was not just the disruption caused by war, but also the crash of a much more deep-seated ruin. The natural surroundings gave them the impression that the Old World had been predestined to be a battlefield and that World War II was simply the result of a long process of rot. The exhausted armies seemed to reflect not just the toll of total war, but also the impotence of an Old World military that had stubbornly clung to its outdated ways. The bankrupt society appeared to tell the story not only of years of warfare, but also of centuries of political cynicism, economic stagnation, and cultural decadence. And finally, the discovery of the Holocaust during the last weeks of the war revealed to the American soldiers as much about Nazi Germany's evil as it did about the Old World's moral ruin.

When in the early 1960s Foster Rhea Dulles wrote the history of American travel to the Old World, he refrained from examining the experience of the millions of GIs in Europe during World War II because he believed that it stood "distinct and apart from the general record of American travel abroad."[1] To be sure, Europe's wartime conditions constituted an exceptional period and America's combat soldiers never experienced the continent as traditional tourists. Yet, rather than a break, or even an interruption, in the Americans' traditional image of the Old World as a cauldron of tyranny, poverty, intolerance, and vice behind a facade of cultural splendor, the GIs' perception of Europe points to a continuation and a culmination.[2] Many of the prejudices against the Old World, which Dulles identified as dominant among the Americans who had traveled to and from it in the previous centuries, became confirmed and strengthened among the GIs by the abominable conditions they encountered in Europe during World War II. It did not matter to the American combat soldiers that they were not always able to determine whether the misery they were seeing was attributable to the current war or to Europe's age-old degeneration, for they were convinced that the plague of war itself was an integral part of the Old World's decline.

If the Great War had already shaken Europe to its corroded foundations, the GIs were convinced that World War II was dealing the ruined continent its deathblow. The war was certainly changing Europe's relationship with the world, as it became glaringly obvious to the GIs that its destiny would henceforth be determined by two extra-European powers: America and the Soviet Union.[3] The American soldiers increasingly pinned their hopes for the containment of the Old World plagues on cooperation with the Soviets. Not because their traditional distrust of the Soviets easily melted away, but rather because Europe itself did not appear to be up to that task anymore. Shocked by Europe's atrophy, the GIs became impressed by the Soviets' vitality. The determination and efficiency with which the Red Army turned out to be fighting asked for an overall reassessment of the Soviet regime. Similarly, the admiration for the Russian military effort led to an appreciation of the Russian people. The New World's confrontation with its Old World antithesis suddenly made it easy for the GIs to find resemblances between America and its Soviet ally. However imperfect Russia's new political system, were they not both revolutionary and anti-imperialist countries that had shown the courage to throw off the yoke of king and czar and to start with a tabula rasa? However experimental the Soviets' economy, were not the industries of America and the Soviet Union the only ones that had proved able to wage a protracted total war with success?[4] By the end of the war it was not preposterous for the GIs to see some poetic justice in the fact that these very countries were able to shake hands as partners amidst the smoking ruins of the Old World.

The perception of Europe that developed among the GIs may not only contribute to a better understanding of how the advances between America and the Soviet Union came to be encouraged during the war, it may also offer an insight into how the honeymoon could turn sour so rapidly after the conflict had ended. The war never succeeded in removing the GIs' distrust of the Soviets entirely. In April 1945, 19 per cent of the American soldiers in Europe still believed that there would be some serious arguments between America and Russia after the war; another 13 per cent even thought that the two countries were likely to fight each other in the future.[5] But these soldiers did not only form a minority, their number had also steadily decreased throughout the war, and so the GIs' expectations of the new ally had become very high by the end of the hostilities. That undoubtedly helps to explain some of the Americans' disappointment and acrimony when the promise of cooperation began to evaporate so soon after the war. More than anyone else, the hundreds of thousands of American soldiers who had fought overseas must have felt betrayed when the Soviets, rather than healthy new actors on the international scene, turned out to be nothing more than intriguers contaminated by the same Old World diseases they had appeared willing to contain. It did not take long before the phrase "Red Fascism" was coined in the US and before Nazi Germany and the Soviet Union merged in the American image of Old World totalitarianism.[6]

The Americans came out of World War II with the conviction that the Old World had grown too weak to set its own house in order. On top of that, they came to believe not long after the war that the Soviet Union was betraying its promise to cooperate with America in that task. Yet, the Americans also emerged from World War II, and the confrontation with the contrasts of the Old World, with an increased awareness of their own country's identity and a new appreciation of its ideological values, such as freedom, democracy, equality, and economic opportunity.[7] If the Great Depression had managed to shake the Americans' confidence in the economic and political viability of their nation during the 1930s, the rise of totalitarianism abroad and the gruesome war that ensued convinced them again in the 1940s that theirs was the best of all countries. As Henry Commager observed of mid-twentieth century America:

> By contrast with the barbarism that so speedily overwhelmed many ancient nations, American failings came to seem superficial, her sins almost innocent.[8]

The experience of World War II caused America to be willing to contain and counteract anything it perceived as another threat to its newly cherished lifestyle with a preponderance of power, if necessary all by itself. Of all the Americans, the soldiers of World War II have proved time and again in the postwar period to be among those most likely to support diplomacy by strength and to favor overwhelming nuclear superiority.[9] That is perhaps the most telling evidence that no Americans obtained a more heightened sense of the New World's uniqueness and exemplariness than those who had seen with their own eyes the Old World at war.

Notes

Preface

1. Stouffer et al., *Combat*, 62–3.
2. Most of the statistics can be found in *What the Soldier Thinks*, a series of War Department reports on the GIs' attitudes, and in Stouffer's two-volume *The American Soldier*. In analyzing the soldiers' personal documents, my emphasis has been on the common experience and on reaching a point of saturation. This method allows the uncovered patterns of perception and experience to be generalized from a sufficiently large sample to the whole social milieu of the American combat soldiers in Europe. The sample for this work consists of the personal stories of some 250 different soldiers (100 unpublished and 150 published ones). For a more detailed exposé on this method and its different applications, see Bertaux and Kohli, "Life Story Approach," 215–37.
3. Robert J. McMahon, "Historiography: The Cold War in Asia: Toward a New Synthesis," *Diplomatic History* 12 (1988): 327.

PART I NATURE

Chapter 1 Nature

1. Baird, "Lend You My Eyes," 287 and Lyon, *Unknown Station*, 108.
2. Phibbs, *Other Side*, 186.
3. Murphy, *Hell*, 84. See also Leinbaugh and Campbell, *Company K*, 17; Egger and Otts, *G Company*, 37; and Sharp to his father, 19 June 1944, 1st AD, SC.
4. Ellis, *Sharp Edge*, 28–9.
5. Giles, *Journal*, 36; Cawthon, *Other Clay*, 57; Freese, "Private Memories," 46, 84th ID, SC; Burgess, "Military Service," 16, 2nd ID, SC; and Cox, "What Did You Do," 220.
6. Mauldin, *Up Front*, 149 and Irgang, *Purple*, 33.
7. Kimball, *Diary*, 113 and Snyder, *My Task*, 36.
8. Rogers, *Chaplain*, 112.
9. Capa, *Out of Focus*, 106–7. See also Bodeen to his girlfriend, 27 August 1944, 36th ID, SC.
10. Huebner, *Long Walk*, 62 and Tsuchida, *Letters*, 28.
11. Huebner, *Long Walk*, 17–18 and 70–1.
12. Risch and Kieffer, *Quartermaster Corps*, vol. 2, 319-23; Murphy, *Hell*, 34; Roche, "Forty Years," 111, RP; Davis, *This Is It*, 219; and Wiltse, *Medical Department*, 162, 240, and 554.
13. Tregaskis, *Invasion*, 140.
14. Krebs, *Rome*, 31 and Wiggans, "Ithaca Boy," 92, 85th ID, SC.
15. Huebner, *Long Walk*, 27 and Wilbur, *Mined Country*, in *Poems*, 18.
16. Parker, *Civilian*, 4 and Jordan, "Bull Sessions," 56, 9th ID, SC.
17. Blumenson, *Breakout*, 10–13.
18. Cawthon, *Other Clay*, 81.
19. Blumenson, *Breakout*, 10–13.
20. Jordan, "Bull Sessions," 160, 9th ID, SC.

21. Mayo, *Ordnance*, 252-5 and Koskimaki, *Eagles*, 195.

22. Tapert, *Lines*, 164 and Blumenson, *Breakout*, 12.

23. Kimball, *Diary*, 123.

24. DeWitt, "Soldier Memories," 73, 14th AD, SC; Morriss, "In the Huertgen Forest," 574; and Irgang, *Purple*, 175.

25. MacDonald, *Commander*, 119; Atwell, *Private*, 121; Irgang, *Purple*, 186; MacDonald, *Siegfried Line*, 492–3; and John S. D. Eisenhower, *The Bitter Woods* (New York: Putnam, 1969).

26. Haygood, "Letters," 116.

27. Sharp to his father, 19 June 1944, 1st AD, SC and Penrose, *Lee Miller*, 15.

28. Sharp, 13 and 14 April 1943, 1st AD, SC and Irgang, *Purple*, 65.

29. Gray, *Warriors*, 9. See also Irgang, *Purple*, 38; Bodeen to his girlfriend, 14 May 1944, 36th ID, SC; Huebner, *Long Walk*, 59; Koskimaki, *Eagles*, 245; Murphy, *Hell*, 120; and Simpson, *The Heroes*, in *Poems*, 54.

30. Arrington, *Infantryman*, 217; Belden, *Still Time*, 278; Houston, *Paratrooper*, 16; Murphy, *Hell*, 237; Huebner, *Long Walk*, 131; Sharp to his parents, 2 February 1945, 1st AD, SC; and Kleber and Birdsell, *Chemical Warfare*, 336–9.

31. Bond, *Cassino*, 109; Ambrose, *Brothers*, 207; Cox, "What Did You Do," 219; and Brink, *God*, 60–1.

32. Brown, *Up Front*, 22; Kelly, *One Man's War*, 26; Hurkala, *Fighting First*, 9; Koskimaki, *Eagles*, 60–4; Egger and Otts, *G Company*, 31–2; and Snyder, *My Task*, 72.

33. Tinsch to his wife, 17 December 1944, 45th ID, SC; McHugh, *Hell to Heaven*, 7; Eustis, *Letters*, 172; Dohmann, "Medic," 12; Brown, *Up Front*, 30, 232, and 256–8; Egger and Otts, *G Company*, 116; and Mauldin, *Brass Ring*, 188.

34. Biddle, *Artist*, 24.

35. *Guide to Northern Ireland*, 3; Ambrose, *Brothers*, 191; and Atwell, *Private*, 69.

36. Duus, *Liberators*, 189 and Boesch, *Huertgen*, 151–3.

37. Rogers, *Chaplain*, 57–8 and Shinn, *Rumors*, 25.

38. Giles, *Journal*, 143.

39. Huebner, *Long Walk*, 155.

40. Boesch, *Huertgen*, 154.

41. Cawthon, *Other Clay*, 25.

42. Bistrica, 25 December 1943, 1st ID, SC; Johnson, *Hill*, 14; Downing, *At War*, 64; Eustis, *Letters*, 191; and Metcalf, *Cross*, 143.

43. Davis, *This Is It*, 195.

44. Eustis, *Letters*, 162; Krebs, *Rome*, 95; and Standifer, *Not in Vain*, 104.

45. Jeske, *WWII Memories*, 272.

46. Peckham and Snyder, *Hoosiers*, 128.

47. Reams diary, 27 March 1943, 1st ID, SC; Jett diary, 26 December 1944, 1st AD, SC; Irgang, *Purple*, 44–5; and Davis, *This Is It*, 195.

48. PFC Frank Elkin to his father, [1942], Box 2/Folder 28, MCC.

49. Eustis, *Letters*, 158 and Giles, *Journal*, 41.

50. Murphy, *Hell*, 26. See also Jordan, "Bull Sessions," 117, 9th ID, SC.

51. Reister, *Medical Statistics*, 738-41 and Wiltse, *Medical Department*, 145, 165, and 172–3.

52. Peyton, *Surgeon's Diary*, 67.

53. Wiltse, *Medical Department*, 260–1 and 316; Hurkala, *Fighting First*, 146; Rogers, *Chaplain*, 196; and Reister, *Medical Statistics*, 738–41.

54. Belden, *Still Time*, 257; Boyer, "My Experiences," 41, 3rd ID, SC; Koskimaki, *Eagles*, 134; Downing, *At War*, 134; Rogers, *Chaplain*, 152; and Boesch, *Huertgen*, 178.

55. *Guide to Northern Ireland*, 3; *Guide to Great Britain*, 6; and John P. Rosendall, 26 October 1942, Box 2/Folder 21, MCC.

56. Rogers, *Chaplain*, 40.
57. Jett diary, 24 November 1943, 1st AD, SC. See also 29 November 1944.
58. Standifer, *Not in Vain*, 117 and Royal Meteorologic Institute of Belgium, letter to author, 30 November 1993.
59. Gurley, 9 November 1944, 100th IDP.
60. Taylor, *Language*, 105 and Faubus, *Faraway Land*, 327.
61. Boesch, *Huertgen*, 161–2.
62. Jordan, "Bull Sessions," 53–4, 9th ID, SC; Hurkala, *Fighting First*, 125; Atwell, *Private*, 29; Houston, *Paratrooper*, 102; Egger and Otts, *G Company*, 19 and 35; and Rogers, *Chaplain*, 46.
63. Reister, *Medical Statistics*, 630–3.
64. Faubus, *Faraway Land*, 383.
65. Kimball, *Diary*, 107; Westrate, *Observer*, 61; Leinbaugh and Campbell, *Company K*, 106.
66. Huebner, *Long Walk*, 124; Egger and Otts, *G Company*, 26; and Frankel and Smith, *Patton's Best*, 80.
67. Beck et al., *Engineers against Germany*, 187; Gravlin, "Combat Engineer," 34–5, 3rd AD, SC; Boesch, *Huertgen*, 154; Lyon, *Unknown Station*, 70, 80, and 89; Kelly, *One Man's War*, 142; Altieri, *Spearheaders*, 311; and Gushwa, *United States Army Chaplaincy*, 156.
68. Eustis, *Letters*, 218–9.
69. Snyder, *My Task*, 96.
70. Litoff et al., *Miss You*, 231; Faubus, *Faraway Land*, 381; and Gushwa, *United States Army Chaplaincy*, 156–7.
71. Colby, *Army Talk*, 168–9. See also *Pocket Guide to Paris*, 23.
72. Gurley, 23 October 1944, 100th IDP. See also Carter, *Devils*, 170.
73. Atwell, *Private*, 218.
74. Mauldin, *Up Front*, 35.
75. Gray, *Warriors*, 58.
76. Kimball, *Diary*, 30 and 130. See also Jett diary, 11 August 1942, 1st AD, SC; and Stankoven diary, 13 October 1942, 1st ID, SC.
77. Huebner, *Long Walk*, 16–17; Hurkala, *Fighting First*, 20; Tregaskis, *Invasion*, 31; and Mauldin, *Brass Ring*, 185.
78. Gossett, 10 December 1944, 42nd IDP.
79. Royal Meteorologic Institute of Belgium, letter to author, 30 November 1993.
80. Burgess, 1 November 1944, 26th ID, SC and Albert, "Duration," 134, 84th ID, SC. See also Atwell, *Private*, 94–5.
81. Lummer diary, 1 May 1945, 11th AD, SC and Giles, *Journal*, 333.
82. McConahey, *Surgeon*, 106; Daly, "Sharpe's Battalion," 170; Davidson, *Cut Off*, 97; and Wagner, "Odyssey," 83.
83. Irgang, *Purple*, 182; Egger and Otts, *G Company*, 105; Faubus, *Faraway Land*, 473; Brander, Q/9b, 2nd AD, SC; Ambrose, *Brothers*, 184; Risch, *Quartermaster Corps*, vol. 1, 90–7 and 102–8; Cawthon, *Other Clay*, 160; Fussell, "My War," 260; Atwell, *Private*, 30 and 83; and Parker, *Civilian*, 28.
84. Gravlin, "Combat Engineer," 24, 3rd AD, SC; Atwell, *Private*, 37–8 and 92; Roche, "Forty Years," 129, RP; Egger and Otts, *G Company*, 118; Lyon, *Unknown Station*, 170; Jordan, "Bull Sessions," 54, 9th ID, SC; Wilson, *Bastogne to Bavaria*, 93; and Burt, "War Memoirs," 16, 2nd AD, SC.
85. Potter, *Liberators*, 192; Snyder, *My Task*, 93 and 153; Grage, "Reflections," 1, 65th ID, SC; Stewart, untitled memoir, 80, 1st ID, SC; Houston, *Paratrooper*, 89–90; Risch, *Quartermaster Corps*, vol. 1, 132–3; and Morphis, *The Bulge Bugle*, August 1990, 1st ID, SC.

86. Lyon, *Unknown Station*, 81.
87. Reister, *Medical Statistics*, 322–3 and 738–41; Atwell, *Private*, 40 and 144; Tsuchida, *Letters*, 99; and Egger and Otts, *G Company*, 207.
88. Ginn et al., *Trench Foot*, 1–2 and 10; Leinbaugh and Campbell, *Company K*, 197; and Standifer, *Not in Vain*, 213.
89. Ginn et al., *Trench Foot*, 1 and 10.
90. Giles, *Journal*, 312.
91. Tsuchida, *Letters*, 107.
92. Irgang, *Purple*, 20. See also Atwell, *Private*, 317 and Huebner, *Long Walk*, 169.
93. Burgett, *Currahee*, 86.
94. Murphy, *Hell*, 146; Huebner, *Long Walk*, 59; Cawthon, *Other Clay*, 91; Burgett, *Currahee*, 136; and Bond, *Cassino*, 134.
95. Ambrose, *Brothers*, 53.

PART II THE SOLDIERS

Chapter 2 The Soldiers – Introduction

1. Scannell, *Poets*, 207–8.
2. Ambrose, *Brothers*, 44; Brown, *Up Front*, 39–40; Koskimaki, *Eagles*, 21–4 and 122.
3. Downing, *At War*, 153; Huebner, *Long Walk*, 40–1; and Engel, "Patrol," 623.
4. Downing, *At War*, 144 and Tregaskis, *Invasion*, 69 and 82.
5. Rontch, *Jewish Youth*, 213 and Daly, "Sharpe's Battalion," 179.
6. Tsuchida, *Letters*, 103.

Chapter 3 The Allies

1. McConahey, *Surgeon*, 20.
2. Gossett to his parents, 10 December 1944, 42nd IDP.
3. Easton, *Love and War*, 119.
4. Letter from an unidentified soldier, 5 July 1943, Box 3/Folder 31, MCC; Wise, *Truly Ours*, 154; and Rontch, *Jewish Youth*, 17.
5. Snyder, *My Task*, 58 and Mauldin, *Up Front*, 105.
6. War Department, *What the Soldier Thinks: Digest*, February 1943, 17; *Guide to Northern Ireland*, 31; and *Guide to Great Britain*, 16.
7. Reynolds, "Inter-Attachment," 407.
8. Jett diary, 1 July 1942, 1st AD, SC.
9. Rogers, *Chaplain*, 49 and letter from Cpl Raymond Dreyer, Box 2/Folder 29, MCC.
10. Letter from an unidentified soldier, [1942], Box 2/Folder 27, MCC.
11. Robinson, *45th*, 66.
12. Downing, *At War*, 146 and 135.
13. Letter from Cpl Raymond Dreyer, 23 May 1943, Box 2/Folder 29, MCC; Raab to his parents, 4 September 1944, RC; Johnson, *Hill*, 22 and 35; Snyder, *My Task*, 58 and 60; and Downing, *At War*, 29.
14. Reynolds, "Inter-Attachment," 407.
15. *Our Cousins*, in *Songs and Ballads*, Page, 126.
16. Downing, *At War*, 173.
17. Unidentified soldier to his parents, 26 September 1943, Box 1/Folder 13, MCC; Cawthon, *Other Clay*, 27; and Carter, *Devils*, 128–9.
18. Giles, *Journal*, 77; Mauldin, *Up Front*, 105; and Downing, *At War*, 25.

19. Reynolds, "Inter-Attachment," 414–15.
20. Ambrose, *Brothers*, 122.
21. Johnson, *Hill*, 12 and Mauldin, *Up Front*, 105.
22. Wiggans, "Ithaca Boy," 99, 85th ID, SC and Ulsaker, "Saga," 252–3, CU.
23. Huebner, *Long Walk*, 29 and 154.
24. Snyder, *My Task*, 137 and Bond, *Cassino*, 125.
25. Tregaskis, *Invasion*, 60; Huebner, *Long Walk*, 154; and Murphy, *Hell*, 66.
26. Murray, "British Effectiveness," 91–5 and 103; Mauldin, *Up Front*, 104–5; Downing, *At War*, 54 and 172; and unidentified soldier to his family, 15 May 1943, Box 2/Folder 29, MCC.
27. *Guide to Northern Ireland*, 31.
28. Reynolds, "Inter-Attachment," 407–8.
29. *Guide to Northern Ireland*, 31.
30. Downing, *At War*, 46 and letter from an unidentified soldier, 6 January 1943, Box 2/Folder 27, MCC.
31. *Guide to Great Britain*, 14.
32. *My Faithless English Rose*, in *Songs and Ballads*, Page, 147.
33. Reynolds, "Inter-Attachment," 408.
34. Page, *Songs and Ballads*, 144 and 146.
35. War Department, *What the Soldier Thinks: Digest*, February 1943, 24 and Reynolds, "Inter-Attachment," 406–22.
36. Tregaskis, *Invasion*, 163; Carter, *Devils*, 146; and Eustis, *Letters*, 229–30.
37. Huebner, *Long Walk*, 154; Hoffman, *Archives*, 116; and Hornsby, *Sevens*, 87.
38. Metcalf, *Cross*, 127 and Huebner, *Long Walk*, 154.
39. Downing, *At War*, 140 and Johnson, *Hill*, 36.
40. Quoted in Murray, "British Effectiveness," 91.
41. Murray, "British Effectiveness," 100 and 128 and d'Este, "Caution," 271–2.
42. Murray, "British Effectiveness," 125–7 and d'Este, "Caution," 277–81.
43. Huebner, *Long Walk*, 154; Carter, *Devils*, 146; and Daly, "Sharpe's Battalion," 168.
44. Carter, *Devils*, 152.
45. Bistrica, Q/40f, 1st ID, SC and Faubus, *Faraway Land*, 316–17.
46. Faubus, *Faraway Land*, 542.
47. Hurkala, *Fighting First*, 111. See also Frucht, "Clem Has Been Here," 40.
48. Murray, "British Effectiveness," 90 and d'Este, "Caution," 278 and 282.
49. d'Este, "Caution," 287.
50. Ambrose, *Brothers*, 163.
51. Ulsaker, "Saga," 252 and 279, CU.
52. Raff, *We Jumped*, 36 and Altieri, *Spearheaders*, 115.
53. Altieri, *Spearheaders*, 114 and Jett diary, 4 November 1942, 1st AD, SC.
54. Huebner, *Long Walk*, 25; Rontch, *Jewish Youth*, 86; Carter, *Devils*, 7; and Downing, *At War*, 90.
55. *Guide to France*, 22.
56. Taylor, *Language*, 127.
57. Letter from an unidentified soldier, 6 January 1943, Box 2/Folder 27, MCC; Raff, *We Jumped*, 84; Downing, *At War*, 115; and Peyton, *Surgeon's Diary*, 15.
58. Altieri, *Spearheaders*, 139.
59. Vigneras, *Rearming the French*, 258–9.
60. Raff, *We Jumped*, 64.
61. Ibid.
62. Hood, "French Effectiveness," 237–39, 240–41, and 247.
63. Altieri, *Spearheaders*, 129–30.
64. Ibid., 133.

65. Howe, *Northwest Africa*, 173.
66. Gurley, 27 April 1945, 100th IDP.
67. Hood, "French Effectiveness," 223, 230, and 235.
68. Downing, *At War*, 78; Rogers, *Chaplain*, 36 and 61; and Westrate, *Observer*, 38–9.
69. Vigneras, *Rearming the French*, 246–9 and 402.
70. Watters, "Invasion of North Africa," 3rd ID, SC and Downing, *At War*, 105.
71. Huebner, *Long Walk*, 15.
72. Egger and Otts, *G Company*, 11; Raab to his parents, 22 May 1944, RC; and Lyon, *Unknown Station*, 3.
73. Hood, "French Effectiveness," 229.
74. Letter from an unidentified private, 6 January 1943, Box 2/Folder 27, MCC.
75. Raff, *We Jumped*, 63.
76. Vigneras, *Rearming the French*, 262 and 264.
77. Letter from an unidentified soldier, 24 May 1943, Box 2/Folder 27, MCC and Vigneras, *Rearming the French*, 254–8.
78. Vigneras, *Rearming the French*, 260–6 and 402.
79. Vigneras, *Rearming the French*, 183, 186, and 194.
80. Watters, "Invasion of North Africa," 11 and 14–15, 3rd ID, SC.
81. Fry, *Combat Soldier*, 42–3. See also Hood, "French Effectiveness," 243.
82. Keefer, *Italian Prisoners of War*, 21–2 and Gray, *Warriors*, 67.
83. Hoffman, *Archives*, 66.
84. Roche, "Forty Years," 50, RP and Fry, *Combat Soldier*, 47.
85. Snyder, *My Task*, 137.
86. Biddle, *Artist*, 99 and Huebner, *Long Walk*, 76 and 81.
87. Roche, "Forty Years," 47, RP and Q/41e, 88th ID, SC.
88. Watters, "Invasion of North Africa," 15, 3rd ID, SC.
89. Vigneras, *Rearming the French*, 247 and Hoffman, *Archives*, 159.
90. Fry, *Combat Soldier*, 43.
91. Huebner, *Long Walk*, 81; Fry, *Combat Soldier*, 43; and Hoffman, *Archives*, 66.
92. Hood, "French Effectiveness," 245–6 and Keegan, *Six Armies*, 305 and 309.
93. Clarkson, "G.I. Joe," 12, 5th ID, SC; Toole, *Battle Diary*, 61; Stewart, untitled memoir, 44–5, 1st ID, SC.

Chapter 4 The Enemies

1. Monks, *College Men*, 103; Arrington, *Infantryman*, 40; and Eustis, *Letters*, 159.
2. Arrington, *Infantryman*, 38.
3. Altieri, *Spearheaders*, 114.
4. Sadkovich, "Rommel and the Italians," 294–5.
5. Gushwa, *United States Army Chaplaincy*, 151.
6. Biddle, *Artist*, 43 and Raff, *We Jumped*, 203.
7. Capa, *Out of Focus*, 74; Eustis, *Letters*, 150–1; and Johnson, *Hill*, 108.
8. Petracarro, "Italian Army in Africa," 115–17 and Knox, "Italian Armed Forces," 152.
9. Altieri, *Spearheaders*, 226, 256, and 294.
10. Johnson, *Hill*, 98.
11. Petracarro, "Italian Army in Africa," 104 and Knox, "Italian Armed Forces," 150–5.
12. Knox, "Italian Armed Forces," 140–1 and 147 and Sadkovich, "Rommel and the Italians," 310.
13. Petracarro, "Italian Army in Africa," 119–21 and Keefer, *Italian Prisoners of War*, 4.
14. Capa, *Out of Focus*, 74.
15. Abbott, *Believers*, 59.

16. Petracarro, "Italian Army in Africa," 103–4 and 109–10 and Knox, "Italian Armed Forces," 140 and 164–6.

17. Eustis, *Letters*, 154.

18. Petracarro, "Italian Army in Africa," 122.

19. Bairnsfather, *Jeeps and Jests* and Fussell, *Wartime*, 123.

20. Altieri, *Spearheaders*, 226 and Biddle, *Artist*, 112.

21. Carter, *Devils*, 29 and Mauldin, *Mauldin's Army*, 99.

22. Bernstein, *Head Down*, 101; Fussell, *Wartime*, 124; and Raab to his parents, 5 June 1944, RC.

23. Biddle, *Artist*, 144 and Altieri, *Spearheaders*, 271.

24. *Guide to Italy*, 8–9.

25. Eustis, *Letters*, 150; Rogers, *Chaplain*, 116; and Mauldin, *Up Front*, 64.

26. Elting, Cragg, and Deal, *Soldier Talk*, 100.

27. Keefer, *Italian Prisoners of War*, XIII, 73, 76, and 87–101 and Blumenson, *Salerno to Cassino*, 184–5.

28. Blumenson, *Salerno to Cassino*, 185 and 276.

29. Raab, 31 October–1 November 1944, RC.

30. According to J. Glenn Gray, philosopher and veteran, only a minority of the American combat soldiers held an "image of the opposing enemy as an essentially decent man who is either temporarily misguided by false doctrines or forced to make war against his better will and desire." As a result, the GIs rarely made a distinction between "Germans" and "Nazis." (*Warriors*, 158–9 and 161.)

31. Some of these names are mentioned in Elting, Cragg, and Deal, *Soldier Talk*, 129, 169, 171, and 178 and in Taylor, *Language*, 103. All others the author encountered while reading the letters, diaries, and memoirs of GIs.

32. For the impact of World War I on the West's (sub)consciousness, see Fussell, *The Great War*.

33. Atwell, *Private*, 164.

34. Cawthon, *Other Clay*, XIV; Brink, *God*, 16; Stouffer et al., *Combat*, 440–1; and Snyder, *My Task*, 10 and 15.

35. Toole, *Battle Diary*, 1 and 6 and Cawthon, *Other Clay*, 126–7.

36. Bond, *Cassino*, 34 and Easton, *Love and War*, 257.

37. Faubus, *Faraway Land*, 190 and Winston, *Combat Medic*, 159.

38. Haygood, "Letters," 111 and Simmons, "Banning of *All Quiet on the Western Front*," 40–60.

39. McIntyre, untitled memoir, 83, MP and Charles, *Troopships*, 12, 20, 30, 32, 47, 53, 59, and 84.

40. Roche, "Forty Years," 42, RP and Faubus, *Faraway Land*, 336 and 515.

41. Gravlin, "Combat Engineer," 10, 3rd AD, SC.

42. Johnson, *Hill*, 8; Connelly, *Assistant*, 28; and Johnnie Anders, Box 2/Folder 21, MCC.

43. Kimball, *Diary*, 57 and Brink, *God*, 34.

44. Peyton, *Surgeon's Diary*, 10; Downing, *At War*, 192; and Adams, "Les Americaines," 184.

45. Boesch, *Huertgen*, 57 and Brown, *Up Front*, 401.

46. Shapiro to his family, 9 March 1945, 28th ID, SC and Davidson, *Cut Off*, 14.

47. Easton, *Love and War*, 257; Atwell, *Private*, 26; and Bodeen, 36th ID, SC.

48. Brown, *Up Front*, 53; Lyon, *Unknown Station*, 66–7; and Murphy, *Hell*, 250.

49. Palmer, *G.I. Songs*, 235.

50. US War Department, *German Military Forces*, 518 and 527–8 and *Field Manual FM 27-10*, 7.

51. Daly, "Sharpe's Battalion," 8 and 19; unidentified lieutenant to his brother, 17 October 1942, Box 2/Folder 27, MCC; and Donald S. Hutcheson, 9 August 1942, Box 1/Folder 13, MCC.
52. Downing, *At War*, 52.
53. Cawthon, *Other Clay*, 46; *Guide to France*, 72; and *Guide to Germany*, 48.
54. Bond, *Cassino*, 66; Lyon, *Unknown Station*, 40; Downing, *At War*, 76; Huebner, *Long Walk*, 68; and Egger and Otts, *G Company*, 102.
55. Burgett, *Currahee*, 172–3; Giles, *Journal*, 57–9; and Brown, *Up Front*, 236.
56. Opal notebook, 1st ID, SC and Ethier diary, 13th AD, SC.
57. Irgang, *Purple*, 59.
58. Murphy, *Hell*, 5.
59. War Department, *What the Soldier Thinks: Digest*, February 1943, 17; Raff, *We Jumped*, 201; and Faubus, *Faraway Land*, 151.
60. Tapert, *Lines*, 215–16 and Brown, *Up Front*, 40.
61. Snyder, *My Task*, 69 and Brown, *Up Front*, 40.
62. Westrate, *Observer*, 118.
63. Peckham and Snyder, *Hoosiers*, 54 and Brown, *Up Front*, 404.
64. Johns, *Clay Pigeons*, 168; Cawthon, *Other Clay*, 100; and Bond, *Cassino*, 126.
65. Leinbaugh and Campbell, *Company K*, 234; Carter, *Devils*, 154; and Frankel and Smith, *Patton's Best*, 95.
66. McConahey, *Surgeon*, 77 and Frankel and Smith, *Patton's Best*, 97.
67. MacDonald, *Commander*, 124-6 and Tsuchida, *Letters*, 77.
68. Seiverling, *Stories*, 18 and Brown, *Up Front*, 456.
69. Toole, *Battle Diary*, 91.
70. Cawthon, *Other Clay*, 133 and Standifer, *Not in Vain*, 106.
71. Roche, "Forty Years," 52, RP and Burgett, *Currahee*, 152.
72. Mauldin, *Up Front*, 160 and Jordan, "Bull Sessions," 58, 9th ID, SC.
73. Cawthon, *Other Clay*, 154.
74. Haygood, "Letters," 106. See also Robinson, *45th*, 113.
75. *Guide to Germany*, 16.
76. Irgang, *Purple*, 131 and Jordan, "Bull Sessions," 60, 9th ID, SC.
77. Giles, *Journal*, 318.
78. Bond, *Cassino*, 110; Winter, "Battle Babies," 54, 99th ID, SC; Brown, *Up Front*, 51–2, 177, 194, and 228; Jordan, "Bull Sessions," 59, 9th ID, SC; Burgess, "Military Service," 23, 2nd ID, SC; and Irgang, *Purple*, 173.
79. Easton, *Love and War*, 285; Davidson, *Cut Off*, 153; Atwell, *Private*, 104; Clarkson, "G.I. Joe," 15, 5th ID, SC; Ulsaker, "Saga," 233, CU; Lyon, *Unknown Station*, 105; Standifer, *Not in Vain*, 165–6; Boesch, *Huertgen*, 50; and Ambrose, *Brothers*, 99.
80. DeWitt, "Soldier Memories," 103, 14th AD, SC.
81. Tregaskis, *Invasion*, 236-7.
82. Jett diary, 13 May 1944, 1st AD, SC and Daly, "Sharpe's Battalion," 68–9.
83. Mauldin, *Up Front*, 93. A US Army survey of wounded combat veterans in the ETO in September–October 1944, for instance, revealed that 52 per cent of the men rated the 88 mm gun as the weapon they feared most. (Stouffer et al., *Combat*, 238.)
84. Egger and Otts, *G Company*, 57 and Giles, *Journal*, 39.
85. Leinbaugh and Campbell, *Company K*, 121.
86. Giles, *Journal*, 53; Burgett, *Currahee*, 152; Hoffman, *Archives*, 105; Atwell, *Private*, 271; and Bond, *Cassino*, 33.
87. Snyder, *My Task*, 77-8. See also Jordan, "Bull Sessions," 56, 9th ID, SC.
88. Stouffer et al., *Combat*, 232-4 and 238 and Arrington, *Infantryman*, 148.
89. Jordan, "Bull Sessions," 44, 9th ID, SC and MacDonald, *Commander*, 123.
90. Burgett, *Currahee*, 103. See also Bond, *Cassino*, 93 and Standifer, *Not in Vain*, 162.

91. Tregaskis, *Invasion*, 127 and Faubus, *Faraway Land*, 465. A US Army survey of wounded enlisted men from the North African campaign, conducted in the summer of 1943, showed that the machine gun belonged to the five most feared German weapons and that 42 per cent of the men were particularly impressed by its rapid rate of fire. (Stouffer et al., *Combat*, 232–4.)

92. Tregaskis, *Invasion*, 123 and 171–2 and MacDonald, *Commander*, 50, 58, 61, and 118.

93. Toole, *Battle Diary*, 10.

94. Freese, "Memories," 104, 84th ID, SC and Leinbaugh and Campbell, *Company K*, 258.

95. US War Department, *German Military Forces*, 384–90.

96. Letter from an unidentified tank operator, 15 May 1943, Box 2/Folder 29, MCC; Cawthon, *Other Clay*, 124; and Jordan, "Bull Sessions," 56–9, 9th ID, SC.

97. US War Department, *German Military Forces*, 390 and Irgang, *Purple*, 8.

98. Easton, *Love and War*, 4.

99. Johns, *Clay Pigeons*, 165; Tapert, *Lines*, 106; Irgang, *Purple*, 99–100 and 105; and Huebner, *Long Walk*, 194.

100. Stewart, untitled memoir, 62, 1st ID, SC.

101. Downing, *At War*, 156. *Soldbuchs*, booklets containing the Germans' personal and unit data, were so routinely confiscated by GIs in the field that screening, processing, and intelligence activities at the POW camps were seriously hampered. (Krammer, *Nazi Prisoners*, 13.)

102. Calhoun, letters to his parents, 22 November 1944 and 2 May 1945, 42nd ID, SC; Faubus, *Faraway Land*, 478; Raab, letter to his parents, 28 May 1944, RC; and Stradling, *Johnny*, 255.

103. Boesch, *Huertgen*, 31. See also Fry, *Combat Soldier*, 261 and Brown, *Up Front*, 459.

104. Eustis, *Letters*, 147. Egger and Otts, *G Company*, 238 and Brown, *Up Front*, 194.

105. Jordan, "Bull Sessions," 58 and 73, 9th ID, SC.

106. Ambrose, *Brothers*, 81; Brown, *Up Front*, 363 and 461; Lyon, *Unknown Station*, 151; Stewart, untitled memoir, 106–7; Fry, *Combat Soldier*, 134; Cawthon, *Other Clay*, 93; and Boesch, *Huertgen*, 234. Even the famous *Forty-Four Blues* eventually reflected the importance of the German pistols. In the 1920s the song featured a .44 or .45 and in the 1930s a .38 or .32. But in the years following World War II, some African-American veterans sang it as the *P-.38 Blues*. (Charters, *Poetry of the Blues*, 45–6.)

107. Ambrose, *Brothers*, 248.

108. *Guide to Italy*, 2 and *Guide to Germany*, 11.

109. Easton, *Love and War*, 277.

110. 1 Mauldin, *Brass Ring*, 150–1; MacDonald, *Commander*, 328–9; and Ethier diary, 9 May 1945, 13th AD, SC.

111. Rontch, *Jewish Youth*, 38 and Mauldin, *Up Front*, 54–5.

112. Faubus, *Faraway Land*, 209. See also Morris, "Adventures," 1, 65th ID, SC.

113. Rontch, *Jewish Youth*, 262; Burt, "War Memoirs," 9, 2nd AD, SC; Frankel and Smith, *Patton's Best*, 4–6; and Elting, Cragg, and Deal, *Soldier Talk*, 264.

114. Shannon, "Replacement," 127, 26th ID, SC.

115. Mauldin, *Up Front*, 52.

116. Gray, *Warriors*, 138–40.

117. Mauldin, *Up Front*, 50 and Stouffer et al., *Combat*, 80.

118. Ambrose, *Brothers*, 103; Murphy, *Hell*, 219; and Atwell, *Private*, 278.

119. Ambrose, *Brothers*, 62. See also Carter, *Devils*, 42.

120. Duus, *Liberators*, 100.

121. War Department, *What the Soldier Thinks: Monthly Digest*, March 1944, 3–4; Coll, Keith, and Rosenthal, *Engineers*, 53–5, 169, 263, 346–7, 468, and 482; Beck et al., *Engineers against Germany*, 100–7, 144, 181, 368, 374, 380, and 564; and US War Department, *German Military Forces*, 484–506.

122. Unidentified soldier to his family, 15 May 1943, Box 2/Folder 29, MCC; Leinbaugh and Campbell, *Company K*, 211; Faubus, *Faraway Land*, 177; and Fry, *Combat Soldier*, 157.

123. Unidentified soldier, 15 May 1943, Box 2/Folder 29, MCC.

124. Biddle, *Artist*, 109 and Raff, *We Jumped*, 201.

125. 2 Downing, *At War*, 85; Cawthon, *Other Clay*, 77; Egger and Otts, *G Company*, 48; and Ambrose, *Brothers*, 62.

126. Atwell, *Private*, 298-9.

127. Kimball, *Diary*, 161; Burt, "War Memoirs," 14–15, 2nd AD, SC; Daly, "Sharpe's Battalion," 40–1; Irgang, *Purple*, 23; and Koskimaki, *Eagles*, 173.

128. Murphy, *Hell*, 44; Irgang, *Purple*, 233–5; and Jordan, "Bull Sessions," 59, 9th ID, SC.

129. Omer Bartov claims that warfare on the Eastern Front was "an essentially different experience" from that on the Western Front because German troops in the East were caught up in a process of systematic barbarization. Yet he adds that although "in the West the Wehrmacht did behave differently, especially in the fighting of 1940 ..., in the latter stages of the war, and not least due to the fact that many soldiers fighting in France in 1944 had already served in Russia, its conduct became increasingly criminal." ("Wehrmacht," 34.)

130. Tsuchida, *Letters*, 18; Daly, "Sharpe's Battalion," 297; MacDonald, *Commander*, 184–5; Baird, "Lend You My Eyes," 294; Egger and Otts, *G Company*, 178: Arrington, *Infantryman*, 57 and 165; and Raff, *We Jumped*, 144. GIs dubbed the hospital area of the Anzio beachhead "Hell's Half Acre." (Elting, Cragg, and Deal, *Soldier Talk*, 150.)

131. Huebner, *Long Walk*, 79; Murphy, *Hell*, 176; Mauldin, *Brass Ring*, 266; Brown, *Up Front*, 426 and 465; Krebs, *Rome*, 39; and Freese, "Private Memories," 38, 84th ID, SC.

132. Stouffer et al., *Combat*, 161–2; Carter, *Devils*, 26; Koskimaki, *Eagles*, 183, 230, and 370; Burgett, *Currahee*, 115–16 and 179; and Irgang, *Purple*, 26. In March–April 1944, a similar US Army survey showed that the same percentage of GIs had witnessed enemy atrocities in the Pacific, but that a considerably larger proportion (45 per cent) had heard about Japanese atrocities from others.

133. Giles, *Journal*, 55.

134. Leinbaugh and Campbell, *Company K*, 43, 92, and 222; Irgang, *Purple*, 53; Arrington, *Infantryman*, 224; Brown, *Up Front*, 206; and Stoner to his wife, 5 January 1945, 42nd IDP.

135. Stouffer et al., *Combat*, 162–4 and Faubus, *Faraway Land*, 475.

136. Coll, Keith, and Rosenthal, *Engineers*, 254.

137. Burgett, *Currahee*, 65.

138. Gray, *Warriors*, 146.

139. Raff, *We Jumped*, 204 and Mauldin, *Up Front*, 13–14 and 50.

140. Huebner, *Long Walk*, 173 and Stouffer et al., *Combat*, 174 and 565.

141. Peckham and Snyder, *Hoosiers*, 71 and Gray, *Warriors*, 51–2.

142. Burgett, *Currahee*, 131 and Leinbaugh and Campbell, *Company K*, 218–9. Taking into account this state of mind among the American combat soldiers, S. L. A. Marshall's findings that only 15 to 25 per cent of the GIs in line companies actually fired at enemy positions during World War II (because of lack of initiative and a fear of killing imposed by Christian tenets) strike one as particularly surprising. In recent years, Marshall's assertions have been attacked by veterans as "absurd, ridiculous, and totally nonsensical," while some professional historians find his ratio-of-fire statistics "misleading and indeed fraudulent." They argue that "[i]n battle's hard school, ordinary people eventually discover, quite by themselves, the knack of skillful killing" and that, as a result, the ratio of fire was much higher in World War II than Marshall indicated. They even suggest a tendency toward "aimless shooting" and "shooting hysteria," caused

by a mixture of fear and anger. (Marshall, *Men against Fire*, chapter 6; Smoler, "Secret of the Soldiers," 40–5; and Spiller, "Ratio of Fire," 68–9.)

143. Engel, "Patrol," 625.
144. Irgang, *Purple*, 86–8 and Atwell, *Private*, 429. James J. Weingartner has pointed out that in the European war theaters such violations were "in large measure the products of a psychological environment created by total war which affected all participants in approximately similar ways, regardless of ideological or national affinities. ("Massacre at Biscari," 39.)
145. Buettner, Q/46e, 1st ID, SC.
146. Ambrose, *Brothers*, 63.
147. Anderson, "War Years," 21, 8th ID, SC.
148. Weingartner, "Massacre at Biscari," 28 and 37. See also Arrington, *Infantryman*, 147 and Winston, *Combat Medic*, 192.
149. Atwell, *Private*, 393 and Motley, *Invisible Soldier*, 153. See also Frankel and Smith, *Patton's Best*, 40 and Faubus, *Faraway Land*, 157.
150. Tapert, *Lines*, 227 and DeWitt, "Soldier Memories," 115, 14th AD, SC. See also Kelly and Martin, *One Man's War*, 86 and Murphy, *Hell*, 43–4.
151. Leinbaugh and Campbell, *Company K*, 143 and Ethier, 13th AD, SC. See also Hovsepian, *Your Son*, 197 and Brown, *Up Front*, 226.
152. Koskimaki, *Eagles*, 370.
153. Leinbaugh and Campbell, *Company K*, 131.
154. Clarkson, "G.I. Joe," 19–20, 5th ID, SC. See also Burt, "War Memoirs," 26, 2nd AD, SC.
155. Jeske, *WWII Memories*, 275; Kennerly, Q/46e, 10th MD, SC; and Brown, *Up Front*, 315–16.
156. Fry, *Combat Soldier*, 69 and Ambrose, *Brothers*, 152.
157. Ulsaker, "Saga," 187–8, CU and Toole, *Battle Diary*, 57.
158. MacDonald, *Commander*, 213–15.
159. Gravlin, "Combat Engineer," 10, 3rd AD, SC; Krebs, *Rome*, 75; Boesch, *Huertgen*, 227; and Biddle, *Artist*, 196. See also Atwell, *Private*, 366.
160. Brown, *Up Front*, 204 and 451 and McGill, "This Is It," 46, 12th AD, SC. See also Leinbaugh and Campbell, *Company K*, 46.
161. Peyton, *Surgeon's Diary*, 35. See also Murphy, *Hell*, 11.
162. Altieri, *Spearheaders*, 211 and Hovsepian, *Your Son*, 113 and 115. See also Wilson, *Bastogne to Bavaria*, 205; Roche, "Forty Years," 55, RP; and Arrington, *Infantryman*, 49.
163. Metcalf, *Cross*, 124 and Faubus, *Faraway Land*, 216. See also Westrate, *Observer*, 58.
164. Monks, *College Men*, 116–17.
165. Wise, *Truly Ours*, 127.
166. Peckham and Snyder, *Hoosiers*, 129; Johns, *Clay Pigeons*, 76; Fry, *Combat Soldier*, 102. See also Leinbaugh and Campbell, *Company K*, 183.
167. Kenneth G. Jones, [December 1942], Box 2/Folder 27, MCC; Griswold to local newspaper, 4 August 1944, 9th ID, SC; Leinbaugh and Campbell, *Company K*, 140; Ambrose, *Brothers*, 150–1; and Gurley, 100th IDP.
168. Boesch, *Huertgen*, 231 and Faubus, *Faraway Land*, 185. Several historians have demonstrated that the Anglo-Americans despised the Japanese more than the Germans during World War II and that "the fighting in the Pacific was more savage than in the European theater." It may be true that this was in large part the result of a "deep-seated racial bias," whereas the hatred for the Germans was "the normal war hate that simply came from direct confrontation." One should not forget, however, that in combat the results often were similar: the Japanese were not the only enemies who became dehumanized and combat did not assume the character of a hunt in the Pacific alone.

Gray contends that the increasingly totalitarian character of war makes it ever more difficult to "fight without an image of the enemy as totally evil, for whom any mercy or sympathy is incongruous, if not traitorous." (Dower, *War without Mercy*, 8–11, 33–5, 79; Weingartner, "Trophies of War," 53–6 and 66–7; and Gray, *Warriors*, 146.)

169. McConahey, *Surgeon*, 47 and MacDonald, *Commander*, 34.
170. Huebner, *Long Walk*, 84.
171. Huebner, *Long Walk*, 51 and Rogers, *Chaplain*, 123.
172. Ambrose, *Brothers*, 86 and Potter, *Liberators*, 172. See also MacDonald, *Commander*, 19.
173. Irgang, *Purple*, 13; MacDonald, *Commander*, 39–40; and Brown, *Up Front*, 419.
174. McGill, "This Is It," 27, 12th AD, SC.
175. Fry, *Combat Soldier*, 222.
176. Leinbaugh and Campbell, *Company K*, 160.
177. Lyon, *Unknown Station*, 163 and Brown, *Up Front*, 60. See also Kelly, *One Man's War*, 35.
178. Rogers, *Chaplain*, 159 and Faubus, *Faraway Land*, 386.
179. Anderson, "War Years," 12, 8th ID, SC and Fry, *Combat Soldier*, 222–3.
180. Murphy, *Hell*, 183 and Fry, *Combat Soldier*, 223.
181. Carter, *Devils*, 165 and MacDonald, *Commander*, 40. See also Peckham and Snyder, *Hoosiers*, 163.
182. Gray, *Warriors*, 136 and 157.
183. Huebner, *Long Walk*, 75; Murphy, *Hell*, 259; and Wagner, "Odyssey," 75.
184. War Department, *What the Soldier Thinks: Quarterly Report*, August 1943, 92. After the obligatory viewing of the *Why We Fight* army propaganda series, which highlighted Nazi oppression and persecution of religion, this percentage increased even further to 83.
185. Downing, *At War*, 201; Kimball, *Diary*, 112; Toole, *Battle Diary*, 42; Bernstein, *Head Down*, 150; and Leinbaugh and Campbell, *Company K*, 137.
186. Jordan, "Bull Sessions," 59, 9th ID, SC.
187. Biddle, *Artist*, 87. See also Boesch, *Huertgen*, 48–9; Notley, "There Were None," 32, 35th ID, SC; and Shinn, *Rumors*, 45. Gray points out that modern totalitarian wars between ideological systems have come to resemble "religious crusades" against "those who oppose the truth." "In this," he contends, "the enemy is conceived to be not merely a loathsome animal, below the human level, but also above it in being a devil or at least demon-possessed and, as such, an enemy of God." (*Warriors*, 146 and 153.)
188. Tsuchida, *Letters*, 83 and Sampson, *Look Out*, 64–5. The Intellectual Diversion Program for the POW camps in the US aimed not only at teaching democratic principles, but also at returning the enemy soldiers to Christian practices. Despite resistance from fervent Nazis, the program was successful and church attendance as well as the demand for religious literature increased rapidly among the German inmates. (Gansberg, *Stalag U.S.A.*, 110–12 and Krammer, *Nazi Prisoners*, 72–4.)
189. Ambrose, *Brothers*, 181. See also Tsuchida, *Letters*, 77.
190. US War Department, *German Military Forces*, 2.
191. Boesch, *Huertgen*, 31; Atwell, *Private*, 333; and Carter, *Devils*, 112–13.
192. Rogers, *Chaplain*, 58 and Burt, "War Memoirs," 24–5, 2nd AD, SC. See also Bernstein, *Head Down*, 142.
193. Stouffer et al., *Combat*, 145–6; Jordan, "Bull Sessions," 53 and 56, 9th ID, SC; Biddle, *Artist*, 86 and 97; Groth, *Europe*, 80; Brown, *Up Front*, 321; Ambrose, *Brothers*, 150; and Koskimaki, *Eagles*, 92. See also US War Department, *German Military Forces*, 541.

194. Burgett, *Currahee*, 152; Boesch, *Huertgen*, 26; Hoffman, *Archives*, 105; Standifer, *Not In Vain*, 105; Toole, *Battle Diary*, 44; and Potter, *Liberators*, 191. See also US War Department, *German Military Forces*, 390 and 395.

195. Förster, "Dynamics," 182, 184, and 187.

196. Raff, *We Jumped*, 51; Kimball, *Diary*, 20; and Johnson, *Hill*, 56.

197. Saidel, 25 March 1943, 1st AD, SC and letter from an unidentified soldier, 23 February 1943, Box 2/Folder 27, MCC.

198. Stouffer et al., *Combat*, 232–4 and Davis, *This Is It*, 193.

199. Abbott, *Believers*, 64.

200. Murray, *Luftwaffe*, 136–8, 183–4, 242, 276–7, and 285–96.

201. Lt Daniel O'Madigan, Jr to a friend, 6 December 1942, Box 2/Folder 27, MCC.

202. Eustis, *Letters*, 142. See also Murray, *Luftwaffe*, 295.

203. Reams diary, 1st ID, SC and Easton, *Love and War*, 295. See also Murray, *Luftwaffe*, 295.

204. Huebner, *Long Walk*, 37; Boyer, "My Experiences," 3rd ID, SC; and Bistrica, Q/36f, 1st ID, SC. See also Murray, *Luftwaffe*, 295–6.

205. Mauldin, *Brass Ring*, 154 and Burt, "War Memoirs," 22, 2nd AD, SC. See also Giles, *Journal*, 293.

206. Ulsaker, "Saga," 255–6, 95th ID, SC.

207. McConahey, *Surgeon*, 85. The GIs' surprise was understandable because the *Wehrmacht*'s military strength had been overestimated as early as the Rhineland crisis of 1936. Following the debacle of May–June 1940, the tendency to exaggerate the *Wehrmacht*'s technological and numerical might had only increased. According to some historians, much of this was the result of Nazi Germany's "flair for shaping images" and the Allies' search for an excuse that would justify a defeat caused mainly by unpreparedness and incompetence. (Bartov, "Wehrmacht," 31–2 and Beaumont, "*Wehrmacht* Mystique.")

208. Wagner, "Odyssey," 74; Koskimaki, *Eagles*, 233; and Baird, "Lend You My Eyes," 291. One of the three infantry regiments of each Volks Grenadier Division was a unit equipped with 625 bicycles. (US War Department, *German Military Forces*, 119.)

209. Burgett, *Currahee*, 169.

210. Lyon, *Unknown Station*, 193.

211. US War Department, *German Military Forces*, 92 and Cole, *Lorraine Campaign*, 124–5 and 312.

212. Cooper, *German Army*, 494 and MacDonald, *Siegfried Line*, 617 and 621–2.

213. Atwell, *Private*, 220.

214. Winter, "Battle Babies," 48, 99th ID, SC and Giles, *Journal*, 251–2. See also MacDonald, *Siegfried Line*, 30–1 and 34–5.

215. Giles, *Journal*, 252. See also MacDonald, *Siegfried Line*, 31, 34, and 74.

216. Johns, *Clay Pigeons*, 75; Peckham and Snyder, *Hoosiers*, 128 and 130; and Hurkala, *Fighting First*, 128.

217. Arrington, *Infantryman*, 172 and Boesch, *Huertgen*, 57.

218. Westrate, *Observer*, 130 and Freese, "Private Memories," 92–3, 84th ID, SC. See also Jett diary, 6 May 1943, 1st AD, SC and Leinbaugh and Campbell, *Company K*, 57 and 148–9.

219. Freese, "Private Memories," 101, 84th ID, SC.

220. Abbott, *Believers*, 125; Wise, *Truly Ours*, 151; and Leinbaugh and Campbell, *Company K*, 261.

221. Ambrose, *Brothers*, 269.

222. Calhoun to his parents, 13 May 1945, 42nd ID, SC.

223. Connelly, *Assistant*, 85. See also Cawthon, *Other Clay*, 182; MacDonald, *Commander*, 364; and Tapert, *Lines*, 263–5.

224. Biddle, *Artist*, 97.
225. Leinbaugh and Campbell, *Company K*, 182 and Groth, *Europe*, 78. See also Hornsby, *Sevens*, III.
226. Toole, *Battle Diary*, 29.
227. Cawthon, *Other Clay*, 137.
228. Letter from an unidentified soldier, 24 May 1943, Box 2/Folder 27, MCC; Saidel, [around 10 May 1943], 1st AD, SC; and Raff, *We Jumped*, 139. See also Abbott, *Believers*, 125.
229. Biddle, *Artist*, 103; Rontch, *Jewish Youth*, 103; Whelan, *Robert Capa*, 235; and Peyton, *Surgeon's Diary*, 140. See also Boesch, *Huertgen*, 32.
230. US War Department, *German Military Forces*, 2. See also Fussell, "My War," 258. The average age of the German army's soldier in 1944 was 31 years. (Förster, "Dynamics," 190.)
231. Groth, *Europe*, 82; Huebner, *Long Walk*, 54; Bernstein, *Head Down*, 99; and Winter, "Battle Babies," 41, 99th ID, SC. See also unidentified soldier, Q/44d(2), 30th ID, SC and Brown, *Up Front*, 28.
232. Giles, *Journal*, 34 and Haygood, "Letters," 114. See also Boesch, *Huertgen*, 110.
233. Fussell, "My War," 258–9 and Brown, *Up Front*, 209.
234. Huebner, *Long Walk*, 54.
235. Ambrose, *Brothers*, 87 and 236. See also Stewart, untitled memoir, 47–8; Engel, "Patrol," 621; and Murphy, *Hell*, 126.
236. Ambrose, *Brothers*, 87; Irgang, *Purple*, 101; and Brown, *Up Front*, 251.
237. Boesch, *Huertgen*, 84; Murphy, *Hell*, 27; Atwell, *Private*, 225; and Giles, *Journal*, 255. See also Tregaskis, *Invasion*, 47.
238. Hoffman, *Archives*, 159; Huebner, *Long Walk*, 125; Brown, *Up Front*, 258; Freese, "Private Memories," 40, 84th ID, SC; Leinbaugh and Campbell, *Company K*, 112; and Krebs, *Rome*, 95.
239. Boesch, *Huertgen*, 62 and Giles, *Journal*, 255. See also McGill, "This Is It," 20, 12th AD, SC.
240. Burgett, *Currahee*, 137 and Jordan, "Bull Sessions," 59, 9th ID, SC. See also Roche, "Forty Years," 103, RP and Irgang, *Purple*, 222.
241. Fussell, "My War," 257; Irgang, *Purple*, 101; and MacDonald, *Commander*, 246.
242. Kelly, *One Man's War*, 72 and 85. See also Raab to his parents, 24 October 1944, RC; Brown, *Up Front*, 203; and MacDonald, *Commander*, 65.
243. Cawthon, *Other Clay*, 137. See also MacDonald, *Commander*, 65; Lyon, *Unknown Station*, 220; and Irgang, *Purple*, 192–3.
244. For the code of masculinity and the role of the combat soldier in the US Army, see Stouffer et al., *Combat*, 131–5.
245. Atwell, *Private*, 292 and Tsuchida, *Letters*, 83. See also Burgett, *Currahee*, 131 and Biddle, *Artist*, 88–9, 97, and 178.
246. Gurley, 11 April 1945, 100th IDP; Tsuchida, *Letters*, 83; and Boesch, *Huertgen*, 32.
247. Gravlin, "Combat Engineer," 28, 3rd AD, SC.
248. Brown, *Up Front*, 470.
249. Stouffer et al., *Combat*, 119–21.
250. Jordan, "Bull Sessions," 62, 9th ID, SC.
251. van Creveld, *Fighting Power*, 21–3 and Förster, "Dynamics," 207–9 and 214. Förster also points out that "Hitler's egalitarian drive both to dismantle social barriers inside the armed forces and to promote new talents under the leadership principle was popular throughout the population."
252. Motley, *Invisible Soldier*, 171.
253. Jordan, "Bull Sessions," 62, 9th ID, SC; Parker, *Civilian*, 74; and Ambrose, *Brothers*, 274–5.

254. Faubus, *Faraway Land*, 209 and Jordan, "Bull Sessions," 136, 9th ID, SC.

255. US War Department, *German Military Forces*, 5.

256. Letter from an unidentified soldier, 24 May 1943, Box 2/Folder 27, MCC and Haygood, "Letters," 114–15.

257. Irgang, *Purple*, 140–1 and MacDonald, *Commander*, 249. See also Boesch, *Huertgen*, 234–5 and Toole, *Battle Diary*, 138. A comparison of the treatment of captured German generals by the Americans and the British has brought to light a similar attitude. The British treated the generals "with the chivalry traditionally reserved for fellow aristocrats and professional soldiers." To the Americans, however, the German senior officers were "relics, antiquated caricatures captured by citizen-soldiers" who "represented the very antithesis of the democratic ideals which America was fighting to restore to Central Europe." As a result, 31 German generals were made to live in wooden houses at hot and humid Camp Clinton, Mississippi, in conditions that were spartan compared to those of the stately homes at Wilton Park where the British housed their German generals. (Krammer, "German Generals," 28, 32–5, 37–8, 42, and 46.)

258. Frankel and Smith, *Patton's Best*, 31–2.

259. Letter from paratrooper Gus Falen, 2 July 1944, Box 1/Folder 16, MCC and Burgett, *Currahee*, 153. See also Faubus, *Faraway Land*, 215. At the time of Operation Overlord, some 60,000 Soviet soldiers were fighting with the Germans in France. (Cooper, *German Army*, 496.)

260. Förster, "Dynamics," 189.

261. Egger and Otts, *G Company*, 123; Jordan, "Bull Sessions," 144, 9th ID, SC; Rogers, *Chaplain*, 177; and Mauldin, *Brass Ring*, 269.

262. Tsuchida, *Letters*, 74. See also Johns, *Clay Pigeons*, 200.

263. Tapert, *Lines*, 162.

264. Cawthon, *Other Clay*, 43–4; Faubus, *Faraway Land*, 158; Huebner, *Long Walk*, 125; and MacDonald, *Commander*, 269.

265. John S. D. Eisenhower, "Introduction," in Winston, *Combat Medic*, XX and Raab to his parents, 10 and 11 July 1944, RC.

266. Gray, *Warriors*, 102 and Brown, *Up Front*, 490. See also Capt. L. A. Varteressian, 22 February 1945, Box 1/Folder 16, MCC and Anderson, "War Years," 21, 8th ID, SC. German boys 18 and younger, for instance, were employed in antiaircraft units. Their number increased from 24,000 in 1940 to 92,500 in 1945. Moreover, male civilians from 16 to 60 were responsible for home defense in the *Volkssturm*, while boys and girls from the Hitler Youth were called up as auxiliaries. (Förster, "Dynamics," 188 and US War Department, *German Military Forces*, 3.)

267. MacDonald, *Commander*, 362.

268. Jordan, "Bull Sessions," 58, 9th ID, SC and Brown, *Up Front*, 490. See also Ethier diary, 28 April 1945, 13th AD, SC and Huebner, *Long Walk*, 90.

269. Brown, *Up Front*, 490.

270. Ethier, 18 April 1945, 13th AD, SC.

271. Brammer, "First Platoon," 89, 44th ID, SC and Grage, "Reflections," 4, 65th ID, SC.

PART III THE CIVILIANS

Chapter 5 The Civilians – Introduction

1. Jordan, "Bull Sessions," 89, 9th ID, SC.

2. Winter, "Battle Babies," 45, 99th ID, SC. See also Toole, *Battle Diary*, 102.

3. Irgang, *Purple*, 73. See also Arrington, *Infantryman*, 104.

4. *Guide to Italian Cities*, 2.
5. Gray, *Warriors*, 10.
6. Frankel and Smith, *Patton's Best*, 19.
7. Fry, *Combat Soldier*, 221; Winston, *Combat Medic*, 130; MacDonald, *Commander*, 88; and Ambrose, *Brothers*, 225.
8. Stewart, untitled memoir, 55, 1st ID, SC; Brown, *Up Front*, 447; and Johns, *Clay Pigeons*, 233–4.
9. Simpson, *Arm in Arm*, in *Poems*, 9. See also Murphy, *Hell*, 260–1 and Brown, *Up Front*, 319.
10. Egger and Otts, *G Company*, 65–6, 111, and 162–4 and Tsuchida, *Letters*, 3, 77, and 134.
11. Ziemke, *Occupation of Germany*, 145 and 185; Egger and Otts, *G Company*, 207; and Freese, "Private Memories," 23, 84th ID, SC.
12. Lyon, *Unknown Station*, 38; Seiverling, *Stories*, 29; Carter, *Devils*, 65; Runyon, "Memories," 20, 92nd ID, SC; Toole, *Battle Diary*, 45; Egger and Otts, *G Company*, 60; and Ziemke, *Occupation of Germany*, 136, 139, 145, and 185.
13. Eustis, *Letters*, 212–13; Arrington, *Infantryman*, 185; and MacDonald, *Commander*, 326.
14. Faubus, *Faraway Land*, 414.
15. Huebner, *Long Walk*, 70 and 83; Rogers, *Chaplain*, 202; Fry, *Combat Soldier*, 107; Haygood, "Letters," 117; and Ziemke, *Occupation of Germany*, 136 and 189.
16. Egger and Otts, *G Company*, 154 and Faubus, *Faraway Land*, 353.
17. Van Way and Ladd, *Leaves*, 1–13.
18. Ibid.
19. Van Way and Ladd, *Leaves*, 1–13 and Winston, *Combat Medic*, 171–2 and 178.
20. Toole, *Battle Diary*, 132 and Van Way and Ladd, *Leaves*, 14–15.

Chapter 6 The Labyrinth of Nations

1. Brown, *Up Front*, 24.
2. Rogers, *Chaplain*, 130.
3. Altieri, *Spearheaders*, 91.
4. Koskimaki, *Eagles*, 19. See also Johnson, *Hill*, 136.
5. Carter, *Devils*, 139; Costello, *Virtue under Fire*, 239; and Jett diary, 28 June 1944, 1st AD, SC.
6. Kimball, *Diary*, 172.
7. Burgett, *Currahee*, 184. See also Houston, *Paratrooper*, 42.
8. Sampson, *Look Out*, 81 and Rogers, *Chaplain*, 131.
9. Ambrose, *Brothers*, 42; Altieri, *Spearheaders*, 83–4; and McConahey, *Surgeon*, 17.
10. Connelly, *Assistant*, 23 and letter home from Capt. Wade, Box 2/Folder 21, MCC. See also Giles, *Journal*, 23 and Clarkson, "G.I. Joe," 6, 5th ID, SC.
11. War Department, *What the Soldier Thinks: Monthly Digest*, January 1944, 15.
12. Connelly, *Assistant*, 20.
13. Stewart, untitled memoir, 22, 1st ID, SC and letter from an unidentified soldier, 30 November 1942, Box 1/Folder 13, MCC.
14. Metcalf, *Cross*, 49 and Faubus, *Faraway Land*, 147. See also Giles, *Journal*, 23.
15. *Guide to Great Britain*, 2 and 4.
16. Connelly, *Assistant*, 25. Hollywood may also have been responsible for the effect of déjà vu. American prewar films, often shot on location and with British actors, had offered a more complete and faithful picture of Britain than of any other country. (Kracauer, "National Types," 61–2.)
17. Rogers, *Chaplain*, 130.

18. Letter from Sgt Joseph Aylward, Jr, 15 November 1942, Box 1/Folder 13, MCC.
19. *Guide to Great Britain*, 2–3, 10, and 35. See also Kracauer, "National Types," 62–4 and Thorne, *Allies*, 147.
20. Donald S. Hutcheson, 17 July 1942, Box 1/Folder 13, MCC.
21. McIntyre, untitled memoir, 90–1, MP.
22. Easton, *Love and War*, 207 and Sampson, *Look Out*, 42–3.
23. Sgt Donald S. Hutcheson, 17 July 1942, Box 1/Folder 13, MCC.
24. Brink, *God*, 20 and PFC Keraus to his family, 29 January 1942, Box 2/Folder 21, MCC.
25. Rogers, *Chaplain*, 28; Donald S. Hutcheson, 8 August 1942, Box 1/Folder 13, MCC; and Eustis, *Letters*, 193–4.
26. Rogers, *Chaplain*, 140 and Cawthon, *Other Clay*, 25. See also Downing, *At War*, 204.
27. Carter, *Devils*, 132–3.
28. Sampson, *Look Out*, 81 and Ambrose, *Brothers*, 108.
29. *Guide to Great Britain*, 2 and 29.
30. Ibid., 1–2.
31. Jett, 25 June 1942, 1st AD, SC.
32. Cawthon, *Other Clay*, 32 and Brown, *Up Front*, 304. See also Kimball, *Diary*, 153 and Metcalf, *Cross*, 50.
33. *Guide to Great Britain*, 17.
34. Cpl Raymond H. Dreyer to his family, 30 March 1942, Box 2/Folder 21, MCC; *Guide to Great Britain*, 12; and Sampson, *Look Out*, 50.
35. Harry L. Belgrade, Box 1/Folder 13, MCC and Eustis, *Letters*, 199.
36. Thorne, *Allies*, 147; Connelly, *Assistant*, 21; and Daly, "Sharpe's Battalion," 21.
37. Jordan, "Bull Sessions" 33, 9th ID, SC and Sampson, *Look Out*, 84–5.
38. Eustis, *Letters*, 194 and Stouffer et al., *Combat*, 575.
39. Kimball, *Diary*, 124 and Eustis, *Letters*, 186. See also Johnson, *Hill*, 127; Rogers, *Chaplain*, 128; and Wise, *Truly Ours*, 93.
40. Wagner, *Correspondents*, 127–8; Cawthon, *Other Clay*, 170; and Giles, *Journal*, 81. See also Sampson, *Look Out*, 79.
41. *Guide to North Africa*, 2.
42. Rogers, *Chaplain*, 34; Sgt Maurice Hollender to his wife, 14 and 19 November 1942, Box 2/Folder 27, MCC; and Kelly, *One Man's War*, 28.
43. Downing, *At War*, 76 and 92.
44. *Guide to North Africa*, 6.
45. Letter from an unidentified soldier, 15 May 1943, Box 2/Folder 29, MCC.
46. Saidel to his family, 7 April 1943 and diary, 8 May 1943, 1st AD, SC.
47. Biddle, *Artist*, 25 and Johnson, *Hill*, 15.
48. Watters, "Invasion of North Africa," 9, 3rd ID, SC; *Guide to North Africa*, 5–6 and 17; and Cpl Raymond Dreyer to his family, 8 January 1943, Box 2/Folder 29, MCC.
49. Cpl Raymond Dreyer to his family, 23 May 1943, Box 2/Folder 29, MCC and Raff, *We Jumped*, 67 and 80.
50. Wagner, *Correspondents*, 79. See also Huebner, *Long Walk*, 12–13.
51. Stradling, *Johnny*, 214 and Tapert, *Lines*, 40.
52. Peyton, *Surgeon's Diary*, 16. See also Rogers, *Chaplain*, 53; Maule, *War Letters*, 107; Stradling, *Johnny*, 211; and Howe, *Northwest Africa*, 109.
53. Mauldin, *Brass Ring*, 140.
54. Rontch, *Jewish Youth*, 236.
55. Mauldin, *Brass Ring*, 140.
56. *Guide to North Africa*, 5 and 41.
57. Stradling, *Johnny*, 204 and Peyton, *Surgeon's Diary*, 15.
58. Huebner, *Long Walk*, 24 and letter from an unidentified soldier, date unknown, Box 2/Folder 30, MCC. See also Mauldin, *Brass Ring*, 140.

59. Cpl Charles E. Hughes to his parents, [1943], Box 2/Folder 27, MCC and *Guide to North Africa*, 42.

60. *Guide to North Africa*, 8 and 42. As late as the eve of the German invasion of May 1940, the chief attack on France by American critics had concerned its imperialism. (Hurstfield, *French Nation*, 35.)

61. Raff, *We Jumped*, 80. See also *Guide to North Africa*, 10–11 and Jett diary, 5 June and 28 August 1943, 1st AD, SC.

62. Abbott, *Believers*, 97–8.

63. Mauldin, *Brass Ring*, 140; Jett diary, 1 June 1943, 1st AD, SC; and Adams, "Mad Days," 69.

64. Raff, *We Jumped*, 47.

65. Raff, *We Jumped*, 104; Krebs, *Rome*, 26; and Rogers, *Chaplain*, 93–4.

66. Brink, *God*, 71. See also Cpl Raymond Dreyer to his family, 23 May 1943, Box 2/Folder 29, MCC and Rogers, *Chaplain*, 53.

67. *Guide to North Africa*, 15–16 and Burt, "War Memoirs," 19, 2nd AD, SC.

68. Robinson, *45th*, 61 and Burt, "War Memoirs," 19–20, 2nd AD, SC. See also Snyder, *My Task*, 120.

69. Unidentified soldier, 5 June 1943, Box 3/Folder 31, MCC.

70. Raff, *We Jumped*, 93; Rogers, *Chaplain*, 86–7; Abbott, *Believers*, 52; Ross and Romanus, *Quartermaster Corps: Germany*, 180; Jett diary, 17 April 1943, 1st AD, SC; and Peyton, *Surgeon's Diary*, 46.

71. Raff, *We Jumped*, 99 and Sgt John Grenfell, 16 November 1942, Box 2/Folder 28, MCC.

72. Wise, *Truly Ours*, 158.

73. Downing, *At War*, 106.

74. Joe Sprung to his brother, [May 1943], Box 2/Folder 30, MCC; Kenneth L. Cooley to his wife, 4 and 29 May 1943, Box 2/Folder 29, MCC; and Altieri, *Spearheaders*, 115.

75. Robinson, *45th*, 70.

76. *Guide to Italy*, 5.

77. Eustis, *Letters*, 148 and 170.

78. Huebner, *Long Walk*, 97 and Tapert, *Lines*, 264.

79. *Guide to Italy*, 1–7, 18, 25, 27, 32–3. American opinion had grown more critical of Mussolini and fascism after the Ethiopian war of 1935. However, when Americans were asked in 1940 to single out the country with the worst influence in Europe, only 1.2 per cent selected Italy. It came after Germany (53 per cent), the Soviet Union (34.2 per cent), and even England (1.8 per cent). When polled in 1942 about how the Axis people had to be dealt with when the war was over, 50 per cent preferred to treat the Italians kindly, humanely, and fairly, whereas 80 per cent demanded a punishment for the Germans harsher than that of Versailles. Americans seemed to remain convinced of "the essential goodness of the tragically misled Italians." (Diggins, *Mussolini*, 324–5 and 426–7.)

80. Belden, *Still Time*, 264 and Mauldin, *Up Front*, 66.

81. Peckham and Snyder, *Hoosiers*, 70. See also Biddle, *Artist*, 104 and Murphy, *Hell*, 21. A 1947 poll in Italy indicated that its people had felt a genuine sympathy for the GIs. When asked which of the Allied soldiers had made the best impression, 62 per cent chose the Americans and only 14 per cent the British. This favorable view was influenced by the GIs' behavior in general and the presence of many Italian-American soldiers in particular, but also by America's economic assistance. (Diggins, *Mussolini*, 441–2, note 19.)

82. *Guide to Italy*, 39–40.

83. Rontch, *Jewish Youth*, 178; Robinson, *45th*, 70; Belden, *Still Time*, 264; and Peyton, *Surgeon's Diary*, 64–5.

84. Peyton, *Surgeon's Diary*, 100 and Murphy, *Hell*, 52.

85. Raab, 8 September and 3 November 1944, RC and Strong to his family, 12 May 1945, 1st AD, SC.

86. Raab to his parents, 16 and 17 June 1944, RC; Strong to his family, 20 August 1944 and 12 May 1945, 1st AD, SC; Roche, "Forty Years," 77–8, RP; and Peyton, *Surgeon's Diary*, 213–14.

87. *Guide to Italy*, 2 and 28. The deluge of wretched Italian immigrants at the end of the nineteenth century had caused the image of an enlightened Italy of antiquity, culture, and art to become overshadowed by that of "a country whose people were suffocating under the dust and dirt of their tragic history." (Diggins, *Mussolini*, 11–12, 59, and 71.)

88. Tregaskis, *Invasion*, 63; Elting, Cragg, and Deal, *Soldier Talk*, 341; Carter, *Devils*, 28 and 53; Bernstein, *Head Down*, 133–4; and Robinson, *45th*, 83. By the late nineteenth century, American travelers already deemed thievishness part of the Italian character, while the press sometimes pictured the Italian immigrant as "a stiletto-wielding criminal." (Diggins, *Mussolini*, 10 and 12.)

89. Dillon, "Normandy," 8, 1st ID, SC.

90. Mauldin, *Up Front*, 64.

91. Snyder, *My Task*, 49.

92. Biddle, *Artist*, 76 and Capa, *Out of Focus*, 74.

93. Murphy, *Hell*, 64–5; Snyder, *My Task*, 150; and Krebs, *Rome*, 82. See also Dillon, "Normandy," 8, 1st ID, SC and Strong to his family, 20 August 1944, 1st AD, SC.

94. Bond, *Cassino*, 133–4.

95. Duus, *Liberators*, 114–15; Hoffman, *Archives*, 72; and Bond, *Cassino*, 133–4.

96. Tregaskis, *Invasion*, 23.

97. Biddle, *Artist*, 80; Peckham and Snyder, *Hoosiers*, 61; and Robinson, *45th*, 100. Traditionally, Americans had blamed much of Italy's wretchedness on Romanism. (Diggins, *Mussolini*, 10.)

98. Robinson, *45th*, 100.

99. Hurstfield, *French Nation*, 55. Hollywood, for instance, guided by the Office of War Information, had the unenviable task of convincing the American public that France remained an ally in the struggle against fascism despite its government's collaboration with Nazi Germany. It tried to accomplish this by making feature films on France that depicted elements of the government as corrupt, but the French people, symbolized by the resistance, "as freedom-loving democrats with courage, integrity, and fighting ability." (Mjagkij, "Occupied Ally," 37–8 and 42–3.)

100. *Guide to France*, 6.

101. Koskimaki, *Eagles*, 148, 169, 188, 232, and 255.

102. Cawthon, *Other Clay*, 76–7 and Rogers, *Chaplain*, 158.

103. Reams diary, 11 June 1944, 1st ID, SC.

104. Koskimaki, *Eagles*, 169; Giles, *Journal*, 46; and Freese, "Private Memories," 17, 84th ID, SC.

105. Peckham and Snyder, *Hoosiers*, 122; Johnson, *Hill*, 142; Irgang, *Purple*, 28; Tapert, *Lines*, 161; and Giles, *Journal*, 46.

106. Dohmann, "Medic," 15; Giles, *Journal*, 46; and Irgang, *Purple*, 43.

107. Easton, *Love and War*, 225.

108. Capa, *Out of Focus*, 163 and Faubus, *Faraway Land*, 265.

109. Faubus, *Faraway Land*, 248.

110. Tapert, *Lines*, 166 and Parker, *Civilian*, 35. See also Capa, *Out of Focus*, 163.

111. Parker, *Civilian*, 85; McConahey, *Surgeon*, 86; and Mauldin, *Up Front*, 204.

112. Baird, "Lend You My Eyes," 304 and Gravlin, "Combat Engineer," 3rd AD, SC; and Stouffer et al., *Combat*, 577.

113. Tsuchida, *Letters*, 31–2; Calhoun to his parents, [5 February] and 30 March 1945, 42nd ID, SC; Toole, *Battle Diary*, 57; Houston, *Paratrooper*, 135; Egger and Otts, *G Company*, 88; and Gossett to his parents, 1 and 13 January 1945, 42nd IDP.

114. Gurley, 3 December 1944, 100th IDP. See also Atwell, *Private*, 90.

115. Winston, *Combat Medic*, 139 and Tsuchida, *Letters*, 32. See also Egger and Otts, *G Company*, 70.

116. Hurstfield, *French Nation*, 40, 99, 102, 115, and 140.

117. Eustis, *Letters*, 197.

118. *Guide to France*, 9. The guidebooks to Northern Ireland, Great Britain, North Africa, Italy, Germany, and Austria consisted respectively of 37, 37, 43, 41, 48, and 33 pages. The *Pocket Guide to France* was 72 pages long. Despite "affectionate bonds" between the US and France, dating back to the American colonies' struggle for independence from Britain, the knowledge of the French language and the interest in French culture had steadily dwindled in the US. (Hurstfield, *French Nation*, 36 and 99–100.)

119. Hovsepian, *Your Son*, 79 and Giles, *Journal*, 40.

120. *Guide to France*, 33 and Ambrose, *Brothers*, 254.

121. Baird, "Lend You My Eyes," 292.

122. *Guide to France*, 41.

123. Winston, *Combat Medic*, 152 and Harlinski to his wife, 12 December 1944, 36th ID, SC.

124. *Guide to France*, 10–11.

125. MacDonald, *Commander*, 225–6 and 277. See also Easton, *Love and War*, 239.

126. McHugh, *Hell to Heaven*, 17 and Easton, *Love and War*, 239.

127. Easton, *Love and War*, 247 and 264; Winston, *Combat Medic*, 127; and Calhoun to his parents, 18 December 1944, 42nd ID, SC.

128. Johnson, *Hill*, 21; Irgang, *Purple*, 48; Durig to his family, 11 March 1945, 97th ID, SC.

129. Raff, *We Jumped*, 69–70.

130. Toole, *Battle Diary*, 22; Mauldin, *Up Front*, 107-8; Irgang, *Purple*, 21–2; and Boesch, *Huertgen*, 35.

131. *Guide to France*, 7–8. Americans widely believed that French culture had "lost its vitality," and it was the general opinion that France's defeat in 1940 had been caused by "internal weaknesses." (Hurstfield, *French Nation*, 31–2, 39–40, and 99.)

132. Gurley, 31 December 1944, 100th IDP and Stouffer et al., *Combat*, 629.

133. Stewart, untitled memoir, 46–7, 1st ID, SC; Rogers, *Chaplain*, 179; Seiverling, *Stories*, 32; and Jordan, "Bull Sessions," 93–4, 9th ID, SC. See also Litoff et al., *Miss You*, 218 and Giles, *Journal*, 112.

134. Stewart, untitled memoir, 50, 1st ID, SC; Seiverling, *Stories*, 33; Shapiro to his family, 3 November 1944, 28th ID, SC; and Winter, "Battle Babies," 25, 99th ID, SC.

135. Beck et al., *Engineers against Germany*, 405.

136. Burt, "War Memoirs," 6–7, 2nd AD, SC. See also *Guide to the Cities of Belgium*, 29.

137. Peckham and Snyder, *Hoosiers*, 151 and Griswold to local newspaper, 3 November 1944, 9th ID, SC. See also Houston, *Paratrooper*, 48 and Hornsby, *Sevens*, 17.

138. Winter, "Battle Babies," 25, 99th ID, SC and Wardlaw, *Missing*, 69. See also letter from an unidentified soldier, 3 January 1945, Box 1/Folder 13, MCC; Peckham and Snyder, *Hoosiers*, 151; Stewart, untitled memoir, 50, 1st ID, SC; and Griswold to local newspaper, 3 November 1944, 9th ID, SC.

139. Stewart, untitled memoir, 50, 1st ID, SC.

140. Litoff et al., *Miss You*, 218; Seiverling, *Stories*, 32–3; and Stewart, untitled memoir, 46–7, 1st ID, SC. See also Jordan, "Bull Sessions," 47, 9th ID, SC.

141. Seiverling, *Stories*, 41 and Gravlin, "Combat Engineer," 13, 3rd AD, SC.

142. Jordan, "Bull Sessions," 124, 9th ID, SC and Winter, "Battle Babies," 35, 99th ID, SC.

143. Atwell, *Private*, 174 and Giles, *Journal*, 117.

144. Leinbaugh and Campbell, *Company K*, 130–1.
145. Ambrose, *Brothers*, 253 and Winter, "Battle Babies," 38, 99th ID, SC. See also Shapiro to his family, 3 January 1945, 28th ID, SC.
146. Irgang, *Purple*, 156; Atwell, *Private*, 159; and Hurkala, *Fighting First*, 157.
147. Litoff et al., *Miss You*, 218; Seiverling, *Stories*, 32; and Egger and Otts, *G Company*, 99–100.
148. Litoff et al., *Miss You*, 218; Atwell, *Private*, 163; and letter from an unidentified soldier, 3 January 1945, Box 1/Folder 13, MCC.
149. Tumey, *G.I.'s View*, 12; Baird, "Lend You My Eyes," 311; Parker, *Civilian*, 96; and Davidson, *Cut Off*, 39.
150. Ambrose, *Brothers*, 128 and Parker, *Civilian*, 102.
151. Houston, *Paratrooper*, 49, 53, and 58; Sampson, *Look Out*, 86 and 90; Ambrose, *Brothers*, 125, 127–8, and 253; Carter, *Devils*, 142; Parker, *Civilian*, 97–8 and 101; Connelly, *Assistant*, 31 and 41; and Faubus, *Faraway Land*, 508 and 532.
152. Connelly, *Assistant*, 30 and 32 and Ambrose, *Brothers*, 127–8 and 253.
153. Houston, *Paratrooper*, 82 and Ambrose, *Brothers*, 167.
154. *Guide to the Cities of the Netherlands*, 1–2, 29–30, and 39.
155. Easton, *Love and War*, 25–6. See also Ambrose, *Brothers*, 253.
156. Houston, *Paratrooper*, 75 and 82. See also Easton, *Love and War*, 26.
157. Sampson, *Look Out*, 88–9 and Houston, *Paratrooper*, 74.
158. Freese, "Private Memories," 19–20, 84th ID, SC; Faubus, *Faraway Land*, 508; Connelly, *Assistant*, 31 and 38; Easton, *Love and War*, 25; Sampson, *Look Out*, 89; Ulsaker, "Saga," 253, CU.
159. Sampson, *Look Out*, 89.
160. Giles, *Journal*, 102 and Easton, *Love and War*, 257. See also Faubus, *Faraway Land*, 501 and Daly, "Sharpe's Battalion," 112.
161. Starr, *Fraternization*, 10–13 and Giles, *Journal*, 252.
162. Phibbs, *Other Side*, 205–6; Roberts, *Texas*, 45; and Atwell, *Private*, 299. See also Hermens, "Viewing Germany," 420.
163. Hovsepian, *Your Son*, 169. See also Gurley to his parents, 20 December 1944, 100th IDP and Lashin to his family, 15 January 1945, 70th ID, SC.
164. Hovsepian, *Your Son*, 167. See also Egger and Otts, *G Company*, 228; Frankel and Smith, *Patton's Best*, 116; and MacDonald, *Commander*, 12.
165. Phibbs, *Other Side*, 232 and Giles, *Journal*, 252. See also Winston, *Combat Medic*, 195; Litoff et al., *Miss You*, 200; and Tsuchida, *Letters*, 65.
166. Ziemke, *Occupation of Germany*, 139. The 45th Infantry Division, for example, encountered civilian resistance at Aschaffenburg on 29 March 1945, and the 42nd Infantry Division at Würzburg on 3 April. Civilian opposition was also reported in the vicinity of Ulm on 30 April. (Starr, *Fraternization*, 18 and 162, note 54.)
167. Phibbs, *Other Side*, 206; Connelly, *Assistant*, 70; Shapiro to his family, 9 March 1945, 28th ID, SC; Gravlin, "Combat Engineer," 40, 3rd AD, SC; Moltmann, "Amerikaklischees," 303 and 306–7; and *Guide to Germany*, 11–12.
168. Phibbs, *Other Side*, 19.
169. Tsuchida, *Letters*, 112. See also Randall, *Doughfeet*, 97; Murphy, *Hell*, 269; Arrington, *Infantryman*, 127; Egger and Otts, *G Company*, 247; and Brown, *Up Front*, 232.
170. Murphy, *Hell*, 270. See also Ziemke, *Occupation of Germany*, 138–9 and 189; Starr, *Fraternization*, 18; and Beck, *German Home Front*, 187–9.
171. Haygood, "Letters," 118.
172. *Guide to Germany*, 6.
173. Shapiro to his family, 26 April 1945, 28th ID, SC; Arrington, *Infantryman*, 118; and Winston, *Combat Medic*, 196.
174. US Twelfth Army Group, *Special Orders*, 3.

175. Starr, *Fraternization*, 1, 5–6, 10–17 and *Guide to Germany*, 2–5.
176. Starr, *Fraternization*, 2 and 17; MacDonald, *Commander*, 218 and 221; Ambrose, *Brothers*, 267; Arrington, *Infantryman*, 107; Brown, *Up Front*, 466 and 476; Atwell, *Private*, 214; Earle to his family, [April 1945], 71st ID, SC; and Shapiro to his family, 9 March 1945, 28th ID, SC.
177. Jacobs, 28 March and 2 April 1945, 44th ID, SC. See also Faubus, *Faraway Land*, 584.
178. Starr, *Fraternization*, 16. See also Ambrose, *Brothers*, 267; MacDonald, *Commander*, 196; Faubus, *Faraway Land*, 528; Brown, *Up Front*, 452; Ulsaker, "Saga," 275, CU; Shapiro to his family, 11 April 1945, 28th ID, SC; Shannon, "Replacement," 70 and 92, 26th ID, SC; and Arrington, *Infantryman*, 202.
179. Starr, *Fraternization*, 23–5 and 27 and Stouffer et al., *Combat*, 565 and 569.
180. Phibbs, *Other Side*, 6 and Stoner, 4 April 1945, 42nd IDP. See also Gurley to his parents, 4 May 1945, 100th IDP.
181. *Guide to Germany*, 30–1; Easton, *Love and War*, 299; and Meissner, "Life as a G.I.," 73, 71st ID, SC.
182. McConahey, *Surgeon*, 138; Arrington, *Infantryman*, 201; Easton, *Love and War*, 19 and 305; Faubus, *Faraway Land*, 578; and Irgang, *Purple*, 210. See also Jacobs to his mother, 31 March 1945, 44th ID, SC and Shannon, "Replacement," 123, 26th ID, SC. Some modern American highways, like the Bronx River Parkway in New York City, had been built by individual states before World War II. But it was only after the war that the US federal government created an Interstate Highway System, based on the German approach.
183. Ambrose, *Brothers*, 256 and 274; Connelly, *Assistant*, 83; Wilson, *Bastogne to Bavaria*, 152; Houston, *Paratrooper*, 138; MacDonald, *Commander*, 219; Tsuchida, *Letters*, 113; Atwell, *Private*, 303; Cawthon, *Other Clay*, 179–80; Shapiro to his family, 9 November 1944, 28th ID, SC; Jacobs to his mother, 28 March 1945, 44th ID, SC; Winston, *Combat Medic*, 198, 208, and 221; and Leinbaugh and Campbell, *Company K*, 257.
184. Gurley to his parents, 24 March 1945, 100th IDP; Jacobs to his mother, 28 March 1945, 44th ID, SC; and Earle to his family, [April 1945], 71st ID, SC.
185. Connelly, *Assistant*, 43 and 70. See also Winston, *Combat Medic*, 208; Wardlaw, *Missing*, 73; and Gurley to his parents, 24 March 1945, 100th IDP.
186. Connelly, *Assistant*, 36 and 77–8.
187. Jacobs to his mother, 26 March 1945, 44th ID, SC; Connelly, *Assistant*, 71 and 77–8; Wilson, *Bastogne to Bavaria*, 324–5; and Haygood, "Letters," 118.
188. Gurley, 24 March, 22 and 29 April 1945, 100th IDP.
189. Arrington, *Infantryman*, 173.
190. Ambrose, *Brothers*, 257 and 265; Jacobs to his mother, 26 and 31 March 1945, 44th ID, SC; and Baird, "Lend You My Eyes," 309 and 313. See also Tsuchida, *Letters*, 119; Easton, *Love and War*, 19; and Atwell, *Private*, 301.
191. Letter from Capt. L. A. Varteressian, 18 April 1945, Box 1/Folder 16, MCC; Wardlaw, *Missing*, 73; Peckham and Snyder, *Hoosiers*, 172; Seiverling, *Stories*, 35; Irgang, *Purple*, 239; Easton, *Love and War*, 290; Connelly, *Assistant*, 33; Carter, *Devils*, 152–3; and *Guide to Germany*, 32.
192. *Guide to France*, 30 and Connelly, *Assistant*, 32–3. See also *Austria: A Soldier's Guide*, 6–7; Sampson, *Look Out*, 77; and Seiverling, *Stories*, 35.
193. Wilson, *Bastogne to Bavaria*, 165. See also Easton, *Love and War*, 282; Shapiro to his family, 18 March 1945, 28th ID, SC; Giles, *Journal*, 352; and Toole, *Battle Diary*, 128. The Nazis harassed the clergy and attempted to undermine the churches' influence in Germany in various ways. However, as the severity of the war increased, they could not prevent the people from seeking the comfort of religion and flocking to churches

in large and ever increasing numbers. (Beck, *German Home Front*, 16, 22–3, 53–5, 87, 120, and 181.)

194. Shapiro to his family, 18 March 1945, 28th ID, SC and Jacobs to his mother, 2 April 1945, 44th ID, SC. See also Connelly, *Assistant*, 33.
195. Wardlaw, *Missing*, 73. See also Wilson, *Bastogne to Bavaria*, 196.
196. *Guide to Germany*, 7–9 and Stouffer et al., *Combat*, 567.
197. Faubus, *Faraway Land*, 593–4 and Stouffer et al., *Combat*, 565.
198. *Guide to Germany*, 13 and 26–30. As early as March 1942, when American ground troops had not yet engaged the German forces, 21 per cent of the American people considered the Germans "inevitably warlike," while another 30 per cent believed "they were too easily led into war by their leaders." (Steele, "American Opinion," 710, note 16.)
199. US Twelfth Army Group, *Special Orders*, 2–3; Ziemke, *Occupation of Germany*, 139; and Atwell, *Private*, 336. See also Faubus, *Faraway Land*, 420; Arrington, *Infantryman*, 86; Kelly, *One Man's War*, 115; Rogers, *Chaplain*, 209; Gurley to his parents, 26 March 1945, 100th IDP; and MacDonald, *Commander*, 215 and 221.
200. Haygood, "Letters," 113.
201. Stouffer et al., *Combat*, 565 and 567.
202. Easton, *Love and War*, 311.
203. Gray, *Warriors*, 9. See also Brown, *Up Front*, 435.
204. US Twelfth Army Group, *Special Orders*, 1. See also *Guide to Germany*, 16.
205. Leinbaugh and Campbell, *Company K*, 222; Freese, "Private Memories," 101, 84th ID, SC; and Stouffer et al., *Combat*, 567. See also Jacobs to his mother, 26 April 1945, 44th ID, SC; Giles, *Journal*, 347–8; Randall, *Doughfeet*, 96; and Jordan, "Bull Sessions," 73, 9th ID, SC.
206. Ziemke, *Occupation of Germany*, 232 and 246 and Ulsaker, "Saga," 258, CU.
207. MacDonald, *Commander*, 256.
208. Whitnah and Erickson, *Occupation of Austria*, 3–9, 15, and 185; Starr, *Fraternization*, 84–6; and *Austria: A Soldier's Guide*, 1, 5–6, 10–11, 15, and 32.
209. Grage, "Reflections," 4, 65th ID, SC; Ponder, "Recollections," 120, 71st ID, SC; and Starr, *Fraternization*, 84–6.
210. Weigley, *Eisenhower's Lieutenants*, 724; McConahey, *Surgeon*, 152; and MacDonald, *Commander*, 352.
211. Starr, *Fraternization*, 84–6 and MacDonald, *Commander*, 352.
212. McConahey, *Surgeon*, 152–4 and MacDonald, *Commander*, 364–7.
213. Hunt, "The Hierarchy of Race," in *Ideology and U.S. Foreign Policy*, 46–91.

Chapter 7 The Limits of Communication

1. Peyton, *Surgeon's Diary*, 288.
2. Kimball, *Diary*, 107.
3. *Guide to Northern Ireland*, 26; *Guide to Great Britain*, 25–6 and 29–32; and William A. Bostick, *England under G.I.'s Reign. Being a Sketchy and Humorous History of that Venerable Kingdom during the American Occupation* (Detroit: Conjure, 1946), 63.
4. Sgt Thomas R. Lyle to his parents, 8 December 1942, Box 2/Folder 27, MCC; Altieri, *Spearheaders*, 271; Jett diary, 30 August 1944, 1st AD, SC; Winston, *Combat Medic*, 141; Clarkson, "G.I. Joe," 8, 5th ID, SC; and Jordan, "Bull Sessions," 65, 9th ID, SC.
5. Easton, *Love and War*, 261 and Murphy, *Hell*, 181. See also Giles, *Journal*, 35.
6. *Guide to Cities of Belgium*, 21.
7. Johns, *Clay Pigeons*, 130.
8. *Guide to Cities of Belgium*, 35 and McHugh, *Hell to Heaven*, 23.

9. *Austria: A Soldier's Guide*, 20; Winston, *Combat Medic*, 176; and Giles, *Journal*, 105.

10. Shapiro to his family, 9 November 1944, 28th ID, SC and Atwell, *Private*, 293.

11. Koskimaki, *Eagles*, 114, 144, 231, and 265.

12. Ulsaker, "Saga," 176–7, CU; Daly, "Sharpe's Battalion," 79; and Swenson, "Personal History," 608, 70th ID, SC.

13. Boesch, *Huertgen*, 85.

14. Connelly, *Assistant*, 31.

15. Robinson, *45th*, 62.

16. Kelly, *One Man's War*, 114 and Faubus, *Faraway Land*, 450.

17. Dohmann, "Medic," 15; Robinson, *45th*, 62; Atwell, *Private*, 169; Baird, "Lend You My Eyes," 306; Winston, *Combat Medic*, 148; and Rogers, *Chaplain*, 57.

18. *Guide to Italy*, 14–15 and Mauldin, *Brass Ring*, 153. About half of the southern Italians who emigrated to the US returned home between 1880 and the early 1920s. The rate peaked in 1908–23, when 60 per cent of them, an estimated 970,000 people, left the US for native soil. (Wyman, *Round-Trip*, 9–11.)

19. *Guide to France*, 12–13; *Guide to Cities of Belgium*, 7 and 13; McHugh, *Heaven to Hell*, 23; Freese, "Private Memories," 20, 84th ID, SC; and *Austria: A Soldier's Guide*, 20.

20. Westrate, *Observer*, 158; Brown, *Up Front*, 51 and 403; and Faubus, *Faraway Land*, 304.

21. Cawthon, *Other Clay*, 75.

22. Raab to his parents, 12 May and 9 June 1944, RC; Morin, *Among the Valiant*, 120; Roche, "Forty Years," 54, RP; Egger and Otts, *G Company*, 94 and 193–4; Shukert and Scibetta, *War Brides*, 98–9; Giles, *Journal*, 8 and 26; Cawthon, *Other Clay*, 135; Davidson, *Cut Off*, 13; Seiverling, *Stories*, 17; Koskimaki, *Eagles*, 101 and 146; Carter, *Devils*, 42; Boesch, *Huertgen*, 124; Brown, *Up Front*, 50; and Burt, "War Memoirs," 28, 2nd AD, SC.

23. Lyon, *Unknown Station*, 27, 153, and 201–2 and Brown, *Up Front*, 169.

24. Giles, *Journal*, 290.

25. See, for instance, Howe, *Northwest Africa*, 101.

26. Bond, *Cassino*, 144–6 and Parker, *Civilian*, 56.

27. Gurley to his parents, 23 October 1944, 100th IDP; Calhoun to his parents, 30 March 1945, 42nd ID, SC; Shapiro to his family, 3 April 1945, 28th ID, SC; and Litoff et al., *Miss You*, 237.

28. Connelly, *Assistant*, 78 and Winston, *Combat Medic*, 135.

29. Kimball, *Diary*, 52; Wolfe, *Testament*, 167; Abbott, *Believers*, 24; Preston, *Letters*, 111; Koskimaki, *Eagles*, 265; Reams diary, 30 June 1944, 1st ID, SC; Calhoun to his parents, 29 December 1944, 42nd ID, SC; Huebner, *Long Walk*, 159; Wise, *Truly Ours*, 111; and Raab to his parents, 20 June 1944, RC.

30. Saidel diary, 31 January 1944, 1st AD, SC.

31. Jordan, "Bull Sessions," 41, 9th ID, SC.

32. Giles, *Journal*, 325.

33. Boesch, *Huertgen*, 31; Seiverling, *Stories*, 17; Tsuchida, *Letters*, 95; Berger, *Diary*, 604; Gustafson, *My Time*, 83; and Brown, *Up Front*, 227.

34. Winston, *Combat Medic*, 166 and unidentified soldier, *Diamond Dust*, 5th ID, SC. See also Standifer, *Not in Vain*, 222.

35. Gurley to his parents, 29 November 1944, 100th IDP.

36. Wilson, *Bastogne to Bavaria*, 144.

37. Brown, *Up Front*, 57 and Jordan, "Bull Sessions," 19, 9th ID, SC. See also Winston, *Combat Medic*, 110 and 226.

38. Connelly, *Assistant*, 49–50.

39. Ambrose, *Brothers*, 60 and 63 and Capa, *Out of Focus*, 144.

40. Simpson, *The Runner*, in *Poems*, 100. See also Johnson, *Hill*, 57.
41. Mauldin, *Up Front*, 130; Lashin to his family, 1 February 1945, 70th ID, SC; Abbott, *Believers*, 99; Jett diary, 26 November 1942, 1st AD, SC; Rontch, *Jewish Youth*, 226; and Risch, *Quartermaster Corps*, vol. 1, 192.
42. Cpl Raymond Dreyer to his family, 7 March 1943, Box 2/Folder 29, MCC and Ambrose, *Brothers*, 144.
43. Risch, *Quartermaster Corps*, vol. 1, 174–201.
44. Risch, *Quartermaster Corps*, vol. 1, 174-5; *Guide to Italy*, 7–8; *Guide to France*, 58; *Guide to Germany*, 1–2; and Stouffer et al., *Combat*, 79.
45. Davidson, *Cut Off*, 29; McHugh, *Heaven to Hell*, 25 and 28–9; Standifer, *Not in Vain*, 150; Sampson, *Look Out*, 84; Giles, *Journal*, 327; Ambrose, *Brothers*, 52 and 104; Mauldin, *Up Front*, 173; Daly, "Sharpe's Battalion," 117–18; Jett diary, 16 December 1942, 1st AD, SC; Ulsaker, "Saga," 169, CU; Rogers, *Chaplain*, 52; Hurkala, *Fighting First*, 138; Huebner, *Long Walk*, 153; Winston, *Combat Medic*, 166; and Tinsch to his wife, 7 October 1944, 45th ID, SC.
46. Giles, *Journal*, 44.
47. Houston, *Paratrooper*, 55; Irgang, *Purple*, 185; Gravlin, "Combat Engineer," 3–4, 3rd AD, SC; and Sampson, *Look Out*, 94.
48. Johnson, *Hill*, 81.
49. Duus, *Liberators*, 183–4; Brown, *Up Front*, 53, 69, and 218; Bernstein, *Head Down*, 83; Wiltse, *Medical Department*, 316–7; Miller to his girlfriend, 18 July 1944, 35th ID, SC; Faubus, *Faraway Land*, 289; Tsuchida, *Letters*, 2; Cawthon, *Other Clay*, 160; Freese, "Private Memories," 94, 84th ID, SC; Egger and Otts, *G Company*, 165–6; and Stewart, untitled memoir, 60, 1st ID, SC.
50. Gurley, 2 February 1945, 100th IDP.
51. Atwell, *Private*, 52; Biddle, *Artist*, 172; and Abbott, *Believers*, 44.
52. Egger and Otts, *G Company*, 99; Atwell, *Private*, 176; Brown, *Up Front*, 455; and Krebs, *Rome*, 55.
53. Raab to his parents, 5 November 1944, RC and Giles, *Journal*, 92.
54. Arrington, *Infantryman*, 116–18; Kelly, *One Man's War*, 92; Rivard, untitled memoir, 58, 1st ID, SC; Egger and Otts, *G Company*, 239; Brown, *Up Front*, 439; and Atwell, *Private*, 297 and 382.
55. Jett diary, 6 February 1945, 1st AD, SC. See also Rontch, *Jewish Youth*, 281 and Kimball, *Diary*, 152.
56. *Guide to North Africa*, 14; *Guide to Italy*, 14; *Guide to France*, 17; and Stewart, untitled memoir, 43, 1st ID, SC.
57. Shannon, "Replacement," 69, 26th ID, SC. See also Raab to his parents, 5 November 1944, RC.
58. Snyder, *My Task*, 157. See also Houston, *Paratrooper*, 73 and Egger and Otts, *G Company*, 59.
59. Raab to his parents, 14 May 1944, RC. See also Tsuchida, *Letters*, 103 and Robinson, *45th*, 65–6.
60. Ambrose, *Brothers*, 63.
61. Johnson, *Hill*, 79; Hoffman, *Archives*, 155; and Altieri, *Spearheaders*, 301.
62. Parker, *Civilian*, 97; Gravlin, "Combat Engineer," 13, 3rd AD, SC; Arrington, *Infantryman*, 81; and MacDonald, *Commander*, 96.
63. Hornsby, *Sevens*, 82; Egger and Otts, *G Company*, 118; and Hovsepian, *Your Son*, 126.
64. Leinbaugh and Campbell, *Company K*, 153 and Brown, *Up Front*, 313.
65. Tapert, *Lines*, 167; Ponder, "Recollections," 120, 71st ID, SC; Jordan, "Bull Sessions," 72, 9th ID, SC; MacDonald, *Commander*, 365; Roche, "Forty Years," 58, RP; Arrington, *Infantryman*, 138; and Jeske, *WWII Memories*, 277.

66. Snyder, *My Task*, 48; Boyer, "My Experiences," 29, 3rd ID, SC; Huebner, *Long Walk*, 33 and 156; Longmate, *G.I.'s*, 177 and 200–1; Abbott, *Believers*, 92; Cawthon, *Other Clay*; and Boesch, *Huertgen*, 98.

67. Mauldin, *Up Front*, 173.

68. See, for instance, Atwell, *Private*, 345.

69. Hovsepian, *Your Son*, 109.

70. Cawthon, *Other Clay*, 145; Leinbaugh and Campbell, *Company K*, 207; Stankoven diary, [February 1943], 1st ID, SC; Miller, 26 July 1944, 35th ID, SC; and Jett diary, 5 January 1945, 1st AD, SC.

71. Murphy, *Hell*, 58.

72. *Guide to Northern Ireland*, 14 and *Guide to Britain*, 23.

73. Ruppenthal, *Logistical Support*, vol. 2, 470–1 and 475; Krebs, *Rome*, 104 and 106–7; Fry, *Combat Soldier*, 250; *Guide to Paris*, 5; *Guide to France*, 45; Ethier diary, 14 February 1945, 13th AD, SC; and Winston, *Combat Medic*, 122–3.

74. Gurley to his parents, 9 November 1944, 100th IDP.

75. Jordan, "Bull sessions," 72, 9th ID, SC; Ulsaker, "Saga," 248, CU; and Boesch, *Huertgen*, 130.

76. *Guide to Cities of the Netherlands*, 7; Connelly, *Assistant*, 32 and 39; and Faubus, *Faraway Land*, 543–4.

77. Tsuchida, *Letters*, 3, 31, and 38–9; Winston, *Combat Medic*, 110; Shapiro to his parents, 4 December 1944, 28th ID, SC; Raab to his parents, 16 May 1944, RC; Calhoun to his parents, 1 and 7 March 1945, 42nd ID, SC; Stradling, *Johnny*, 257; Tinsch to his wife, 7 October 1944, 45th ID, SC; and Baird, "Lend You My Eyes," 298.

78. Preston, *Letters*, 99.

79. Shapiro to his parents, 17 February 1945, 28th ID, SC and Easton, *Love and War*, 300.

80. Pitkin, "The American: How He Lives," 191; Kimball, *Diary*, 173; and Jordan, "Bull Sessions," 8D, 9th ID, SC.

81. Ambrose, *Brothers*, 144. See also Rogers, *Chaplain*, 52.

82. Rogers, *Chaplain*, 99. See also *Guide to North Africa*, 15.

83. Burgett, *Currahee*, 1.

84. Lashin to his family, 17 December 1944, 70th ID, SC; Faubus, *Faraway Land*, 270; and Egger and Otts, *G Company*, 170.

85. Hyer et al., *Military Justice*, 15; Standifer, *Not in Vain*, 214; and Jordan, "Bull Sessions," 53, 9th ID, SC.

86. *Guide to Italy*, 14 and 38; Stankoven diary, [April 1943], 1st ID, SC; Wolfe, *Testament*, 128; Kelly, *One Man's War*, 113; Snyder, *My Task*, 140; Mauldin, *Brass Ring*, 188; and Dohmann, "Medic," 11.

87. Parker, *Civilian*, 35–6 and 68.

88. Egger and Otts, *G Company*, 182.

89. *Guide to Italy*, 13; *Guide to Northern Ireland*, 29–30; *Guide to France*, 17; and *Guide to Germany*, 17.

90. Shapiro to his parents, 3 April 1945, 28th ID, SC.

91. Krebs, *Rome*, 121; *Guide to Italy*, 13; and Stewart, untitled memoir, 26, 1st ID, SC.

92. *Guide to Italy*, 13; Standifer, *Not in Vain*, 152; Hurkala, *Fighting First*, 31; Egger and Otts, *G Company*, 166; Brown, *Up Front*, 197; Shapiro to his parents, 9 March 1945, 28th ID, SC; and Raab to his parents, 2 May 1944, RC.

93. *Guide to Italy*, 13; Brown, *Up Front*, 235; and Burgett, *Currahee*, 154.

94. Calhoun to his parents, 14 April 1945, 42nd ID, SC and *Guide to Paris*, 6. See also Shapiro to his parents, 3 April 1945, 28th ID, SC.

95. Mauldin, *Up Front*, 88–90.

96. Standifer, *Not in Vain*, 137; Koskimaki, *Eagles*, 374; Reams diary, 3 and 8 July 1944, 1st ID, SC; Faubus, *Faraway Land*, 334; and Ambrose, *Brothers*, 139, 185, and 207.

97. Giles, *Journal*, 49, 71, and 345.

98. Mauldin, *Up Front*, 84–8.

99. Downing, *At War*, 127 and 172; Randall, *Doughfeet*, 56; Egger and Otts, *G Company*, 65; Jeske, *WWII Memories*, 265; and Ulsaker, "Saga," 230–2, CU.

100. *Guide to Northern Ireland*, 14; *Guide to Great Britain*, 13; and *Guide to France*, 34 and 36.

101. Faubus, *Faraway Land*, 248; Toole, *Battle Diary*, 57; Rogers, *Chaplain*, 179; Ambrose, *Brothers*, 125; Saidel diary, 8 May 1943 and 5 September 1944, 1st AD, SC; Downing, *At War*, 104; Huebner, *Long Walk*, 115 and 150; and Winston, *Combat Medic*, 232.

102. Ambrose, *Brothers*, 90.

103. Faubus, *Faraway Land*, 294.

104. Ambrose, *Brothers*, 277–9.

105. Easton, *Love and War*, 237 and Hovsepian, *Your Son*, 127.

106. *Guide to Cities of Southern France*, 8 and *Guide to Italian Cities*, 10.

107. Burgett, *Currahee*, 167.

108. Clarkson, "G.I. Joe," 13, 5th ID, SC.

109. Freese, "Private Memories," 102, 84th ID, SC.

110. Sampson, *Look Out*, 88; Standifer, *Not in Vain*, 200 and 217; Snyder, *My Task*, 119; Winter, "Battle Babies," 53, 99th ID, SC; Elting, Cragg, and Deal, *Soldier Talk*, 175 and 308; Baird, "Lend You My Eyes," 301; Huebner, *Long Walk*, 163; Jordan, "Bull Sessions," 21, 9th ID, SC; Rogers, *Chaplain*, 166; Ambrose, *Brothers*, 241; and Ethier diary, 4 April 1945, 13th AD, SC.

111. Jacobs, 11 April 1945, 44th ID, SC.

112. Davidson, *Cut Off*, 29 and Faubus, *Faraway Land*, 506.

113. Hurkala, *Fighting First*, 35, 37, 65, and 109; Egger and Otts, *G Company*, 163; Jordan, "Bull Sessions," 23, 9th ID, SC; and DeWitt, "Soldier Memories," 103, 14th AD, SC.

114. Ambrose, *Brothers*, 86; Arrington, *Infantryman*, 100; Atwell, *Private*, 112; and Gurley to his parents, 29 November 1944, 100 IDP.

115. Hovsepian, *Your Son*, 101.

116. *Guide to Great Britain*, 13; *Guide to Paris*, 41; *Guide to Cities of the Netherlands*, 7; and *Austria: A Soldier's Guide*, 19.

117. MacDonald, *Commander*, 347. See also Winston, *Combat Medic*, 202.

118. Kelly, *One Man's War*, 93. See also Ambrose, *Brothers*, 174.

119. Easton, *Love and War*, 278.

120. Downing, *At War*, 126 and Egger and Otts, *G Company*, 229.

121. Peyton, *Surgeon's Diary*, 154 and Atwell, *Private*, 332–3 and 422. See also Ethier diary, 30 April 1945, 13th AD, SC.

122. Mauldin, *Brass Ring*, 151.

123. Ambrose, *Brothers*, 135. See also Brown, *Up Front*, 277–8 and 467.

124. Roche, "Forty Years," 114, RP and Ambrose, *Brothers*, 169.

125. Hyer et al., *Military Offender*, 8 and 27.

126. Mauldin, *Up Front*, 69.

127. Wiltse, *Medical Department*, 11 and 17.

128. Jett diary, 1st AD, SC; Robinson, *45th*, 124–5; Huebner, *Long Walk*, 113, 116, and 167; and Krebs, *Rome*, 36.

129. Mauldin, *Up Front*, 69.

130. Huebner, *Long Walk*, 83, 113, and 167 and Wiltse, *Medical Department*, 260, 286–7, and 362–5.

131. Cosmas and Cowdrey, *Medical Department*, 173; Koskimaki, *Eagles*, 363 and 372; and Kimball, *Diary*, 171. See also Irgang, *Purple*, 80–2.

132. Cosmas and Cowdrey, *Medical Department*, 172, 539, and 553–7; Beck, *German Home Front*, 146–7 and 164; and Atwell, *Private*, 261.

133. Winston, *Combat Medic*, 156–7.
134. Winston, *Combat Medic*, 133. See also Clarkson, "G.I. Joe," 6, 5th ID, SC and Kimball, *Diary*, 188.
135. *Guide to Great Britain*, 14 and Kimball, *Diary*, 73–4.
136. Wilson, *Bastogne to Bavaria*, 238.
137. Rontch, *Jewish Youth*, 87.
138. Mauldin, *Up Front*, 69.
139. Wise, *Truly Ours*, 183.
140. Rogers, *Chaplain*, 131–2; Snyder, *My Task*, 49; and Shannon, "Replacement," 48, 26th ID, SC.
141. Tsuchida, *Letters*, 2; *Guide to France*, 45; and Winston, *Combat Medic*, 177.
142. Preston, *Letters*, 133.
143. Stradling, *Johnny*, 215.
144. Davidson, *Cut Off*, 54 and Boesch, *Huertgen*, 130.
145. Connelly, *Assistant*, 77. Immediately after the war, the plight of Europe's children received much international attention. Concerned doctors, psychologists, and educators examined the problem of young war victims at a conference in Zurich, of moral rehabilitation at a symposium in France, and of juvenile delinquency at a convention in Geneva, while the United Nations tried to decide the fate of the many war orphans. (Wyman, *DP*, 88–9.)
146. Litoff et al., *Miss You*, 213.
147. Raab to his parents, 10 June 1944, RC; *Guide to North Africa*, 44; and Downing, *At War*, 98.
148. Ziemke, *Occupation of Germany*, 322–4.
149. Haygood, "Letters," 118–19. See also Baird, "Lend You My Eyes," 309.
150. Clarkson, "G.I. Joe," 14, 5th ID, SC; Easton, *Love and War*, 229; Peckham and Snyder, *Hoosiers*, 69; Kimball, *Diary*, 191; and Huebner, *Long Walk*, 162–3.
151. Connelly, *Assistant*, 39–40.
152. Ambrose, *Brothers*, 263. See also Huston, *Face of France*, 16 and Parker, *Civilian*, 52.
153. Rontch, *Jewish Youth*, 73.
154. Gray, *Warriors*, 61.
155. Eakins diary, 2nd AD, SC; Johnson, *Hill*, 6; and Clarkson, "G.I. Joe," 4, 5th ID, SC.
156. Jordan, "Bull Sessions," 31, 9th ID, SC and Hoffman, *Archives*, 155.
157. Downing, *At War*, 202–3. See also Bernstein, *Head Down*, 98.
158. Clarkson, "G.I. Joe," 11, 13, and 23, 5th ID, SC and Huebner, *Long Walk*, 40.
159. Giles, *Journal*, 51.
160. Johnson, *Hill*, 150 and MacDonald, *Commander*, 189 and 193. "Zig zig" was soldier slang for "sexual intercourse of the casual kind." (Elting, Cragg, and Deal, *Soldier Talk*, 347.)
161. Page, *Songs and Ballads*, 11; Stradling, *Johnny*, 215; and Gray, *Warriors*, 61. See also Palmer, *G.I. Songs*, 5–6.
162. Faubus, *Faraway Land*, 513.
163. Kennerly diary, 25 February 1945, 10th MD, SC and Costello, *Virtue under Fire*, 101.
164. Brown, *Up Front*, 130 and Bérubé, *Coming Out*, 186–93.
165. Arrington, *Infantryman*, 44.
166. Brown, *Up Front*, 406.
167. Elkin, "Erotic Tendencies," 409–10 and Gray, *Warriors*, 63.
168. Easton, *Love and War*, 210. See also Gray, *Warriors*, 62–3.
169. Costello, *Virtue under Fire*, 97–8 and 100 and Wiltse, *Medical Department*, 257 and 317.
170. Boesch, *Huertgen*, 63–4.
171. Gray, *Warriors*, 26 and 64–5.

172. Cosmas and Cowdrey, *Medical Department*, 21–2 and 142–7 and Page, *Songs and Ballads*, 116.

173. Wiltse, *Medical Department*, 317.

174. Mauldin, *Up Front*, 128.

175. Palmer, *G.I. Songs*, 102–3.

176. Wiltse, *Medical Department*, 215, 257–8, 317, 354, 411–12, and 513; Stouffer et al., *Adjustment*, 177–8; Costello, *Virtue under Fire*, 222–6; Krebs, *Rome*, 31; Carter, *Devils*, 53; and Tregaskis, *Invasion*, 237.

177. Wiltse, *Medical Department*, 411–12; Cosmas and Cowdrey, *Medical Department*, 172–3, 235, and 539–42; Costello, *Virtue under Fire*, 246–9; Shapiro to his parents, 9 March 1945, 28th ID, SC; *Guide to France*, 16; Egger and Otts, *G Company*, 170–1; Hornsby, *Sevens*, 13; Duus, *Liberators*, 221; Elting, Cragg, and Deal, *Soldier Talk*, 31 and 150; Boesch, *Huertgen*, 102–3; and Jordan, "Bull Sessions," 87, 9th ID, SC.

178. Huebner, *Long Walk*, 102 and Cosmas and Cowdrey, *Medical Department*, 542.

179. Hyer et al., *Military Offender*, 7; Brown, *Up Front*, 123; and Egger and Otts, *G Company*, 238.

180. Starr, *Fraternization*, 80–4. Undoubtedly, not all German rape victims had the courage to file complaints against the American occupiers. Nevertheless, those complaints that were filed are a good indication of the surge in incidences of rape. Whereas there were 18 and 31 complaints in January and February 1945 respectively, the numbers increased to 402 and 501 in March and April and then dropped off to 241 and 63 in May and June. Between 18 July 1942 and 31 October 1945, 13.27 per cent of the complainants in ETO rape cases were English and 2.10 per cent Austrian. In each of the other ETO countries the numbers formed less than 1 per cent of the cases.

181. Costello, *Virtue under Fire*, 250; Starr, *Fraternization*, 47; Ziemke, *Occupation of Germany*, 327; *Guide to Germany*, 2; and Arrington, *Infantryman*, 207.

182. Atwell, *Private*, 444–5.

183. Starr, *Fraternization*, 80–4. For descriptions of rape cases involving American combat soldiers, see the multivolume series *Holdings and Opinions. Board of Review. Branch Office of the Judge Advocate General. European Theater of Operations* (Washington, DC: Office of the Judge Advocate General, 1945–6). See also Leinbaugh and Campbell, *Company K*, 235 and Randall, *Doughfeet*, 64–5.

184. Brown, *Up Front*, 408–10.

185. Gray, *Warriors*, 62 and 71 and Brown, *Up Front*, 366. See also Stouffer et al., *Combat*, 79–80.

186. Huebner, *Long Walk*, 101 and 104.

187. See, for instance, Eakins diary, 2nd AD, SC.

188. Ethier diary, 28 May 1945, 13th AD, SC. See also Egger and Otts, *G Company*, 69.

189. Rontch, *Jewish Youth*, 110.

190. Gossett, 10 and 18 December 1944, 42nd IDP. See also Faubus, *Faraway Land*, 450 and Eustis, *Letters*, 175.

191. Hurkala, *Fighting First*, 76 and Huebner, *Long Walk*, 119–20 and 165.

192. Gray, *Warriors*, 72 and Duus, *Liberators*, 221–2.

193. Gray, *Warriors*, 74.

194. Shukert and Scibetta, *War Brides*, 2, 20, 118, 124, 128, 142, and 144; Reynolds, *Rich Relations*, 420–2; *Guide to France*, 20; *Guide to Germany*, 17–18; Kimball, *Diary*, 121; Altieri, *Spearheaders*, 91–2; Rogers, *Chaplain*, 131; and Ziemke, *Occupation of Germany*, 321–7.

195. Gray, *Warriors*, 74 and 76.

196. Winston, *Combat Medic*, 116 and Kimball, *Diary*, 10.

197. Peyton, *Surgeon's Diary*, 231; Palmer, *G.I. Songs*, 73; and Jeske, *WWII Memories*, 265. See also Gossett to his parents, 27 December 1944, 42nd IDP; Raab to his parents, 18 June 1944, RC; and Groth, *Europe*, 234.

198. Tsuchida, *Letters*, 73. See also Atwell, *Private*, 163–4 and Jordan, "Bull Sessions," 94, 9th ID, SC.

199. Letter home from an unidentified soldier, 17 November 1942, Box 2/Folder 27, MCC and Connelly, *Assistant*, 42 and 57. See also Atwell, *Private*, 418.

200. *Guide to Northern Ireland*, 27 and 29.

201. *Guide to France*, 1 and 19–20 and Boesch, *Huertgen*, 139. The doughboys returned from France with plenty of bawdy tales. The title of the 17th Engineers' history, *The 'Oo la la' Times: A Journal Printed with the Hopes of Passing the Censor and for Those at Home Who Care*, is just one example. In "I Want to Go Home," the GIs sang about the French women, inspired by their fathers' stories: "Oh send me over the sea, Where the wild women can't get at me." (Palmer, *G.I. Songs*, 243.)

202. Kimball, *Diary*, 8; Adams, "Americaines," 178; Inez Robb, *Philadelphia Bulletin*, 16 February 1943, Box 2/Folder 30, MCC; Ambrose, *Brothers*, 263; and Atwell, *Private*, 414. In *The American Troops and the British Community*, written during the war, anthropologist Margaret Mead observed that Americans began dating at a much earlier age than their British peers. She ascribed the success of the GIs with British females in part to their having had more practice, which easily swept inexperienced girls off their feet. (Costello, *Virtue under Fire*, 237.)

203. Atwell, *Private*, 405.

204. Ambrose, *Brothers*, 46 and Easton, *Love and War*, 210.

205. Fishman, *We Will Wait*, XII, 55, 57–9, and 69 and Shukert and Scibetta, *War Brides*, 130 and 135–6.

206. Lyon, *Unknown Station*, 10; quoted in Costello, *Virtue under Fire*, 248; and Atwell, *Private*, 444.

207. Downing, *At War*, 122; Easton, *Love and War*, 243; and Raab to a friend, 8 August 1944, RC.

208. Palmer, *G.I. Songs*, 109 and Griswold, newspaper clipping, 9th ID, SC.

209. *Guide to Great Britain*, 21–2.

210. Adams, "Mad Days," 65; Atwell, *Private*, 90; and Wise, *Truly Ours*, 170.

211. Cawthon, *Other Clay*, 156.

212. Robert L. Maier to his family, 22 November 1942, Box 1/Folder 13, MCC.

213. Inez Robb, *Philadelphia Bulletin*, 16 February 1943, Box 2/Folder 30, MCC.

214. Brown, *Up Front*, 405; Jett diary, 18 December 1944, 1st AD, SC; and Penrose, *Lee Miller*, 51.

215. Kelly, *One Man's War*, 131–2 and Irgang, *Purple*, 103.

Chapter 8 The Totality of War

1. *Guide to Germany*, 5.

2. Ziemke, *Occupation of Germany*, 134–5. See also Brown, *Up Front*, 464.

3. Egger and Otts, *G Company*, 62–3, 72–3, and 93.

4. *Guide to France*, 15–16 and Starr, *Fraternization*, 10–13. See also Brown, *Up Front*, 377 and *Guide to Italy*, 10.

5. Fry, *Combat Soldier*, 110 and 157. See also Hunter, Q/41a,b, and c, 92nd ID, SC.

6. Boesch, *Huertgen*, 84–5 and Standifer, *Not in Vain*, 126 and 130.

7. Ryan, Q/41a, 1st ID, SC. See also Frankel and Smith, *Patton's Best*, 31 and Jordan, "Bull Sessions," 94, 9th ID, SC.

8. Hornsby, *Sevens*, 28.

9. Downing, *At War*, 25 and Sgt Donald S. Hutcheson, 17 July and 8 August 1942, Box 1/Folder 13, MCC.

10. *Guide to Great Britain*, 21 and 23–4. Some 125,000 British women were drafted, while another 430,000 volunteered. They were assigned to defensive units and most of them manned, but did not fire, antiaircraft batteries. (Campbell, "Women in Combat," 306–13.)

11. Sgt Donald S. Hutcheson, 17 July and 8 August 1942, Box 1/Folder 13, MCC and Gurley, [mid-May 1945], 100th IDP.

12. Arrington, *Infantryman*, 94 and 110.

13. Campbell, "Women in Combat," 314–18.

14. Huston, *Face of France*, 171.

15. Jeske, *WWII Memories*, 260; Krebs, *Rome*, 35 and 96; Rogers, *Chaplain*, 113–14 and 173; Bond, *Cassino*, 75; and Gravlin, "Combat Engineer," 6, 3rd AD, SC.

16. Burgett, *Currahee*, 155. See also Kelly, *One Man's War*.

17. Gray, *Warriors*, 237–8.

18. Peckham and Snyder, *Hoosiers*, 65; Bond, *Cassino*, 133; Davidson, *Cut Off*, 39; and Cawthon, *Other Clay*, 158.

19. Faubus, *Faraway Land*, 227.

20. Rogers, *Chaplain*, 128 and Wagner, *War Correspondents*, 70.

21. Gray, *Warriors*, 83.

22. Freese, "Private Memories," 34, 84th ID, SC and Huebner, *Long Walk*, 160–1.

23. Brown, *Up Front*, 294 and 326–7 and Toole, *Battle Diary*, 83.

24. Daly, "Sharpe's Battalion," 107; Kimball, *Diary*, 88; and Groth, *Europe*, 96.

25. Orville W. Arends to his parents, [1942], Box 2/Folder 21, MCC.

26. Cawthon, *Other Clay*, 162.

27. Wardlaw, *Missing*, 49. See also Huston, *Face of France*, 93 and Parker, *Civilian*, 4.

28. MacDonald, *Commander*, 15 and Novich, untitled memoir, 15, 29th ID, SC. See also Giles, *Journal*, 76 and Burgett, *Currahee*, 154–5.

29. Hurkala, *Fighting First*, 134; McConahey, *Surgeon*, 82–3; and Boesch, *Huertgen*, 200.

30. Ambrose, *Brothers*, 220, footnote and Frankel and Smith, *Patton's Best*, 32–3. See also Freese, "Private Memories," 95, 84th ID, SC; Murphy, *Hell*, 187–8; and Gray, *Warriors*, 108.

31. Krebs, *Rome*, 81 and Cawthon, *Other Clay*, 94.

32. McConahey, *Surgeon*, 120. See also Johns, *Clay Pigeons*, 204; Leinbaugh and Campbell, *Company K*, 189; and Krebs, *Rome*, 45.

33. Freese, "Private Memories," 94, 84th ID, SC.

34. Leinbaugh and Campbell, *Company K*, 190 and Anderson, "War Years," 11, 8th ID, SC. See also Irgang, *Purple*, 220.

35. Ambrose, *Brothers*, 133.

36. Bodeen to his girlfriend, 3 June 1944, 36th ID, SC and Maule, *War Letters*, 108. See also Sampson, *Look Out*, 95.

37. *Guide to Great Britain*, 20; Faubus, *Faraway Land*, 147; Connelly, *Assistant*, 26; and Freese, "Private Memories," 11, 84th ID, SC.

38. Huebner, *Long Walk*, 32 and Wilson, *Bastogne to Bavaria*, 68–9. See also Jacobs to his mother, 16 September 1944, 44th ID, SC.

39. Beck, *German Home Front*, 84 and 214, note 1.

40. Connelly, *Assistant*, 65; Ethier diary, 19 April 1945, 13th AD, SC; Easton, *Love and War*, 305; Calhoun to his parents, 7 May 1945, 42nd ID, SC; Ulsaker, "Saga," 276, CU; and Houston, *Paratrooper*, 110.

41. MacDonald, *Commander*, 99.

42. Leinbaugh and Campbell, *Company K*, 200–1; Metcalf, *Cross*, 144; Griswold to local newspaper, 3 November 1944, 9th ID, SC; Giles, *Journal*, 219 and 222; Irgang, *Purple*, 161; and Connelly, *Assistant*, 26.
43. Peckham and Snyder, *Hoosiers*, 66.
44. Letter from an unidentified soldier, 30 November 1942, Box 1/Folder 13, MCC and Eustis, *Letters*, 192.
45. Bond, *Cassino*, 173; Tregaskis, *Invasion*, 180; Hurkala, *Fighting First*, 150; and Huebner, *Long Walk*, 140. See also Peckham and Snyder, *Hoosiers*, 161.
46. *Guide to France*, 26–7 and *Guide to Germany*, 12.
47. Mauldin, *Brass Ring*, 176–7 and Houston, *Paratrooper*, 82.
48. Connelly, *Assistant*, 36; Baird, "Lend You My Eyes," 310; and Eustis, *Letters*, 157–8 and 182–3. Polls showed that – unlike the lieutenant's mother – the vast majority of Americans did not object to the strategic bombing campaigns against Germany and Japan. (Hopkins, "Bombing," 451.)
49. Bond, *Cassino*, 40 and 114 and Blumenson, *Salerno to Cassino*, 397–416.
50. Wagner, "Odyssey," 84. See also Stradling, *Johnny*, 242.
51. *Guide to Italy*, 7–8; *Guide to Germany*, 1; Leinbaugh and Campbell, *Company K*, 258; and Brown, *Up Front*, 300 and 411.
52. Ambrose, *Brothers*, 268. See also Hyer et al., *Military Justice*, 18–19.
53. Gray, *Warriors*, 81–2.
54. Kelly, *One Man's War*, 149–50 and Johns, *Clay Pigeons*, 213–14.
55. Kelly, *One Man's War*, 149–50 and Gray, *Warriors*, 81–2.
56. Fry, *Combat Soldier*, 139–40 and Calhoun to his parents, 14 April and 2 May 1945, 42nd ID, SC.
57. Jordan, "Bull Sessions," 72, 9th ID, SC; Irgang, *Purple*, 46–7; Leinbaugh and Campbell, *Company K*, 216; Giles, *Journal*, 296–7; and Winston, *Combat Medic*, 219.
58. Egger and Otts, *G Company*, 237.
59. Brown, *Up Front*, 236; Irgang, *Purple*, 52 and 224; Randall, *Doughfeet*, 98–9; Arrington, *Infantryman*, 194; and Atwell, *Private*, 328 and 420.
60. *Guide to France*, 40; Faubus, *Faraway Land*, 266; and Jordan, "Bull Sessions," 72, 9th ID, SC.
61. Cawthon, *Other Clay*, 67; Ambrose, *Brothers*, 145; and Ryan et al., *Civil Affairs*, 31–3.
62. Atwell, *Private*, 186–7.
63. Roche, Q/29, 88th ID, SC and Brown, *Up Front*, 259.
64. Ambrose, *Brothers*, 277 and Easton, *Love and War*, 14.
65. Giles, *Journal*, 88 and 272 and Elisabeth Rigo, interview by author, Hasselt, Belgium, 8 March 1985.
66. Atwell, *Private*, 370–1; Meissner, "Life As a G.I.," 74, 71st ID, SC; and Ziemke, *Occupation of Germany*, 228–31.
67. Winston, *Combat Medic*, 200. See also, Daly, "Sharpe's Battalion," 163; Atwell, *Private*, 186; Brown, *Up Front*, 401; Earle to his family, [April 1945], 71st ID, SC; Easton, *Love and War*, 297; Egger and Otts, *G Company*, 183; and Cawthon, *Other Clay*, 180.
68. Leinbaugh and Campbell, *Company K*, 34. See also Irgang, *Purple*, 66; Egger and Otts, *G Company*, 233; and Boesch, *Huertgen*, 227.
69. Giles, *Journal*, 339–40. See also Toole, *Battle Diary*, 127; Jordan, "Bull Sessions," 72, 9th ID, SC; Atwell, *Private*, 186; and Cawthon, *Other Clay*, 180; and Stouffer et al., *Combat*, 171.
70. Charles E. Dornbusch, *Histories of American Army Units: World Wars I and II and Korean Conflict, with Some Earlier Histories* (Washington, DC: Department of the Army, 1956), 189.
71. Wagner, "Odyssey," 78–9.

72. Huebner, *Long Walk*, 187. See also Fry, *Combat Soldier*, 158.
73. Jordan, "Bull Sessions," 79, 9th ID, SC. See also Irgang, *Purple*, 28; Wilson, *Bastogne to Bavaria*, 368–70; and Duus, *Liberators*, 175–6.
74. Gray, *Warriors*, 167–8 and Davidson, *Cut Off*, 90–3. See also Bernstein, *Head Down*, 134–5.
75. Toole, *Battle Diary*, 51. See also Bodeen to his girlfriend, 6 August 1944, 36th ID, SC.
76. Arrington, *Infantryman*, 244; Palmer, *G.I. Songs*, 6; Atwell, *Private*, 87 and 169; Brown, *Up Front*, 179, 280, and 284; Leinbaugh and Campbell, *Company K*, 33 and 123; Baird, "Lend You My Eyes," 301; Miller to his mother, 10 August 1944, 35th ID, SC; Ambrose, *Brothers*, 115; Faubus, *Faraway Land*, 400–1; Ryan, Q/30f(2), 1st ID, SC; Easton, *Love and War*, 243; Standifer, *Not in Vain*, 139; and McConahey, *Surgeon*, 19.
77. Peyton, *Surgeon's Diary*, 170.
78. Bistrica, Q/30f(1) and (2), 1st ID, SC; Davidson, *Cut Off*, 23; Bodeen to his girlfriend, 11 November 1944, 36th ID, SC; Jordan, "Bull Sessions," 85, 9th ID, SC; Atwell, *Private*, 169–70, 332, and 419; Mauldin, *Up Front*, 50; and Peyton, *Surgeon's Diary*, 245.
79. Atwell, *Private*, 258.
80. Brown, *Up Front*, 199 and Ambrose, *Brothers*, 256. See also Arrington, *Infantryman*, 43–4.
81. Jordan, "Bull Sessions," 50, 9th ID, SC; Giles, *Journal*, 44; Jett diary, 1 September 1944, 1st AD, SC; Leinbaugh and Campbell, *Company K*, 34 and 128; and Atwell, *Private*, 185.
82. *Guide to Italian Cities*, 8.
83. Leinbaugh and Campbell, *Company K*, 201 and 205. See also MacDonald, *Commander*, 187.
84. Raab, 5 June 1944, RC. See also Stouffer et al., *Combat*, 87–8.
85. Abbott, *Believers*, 16.
86. Murphy, *Hell*, 163.
87. *Guide to Paris*, 26 and Boesch, *Huertgen*, 139. See also Toole, *Battle Diary*, 52, note 6; Sgt Donald S. Hutcheson to his family, 8 August 1942, Box 1/Folder 13, MCC; Griswold to local newspaper, 22 September 1944, 9th ID, SC; Huebner, *Long Walk*, 122; Winston, *Combat Medic*, 181 and 183; and Atwell, *Private*, 437.
88. Carter, *Devils*, 128; Raab to his parents, 5 June 1944, RC; Cawthon, *Other Clay*, 26; and Boesch, *Huertgen*, 137.
89. Boyer, "My Experiences," 39, 3rd ID, SC and *Guide to Paris*, 1 and 62. See also Murphy, *Hell*, 167 and 231 and Ambrose, *Brothers*, 128.
90. Egger and Otts, *G Company*, 171–2.
91. Calhoun to his parents, [5 February] and 27 March 1945, 42nd ID, SC. See also Egger and Otts, *G Company*, 140 and Peyton, *Surgeon's Diary*, 132.
92. Winter, "Battle Babies," 49, 99th ID, SC and Gurley, 21 November 1944, 100th IDP. See also Rogers, *Chaplain*, 135 and Sharp to his parents, 13 July 1944, 1st AD, SC.
93. *Guide to Italy*, 15. See also War Department, *What the Soldier Thinks: Monthly Digest*, February 1945, 14–16; Egger and Otts, *G Company*, 94; and Raab to his parents, 30 July 1944, RC.
94. *Guide to Great Britain*, 3 and 26–8 and *Guide to Germany*, 33–4.
95. Jordan, "Bull Sessions," 17, 9th ID, SC; Gurley to his parents, 26 January 1945, 100th IDP; Stankoven diary, 23 June 1943, 1st ID, SC; *Austria: A Soldier's Guide*, 15–16; Brown, *Up Front*, 408 and 410–11; Arrington, *Infantryman*, 77; McHugh, *Hell to Heaven*, 31; and Ambrose, *Brothers*, 268.
96. Jordan, "Bull Sessions," 92, 9th ID, SC. See also Egger and Otts, *G Company*, 118.
97. Wilson, *Bastogne to Bavaria*, 325. See also Shapiro to his parents, 9 March 1945, 28th ID, SC; Tinsch to his wife, 13 October and 8 November 1944, 45th ID, SC; and Parker, *Civilian*, 126.

98. Winston, *Combat Medic*, 178 and 182–3; Eustis, *Letters*, 192; Clarkson, "G.I. Joe," 36, 5th ID, SC; Tinsch to his wife, 14 and 28 June 1944, 45th ID, SC; and Litoff et al., *Miss You*, 236–7.

99. Kimball, *Diary*, 23; letter from an unidentified soldier, 6 January 1943, Box 2/Folder 27, MCC; Calhoun to his parents, 18 December 1944, 42nd ID, SC; and Earle to his mother, [May 1945], 71st ID, SC.

100. Bob Hope, *I Never Left Home* (New York: Simon and Schuster, 1944), 153–4 and Calhoun to his parents, 30 March 1945, 42nd ID, SC. See also Eustis, *Letters*, 170; and Sharp to his parents, 30 March 1944, 1st AD, SC.

101. Gossett to his parents, 8 May 1945, 42nd IDP; Randall, *Doughfeet*, 88–9; Bodeen to his girlfriend, 26 October 1944, 36th ID, SC; Meissner, "Life As a G.I.," 78 and 84, 71st ID, SC; and Winter, "Battle Babies," 39, 99th ID, SC.

102. Page III of the various GI guides to European cities.

103. *Guide to Italian Cities*, 49; *Guide to France*, 50; *Guide to Cities of the Netherlands*, 48; and *Guide to Cities of Belgium*, 31.

104. Jett diary, 1st AD, SC and *Guide to Italian Cities*, 3. See also Connelly, *Assistant*, 36.

105. Unidentified soldier, Box 1/Folder 13, MCC.

106. *Guide to Italian Cities*, 2; Jett diary, 7 March 1945, 1st AD, SC; and Ryan et al., *Civil Affairs*, 26–8.

107. Adams, "Americaines," 178; Haygood, "Letters," 106; and Gossett, 18 December 1944, 42nd IDP.

108. Gurley to his parents, [around VE-Day], 100th IDP. See also Boesch, *Huertgen*, 95.

109. Litoff et al., *Miss You*, 236. See also Irgang, *Purple*, 147–8.

110. Ulsaker, "Saga," 233, CU and Boesch, *Huertgen*, 139. See also Egger and Otts, *G Company*, 170.

111. Burgett, *Currahee*, 62. See also Ambrose, *Brothers*, 102 and Lyon, *Unknown Station*, 153.

112. Irgang, *Purple*, 19. See also Burgett, *Currahee*, 181; Duus, *Liberators*, 220–1; Wiggans, "Ithaca Boy," 98, 85th ID, SC; and Bond, *Cassino*, 143.

113. Clarkson, "G.I. Joe," 14, 5th ID, SC.

114. Tsuchida, *Letters*, 10. See also Saidel to his parents, 20 April 1943, 1st AD, SC; Winston, *Combat Medic*, 133; and Winter, "Battle Babies," 38, 99th ID, SC.

115. Litoff et al., *Miss You*, 230 and Stoner, 3 January and 9 March 1945, 42nd IDP. See also Atwell, *Private*, 362; Roche to his parents, 2 June 1944 and "Forty Years," 85, RP; and Winston, *Combat Medic*, 176.

116. *Guide to Paris*, 17.

117. Kimball, *Diary*, 130–1; Wise, *Truly Ours*, 119–20; Raab to his parents, 28 July 1944, RC; and Brown, *Up Front*, 147. See also Egger and Otts, *G Company*, 155.

118. *Guide to Italian Cities*, 44.

119. Standifer, *Not in Vain*, 220 and Griswold to local newspaper, 6 October 1943, 9th ID, SC.

120. Joseph Aylward, Jr to his family, 15 November 1942, Box 1/Folder 13, MCC and Litoff et al., *Miss You*, 239. See also *Guide to Paris*, 4–5 and Gurley to his parents, [around VE-Day], 100th IDP.

121. Carter, *Devils*, 128. See also Toole, *Battle Diary*, 19.

Chapter 9 The Old World

1. Wilson, *Bastogne to Bavaria*, 37.

2. Private Charles Hammons to his mother, 10 March 1942, Box 2/Folder 21, MCC and Griswold to local newspaper, 6 October 1943, 9th ID, SC.

3. Sharp to his mother, 11 June 1944, 1st AD, SC.
4. Connelly, *Assistant*, 20. See also Wardlaw, *Missing*, 43.
5. Brink, *God*, 62–3; Snyder, *My Task*, 130; Rogers, *Chaplain*, 126; Gravlin, "Combat Engineer," 3, 3rd AD, SC; and Eustis, *Letters*, 145.
6. Peyton, *Surgeon's Diary*, 101; Snyder, *My Task*, 54; and Belden, *Still Time*, 241.
7. Rogers, *Chaplain*, 137; Fry, *Combat Soldier*, 85; and Kimball, *Diary*, 128.
8. Wardlaw, *Missing*, 43 and Rogers, *Chaplain*, 136.
9. Connelly, *Assistant*, 23.
10. Gray, *Warriors*, 34.
11. Johnson, *Hill*, 149–50 and Bond, *Cassino*, 191.
12. Peyton, *Surgeon's Diary*, 80; Fry, *Combat Soldier*, 107–8; and Cawthon, *Other Clay*, 80.
13. Atwell, *Private*, 355 and Fry, *Combat Soldier*, 110.
14. Boesch, *Huertgen*, 65–6; Frankel and Smith, *Patton's Best*, 71–2; and Easton, *Love and War*, 6–7 and 10–11.
15. Bernstein, *Head Down*, 91; Cawthon, *Other Clay*, 25; and Wilson, *Bastogne to Bavaria*, 321.
16. Bond, *Cassino*, 79; Irgang, *Purple*, 66; and Johnson, *Hill*, 104–5.
17. *Guide to Northern Ireland*, 3; *Guide to Great Britain*, 5; *Guide to France*, 27; and *Guide to Germany*, 30.
18. Boyer, "My Experiences," 26, 3rd ID, SC; Kelly, *One Man's War*, 153; and Connelly, *Assistant*, 54.
19. *Guide to Great Britain*, 6; Frankel and Smith, *Patton's Best*, 57; and Giles, *Journal*, 290.
20. Kimball, *Diary*, 145; Wardlaw, *Missing*, 46; C. L. Newton to his father, 12 April 1942, Box 2/Folder 21, MCC; and Jacobs to his mother, 31 March 1945, 44th ID, SC.
21. *Guide to France*, 42; *Guide to Northern Ireland*, 6; letter home from Cpl Raymond H. Dreyer, [early 1942], Box 2/Folder 21, MCC; and Winter, "Battle Babies," 33, 99th ID, SC.
22. Kimball, *Diary*, 151.
23. Stewart, untitled memoir, 22, 1st ID, SC; Jordan, "Bull Sessions," 142, 9th ID, SC; McConahey, *Surgeon*, 129; and Huebner, *Long Walk*, 63.
24. Frankel and Smith, *Patton's Best*, 21 and 143 and Daly, "Sharpe's Battalion," 166.
25. Snyder, *My Task*, 51; Litoff et al., *Miss You*, 240; and Kimball, *Diary*, 186.
26. *Guide to Great Britain*, 10.
27. *Guide to Northern Ireland*, 23 and Sampson, *Look Out*, 50.
28. Easton, *Love and War*, 231. See also *Guide to Italy*, 39 and *Guide to France*, 51 and 53.
29. Bond, *Cassino*, 19 and Pyle, *Brave Men*, 75.
30. Wood, untitled memoir, 2, 66th ID, SC.
31. Burgett, *Currahee*, 51 and 53. See also Downing, *At War*, 40 and 137 and Ulsaker, "Saga," 159, CU.
32. Lyon, *Unknown Station*, 3–4 and Freese, "Private Memories," 32, 84th ID, SC.
33. Pyle, *Brave Men*, 75. See also Johnson, *Hill*, 7; Kimball, *Diary*, 139; and Jeske, *WWII Memories*, 274.
34. Easton, *Love and War*, 282. See also *Guide to Great Britain*, 14; McIntyre, untitled memoir, 92, MP; and Johnson, *Hill*, 113.
35. Krebs, *Rome*, 103 and Sharp to his family, 2 July 1944, 1st AD, SC.
36. Private John Rosendall to his sister, 26 October 1942, Box 2/ Folder 21, MCC; Easton, *Love and War*, 308; and Bodeen, 3 June 1944, 36th ID, SC.
37. Wise, *Truly Ours*, 197; Saidel diary, 10 May and 12 November 1943, 1st AD, SC; Phibbs, *Other Side*, 185–92; and Tsuchida, *Letters*, 24.
38. Carter, *Devils*, 34.
39. Davidson, *Cut Off*, 88.

40. Jett diary, 30 November 1944, 1st AD, SC and Easton, *Love and War*, 236–7. See also Runyon, "Memories," 32–3, 92nd ID, SC.
41. Connelly, *Assistant*, 48 and Frankel and Smith, *Patton's Best*, 77.
42. *Guide to France*, 40–1; *Guide to Northern Ireland*, 30–1 and 33; *Guide to Italy*, 39; and *Guide to Great Britain*, 3 and 8.
43. Sgt Lewis M. Tenneriello, [1942], Box 2/Folder 27 and letter home from Sgt Tom Syers, 3 January 1943, Box 1/Folder 13, MCC.
44. Stankoven diary, [1942], 1st ID, SC; Wilson, *Bastogne to Bavaria*, 64; and Jacobs to his mother, 16 September 1944, 44th ID, SC.
45. *Guide to France*, 42; Shapiro to his family, 20 October 1944, 28th ID, SC; and Litoff et al., *Miss You*, 211.
46. Boyer, "My Experiences," 32, 3rd ID, SC and Kimball, *Diary*, 185.
47. Jett diary, 31 May 1942, 1st AD, SC; Eustis, *Letters*, 161; *Guide to France*, 57–8; and Connelly, *Assistant*, 59.
48. *Guide to France*, 58; Metcalf, *Cross*, 44; and Huebner, *Long Walk*, 161.
49. Brown, *Up Front*, 151; Kimball, *Diary*, 10; Irgang, *Purple*, 115; and Sgt Ray Salisbury to his sister, 12 August 1943, Box 3/Folder 31, MCC.
50. Wilson, *Bastogne to Bavaria*, 119.
51. *Guide to France*, 48 and letter home from Cpl Oscar F. Deneault, 31 October 1942, Box 1/Folder 13, MCC.
52. *Guide to Northern Ireland*, 17 and *Guide to France*, 33–4.
53. Letter home from Cpl Raymond Dreyer, 30 March 1942, Box 2/Folder 21, MCC and Winter, "Battle Babies," 28, 99th ID, SC.
54. Biddle, *Artist*, 65; Snyder, *My Task*, 71; and Boyer, "My Experiences," 29, 3rd ID, SC.
55. *Guide to France*, 41–2 and Stewart, untitled memoir, 37, 1st ID, SC.
56. Letter home from Sgt Henry Stadnicki, 31 October 1942, Box 1/Folder 13, MCC; Griswold to local newspaper, 22 September 1944, 9th ID, SC; and Egger and Otts, *G Company*, 170.
57. *Guide to France*, 52; Cawthon, *Other Clay*, 24; *Guide to Great Britain*, 17; Shannon, "Replacement," 46, 26th ID, SC; and McConahey, *Surgeon*, 24.
58. Jett diary, 18–19 July 1942, 1st AD, SC; private Robert Taylor to his mother, 9 April 1942, Box 2/Folder 21, MCC; and Gustafson, *My Time*, 86.
59. *Guide to Great Britain*, 17; Gustafson, *My Time*, 87; and Calhoun to his parents, 14 April 1945, 42nd ID, SC.
60. Gray, *Warriors*, 6. See also Rogers, *Chaplain*, 168 and Lummer diary, 3 April 1945, 11th AD, SC.
61. Biddle, *Artist*, 164. See also Rogers, *Chaplain*, 138; Koskimaki, *Eagles*, 107; Irgang, *Purple*, 125–6; and Johnson, *Hill*, 122.
62. Quoted from *Meet the Americans*, British Army Bureau of Current Affairs Bulletin, no. 22, 18 July 1942, in *Guide to Great Britain*, 36.
63. Sgt Ray Salisbury to his sister, 6 July 1943, Box 3/Folder 31, MCC; Easton, *Love and War*, 227; and Winston, *Combat Medic*, 152.
64. Penrose, *Lee Miller*, 24; Wilson, *Bastogne to Bavaria*, 159; and Swenson, "Personal History," 597, 70th ID, SC.
65. Shapiro to his family, 3 December 1944, 28th ID, SC.
66. Jett diary, 16 January 1943, 1st AD, SC; Rogers, *Chaplain*, 55 and 93; Kimball, *Diary*, 140–1; Abbott, *Believers*, 73; and Roche, "Forty Years," 53, RP.
67. Kimball, *Diary*, 177; Gustafson, *My Time*, 87; Freese, "Private Memories," 20, 84th ID, SC; Abbott, *Believers*, 98; Pyle, *Your War*, 276; and Brown, *Up Front*, 412.
68. *Guide to Northern Ireland*, 26; *Guide to France*, 13; and Louis E. Rossetti, *APO 451* (New York: Carlton, 1969).

69. Preston, *Letters*, 55. On the popularity of American music in the Third Reich, see Beck, "Swing Youth," 45–53 and Kater, *Different Drummers*.

70. Reams diary, 1st ID, SC and Penrose, *Lee Miller*, 15.

71. Easton, *Love and War*, 240 and Gurley to his parents, 23 October 1944, 100th IDP.

72. *Guide to Northern Ireland*, 29; *Austria: A Soldier's Guide*, 13–14; Earle to his family, 9 March 1945, 71st ID, SC; and Gurley, 100th IDP.

73. Cpl Raymond Dreyer to his family, 11 June 1943, Box 2/Folder 29, MCC.

74. PFC Frank Elkin, [1942], Box 2/Folder 28, MCC; Ryan, Q/41d, 1st ID, SC; *Guide to Germany*, 10; Mauldin, *Up Front*, 74; and Wise, *Truly Ours*, 101.

75. Rogers, *Chaplain*, 138.

76. Connelly, *Assistant*, 64.

77. PFC Frank Elkin to his father, [1942], Box 2/Folder 28, MCC and Baird, "Lend You My Eyes," 306.

78. Litoff et al., *Miss You*, 209 and Raab to his parents, 12 November 1944, RC.

79. *Guide to Italy*, 29; *Guide to France*, 17; *Austria: A Soldier's Guide*, 6; and *Guide to Germany*, 16–17.

80. Kimball, *Diary*, 28 and Bond, *Cassino*, 56.

81. Winston, *Combat Medic*, 161. See also Jeske, *WWII Memories*, 273 and Atwell, *Private*, 304.

82. Downing, *At War*, 105.

83. *Guide to Italy*, 13. See also Clarkson, "G.I. Joe," 14, 5th ID, SC and Hornsby, *Sevens*, V.

84. McConahey, *Surgeon*, 16; Robinson, *45th*, 82; *Guide to Italy*, 30; Brown, *Up Front*, 197; and Peyton, *Surgeon's Diary*, 50.

85. Clarkson, "G.I. Joe," 8, 5th ID, SC; Gossett to his family, 10 December 1944, 42nd IDP; and Arrington, *Infantryman*, 38.

86. Jordan, "Bull Sessions," 49, 9th ID, SC and Baird, "Lend You My Eyes," 306. See also Rogers, *Chaplain*, 120; Cawthon, *Other Clay*, 144–5; and Burgett, *Currahee*, 140.

87. Atwell, *Private*, 146.

88. Wiggans, "Ithaca Boy," 104, 85th ID, SC.

89. *Guide to Paris*, 1; Egger and Otts, *G Company*, 170; and Sampson, *Look Out*, 101.

90. Sampson, *Look Out*, 98; Ethier diary, 17 March 1945, 13th AD, SC; and Mayo, *No Time*, 29.

91. *Guide to Italy*, 10; *Guide to France*, 16–17; and Tapert, *Lines*, 233.

92. Groth, *Europe*, 240 and Gossett, 18 December 1944, 42nd IDP.

93. Ambrose, *Brothers*, 275.

94. Giles, *Journal*, 304; DeWitt, "Soldier Memories," 113, 14th AD, SC; Phibbs, *Other Side*, 319–22; and Ulsaker, "Saga," 281, CU.

95. Gurley, 100th IDP.

96. Boesch, *Huertgen*, 48. See also Faubus, *Faraway Land*, 472.

97. Gurley to his parents, 29 November 1944, 100th IDP and Jeske, *WWII Memories*, 255. See also *Guide to France*, 49.

98. Koskimaki, *Eagles*, 166–7 and 180; Roche, "Forty Years," 81, RP; and Cawthon, *Other Clay*, 153.

99. Faubus, *Faraway Land*, 508.

100. Huebner, *Long Walk*, 82 and Gravlin, "Combat Engineer," 8, 3rd AD, SC.

101. *Guide to Northern Ireland*, 19 and 22; *Guide to Great Britain*, 14; and *Guide to France*, 30.

102. Tsuchida, *Letters*, 75; Winston, *Combat Medic*, 233; and Kimball, *Diary*, 177.

103. Atwell, *Private*, 259; Gray, *Warriors*, 11; and Krebs, *Rome*, 84.

104. Raab, 5 June 1944, RC; Mayo, *No Time*, 14; and Wilson, *Bastogne to Bavaria*, 357.

105. Wilson, *Bastogne to Bavaria*, 118–19 and 166.

106. Brink, *God*, 27–8 and *Guide to Northern Ireland*, 22.
107. Letter from an unidentified soldier, 6 January 1943, Box 2/Folder 27, MCC; Kimball, *Diary*, 112; *Guide to Northern Ireland*, 2 and 10; and *Guide to Great Britain*, 25.
108. Biddle, *Artist*, 107 and 113; Frankel and Smith, *Patton's Best*, 31; and Cawthon, *Other Clay*, 179.
109. *Guide to Paris*, 43 and *Guide to Italy*, 37.
110. Parker, *Civilian*, 96; Fry, *Combat Soldier*, 123; and Gray, *Warriors*, 10–11.
111. Atwell, *Private*, 38.
112. Raff, *We Jumped*, 54 and Preston, *Letters*, 58.
113. Wade, Box 2/Folder 21, MCC.
114. Mauldin, *Up Front*, 72 and 173 and Eliach and Gurewitsch, *Liberators*, 30.
115. Swenson, "Personal History," 600, 70th ID, SC. See also Fisher, *Cassino to the Alps*, 178–80, 341, and 366–7 and Ambrose, *Brothers*, 219.
116. Blumenson, *Salerno to Cassino*, 383; Freese, "Private Memories," 17, 84th ID, SC; Burgett, *Currahee*, 93; and Irgang, *Purple*, 39.
117. Lyon, *Unknown Station*, 135.
118. *Guide to France*, 25 and 29; *Guide to Germany*, 15; and *Guide to Great Britain*, 15.
119. Mauldin, *Up Front*, 35 and 173; Fussell, "My War," 258; Ambrose, *Brothers*, 161; and Winston, *Combat Medic*, 223.
120. Connelly, *Assistant*, 34.
121. Sgt Ray Salisbury, 20 April 1943, Box 3/Folder 31, MCC and Wise, *Truly Ours*, 157.
122. Connelly, *Assistant*, 47. See also Wagner, "Odyssey," 74; Jordan, "Bull Sessions," 118, 9th ID, SC; and Gurley to his parents, 3 December 1944, 100th IDP.
123. Easton, *Love and War*, 296.

PART IV THE APOCALYPSE

Chapter 10 The Apocalypse

1. Gray, *Warriors*, 15.
2. Leonidas E. Hill, review of *Inside the Vicious Heart: Americans and the Liberation of Nazi Concentration Camps*, by Robert H. Abzug, *Journal of American History* 73 (December 1986), 803.
3. Daly, "Sharpe's Battalion," 202–3 and MacDonald, *Commander*, 189–349.
4. Easton, *Love and War*, 29.
5. MacDonald, *Commander*, 209 and 363.
6. Wyman, *Abandonment*, 326 and *Guide to Germany*, 19.
7. Bohnen, "Rabbi," 84–5 and Frankel and Smith, *Patton's Best*, 164.
8. Adams, "Americaines," 184–5; Rogers, *Chaplain*, 84–5; and Rontch, *Jewish Youth*, 48–9.
9. Rontch, *Jewish Youth*, 14. See also Gushwa, *United States Army Chaplaincy*, 153–4.
10. Abzug, *Vicious Heart*, 10.
11. Wyman, *Abandonment*, 321–3 and Ambrose, *Brothers*, 254–7.
12. Wyman, *Abandonment*, 9–15 and Elting, Cragg, and Deal, *Soldier Talk*, 169.
13. Rontch, *Jewish Youth*, 43 and 111–12. See also McHugh, *Hell to Heaven*, 1–2.
14. Stouffer et al., *Combat*, 585.
15. Faubus, *Faraway Land*, 598. See also Bennett and Floyd, *Displaced Persons*, 36–7 and 43–4.
16. Bennett and Floyd, *Displaced Persons*, 3–5.
17. Cawthon, *Other Clay*, 179.

18. Peyton, *Surgeon's Diary*, 290.
19. Faubus, *Faraway Land*, 583. See also McConahey, *Surgeon*, 142.
20. Hyer, May, and Sudarsky, *War Crimes*, 3–4. See also Brown, *Up Front*, 471.
21. Arrington, *Infantryman*, 111 and Toole, *Battle Diary*, 122.
22. Bennett and Floyd, *Displaced Persons*, 6.
23. Ibid., 3.
24. Eliach and Gurewitsch, *Liberators*, 3, 12, 21, and 34. See also Tapert, *Lines*, 267.
25. Eliach and Gurewitsch, *Liberators*, 40.
26. Ibid.
27. Bridgman, *Holocaust*, 106–8. Special thanks to Dr Gie Van Den Berghe for information on this subject.
28. Potter, *Liberators*, 217–18; Eliach and Gurewitsch, *Liberators*, 23–4; Wilson, *Bastogne to Bavaria*, 288–9; and Baird, "Lend You My Eyes," 308.
29. Potter, *Liberators*, 219. See also Baird, "Lend You My Eyes," 308 and McConahey, *Surgeon*, 144.
30. Tapert, *Lines*, 268–9.
31. Eliach and Gurewitsch, *Liberators*, 32 and 38 and Ambrose, *Brothers*, 269–70.
32. Wilson, *Bastogne to Bavaria*, 287 and Eliach and Gurewitsch, *Liberators*, 4, 12–13, and 23.
33. Atwell, *Private*, 376.
34. Leinbaugh and Campbell, *Company K*, 261. See also letter home from PFC Joseph Dolin, 8 April 1945, Box 2/Folder 17, MCC.
35. Quoted in MacDonald, *Last Offensive*, 392.
36. Easton, *Love and War*, 231 and Wilson, *Bastogne to Bavaria*, 342.
37. Stouffer et al., *Adjustment*, 431–2.
38. Stouffer et al., *Combat*, 151–3 and 587–8.
39. Ibid., 136–8, 153, and 589.
40. Faubus, *Faraway Land*, 154–5 and 545. See also Carter, *Devils*, 139; Hoffman, *Archives*, 100; and Bodeen to his girlfriend, 20 November 1944, 36th ID, SC.
41. Letter home from an unidentified tank operator, 15 May 1943, Box 2/Folder 29, MCC; Saidel diary, 5 September 1944, 1st AD, SC; and Gray, *Warriors*, 11.
42. Seiverling, *Stories*, 33. See also letter home from Sgt Lewis M. Tenneriello, [1942], Box 2/Folder 27, MCC.
43. Abzug, *Vicious Heart*, 52 and 92–3.
44. Motley, *Invisible Soldier*, 154–5. See also Gravlin, "Combat Engineer," 42, 3rd AD, SC.
45. Winston, *Combat Medic*, 195. See also MacDonald, *Commander*, 365–6 and Frankel and Smith, *Patton's Best*, 129–30.
46. Connelly, *Assistant*, 89.
47. Tapert, *Lines*, 254.
48. Stouffer et al., *Combat*, 590–1.
49. Easton, *Love and War*, 296.
50. Levering, *Russian Alliance*, 203.
51. Ibid., 17, 50, and 143.
52. Ibid., 127.
53. Saidel diary, [early February 1944], 1st AD, SC and Easton, *Love and War*, 257. See also Jett diary, 1 October 1942, 1st AD, SC.
54. Gurley, 26 January 1945, 100th IDP and Faubus, *Faraway Land*, 495. See also Winston, *Combat Medic*, 167–8.
55. Jett diary, 1st AD, SC.
56. Winston, *Combat Medic*, 149.
57. Jett diary, 22 March 1945, 1st AD, SC.

58. Atwell, *Private*, 151.
59. Peckham and Snyder, *Hoosiers*, 56; Koskimaki, *Eagles*, 188; Ambrose, *Brothers*, 224; Tregaskis, *Invasion*, 33; Biddle, *Artist*, 185; and Faubus, *Faraway Land*, 413.
60. Rontch, *Jewish Youth*, 262–3 and Biddle, *Artist*, 185. See also Peckham and Snyder, *Hoosiers*, 56.
61. Faubus, *Faraway Land*, 208. See also Connelly, *Assistant*, 57; Giles, *Journal*, 262; and Baird, "Lend You My Eyes," 304.
62. Gurley, 100th IDP.
63. Stouffer et al., *Combat*, 574.
64. McConahey, *Surgeon*, 154 and Connelly, *Assistant*, 94–5.
65. Connelly, *Assistant*, 95.
66. Leinbaugh and Campbell, *Company K*, 263; Meissner, "Life As a G.I.," 79, 71st ID, SC; Brown, *Up Front*, 504–5; and Connelly, *Assistant*, 95–6.
67. Stouffer et al., *Combat*, 627–30.
68. Anderson, "War Years," 27, 8th ID, SC.
69. Connelly, *Assistant*, 95; Ponder, "Recollections," 125, 71st ID, SC; and Gurley to his parents, 4 May 1945, 100th IDP. See also McConahey, *Surgeon*, 154 and Potter, *Liberators*, 254–5.
70. Leinbaugh and Campbell, *Company K*, 263 and Potter, *Liberators*, 252. See also Brown, *Up Front*, 505–6; Morris, "Adventures," 4, 65th ID, SC; and Connelly, *Assistant*, 97.
71. Toole, *Battle Diary*, 125; Faubus, *Faraway Land*, 468 and 501; Easton, *Love and War*, 29; and Engel, "Patrol," 627.
72. Brown, *Up Front*, 455 and 498 and Cawthon, *Other Clay*, 180–1.
73. Winston, *Combat Medic*, 226. See also Giles, *Journal*, 348.
74. Toole, *Battle Diary*, XXXI.

Epilogue

1. Dulles, *Americans Abroad*, 153.
2. For a description of how tenaciously these age-old prejudices against Europe have remained rooted in the American imagination until well into the twentieth century, see Dulles, *Americans Abroad*, 4–7, 149, and 155, but also, for instance, Strout, *The American Image*, 155–6, 170–6, and 192–3 and Boorstin, *America and the Image of Europe*, 22–5.
3. For an insightful interpretation of this turning point, see Lukacs, *The Last European War*.
4. For a similar kind of reasoning in the American press, see Small, "How We Learned to Love the Russians," 455–78.
5. Stouffer et al., *Combat*, 574. In an Army survey in the US in July 1943, those percentages had still been respectively 22 and 19. By August 1945, on the other hand, they had further been reduced to 19 and 9 in the ETO.
6. Adler and Paterson, "Red Fascism," 1046–64.
7. For the great ideological reawakening the war brought about among Americans, see Gleason, "Americans All," 501–2, 511–12, and 515–16.
8. Commager, *The American Mind*, 433.
9. Phillips, "Militarism," 629, 636–8, and 640.

Bibliography

PRIMARY SOURCES

I Manuscripts

(A) The United States Army Military History Institute, Carlisle Barracks, Pennsylvania
1. The World War II Survey Collection
1st Infantry Division
Bistrica, John E. Questionnaire and letters to his mother.
Buettner, Henry J. Questionnaire.
Dillon, William T. Memoir: "Pearl Harbor to Normandy and Beyond."
Morphis, Bert H. Questionnaire.
Opal, Edward A. Questionnaire and notebook.
Reams, Quinton F. Diary.
Rivard, Richard P. Untitled memoir.
Ryan, Charles J. Questionnaire.
Stankoven, Charles F. Diary.
Stewart, Leroy N. Untitled memoir.
Swartzbeck, Charles. Questionnaire.
2nd Infantry Division
Burgess, Raymond. Memoir: "World War II. Military Service: July 1, 1944 to April 21, 1946."
3rd Infantry Division
Boyer, Robert H. Memoir: "My Experiences in World War II."
Watters, Joseph A. Memoir: "The Invasion of North Africa at Fedala and Casablanca, French Morocco."
5th Infantry Division
Clarkson, Karl T. Memoir: "The Story of G.I. Joe (Karl). A Combat Infantryman in World War II."
Unidentified soldier. *Diamond Dust*, 8 May 1945, 5th Infantry Division newspaper.
8th Infantry Division
Anderson, Daniel V. Memoir: "The War Years, 1941–1945."
9th Infantry Division
Griswold, Alvin H. Letters to local newspaper.
Jordan, Chester H. Memoir: "Bull Sessions. World War II, Company K, 47th Inf., 9th Div. from Normandy to Remagen."
O'Connor, Ronald C., Jr. Untitled memoir.
10th Mountain Division
Kennerly, Dan L. Questionnaire and diary.
26th Infantry Division
Burgess, Joseph W. Letters to his mother and sister.
Shannon, Paul D. Memoir: "Replacement."
28th Infantry Division
Shapiro, Murray. Letters home.
29th Infantry Division
Novich, Max M. Untitled memoir.
30th Infantry Division
Unidentified soldier. Questionnaire.

35th Infantry Division
Miller, George D. Letters to his mother and girlfriend.
Notley, William C. Memoir: "And Then There Were None."
36th Infantry Division
Bodeen, Russell. Letters to his girlfriend.
Harlinski, Anthony. Letters to his wife.
42nd Infantry Division
Calhoun, Robert J. Letters to his parents.
44th Infantry Division
Brammer, Harry M. Memoir: "The First Platoon of the 44th Cavalry Reconnaissance Troop."
Jacobs, John D. Letters to his mother.
45th Infantry Division
Tinsch, Frank E. Letters to his wife.
65th Infantry Division
Grage, Armond H. Memoir: "Reflections."
Morris, Leonard F. Memoir: "Adventures of Leonard F. Morris."
66th Infantry Division
Wood, Morton, Jr. Untitled memoir.
70th Infantry Division
Lashin, Abraham I. Letters to his family.
Swenson, Paul A. Memoir: "Family and Personal History."
71st Infantry Division
Earle, John W. Letters to his family.
Meissner, William L. Memoir: "Life As a G.I."
Ponder, Lewington S. Memoir: "Recollections of World War II."
80th Infantry Division
Loughlin, Martin F. Untitled memoir.
84th Infantry Division
Albert, Wendell E. Memoir: "For the Duration ... and Six Months."
Freese, Frank. Memoir: "Private Memories of World War II. (A Small Piece of a Big War.)"
85th Infantry Division
Wiggans, Robert L. Memoir: "The Hazardous Trail: Journeys of an Ithaca Boy."
88th Infantry Division
Roche, John J. Questionnaire.
92nd Infantry Division
Hunter, Jehu C. Questionnaire.
Moore, Spencer C. Questionnaire.
Runyon, Jack F. Memoir: "Memories of the 92nd Infantry Division."
97th Infantry Division
Durig, Richard F. Letters to his family.
99th Infantry Division
Winter, Milton Shipman, Jr. "Battle Babies: The Story of the 99th Infantry Division – Letters from PFC. Milton S. Winter, Jr.: August 13, 1943 through June 11, 1945."
104th Infantry Division
Pendleton, Roger Lee. Letters to his parents.
1st Armored Division
Jett, Oswald G. Diary.
Saidel, Raymond. Diary and letters to his parents.
Sharp, Wendell C. Letters to his parents.
Strong, Paul. Letters to his family.
2nd Armored Division
Brander, Robert Lee. Questionnaire.

Burt, James M. Memoir: "War Memoirs." ·
Eakins, Horace G. Diary.
3rd Armored Division
Gravlin, Robert T. Memoir: "World War II As a Combat Engineer with the Third Armored
    Division."
7th Armored Division
Shuster, Walter J. Memoir: "A Medic's Day in St. Vith."
11th Armored Division
Lummer, Kenneth. Diary.
12th Armored Division
McGill, Ward D. Memoir: "This Is 'It,' the Real Thing: Chronicling the Events of B Co.,
    66th AIB during December 1944 and January 1945."
13th Armored Division
Ethier, Glen Evan. Diary.
14th Armored Division
DeWitt, Jack R. Memoir: "Soldier Memories."
2. The 42nd Infantry Division Papers
Gossett, Edward F. Letters to his parents.
Stoner, Roy W. Letters to his wife.
3. The 100th Infantry Division Papers
Gurley, Franklin L. Letters to his parents.
4. The 4th Armored Division Papers
Calvert, Robert, Jr. Memoir: "The Battle of the Bulge: A Personal Diary."
5. The George E. McIntyre Papers
Untitled Memoir. (4th Infantry Division)
6. The Raab Family Collection
Raab, Herbert. Letters to his parents. (88th Infantry Division)
7. The John J. Roche Papers
Memoir: "Forty Years After." (88th Infantry Division)
8. The Carl Ulsaker Papers
Memoir: "The Ulsaker Saga." (95th Infantry Division)

(B) Yale University Library, New Haven, Connecticut
The Mina Curtiss Collection
Group 1206, Series I, Boxes 1–3, Folders with GI letters from:
13: England, 1942–4
16: France, 1943–5
17: Germany, 1941–5
21: Ireland, 1942
22: Italy, 1943–4
27: North Africa, 1942
28: North Africa, 1942
29: North Africa, 1943
30: North Africa, 1943
31: North Africa, 1943
32: North Africa, 1943
37: Scotland, 1942–3

II Letters, Diaries, Poems, and Memoirs

Abbott, Harry P. *The Nazi '88' Made Believers*. Dayton, Ohio: Otterbein, 1946.

Altieri, James. *The Spearheaders: A Personal History of Darby's Rangers*. Washington, DC: Zenger, 1979.

Arrington, Grady P. *Infantryman at the Front*. New York: Vantage, 1959.

Atwell, Lester. *Private*. New York: Simon and Schuster, 1958.

Belden, Jack. *Still Time to Die*. New York: Harper, 1944.

Berger, Josef and Dorothy, eds. *Diary of America*. New York: Simon and Schuster, 1957.

Bernstein, Walter. *Keep Your Head Down*. New York: Viking, 1945.

Biddle, George. *Artist at War*. New York: Viking, 1944.

Boesch, Paul. *Road to Huertgen – Forest in Hell*. Houston: Gulf, 1962.

Bond, Harold L. *Return to Cassino: A Memoir of the Fight for Rome*. Garden City, New York: Doubleday, 1964.

Bourke-White, Margaret. *They Called It "Purple Heart Valley:" A Combat Chronicle of the War in Italy*. New York: Simon and Schuster, 1944.

Brink, Ebenezer Cobb. *And God Was There*. Philadelphia: Westminster, 1944.

Brown, Walter L. *Up Front with U.S.* Oakland, Maine: privately published, 1979.

Burgett, Donald. *Currahee! "We Stand Alone!": A Paratrooper's Account of the Normandy Invasion*. London: Hutchinson, 1967.

Capa, Robert. *Slightly Out of Focus*. New York: Henry Holt, 1947.

Carter, Ross S. *Those Devils in Baggy Pants*. New York: Signet, 1957.

Cawthon, Charles R. *Other Clay: A Remembrance of the World War II Infantry*. New York: Dell, 1990.

Connelly, Kenneth A. *Chaplain's Assistant: From the Correspondence of Corporal Kenneth A. Connelly, Jr.* Seattle: Craftsman, 1945.

Curtiss, Mina, ed. *Letters Home*. Boston: Little, Brown, 1944.

Davidson, Bill. *Cut Off*. New York: Stein and Day, 1972.

Davis, Harry, ed. *This Is It!* New York: Vanguard, 1944.

Downing, John P. *At War with the British*. Daytona Beach, Florida: privately published, 1980.

Easton, Robert and Jane. *Love and War: Pearl Harbor through V-J Day*. Norman: University of Oklahoma Press, 1991.

Egger, Bruce E. and Lee MacMillan Otts. *G Company's War: Two Personal Accounts of the Campaigns in Europe, 1944–1945*. Edited by Paul Roley. Tuscaloosa: University of Alabama Press, 1992.

Eliach, Yaffa and Brana Gurewitsch, eds. *Liberation Day: Oral History Testimonies of American Liberators from the Archives of the Center for Holocaust Studies*. Vol. 1 of *The Liberators: Eyewitness Accounts of the Liberation of Concentration Camps*. Brooklyn: Center for Holocaust Studies Documentation and Research, 1981.

Eustis, Morton. *War Letters of Morton Eustis to His Mother: February 6, 1941 to August 10, 1944*. New York: Spiral, 1945.

Faubus, Orval Eugene. *In this Faraway Land*. Conway, Arkansas: River Road, 1971.

Frankel, Nat and Larry Smith. *Patton's Best: An Informal History of the 4th Armored Division*. New York: Hawthorn, 1978.

Fry, James C. *Combat Soldier*. Washington, DC: National, 1968.

Fussell, Paul. "My War." In *The Boy Scout Handbook and Other Observations*. New York: Oxford University Press, 1982.

Giles, Henry. *The G.I. Journal of Sergeant Giles*. Boston: Houghton Mifflin, 1965.

Gray, J. Glenn. *The Warriors: Reflections on Men in Battle*. New York: Harper and Row, 1967.

Groth, John. *Studio: Europe*. New York: Vanguard, 1945.

Gustafson, Walter. *My Time in the Army: The Diary of a World War II Soldier*. Chicago: Adams, 1968.

Hoffman, Alice M. and Howard S. *Archives of Memory: A Soldier Recalls World War II*. Lexington: University Press of Kentucky, 1990.

Hornsby, Henry H., Jr. *The Trey of Sevens*. Dallas: Mathis Van Nort, 1946.

Houston, Robert J. *D-Day to Bastogne: A Paratrooper Recalls World War II*. Smithtown, New York: Exposition, 1980.

Hovsepian, Aramais Akob. *Your Son and Mine*. New York: Duell, Sloan and Pearce, 1950.

Huebner, Klaus H. *Long Walk through War: A Combat Doctor's Diary*. College Station: Texas A & M University Press, 1987.

Hurkala, John. *The Fighting First Division: A True Story*. New York: Greenwich, 1957.

Irgang, Frank J. *Etched in Purple*. Caldwell, Idaho: Caxton, 1949.

Jeske, Russell G. *WWII Memories Recalled: A GI's Diary of Letters*. Elm Grove, Wisconsin: Sycamore, 1992.

Johns, Glover S. *The Clay Pigeons of St. Lô*. Harrisburg, Pennsylvania: Military Service, 1958.

Johnson, Franklyn A. *One More Hill*. New York: Bantam, 1987.

Kelly, Charles E. and Pete Martin. *One Man's War*. New York: Alfred A. Knopf, 1944.

Kimball, Clyde E. *A Diary of My Work Overseas*. Nashua, New Hampshire: privately published, 1947.

Koskimaki, George E. *D-Day with the Screaming Eagles*. Madelia, Minnesota: House of Print, 1970.

Krebs, John E. *To Rome and Beyond: Battle Adventures of Company 'B', 760th Tank Battalion, Italy 1943–1945*. Weatherford, Texas: privately published, 1981.

Leinbaugh, Harold P. and John D. Campbell. *The Men of Company K: The Autobiography of a World War II Rifle Company*. New York: William Morrow, 1985.

Litoff, Judy Barrett, et al. *Miss You: The World War II Letters of Barbara Wooddall Taylor and Charles E. Taylor*. Athens: University of Georgia Press, 1990.

Lyon, Allan. *Toward an Unknown Station*. New York: Macmillan, 1948.

MacDonald, Charles B. *Company Commander*. New York: Bantam, 1982.

Mauldin, William H. *Up Front*. Cleveland, Ohio: World, 1945.

Mauldin, William H. *The Brass Ring*. New York: W.W. Norton, 1971.

Maule, Harry E. *A Book of War Letters*. New York: Random House, 1943.

Mayo, Andrew R. *No Time for Glory*. New York: Pageant, 1955.

McConahey, William M. *Battalion Surgeon*. Rochester, Minnesota: privately published, 1966.

McGuire, Phillip. *Taps for a Jim Crow Army: Letters from Black Soldiers in World War II*. Santa Barbara, California: ABC-Clio, 1983.

McHugh, Vernon D. *From Hell to Heaven: Memoirs from Patton's Third Army*. Ardmore, Pennsylvania: Dorrance, 1980.

Metcalf, George R. *With Cross and Shovel: A Chaplain's Letters from England, France, and Germany, 1942–1945*. Duxbury, Massachusetts: n.p., 1957.

Motley, Mary Penick, ed. *The Invisible Soldier: The Experience of the Black Soldier, World War II*. Detroit: Wayne State University Press, 1975.

Murphy, Audie. *To Hell and Back*. New York: Holt, Rinehart and Winston, 1971.

Parker, Kenneth C. *Civilian at War*. Traverse City, Michigan: privately published, 1984.

Peckham, Howard H. and Shirley A. Snyder, eds. *Letters from Fighting Hoosiers*. Vol. 2 of *Indiana in World War II*. Bloomington, Indiana: Indiana War History Commission, 1948.

Penrose, Antony, ed. *Lee Miller's War: Photographer and Correspondent with the Allies in Europe*. Boston: Bulfinch, 1992.

Peyton, Frank W. *A Surgeon's Diary: 15th Evacuation Hospital, Experiences in World War II, North Africa – Sicily – Italy*. Crawfordsville, Indiana: privately published, 1987.

Phibbs, Brandon. *The Other Side of Time*. Boston: Little, Hart, 1987.

Preston, William P.T., ed. *Letters of William P.T. Preston, Jr. Written to His Family from the U.S. and Overseas during World War II*. N.p.: privately published, 1950.

Pyle, Ernest T. *Here Is Your War*. New York: Holt, 1943.

Pyle, Ernest T. *Brave Men*. New York: Holt, 1944.

Raff, Edson D. *We Jumped to Fight*. New York: Eagle, 1944.

Randall, Howard M. *Dirt and Doughfeet: Combat Experiences of a Rifle-Platoon Leader*. New York: Exposition, 1955.

Roberts, Cecil E. *A Soldier from Texas*. Fort Worth: Branch-Smith, 1978.

Robinson, Don. *News of the 45th*. Norman: University of Oklahoma Press, 1944.

Rogers, Edward K. *Doughboy Chaplain*. Boston: Meador, 1946.

Rontch, Isaac E. *Jewish Youth at War: Letters from American Soldiers*. New York: Marstin, 1945.

Sampson, Francis L. *Look Out Below!: A Story of the Airborne by a Paratrooper Padre*. Washington, DC: Catholic University of America, 1958.

Seiverling, Richard F. *Short Stories of World War II*. Palmyra, Pennsylvania: Cornell, 1947.

Shinn, Roger Lincoln. *Wars and Rumors of Wars*. Nashville, Tennessee: Abingdon, 1972.

Simpson, Louis. *Collected Poems*. New York: Paragon House, 1988.

Snyder, Robert Strong. *And When My Task on Earth Is Done: The Day by Day Experiences of a Christian GI, Written in His Diary which Was Sent Home by the War Department*. Kansas City, Missouri: Graphic Laboratory, 1950.

Standifer, Leon C. *Not in Vain: A Rifleman Remembers World War II*. Baton Rouge: Louisiana State University Press, 1992.

Stradling, Harriet, ed. *Johnny*. Salt Lake City: Bookcraft, 1946.

Tapert, Annette, ed. *Lines of Battle: Letters from American Servicemen, 1941–1945*. New York: Times, 1987.

Terkel, Studs. *"The Good War:" An Oral History of World War II*. New York: Pantheon, 1984.

Toole, John H. *Battle Diary*. Missoula, Montana: Vigilante, 1978.

Tregaskis, Richard W. *Invasion Diary*. New York: Random House, 1944.

Tsuchida, William Shinji. *Wear It Proudly: Letters by William Shinji Tsuchida*. Berkeley and Los Angeles: University of California Press, 1947.

Tumey, Ben. *G.I.'s View of World War II: The Diary of a Combat Private*. Hicksville, New York: Exposition, 1959.

Vining, Donald, ed. *American Diaries of World War II*. New York: Pepys, 1982.

Wardlaw, Frederick C., ed. *Missing in Action: Letters of a Medic*. Raleigh, North Carolina: Sparks, 1983.

Westrate, Edwin V. *Forward Observer*. Philadelphia: Blakiston, 1944.

Wilbur, Richard. *Poems, 1943–1956*. London: Faber and Faber, 1964.

Wilson, Charles E. *From Bastogne to Bavaria with the Fighting Fourth Armored Division, 1944–1945: Scenes from the War and Holocaust*. Lewiston, New York: Edwin Mellen, 1993.

Winston, Keith. *V...-Mail: Letters of a World War II Combat Medic*. Chapel Hill, North Carolina: Algonquin, 1985.

Wise, James Waterman, ed. *Very Truly Ours: Letters from America's Fighting Men*. New York: Dial, 1943.

Wolfe, Don M., ed. *The Purple Testament*. Garden City, New York: Doubleday, 1947.

III Songs, Jokes, and Cartoons

Bairnsfather, Bruce. *Jeeps and Jests*. New York: Putnam's Sons, 1943.

Hersey, Harold, ed. *More G.I. Laughs: Real Army Humor*. New York: Sheridan House, 1944.

Mauldin, William H. *Bill Mauldin's Army*. Novato, California: Presidio, 1983.

Murdoch, Brian. *Fighting Songs and Warring Words: Popular Lyrics of Two World Wars*. London: Routledge, 1990.

Page, Martin. *Kiss Me Goodnight, Sergeant Major: The Songs and Ballads of World War II.* Frogmore, England: Panther, 1975.

Palmer, Edgar A., ed. *G.I. Songs: Written, Composed and/or Collected by the Men in the Service.* New York: Sheridan House, 1944.

Scannell, Vernon. *Not Without Glory: Poets of the Second World War.* London: Woburn, 1976.

IV Articles by Participants

Adams, John G. "Les Americaines." *North Dakota Quarterly* 54, no. 4 (1986): 170–85.

Adams, John G. "The Mad Days." *North Dakota Quarterly* 55, no. 3 (1987): 62–72.

Bohnen, Eli A. "Our Rabbi with the Rainbow Division: A World War II Reminiscence." *Rhode Island Jewish Historical Notes* 8, no. 2 (1980): 81–90.

Bruff, Thomas B. "D-Day: As Seen by a Paratrooper." *New York Times Magazine*, 6 June 1954.

Campbell, Eugene E. "I Wanted to Be a Chaplain: A Reminiscence of World War II." *Utah Historical Quarterly* 60, no. 3 (1992): 277–84.

Dohmann, George W. "A Medic in Normandy." *American History Illustrated* 4, no. 3 (1969): 8–17.

Engel, Russ. "The Incredible Patrol." In *Combat WW II: European Theater of Operations.* Edited by Don Congdon. New York: Arbor House, 1983. Originally published in *Life*, 15 January 1945.

Goldsmith, Adolph O. "Sounds of War." *MHQ* 3 (1991): 112.

Hargrove, Hondon. "Il Corsaro: A Story of War and Friendship." *Michigan History* 64, no. 1 (1980): 14–19.

Haygood, William C. "A GI's Wartime Letters." *Wisconsin Magazine of History* 59, no. 2 (1975–6): 101–35.

Morriss, Mack. "In the Huertgen Forest." In *Combat WW II: European Theater of Operations.* Edited by Don Congdon. New York: Arbor House, 1983. Originally published in *Yank: The GI Story of the War.* New York: Duell, Sloan and Pearce, 1947.

Shaw, John. "Battle of the Bulge: As Seen by a G.I." *New York Times Magazine*, 12 December 1954.

Sonnen, John S. "Out of the Attic, Or What Price Memorabilia? A Minnesota Couple's World War II Letters." *Minnesota History* 53, no. 2 (1992): 56–67.

V Government Publications

Ginn, L. Holmes, Jr., et al. *Trench Foot (Cold Injury, Ground Type).* Reports of the General Board, United States Forces, European Theater, no. 94.

Hyer, Julien C., Ernest May, and Joseph S. Sudarsky. *War Crimes and Punishment of War Criminals.* Reports of the General Board, United States Forces, European Theater, no. 86.

Hyer, Julien C., et al. *Military Justice Administration in the Theater of Operations.* Reports of the General Board, United States Forces, European Theater, no. 83.

Hyer, Julien C., et al. *The Military Offender in the Theater of Operations.* Reports of the General Board, United States Forces, European Theater, no. 84.

MTOUSA. Information and Education Section. *Austria: A Soldier's Guide.* N.p., n.d.

Office of the Judge Advocate General. *Holdings and Opinions. Board of Review. Branch Office of the Judge Advocate General. European Theater of Operations.* Washington, DC, 1945–6.

Pocket Guide to Germany. N.p., 1944.

Ryan, C.E., et al. *Civil Affairs and Military Government Activities in Connection with Monuments, Fine Arts, and Archives.* Reports of the General Board, United States Forces, European Theater, no. 36.

US Twelfth Army Group. Europe. Headquarters. *Special Orders for German–American Relations.* [1944].

US War Department. *Handbook on German Military Forces.* Washington, DC, 1945; reprint, Baton Rouge: Louisiana State University Press, 1990.

Van Way, Charles, Jr. and John I. Ladd. *Leaves, Furloughs, and Passes in the Theater.* Reports of the General Board, United States Forces, European Theater, no. 4.

War Department. *Basic Field Manual, FM 27–10: Rules of Land Warfare* Washington, DC, 1940.

War Department. *Pocket Guide to the Cities of Belgium and Luxembourg.* Washington, DC, 1944.

War Department. *Pocket Guide to the Cities of the Netherlands.* Washington, DC, 1944.

War Department. *Pocket Guide to the Cities of Southern France.* Washington, DC, 1944.

War Department. *Pocket Guide to Italian Cities.* Washington, DC, 1944.

War Department. *Pocket Guide to Paris and the Cities of Northern France.* Washington, DC, 1944.

War Department. Services of Supply. Special Service Division. Information and Education Division. Research Branch. *What the Soldier Thinks: Digest, with Charts, of a Year's Research Studies Indicating the Attitudes, Prejudices, and Desires of American Troops.* February 1943.

War Department. Army Service Forces. Special Service Division. Information and Education Division. Research Branch. *What the Soldier Thinks: Quarterly Report, with Charts, of Research Studies Indicating the Attitudes, Prejudices and Desires of American Troops.* August 1943.

War Department. Army Service Forces. Morale Services Division. *What the Soldier Thinks: A Monthly Digest of War Department Studies on the Attitudes of American Troops.* January 1944–September 1945.

War and Navy Departments. *Pocket Guide to North Africa.* Washington, DC, 1942.

War and Navy Departments. *A Guide to the Occupation of Enemy Territory: Italy.* Washington, DC, 1943.

War and Navy Departments. *Pocket Guide to France.* Washington, DC, 1944.

War and Navy Departments. *A Pocket Guide to the USSR.* Washington, DC, 1944.

War and Navy Departments. *A Pocket Guide to Northern Ireland.* Washington, DC, n.d.

War and Navy Departments. *A Short Guide to Great Britain.* Washington, DC, n.d.

VI Document Collections

Friedman, Leon, ed. *The Law of War: A Documentary History.* Vol. 1. New York: Random House, 1972.

SECONDARY SOURCES

I Government Publications

Beck, Alfred M., et al. *The Corps of Engineers: The War against Germany.* United States Army in World War II: The Technical Services. Washington, DC: Office of the Chief of Military History, Department of the Army, 1985.

Bennett, Linda and Marcus W. Floyd. *Displaced Persons.* Occupation Forces in Europe Series. Frankfurt-am-Main: Office of the Chief Historian, European Command, 1947.

Blumenson, Martin. *Breakout and Pursuit*. United States Army in World War II: The European Theater of Operations. Washington, DC: Office of the Chief of Military History, Department of the Army, 1961.

Blumenson, Martin. *Salerno to Cassino*. United States Army in World War II: The Mediterranean Theater of Operations. Washington, DC: Office of the Chief of Military History, United States Army, 1969.

Cole, Hugh M. *The Lorraine Campaign*. United States Army in World War II: The European Theater of Operations. Washington, DC: Historical Division, Department of the Army, 1950.

Coll, Blanche D., Jean E. Keith, and Herbert H. Rosenthal. *The Corps of Engineers: Troops and Equipment*. United States Army in World War II: The Technical Services. Washington, DC: Office of the Chief of Military History, Department of the Army, 1958.

Cosmas, Graham A. and Albert E. Cowdrey. *The Medical Department: Medical Service in the European Theater of Operations*. United States Army in World War II: The Technical Services. Washington, DC: Center of Military History, United States Army, 1992.

Fisher Ernest F., Jr. *Cassino to the Alps*. United States Army in World War II: The Mediterranean Theater of Operations. Washington, DC: Center of Military History, United States Army, 1977.

Gushwa, Robert L. *The Best and Worst of Times: The United States Army Chaplaincy, 1920–1945*. Vol. 4. Washington, DC: Office of the Chief of Chaplains, Department of the Army, 1977.

Howe, George F. *Northwest Africa: Seizing the Initiative in the West*. United States Army in World War II: The Mediterranean Theater of Operations. Washington, DC: Office of the Chief of Military History, Department of the Army, 1957.

Kleber, Brooks E. and Dale Birdsell. *The Chemical Warfare Service: Chemicals in Combat*. United States Army in World War II: The Technical Services. Washington, DC: Office of the Chief of Military History, Department of the Army, 1966.

MacDonald, Charles B. *The Last Offensive*. United States Army in World War II: The European Theater of Operations. Washington, DC: Center of Military History, United States Army, 1990.

MacDonald, Charles B. *The Siegfried Line Campaign*. United States Army in World War II: The European Theater of Operations. Washington, DC: Office of the Chief of Military History, Department of the Army, 1963.

Mayo, Lida. *The Ordnance Department: On Beachhead and Battlefront*. United States Army in World War II: The Technical Services. Washington, DC: Office of the Chief of Military History, Department of the Army, 1968.

Reister, Frank A., ed. *Medical Statistics in World War II*. Washington, DC: Office of the Surgeon General, Department of the Army, 1975.

Risch, Erna. *The Quartermaster Corps: Organization, Supply, and Services*. Vol. 1. United States Army in World War II: The Technical Services. Washington, DC: Office of the Chief of Military History, Department of the Army, 1953.

Risch, Erna and Chester L. Kieffer. *The Quartermaster Corps: Organization, Supply, and Services*. Vol. 2. United States Army in World War II: The Technical Services. Washington, DC: Office of the Chief of Military History, Department of the Army, 1955.

Ross, William F. and Charles F. Romanus. *The Quartermaster Corps: Operations in the War against Germany*. United States Army in World War II: The Technical Services. Washington, DC: Office of the Chief of Military History, Department of the Army, 1965.

Ruppenthal, Roland G. *May 1941 – September 1944*. Vol. 1 of *Logistical Support of the Armies*. United States Army in World War II: The European Theater of Operations. Washington, DC: Office of the Chief of Military History, Department of the Army, 1953.

Ruppenthal, Roland G. *September 1944 – May 1945*. Vol. 2 of *Logistical Support of the Armies*. United States Army in World War II: The European Theater of Operations. Washington, DC: Office of the Chief of Military History, Department of the Army, 1959.

Starr, Joseph R. *Fraternization with the Germans in World War II*. Occupation Forces in Europe Series. Frankfurt-am-Main: Office of the Chief Historian, European Command, 1947.

Vigneras, Marcel. *Rearming the French*. United States Army in World War II: Special Studies. Washington, DC: Office of the Chief of Military History, Department of the Army, 1957.

Wiltse, Charles M. *The Medical Department: Medical Service in the Mediterranean and Minor Theaters*. United States Army in World War II: The Technical Services. Washington, DC: Office of the Chief of Military History, Department of the Army, 1965.

Ziemke, Earl F. *The U.S. Army in the Occupation of Germany, 1944–1946*. Army Historical Series. Washington, DC: Center of Military History, United States Army, 1975.

II Dissertations

Daly, Charlotte Sharpe. "Sharpe's Battalion in World War II." Florida State University, 1989.

III Books

Abzug, Robert H. *Inside the Vicious Heart: Americans and the Liberation of Nazi Concentration Camps*. New York: Oxford University Press, 1985.

Alexander, Charles C. *Nationalism in American Thought, 1930–1945*. Chicago: Rand McNally, 1973.

Ambrose, Stephen E. *Band of Brothers. E Company, 506th Regiment, 101st Airborne. From Normandy to Hitler's Eagle's Nest*. New York: Simon and Schuster, 1992.

Beck, Earl R. *Under the Bombs: The German Home Front, 1942–1945*. Lexington: University Press of Kentucky, 1986.

Bérubé, Allan. *Coming Out under Fire: The History of Gay Men and Women in World War Two*. New York: Free Press, 1990.

Boorstin, Daniel J. *America and the Image of Europe: Reflections on American Thought*. Gloucester, Massachusetts: Peter Smith, 1976.

Bridgman, Jon. *The End of the Holocaust: The Liberation of the Camps*. Portland, Oregon: Areopagitica Press, 1990.

Charles, Roland W. *Troopships of World War II*. Washington, DC: Army Transportation Association, 1947.

Charters, Samuel. *The Poetry of the Blues*. New York: Oak, 1963.

Colby, Elbridge. *Army Talk: A Familiar Dictionary of Soldier Speech*. Princeton, New Jersey: Princeton University Press, 1942.

Commager, Henry Steele. *The American Mind: An Interpretation of American Thought and Character since the 1880s*. New Haven: Yale University Press, 1950.

Cooper, Matthew. *The German Army, 1933–1945: Its Political and Military Failure*. Chelsea, Michigan: Scarborough House, 1991.

Costello, John. *Virtue under Fire: How World War II Changed Our Social and Sexual Attitudes*. Boston: Little, Brown, 1985.

d'Este, Carlo. "Caution." In *Decision in Normandy: The Unwritten Story of Montgomery and the Allied Campaign*. London: Collins, 1983.

Diggins, John P. *Mussolini and Fascism: The View from America*. Princeton, New Jersey: Princeton University Press, 1972.

Dower, John W. *War Without Mercy: Race and Power in the Pacific War*. New York: Pantheon, 1986.

Dulles, Foster Rhea. *Americans Abroad: Two Centuries of European Travel.* Ann Arbor: University of Michigan Press, 1964.

Duus, Masayo Umezawa. *Unlikely Liberators: The Men of the 100th and 442nd.* Honolulu: University of Hawaii Press, 1987.

Ellis, John. *The Sharp Edge: The Fighting Man in World War II.* New York: Scribners, 1980.

Elting, John R., Dan Cragg, and Ernest L. Deal. *A Dictionary of Soldier Talk.* New York: Charles Scribner's Sons, 1984.

Fishman, Sarah. *We Will Wait: Wives of French Prisoners of War, 1940–1945.* New Haven: Yale University Press, 1991.

FitzGerald, Frances. *America Revised: History Schoolbooks in the Twentieth Century.* Boston: Atlantic – Little, Brown, 1979.

Förster, Jürgen E. "The Dynamics of *Volksgemeinschaft*: The Effectiveness of the German Military Establishment in the Second World War." In *The Second World War.* Vol. 3 of *Military Effectiveness.* Edited by Allan R. Millett and Williamson Murray. Boston: Allen and Unwin, 1988.

Fussell, Paul. *The Great War and Modern Memory.* New York: Oxford University Press, 1979.

Fussell, Paul. *Wartime: Understanding and Behavior in the Second World War.* New York: Oxford University Press, 1989.

Gansberg, Judith M. *Stalag U.S.A.: The Remarkable Story of German POWs in America.* New York: Thomas Y. Crowell, 1977.

Hood, Ronald Chalmers, III. "Bitter Victory: French Military Effectiveness during the Second World War." In *The Second World War.* Vol. 3 of *Military Effectiveness.* Edited by Allan R. Millett and Williamson Murray. Boston: Allen and Unwin, 1988.

Hunt, Michael H. *Ideology and U.S. Foreign Policy.* New Haven, Connecticut: Yale University Press, 1987.

Hurstfield, Julian G. *America and the French Nation, 1939–1945.* Chapel Hill: University of North Carolina Press, 1986.

Huston, James A. *Across the Face of France: Liberation and Recovery, 1944–63.* N.p.: Purdue University Studies, 1963.

Kater, Michael H. *Different Drummers: Jazz in the Culture of Nazi Germany.* New York: Oxford University Press, 1992.

Keefer, Louis E. *Italian Prisoners of War in America, 1942–1946: Captives or Allies?* New York: Praeger, 1992.

Keegan, John. *Six Armies in Normandy: From D-Day to the Liberation of Paris, June 6th – August 25th, 1944.* New York: Viking, 1982.

Kennett, Lee. *G.I.: The American Soldier in World War II.* New York: Charles Scribner's Sons, 1987.

Knox, MacGregor. "The Italian Armed Forces, 1940–3." In *The Second World War.* Vol. 3 of *Military Effectiveness.* Edited by Allan R. Millett and Williamson Murray. Boston: Allen and Unwin, 1988.

Krammer, Arnold. *Nazi Prisoners of War in America.* Briarcliff Manor, New York: Stein and Day, 1979.

Leed, Eric J. *The Mind of the Traveler: From Gilgamesh to Global Tourism.* New York: Basic Books, 1991.

Levering, Ralph B. *American Opinion and the Russian Alliance, 1939–1945.* Chapel Hill: University of North Carolina Press, 1976.

Longmate, Norman. *The G.I.'s: The Americans in Britain, 1942–1945.* London: Hutchinson, 1975.

Lukacs, John. *The Last European War, September 1939/December 1941.* Garden City, New York: Anchor Press/Doubleday, 1976.

Marshall, S. L. A. *Men against Fire: The Problem of Battle Command in Future War.* Washington, DC: Combat Forces, 1954.

Millett, Allan R. "The United States Armed Forces in the Second World War." In *The Second World War*. Vol. 3 of *Military Effectiveness*. Edited by Allan R. Millett and Williamson Murray. Boston: Allen and Unwin, 1988.

Monks, John P. *College Men at War*. Vol. 24 of *Memoirs of the American Academy of Arts and Sciences*. Boston: American Academy of Arts and Sciences, 1957.

Morin, Raul. *Among the Valiant: Mexican-Americans in WW II and Korea*. Los Angeles: Borden, 1963.

Murray, Williamson. *Luftwaffe*. Baltimore: Nautical and Aviation Publishing Company of America, 1985.

Murray, Williamson. "British Military Effectiveness in the Second World War." In *The Second World War*. Vol. 3 of *Military Effectiveness*. Edited by Allan R. Millett and Williamson Murray. Boston: Allen and Unwin, 1988.

Pitkin, Walter B. "The American: How He Lives." In *Culture and Commitment, 1929–1945*. Edited by Walter Susman. New York: George Braziller, 1973.

Potter, Lou, William Miles, and Nina Rosenblum. *Liberators: Fighting on Two Fronts in World War II*. New York: Harcourt Brace Jovanovich, 1992.

Reynolds, David. *Rich Relations: The American Occupation of Britain, 1942–1945*. New York: Random House, 1995.

Rosenberg, Emily S. *Spreading the American Dream: American Economic and Cultural Expansion, 1890–1945*. New York: Hill and Wang, 1982.

Sanford, Charles L. *The Quest for Paradise: Europe and the American Moral Imagination*. Urbana, Illinois: University of Illinois Press, 1961.

Shukert, Elfrieda B. and Barbara S. Scibetta. *War Brides of World War II*. Novato, California: Presidio, 1988.

Stanton, Shelby L. *Order of Battle: U.S. Army, World War II*. Novato, California: Presidio, 1984.

Stouffer, Samuel A., et al. *The American Soldier: Adjustment during Army Life*. Vol. 1 of *Studies in Social Psychology in World War II*. Princeton, New Jersey: Princeton University Press, 1949.

Stouffer, Samuel A., et al. *The American Soldier: Combat and Its Aftermath*. Vol. 2 of *Studies in Social Psychology in World War II*. Princeton, New Jersey: Princeton University Press, 1949.

Strout, Cushing. *The American Image of the Old World*. New York: Harper & Row, 1963.

Taylor, A. Marjorie. *The Language of World War II: Abbreviations, Captions, Slogans, Titles and Other Terms and Phrases*. New York: H.H. Wilson, 1948.

Thorne, Christopher. *Allies of a Kind: The United States, Britain and the War against Japan, 1941–1945*. New York: Oxford University Press, 1978.

van Creveld, Martin. *Fighting Power: German and U.S. Army Performance, 1939–1945*. Contributions in Military History, no. 32. Westport, Connecticut: Greenwood Press, 1982.

Wagner, Lilya. *Women War Correspondents of World War II*. Contributions in Women's Studies, no. 104. Westport, Connecticut: Greenwood Press, 1989.

Weigley, Russell F. *Eisenhower's Lieutenants: The Campaign of France and Germany, 1944–1945*. Bloomington: Indiana University Press, 1990.

Whelan, Richard. *Robert Capa: A Biography*. London: Faber and Faber, 1985.

Whitnah, Donald R. and Edgar L. Erickson. *The American Occupation of Austria: Planning and Early Years*. Contributions in Military Studies, no. 46. Westport, Connecticut: Greenwood Press, 1985.

Wyman, David S. *The Abandonment of the Jews: America and the Holocaust, 1941–1945*. New York: Pantheon, 1984.

Wyman, Mark. *DP: Europe's Displaced Persons, 1945–1951*. Philadelphia: The Balch Institute Press, 1989.

Wyman, Mark. *Round-Trip to America: The Immigrants Return to Europe, 1880–1930.* Ithaca, New York: Cornell University Press, 1993.

IV Articles

Adler, Les K. and Thomas G. Paterson. "Red Fascism: The Merger of Nazi Germany and Soviet Russia in the American Image of Totalitarianism, 1930s–1950s." *American Historical Review* 75, no. 4 (1970): 1046–64.

Baird, Nancy Disher. "'To Lend You My Eyes...:' The World War II Letters of Special Services Officer Harry Jackson." *Register of the Kentucky Historical Society* 88, no. 3 (1990): 287–317.

Bartov, Omer. "The Myths of the Wehrmacht." *History Today,* April 1992: 30–36.

Beaumont, Roger A. "On the *Wehrmacht* Mystique." *Military Review* 66, no. 7 (1986): 44–56.

Beck, Earl R. "The Anti-Nazi 'Swing Youth,' 1942–1945." *Journal of Popular Culture* 19, no. 3 (1985): 45–53.

Bertaux, Daniel and Martin Kohli. "The Life Story Approach: A Continental View." *Annual Review of Sociology* 10 (1984): 215–37.

Campbell, D'Ann. "Women in Combat: The World War II Experience in the United States, Great Britain, Germany, and the Soviet Union." *Journal of Military History* 57, no. 2 (1993): 301–23.

Coates, Ken and W.R. Morrison. "The American Rampant: Reflections on the Impact of United States Troops in Allied Countries during World War II." *Journal of World History* 2, no. 2 (1991): 201–21.

Cox, Lori. "What Did You Do in the War?" *Nebraska History* 72, no. 4 (1991): 158–256.

Elkin, Frederick. "The Soldier's Language." *American Journal of Sociology* 51 (1946): 414–422.

Elkin, Henry. "Aggressive and Erotic Tendencies in Army Life." *American Journal of Sociology* 51 (1946): 408–13.

Frucht, Karl. "Clem Has Been Here: Second Thoughts on the American Soldier in Europe." *Commentary* 1 (March 1946): 39–45.

Glaser, Daniel. "The Sentiments of American Soldiers Abroad toward Europeans." *American Journal of Sociology* 51 (1946): 433–8.

Gleason, Philip. "Americans All: World War II and the Shaping of American Identity." *Review of Politics* 43, no. 4 (1981): 483–518.

Hermens, Ferdinand A. "The Danger of Stereotypes in Viewing Germany." *Public Opinion Quarterly* 9 (winter 1945–6): 418–27.

Hopkins, George E. "Bombing and the American Conscience during World War II." *Historian* 28, no. 3 (1966): 451–73.

Jones, David Lloyd. "Marketing the Allies to America." *Midwest Quarterly* 29, no. 3 (1988): 366–83.

Kohn, Richard H., ed. "The Scholarship on World War II: Its Present Condition and Future Possibilities." *Journal of Military History* 55, no. 3 (1991): 365–93.

Kracauer, Siegfried. "National Types as Hollywood Presents Them." *Public Opinion Quarterly* 13 (spring 1949): 53–72.

Krammer, Arnold. "American Treatment of German Generals during World War II." *Journal of Military History* 54, no. 1 (1990): 27–46.

Lilley, Charles R. and Michael H. Hunt. "On Social History, the State, and Foreign Relations: Commentary on 'The Cosmopolitan Connection.'" *Diplomatic History* 11, no. 3 (1987): 243–50.

Mjagkij, Nina. "Know Your Occupied Ally: The Image of France in *Passage to Marseilles.*" *Film and History* 20, no. 2 (1990): 37–43.

Moltmann, Günter. "Amerikaklischees der deutschen Kriegspropaganda, 1941–1945." *Amerikastudien/American Studies* 31, no. 3 (1986): 303–14.

Petracarro, Domenico. "The Italian Army in Africa, 1940–1943: An Attempt at Historical Perspective." *War & Society* 9 (1991): 103–27.

Phillips, Nancy Edelman. "Militarism and Grass-Roots Involvement in the Military-Industrial Complex." *Journal of Conflict Resolution* 17, no. 4 (1973): 625–55.

Reynolds, David. "GI and Tommy in Wartime Britain: The Army 'Inter-Attachment' Scheme of 1943–44." *Journal of Strategic Studies* 7, no. 4 (1984): 406–22.

Sadkovich, James J. "Of Myths and Men: Rommel and the Italians in North Africa, 1940–1942." *International History Review* 13, no. 2 (1991): 284–313.

Simmons, Jerold. "Film and International Politics: The Banning of *All Quiet on the Western Front* in Germany and Austria, 1930–1931." *Historian* 52, no. 1 (1989): 40–60.

Small, Melvin. "How We Learned to Love the Russians: American Media and the Soviet Union during World War II." *Historian* 36, no. 3 (1974): 455–78.

Smoler, Fredric. "The Secret of the Soldiers Who Didn't Shoot." *American Heritage* 40, no. 2 (1989): 36–45.

Spiller, Roger J. "S. L. A. Marshall and the Ratio of Fire." *RUSI Journal* 133, no. 4 (1988): 63–71.

Steele, Richard W. "American Popular Opinion and the War against Germany: The Issue of Negotiated Peace, 1942." *Journal of American History* 65, no. 3 (1978): 704–23.

Wagner, Robert L. "The Odyssey of a Texas Citizen Soldier." *Southwestern History Quarterly* 72, no. 1 (1968): 60–87.

Weingartner, James J. "Massacre at Biscari: Patton and an American War Crime." *Historian* 52, no. 1 (1989): 24–39.

Weingartner, James J. "Trophies of War: U.S. Troops and the Mutilation of Japanese War Dead, 1941–1945." *Pacific Historical Review* 61, no. 1 (1992): 53–67.

White, Richard. "The Soldier as Tourist: The Australian Experience of the Great War." *War & Society* 5, no. 1 (1987): 63–77.

Index